Linux

ALL-IN-ONE

A Wiley Brand

Linux®

ALL-IN-ONE

6th Edition

by Emmett Dulaney

Linux® All-in-One For Dummies®, 6th Edition

Published by: **John Wiley & Sons, Inc.,** 111 River Street, Hoboken, NJ 07030-5774, www.wiley.com

Copyright © 2018 by John Wiley & Sons, Inc., Hoboken, New Jersey

Published simultaneously in Canada

For general information on our other products and services, please contact our Customer Care Department within the U.S. at 877-762-2974, outside the U.S. at 317-572-3993, or fax 317-572-4002. For technical support, please visit https://hub.wiley.com/community/support/dummies.

Wiley publishes in a variety of print and electronic formats and by print-on-demand. Some material included with standard print versions of this book may not be included in e-books or in print-on-demand. If this book refers to media such as a CD or DVD that is not included in the version you purchased, you may download this material at http://booksupport.wiley.com. For more information about Wiley products, visit www.wiley.com.

Library of Congress Control Number: 2018943541

ISBN: 978-1-119-49046-3 (pbk); 978-1-119-49052-4 (ebk); 978-1-119-49045-6 (ebk)

Manufactured in the United States of America

V087206_060718

Contents at a Glance

Introduction 1

Book 1: Getting Started with Linux 7
CHAPTER 1: Introducing Linux 9
CHAPTER 2: Installing Linux 29
CHAPTER 3: Troubleshooting and Configuring Linux 39
CHAPTER 4: Trying Out Linux 57

Book 2: Linux Desktops 67
CHAPTER 1: GNOME and Its Derivatives 69
CHAPTER 2: The KDE Plasma Desktop 75
CHAPTER 3: Commanding the Shell 83
CHAPTER 4: Navigating the Linux File System 105
CHAPTER 5: Introducing Linux Applications 123
CHAPTER 6: Using Text Editors 137

Book 3: Networking 151
CHAPTER 1: Connecting to the Internet 153
CHAPTER 2: Setting Up a Local Area Network 167
CHAPTER 3: Going Wireless 181
CHAPTER 4: Managing the Network 191

Book 4: The Internet 203
CHAPTER 1: Browsing the Web 205
CHAPTER 2: Using FTP 217
CHAPTER 3: Hosting Internet Services 229
CHAPTER 4: Managing Mail Servers 245
CHAPTER 5: Managing DNS 259

Book 5: Administration 281
CHAPTER 1: Introducing Basic System Administration 283
CHAPTER 2: Managing Users and Groups 319
CHAPTER 3: Managing File Systems 331
CHAPTER 4: Working with Samba and NFS 353

Book 6: Security 363

CHAPTER 1: Introducing Linux Security 365

CHAPTER 2: Securing Linux 381

CHAPTER 3: Vulnerability Testing and Computer Security Audits 413

Book 7: Scripting 429

CHAPTER 1: Introductory Shell Scripting 431

CHAPTER 2: Working with Advanced Shell Scripting 443

CHAPTER 3: Programming in Linux 451

Book 8: Linux Certification 477

CHAPTER 1: Studying for the Linux Essentials Certification Exam 479

CHAPTER 2: Studying for the CompTIA Linux+ Powered by
LPI Certification Exams 489

CHAPTER 3: Other Linux Certifications 507

Index 509

Table of Contents

INTRODUCTION 1

About This Book...2

Foolish Assumptions...3

Icons Used in This Book 4

Beyond the Book..4

Where to Go from Here 5

BOOK 1: GETTING STARTED WITH LINUX.................... 7

CHAPTER 1: **Introducing Linux**.. 9

What Is Linux? 9

    Linux distributions...10

    Making sense of version numbers 13

    Linux Standard Base (LSB) 14

Contents of a Linux Distribution......................................15

    GNU software..15

    GUIs and applications..16

    Networks..19

    Internet servers 19

    Software development 20

    Online documentation 22

Managing Your PC with Linux 23

    Distribution media...23

    Peripheral devices...24

    File systems and sharing 25

    Network 25

Getting Started..26

    Step 1: Install 26

    Step 2: Configure..26

    Step 3: Explore..27

    Step 4: Find out more 27

CHAPTER 2: **Installing Linux**... 29

Following the Installation Steps......................................29

Checking Your PC's Hardware 31

Setting Aside Space for Linux 33

Trying a Live CD 34

Installing Linux on a Flash Drive......................................35

    Creating the bootable flash drive 35

    Troubleshooting the workstation 36

    Working daily with the new drive 37

CHAPTER 3: **Troubleshooting and Configuring Linux**............39

Using Text Mode Installation....................................40
Troubleshooting X..40
Resolving Other Installation Problems.........................42
    Using Knoppix boot commands 42
    Handling the fatal signal 11 error.....................45
    Getting around the PC reboot problem...................45
    Using Linux kernel boot options........................48
Setting Up Printers..48
Managing DVDs, CD-ROMs, and Flash Drives......................51
Installing Other Software..51
    Installing software in Debian and Ubuntu...............52
    Installing software in Fedora..........................54
    Installing software in SUSE............................55

CHAPTER 4: **Trying Out Linux**....................................57

Starting Linux...57
Playing with the Shell...60
    Starting the bash shell 61
    Understanding shell commands...........................62
    Trying a few Linux commands............................62
Shutting Down..64

BOOK 2: LINUX DESKTOPS...67

CHAPTER 1: **GNOME and Its Derivatives**..........................69

Getting to Know the GNOME Desktop.............................70
Understanding the GNOME Panels.................................72
    The top panel...72
    The desktop...72
    The bottom panel 73
Looking at Unity...73
Looking at Cinnamon...73
Looking at MATE...74

CHAPTER 2: **The KDE Plasma Desktop**.............................75

Getting to Know the Plasma Desktop............................75
    Desktop contextual menus 77
    Icon contextual menus..................................77
Understanding the Plasma Panel.................................78
    The Main Menu button...................................79
    Panel icons...80
Configuring the Plasma Bottom Panel............................81
Configuring the Plasma Desktop.................................81

CHAPTER 3: **Commanding the Shell** 83

Opening Terminal Windows and Virtual Consoles 83
Using the bash Shell 84
    Understanding the syntax of shell commands 85
    Combining shell commands 86
    Controlling command input and output 87
    Typing less with automatic command completion. 89
    Going wild with asterisks and question marks 90
    Repeating previously typed commands. 91
Discovering and Using Linux Commands 92
    Becoming root (superuser) 97
    Managing processes 97
    Working with date and time. 99
    Processing files 100
Writing Shell Scripts 102

CHAPTER 4: **Navigating the Linux File System** 105

Understanding the Linux File System. 105
Navigating the File System with Linux Commands. 110
    Commands for directory navigation. 110
    Commands for directory listings and permissions. 112
    Commands for changing permissions and ownerships 114
    Commands for working with files. 116
    Commands for working with directories .117
    Commands for finding files 118
    Commands for mounting and unmounting 119
    Commands for checking disk-space use .120

CHAPTER 5: **Introducing Linux Applications** 123

Taking Stock of Linux Applications 124
Introducing Office Applications and Tools. 124
    LibreOffice.org office suite. 125
    Calendars 128
    Calculators 128
Checking out Multimedia Applications. 129
    Using a digital camera. 130
    Playing audio CDs 131
    Playing sound files. 131
    Burning a DVD or CD. 132
Using Graphics and Imaging Apps 133
    The GIMP 133
    GNOME Ghostview 134

CHAPTER 6: **Using Text Editors** 137

Using GUI Text Editors 137

Text Editing with ed and vi 140

Using ed 141

Using vi 145

BOOK 3: NETWORKING 151

CHAPTER 1: **Connecting to the Internet** 153

Understanding the Internet 154

Deciding How to Connect to the Internet 155

Connecting with DSL 156

How DSL works 156

DSL alphabet soup: ADSL, IDSL, SDSL .157

Typical DSL setup 158

Connecting with a Cable Modem 162

How a cable modem works 162

Typical cable modem setup 164

CHAPTER 2: **Setting Up a Local Area Network** 167

Understanding TCP/IP 167

IP addresses 169

Internet services and port numbers 170

Setting Up an Ethernet LAN 172

How Ethernet works 173

Ethernet cables 174

Configuring TCP/IP Networking 176

Connecting Your LAN to the Internet 178

CHAPTER 3: **Going Wireless** 181

Understanding Wireless Ethernet Networks 181

Understanding infrastructure and ad hoc modes 183

Understanding Wired Equivalent Privacy (WEP) 183

Setting Up Wireless Hardware 184

Configuring the Wireless Access Point 185

Configuring Wireless Networking 186

CHAPTER 4: **Managing the Network** 191

Discovering the TCP/IP Configuration Files 191

/etc/hosts 192

/etc/networks 193

/etc/host.conf 193

/etc/resolv.conf 193

/etc/hosts.allow 194

/etc/hosts.deny 195
/etc/nsswitch.conf 195
Checking Out TCP/IP Networks 196
Checking the network interfaces 196
Checking the IP routing table 196
Checking connectivity to a host 197
Checking network status 198
Sniffing network packets 199
Using GUI tools 200
Configuring Networks at Boot Time 201

BOOK 4: THE INTERNET 203

CHAPTER 1: **Browsing the Web** 205
Surfing the Web 205
Like a giant spider's web 206
Links and URLs 206
Web servers and web browsers 209
Web Browsing in Linux 209
Checking out web browsers for Linux 210
Introducing Firefox's user interface 210
Changing your home page 213
Surfing the Internet with Firefox 214

CHAPTER 2: **Using FTP** 217
Using Graphical FTP Clients 218
Using gFTP 218
Introducing FileZilla 220
Using a web browser as an FTP client 221
Using the Command-Line FTP Client 223

CHAPTER 3: **Hosting Internet Services** 229
Understanding Internet Services 229
TCP/IP and sockets 230
Internet services and port numbers 233
Using the Internet Super Server 235
Using inetd 236
Using xinetd 237
Running Stand-Alone Servers 239
Starting and stopping servers manually 240
Starting servers automatically at boot time 240

CHAPTER 4: **Managing Mail Servers** 245
    Installing the Mail Server 245
        Using sendmail 245
        A mail-delivery test 246
        The mail-delivery mechanism 247
        The sendmail configuration file. 247
        Syntax of the sendmail.cf file. 253
        Other sendmail files 254
        The .forward file. 256
        The sendmail alias file. 257

CHAPTER 5: **Managing DNS**. 259
    Understanding the Domain Name System (DNS). 259
        What is DNS? 260
        Discovering hierarchical domain names 261
        Exploring BIND. 262
    Configuring DNS 266
        Configuring the resolver. 266
        Configuring a caching name server 267
        Configuring a primary name server 278

BOOK 5: ADMINISTRATION 281

CHAPTER 1: **Introducing Basic System Administration** 283
    Taking Stock of System Administration Tasks. .284
    Becoming root 285
        Using the su - command. 285
        Recovering from a forgotten root password. 286
    Understanding How Linux Boots 287
        Understanding the init process. 288
        Examining the /etc/inittab file 289
        Trying a new run level with the init command 291
        Understanding the Linux startup scripts 291
        Manually starting and stopping servers. 292
        Automatically starting servers at system startup. 293
    Taking Stock of Linux System Configuration Files 294
    Monitoring System Performance 296
        Using the top utility. 297
        Using the uptime command 298
        Using the vmstat utility. 299
        Checking disk performance and disk usage 300
    Viewing System Information with the /proc File System. 302
    Understanding Linux Devices 305
        Device files 305
        Persistent device naming with udev. 307

Managing Loadable Driver Modules. 308
    Loading and unloading modules. 308
    Understanding the /etc/modprobe.d files. 309
Scheduling Jobs in Linux. 310
    Scheduling one-time jobs. 310
    Scheduling recurring jobs. 312
Introducing Some GUI System Administration Tools. 316

CHAPTER 2: **Managing Users and Groups**. 319
Adding User Accounts. 320
    Managing user accounts by using a GUI user manager 320
    Managing user accounts by using commands 322
Understanding the /etc/passwd File. 323
Managing Groups 324
Setting Other User and Group Administration Values. 325
Exploring the User Environment. 326
Changing User and Group Ownership of Files 328

CHAPTER 3: **Managing File Systems** 331
Exploring the Linux File System. 331
    Understanding the file-system hierarchy. 333
    Mounting a device on the file system. 336
    Examining the /etc/fstab file 337
Sharing Files with NFS. 339
    Exporting a file system with NFS. 340
    Mounting an NFS file system 341
Backing Up and Restoring Files. 341
    Selecting a backup strategy and media .342
    Commercial backup utilities for Linux 343
    Using the tape archiver: tar 343
Accessing a DOS or Windows File System 348
    Mounting a DOS or Windows disk partition 348
    Mounting those ancient DOS floppy disks. 349
Mounting an NTFS partition. 351

CHAPTER 4: **Working with Samba and NFS**. 353
Sharing Files with NFS. 353
    Exporting a file system with NFS. 354
    Mounting an NFS file system 357
Setting Up a Windows Server Using Samba 357
    Installing Samba 359
    Configuring Samba 359
    Trying out Samba. 360

BOOK 6: SECURITY 363

CHAPTER 1: **Introducing Linux Security** 365

Why Worry about Security? 366
Establishing a Security Framework 366
    Determining business requirements for security 368
    Performing risk analysis 368
    Establishing a security policy 370
    Implementing security solutions (mitigation) 371
    Managing security 372
Securing Linux 372
    Understanding the host-security issues 373
    Understanding network-security issues 374
Delving Into Computer Security Terminology and Tools 375
Keeping Up with Security News and Updates 379

CHAPTER 2: **Securing Linux** 381

Securing Passwords 382
    Shadow passwords 382
    Pluggable authentication modules (PAMs) 383
Protecting Files and Directories 384
    Viewing ownerships and permissions 385
    Changing file ownerships 385
    Changing file permissions 385
    Setting default permission 386
    Checking for set user ID permission 388
Encrypting and Signing Files with GnuPG 389
    Understanding public key encryption 389
    Understanding digital signatures 390
    Using GPG 391
Monitoring System Security 396
Securing Internet Services 397
    Turning off stand-alone services 397
    Configuring the Internet super server 398
    Configuring TCP wrapper security 398
Using Secure Shell for Remote Logins 399
Setting Up Simple Firewalls 402
    Using NAT 405
    Enabling packet filtering on your Linux system 406
Security Files to Be Aware Of 411

CHAPTER 3: **Vulnerability Testing and Computer Security Audits** 413

    Understanding Security Audits 414

        Nontechnical aspects of security audits. 414

        Technical aspects of security audits 415

    Implementing a Security Test Methodology 416

        Some common computer vulnerabilities. 417

        Host-security review 418

        Network-security review. 422

    Vulnerability Testing Types 424

    Exploring Security Testing Tools 425

BOOK 7: SCRIPTING 429

CHAPTER 1: **Introductory Shell Scripting** 431

    Trying Out Simple Shell Scripts 432

    Exploring the Basics of Shell Scripting 433

        Storing stuff 434

        Calling shell functions. 435

        Controlling the flow. 435

        Exploring bash's built-in commands. 439

CHAPTER 2: **Working with Advanced Shell Scripting** 443

    Trying Out sed 443

    Working with awk and sed. 446

        Step 1: Pull out the ISBN. 447

        Step 2: Calculate the 13th digit 448

        Step 3: Add the 13th digit to the other 12 449

        Step 4: Finish the process. 450

    Final Notes on Shell Scripting 450

CHAPTER 3: **Programming in Linux** 451

    An Overview of Programming 452

    Exploring the Software-Development Tools in Linux. 453

        GNU C and C++ compilers 454

        The GNU make utility 458

        The GNU debugger 466

    Understanding the Implications of GNU Licenses 473

        The GNU General Public License. 473

        The GNU Library General Public License 474

BOOK 8: LINUX CERTIFICATION 477

CHAPTER 1: **Studying for the Linux Essentials Certification Exam** 479

Overview of Linux Essentials 479
The Linux Community and a Career in Open Source 480
Finding Your Way on a Linux System 482
The Power of the Command Line 483
The Linux Operating System 485
Security and File Permissions 486

CHAPTER 2: **Studying for the CompTIA Linux+ Powered by LPI Certification Exams** 489

Overview of the CompTIA Linux+ Exams 489
System Architecture 490
Linux Installation and Package Management 492
GNU and Unix Commands 494
Devices, Linux File Systems, Filesystem Hierarchy Standard 495
Shells, Scripting, and Data Management 497
User Interfaces and Desktops 498
Administrative Tasks 500
Essential System Services 501
Networking Fundamentals 502
Security 504

CHAPTER 3: **Other Linux Certifications** 507

Vendor-Neutral Certifications 507
Vendor-Specific Certifications 508

INDEX 509

Introduction

L inux is truly amazing when you consider how it originated and how it continues to evolve. From its modest beginning as the hobby of one person — Linus Torvalds of Finland — Linux has grown into a full-fledged operating system with features that rival those of any commercial Unix operating system. To top it off, Linux — with all its source code — is available free to anyone. All you have to do is download it from an Internet site or get it on CDs or a DVD for a nominal fee from one of many Linux CD vendors.

Linux certainly is an exception to the rule that "you get what you pay for." Even though Linux is free, it's no slouch when it comes to performance, features, and reliability. The robustness of Linux has to do with the way it is developed and updated. Developers around the world collaborate to add features. Incremental versions are continually downloaded by users and tested in a variety of system configurations. Linux revisions go through much more rigorous beta testing than any commercial software does.

Since the release of Linux kernel 1.0 on March 14, 1994, the number of Linux users around the world has grown exponentially. Many Linux distributions — combinations of the operating system with applications and installation tools — have been developed to simplify installation and use. Some Linux distributions are commercially sold and supported, while many continue to be freely available.

Linux, unlike many freely available software programs, comes with extensive online information on topics such as installing and configuring the operating system for a wide variety of PCs and peripherals. A small group of hard-core Linux users are expert enough to productively use Linux with the online documentation alone. A much larger number of users, however, move to Linux with some specific purpose in mind (such as setting up a web server or learning Linux). Also, many Linux users use their systems at home. For these new users, the online documentation is not easy to use and typically does not cover the specific uses of Linux that each user may have in mind.

If you're beginning to use Linux, what you need is a practical guide that not only gets you going with Linux installation and setup, but also shows you how to use Linux for a specific task. You may also want to try out different Linux distributions before settling on one.

About This Book

Linux All-in-One For Dummies gives you eight quick-reference guides in a single book. Taken together, these eight minibooks provide detailed information on installing, configuring, and using Linux, as well as pointers for passing the vendor-neutral certification exams available from the Linux Professional Institute (LPI) to authenticate your skills.

What you'll like most about this book is that you don't have to sequentially read the whole thing chapter by chapter — or even read through each section in a chapter. You can pretty much turn to the topic you want and quickly get the answer to your pressing questions about Linux, whether they're about using the LibreOffice.org word processor, setting up the Apache web server, or a wide range of topics.

Here are some of the things you can do with this book:

>> Install and configure Linux using the information given in this book.

>> Connect the Linux PC to the Internet through a DSL or cable modem.

>> Add a wireless Ethernet to your existing network.

>> Get tips, techniques, and shortcuts for specific uses of Linux, such as

- Setting up and using Internet services

- Setting up a Windows server using Samba

- Using Linux commands

- Using shell programming

- Using the LibreOffice.org office suite and other applications that come with Linux

>> Understand the basics of system and network security.

>> Perform system administration tasks.

I use a simple notational style in this book. All listings, filenames, function names, variable names, and keywords are typeset in a monospace font for ease of reading. I *italicize* the first occurrences of new terms and concepts and then provide a definition right there. I show typed commands in **boldface**. The output of commands and any listing of files are shown in a monospace font.

Topics that correspond to the certification objectives are important after you've become comfortable enough with the operating system to consider taking the certification exams. As we discuss the material, Tips draw your attention to the key concepts and topics tested in the LX0-103 and LX0-104 exams (both of which you must pass to become certified by the Linux Professional Institute). Note, though, that not all Tips indicate material that's on the exams; I also share other types of information in Tips.

If you are a novice to Linux, overlook the certification objective information as you read. Only after you become comfortable with the operating system, and are considering authenticating your skills by taking the LPI exams, should you revisit the book and look for this information.

Each minibook zeros in on a specific task area — such as using the Internet or running Internet servers — and then provides hands-on instructions on how to perform a series of related tasks. You can jump right to a section and read about a specific task. You don't have to read anything but the few paragraphs or the list of steps that relate to your question. Use the Table of Contents or the Index to locate the pages relevant to your question.

You can safely ignore text next to the Technical Stuff icons, as well as text in sidebars. However, if you're the kind of person who likes to know some of the hidden details of how Linux works, then, by all means, dig into the Technical Stuff icons and the sidebars.

Foolish Assumptions

I assume that you're familiar with a PC — you know how to turn it on and off and you've dabbled with Windows. (Considering that most new PCs come preloaded with Windows, this assumption is safe, right?) And I assume that you know how to use some Windows applications, such as Microsoft Office.

When installing Linux on your PC, you may want to retain your Windows installations. I assume that you don't mind shrinking the Windows partition to make room for Linux. For this procedure, you can invest in a good disk-partitioning tool or use one of the partitioning tools included with most Linux distributions.

I also assume that you're willing to accept the risk that when you try to install Linux, some things may not quite work. Problems can happen if you have some uncommon types of hardware. If you're afraid of ruining your system, try finding a slightly older, spare Pentium PC that you can sacrifice and then install Linux on that PC.

Linux All-in-One Desk Reference For Dummies has eight minibooks, each of which focuses on a small set of related topics. If you're looking for information on a specific topic, check the minibook names on the thumbtabs or consult the Table of Contents.

Icons Used in This Book

Following the time-honored tradition of the *All-in-One For Dummies* series, I use icons to help you quickly pinpoint useful information. The icons include the following:

DISTRIBUTION SPECIFIC

The Distribution Specific icon points out information that applies to specific Linux distributions that this book covers: Debian, Fedora, Knoppix, SUSE, and Ubuntu.

REMEMBER

The Remember icon marks a general, interesting fact — something that you want to know and remember as you work with Linux. You might even find interesting trivia worth bringing up at an evening dinner party.

TIP

When you see the Tip icon, you're about to read about something you can do to make your job easier. Long after you've finished with the first reading of this book, you can skim the book, looking for only the tips.

WARNING

I use the Warning icon to highlight potential pitfalls. With this icon, I'm telling you: "Watch out! Whatever is being discussed could hurt your system." They say that those who are forewarned are forearmed, so I hope these entities will save you some frustration.

TECHNICAL STUFF

The Technical Stuff icon marks technical information that could be of interest to an advanced user (or those aspiring to be advanced users).

Beyond the Book

This book does not stop with the physical copy you hold in your hands. In addition to the content that is here, you'll find a Cheat Sheet worth looking at on the Dummies website. It includes quick tips for performing common tasks with Linux. You can find the Cheat Sheet at www.dummies.com.

Occasionally, we have updates to our technology books. If this book does have any technical updates, they'll be posted at www.dummies.com.

Where to Go from Here

It's time to get started on your Linux adventure. Turn to any chapter and let the fun begin. Use the Table of Contents and the Index to figure out where you want to go. Before you know it, you'll become an expert at Linux!

I hope you enjoy consulting this book as much as I enjoyed writing it!

1

Getting Started with Linux

Contents at a Glance

CHAPTER 1: Introducing Linux 9

What Is Linux? 9

Contents of a Linux Distribution 15

Managing Your PC with Linux 23

Getting Started. 26

CHAPTER 2: Installing Linux 29

Following the Installation Steps. 29

Checking Your PC's Hardware 31

Setting Aside Space for Linux 33

Trying a Live CD 34

Installing Linux on a Flash Drive 35

CHAPTER 3: Troubleshooting and Configuring Linux 39

Using Text Mode Installation 40

Troubleshooting X. 40

Resolving Other Installation Problems. 42

Setting Up Printers 48

Managing DVDs, CD-ROMs, and Flash Drives 51

Installing Other Software 51

CHAPTER 4: Trying Out Linux 57

Starting Linux. 57

Playing with the Shell 60

Shutting Down 64

» **Looking at what Linux distributions typically include**

» **Discovering what Linux helps you manage**

» **Getting started with Linux**

Chapter **1**

Introducing Linux

By virtue of your holding this book in your hands, it's a safe bet that you've heard something about Linux. If you're wondering exactly what Linux is, whether it's worth serious consideration, and what it can help you do, this chapter is for you. Here, I provide a broad picture of Linux and tell you how you can start using it right away.

TECHNICAL STUFF

Although Linux can run on many hardware platforms, this book focuses on Linux for Intel Pentium-based processors (basically, any PC that can run any flavor of Windows).

What Is Linux?

You can think of a PC as being a combination of *hardware* — things you can touch, such as the system box, monitor, keyboard, and mouse. The system box contains the most important hardware of all: the *central processing unit* (CPU), the microchip that runs the *software* (any program that tells the computer how to do your bidding), which you can't actually touch. In a typical Pentium-based PC, the Pentium microprocessor is the CPU. Other important hardware in the system box includes the memory (RAM chips) and the hard drive.

The *operating system* is the program that has to interact with all the hardware and get it to play nice. The operating-system software manages all that hardware and runs other software at your command. You, the user, provide those commands by choosing menus, clicking icons, or typing cryptic text. Linux is an operating system — as are Unix, macOS, Windows 10, and even older Windows versions. The Linux operating system is modeled after Unix; in its most basic, no-frills form, the Linux operating system also goes by *Linux kernel*.

The operating system gives a computer — any computer — its personality. You can run Windows on a PC, for example, and on that same PC, you can also install and run Linux. Then, depending on which operating system is installed and running at any particular time, the same PC can operate as a Windows system or as a Linux system.

The primary job of an operating system is to load software (computer programs) from the hard drive (or other permanent storage) into the memory and get the CPU to run those programs. Everything you do with your computer is possible because of the operating system, so if the operating system somehow messes up, the entire system freezes. You may know how infuriating it can be when your favorite operating system — maybe even the one that came with your PC — suddenly calls it quits just as you were about to click the Send button after composing that long email to your friend. You try several things frantically, but nothing happens. Then it's time to press the Reset button (or pull the cord from the back of the machine if your computer's builders weren't wise enough to include a Reset button). Luckily, that sort of thing almost never happens with Linux; it has a reputation for being a very reliable operating system.

TECHNICAL STUFF

In technical mumbo jumbo, Linux is a *multiuser, multitasking operating system.* Those terms just mean that Linux enables multiple users to log in, and each of those users can run more than one program at the same time. Nearly all operating systems are multiuser and multitasking these days, but when Linux started in 1993, *multiuser* and *multitasking* were big selling points.

Linux distributions

A *Linux distribution* consists of the Linux *kernel* (the operating system) and a collection of applications together with an easy-to-use installation program.

TIP

Most people just say *Linux* to refer to a specific Linux distribution.

Many Linux distributions are available, and each includes the standard Linux operating system and the following major packages:

>> **The X Window System:** It's the graphical user interface.

>> **One or more graphical desktops:** Among the most popular are GNOME and KDE Plasma.

DOES LINUX REALLY RUN ON ANY COMPUTER?

TECHNICAL STUFF

Linux runs on many types of computer systems, and there are so many distributions that it does seem able to run on nearly any type of computer.

Linus Torvalds and other programmers developed Linux for the Intel 80x86 (and compatible) line of processors. This book covers Linux for Intel 80x86 and Pentium processors (known as the *IA32 architecture* processors, or *i386*, because they support the instruction set of the 80386 processor).

Nowadays, Linux is also available for systems based on other processors as well, and IBM has released its own version of Linux for its zSeries mainframes. Several popular Linux distributions, including Ubuntu and Fedora, can even be run on Sony's PlayStation video game system.

>> **A selection of applications:** Linux programs come in the form of ready-to-run software, but the *source code* (the commands we humans use to tell the computer what to do) is included (or available), as is its documentation.

Current Linux distributions include a huge selection of software — so much that some distributions usually require multiple DVD-ROMs for installation.

TIP

The development and maintenance of the Linux kernel, the software packages in a Linux distribution, and the Linux distributions themselves are organized as open-source projects. In a nutshell, *open-source* means access to the source code and the right to freely redistribute the software without any restrictions. The definition involves a lot more than this succinct note, however. To find out the details of what open-source means and the acceptable open-source licenses, you can visit the Open Source Initiative website at https://opensource.org.

Table 1-1 lists a few major Linux distributions and gives a brief description of each one. Note, however, that many more Linux distributions exist than the ones shown in Table 1-1. To find out more about Linux distributions, visit DistroWatch.com at http://distrowatch.com. At that website, you can read up on specific distributions, as well as find links for downloading or ordering DVDs for specific distributions.

As you can see from the brief descriptions in Table 1-1, some Linux distributions, such as Knoppix and MEPIS, are available in the form of Live media (USBs, CDs, or DVDs). A *Live* version includes a Linux kernel that you can boot and run directly from the USB, CD, or DVD without having to install it on your hard drive. Such Live distributions can be handy if you want to try a distribution before you decide whether to install it.

TABLE 1-1 **Major Linux Distributions**

Distribution	Description
Debian GNU/Linux	This noncommercial distribution started in 1993 and continues to be a popular distribution, with many volunteer developers around the world contributing to the project. Debian is a huge distribution that takes some time to install. After you install the base Debian system, you can install and upgrade Debian packages easily with a package installer called apt–get (where *apt* stands for the Advanced Packaging Tool). Debian is available free of charge from https://www.debian.org. Debian is the basis for several other recent distributions, including Knoppix, MEPIS, and Ubuntu. At this writing, the most recent release of Debian is Debian 9, code-named Stretch.
Fedora	This distribution, once known as Fedora Core, is the successor to Red Hat Linux, which is the Linux distribution from Red Hat. Fedora Core 1, released in November 2003, was the successor to Red Hat Linux 9. The alpha release of Fedora 27 occurred in 2017. Fedora is freely available and uses Red Hat Package Manager (RPM) format for its software packages. You can download Fedora at https://getfedora.org.
Gentoo Linux	This noncommercial, *source-based* (all software provided in source-code form) distribution first appeared in 2002. The installer provides some binary packages to get Linux going, but the idea is to compile all source packages on the user's computer. The requirement to install so much makes it time-consuming to build a full-fledged Gentoo system with the latest graphical desktops, multimedia, and development tools, because all the packages have to be downloaded and compiled. Gentoo Linux is freely available at https://www.gentoo.org.
Knoppix	This Live distribution is based on Debian and named after its developer, Klaus Knopper of Germany. Knoppix can be used as a recovery tool to fix problems with an installed Linux system because you can run Knoppix directly from a CD without having to install it on the hard drive. first (Although other distributions have this capability, Knoppix is ideally suited for the task.) Knoppix uses Debian package management. For information on downloading Knoppix free of charge, visit the Knoppix website at www.knopper.net/knoppix/index–en.html.
Linspire	This commercial distribution was first released in 2002 under the name LindowsOS. Linspire uses Debian package format and offers software downloads for a fee through what it calls the Click-N-Run web-based interface. Though you can still find it and download it from some locations, Linspire was acquired by Xandros in 2008 and has since been discontinued as a Linux distribution.
MEPIS Linux	This Debian-based Live distribution was first released in July 2003. It includes a graphical installer that can be launched from the Live distribution to install MEPIS on the hard drive. MEPIS has good hardware detection and comes with Java and multimedia software, which makes it popular. MEPIS uses Debian package format. You can download it from www.mepis.org.
Slackware Linux	This distribution is one of the oldest, first released in 1992. Slackware uses compressed tar files for its packages and provides a text-based installer with limited automatic detection of hardware. You do all software configurations by editing text files. Slackware is freely available from www.slackware.com.

Distribution	Description
SUSE Linux	This commercial distribution switched to a community development project called openSUSE in August 2005. SUSE Linux Open Source Software (OSS) is now freely available, and retail SUSE Linux is based on the open-source version. SUSE comes with the YaST installation and configuration tool, which is one of the best administration tools available. SUSE Linux uses RPM packages. The openSUSE project provides the ISO image files from various mirror sites. Visit https://www.opensuse.org for more information.
Ubuntu Linux	This Debian-based, noncommercial Linux distribution has become very popular since its initial release in 2004. Ubuntu is available as both an install distribution and a Live distribution. Because it's Debian-based, you can install the basic desktop system from the install media and then use the apt-get tool to install other packages and keep the system up to date. You can download Ubuntu free of charge from https://www.ubuntu.com/download.

Many Linux distributions are commercial products that you can buy online or in computer stores and bookstores. If you've heard about open-source and the *GNU* (which stands for GNU's Not Unix) license, you may think that no one can sell Linux for profit. Luckily for companies that sell Linux distributions, the GNU license — also called the GNU General Public License (GPL) — does allow commercial, for-profit distribution (but requires that the software be distributed in source-code form) and stipulates that anyone may copy and distribute the software in source-code form to anyone else. Several Linux distributions are available free of charge under the GPL, which means that you can download as many copies of the OS as you like.

Making sense of version numbers

TIP

The Linux kernel — and each Linux distribution — has its own version number. Additional software programs (such as GNOME and KDE Plasma desktops) that come with the Linux distribution have their own version numbers as well. The version numbers for the Linux kernel and the Linux distributions are unrelated, but each has particular significance. Version numbers are in the form of three integers separated by periods — *major.minor.patch*, where *major* and *minor* are numbers denoting the major and minor version numbers, and *patch* is another number representing the patch level (for example 4.15.7).

TIP

You can find out about the latest version of the Linux kernel online at https://www.kernel.org.

Each version of a Linux distribution includes specific versions of the Linux kernel and other major components, such as GNOME, KDE, and various applications.

The developers of active Linux distributions usually release new versions of their distribution on a regular basis — about every six to nine months. Ubuntu 17.10, for example, was released in October 2017; the next version was scheduled for release in April 2018. Typically, each new major version of a Linux distribution provides significant new features.

DISTRIBUTION SPECIFIC

Debian always has at least three releases at any time:

>> **Stable:** Most users prefer this type of release because it's the latest officially released distribution.

>> **Unstable:** The developers are working on this release.

>> **Testing:** The release contains packages that have gone through some testing but aren't ready for inclusion in the stable release.

Linux Standard Base (LSB)

Linux has become important enough that it has a standard called the Linux Standard Base (LSB). *LSB* is a set of binary standards that should help reduce variations among the Linux distributions and promote portability of applications. The idea behind LSB is to provide an application binary interface so that software applications can run on any Linux (or other Unix) systems that conform to the LSB standard. The LSB specification references POSIX (Portable Operating System Interface) standards as well as many other standards, such as the C and C++ programming language standards, the X Window System version 11 release 6 (X11R6), and the Filesystem Hierarchy Standard (FHS). LSB version 1.2 (commonly referred to as *LSB 1.2*) was released on June 28, 2002. LSB 2.0 was released on August 30, 2004, and LSB 4.0 was released on November 11, 2008. Version 4.1 followed on February 16, 2011, essentially removing Java; version 5.0, the most recent version, was released June 2, 2015.

The LSB specification is organized into two parts: a common specification that remains the same across all types of processors and a set of hardware-specific specifications, one for each type of processor architecture. LSB 1.2, for example, has architecture-specific specifications for Intel 32-bit (IA32) and PowerPC 32-bit (PPC32) processors. LSB 1.3 adds a specification for the Intel 64-bit (IA64) architecture and IBM zSeries 31-bit (S/390) and 64-bit (S390X) processors, in addition to the ones for IA32 and PPC32. LSB 2.0 added a specification for the AMD 64-bit (AMD64 or X86_64) processors. LSB 4.0, which is the current specification, supports seven processor architectures: IA32, IA64, PPC32, PPC64 (64-bit PowerPC), S390, S390X, and X86_64.

An LSB certification program exists. Several Linux distributions are certified to be LSB-compliant, IA32 runtime environments. To discover more about LSB, visit `https://wiki.linuxfoundation.org/lsb/start`.

Contents of a Linux Distribution

A Linux distribution comes with the Linux kernel and a lot more software. These software packages include everything from graphical desktops to Internet servers to programming tools for creating new software. In this section, I briefly describe some major software packages that are bundled with typical Linux distributions. Without this bundled software, Linux wouldn't be as popular as it is today.

GNU software

At the heart of a Linux distribution is a collection of software that came from the GNU Project (see the nearby sidebar). You get to know these GNU utilities only if you use your Linux system through a *text terminal:* basic command-line interface that doesn't use onscreen visuals but instead shows a prompt at which you type your commands. (Alternatively, you could use a graphical window that mimics a text terminal and still use GNU utilities.) The GNU software is a basic part of any Linux distribution.

WHAT IS THE GNU PROJECT?

GNU is a recursive acronym that stands for GNU's Not Unix. Richard Stallman launched the GNU Project in 1984 to develop a complete Unix-like operating system. The GNU Project developed nearly everything needed for a complete operating system except the operating-system kernel.

All GNU software was distributed under the GNU General Public License (GPL). GPL essentially requires the software to be distributed in source-code form and stipulates that any user may copy, modify, and distribute the software to anyone else in source-code form. Users may have to pay for their individual copies of GNU software, however.

The Free Software Foundation is a tax-exempt charity that raises funds for work on the GNU Project. To find out more about the GNU Project, visit its home page at www.gnu.org. The home page is also where you can find information about how to contact the Free Software Foundation and how to help the GNU Project.

As a Linux user, you may not realize the extent to which all Linux distributions rely on GNU software. Nearly all the tasks you perform in a Linux system involve one or more GNU software packages. The GNOME graphical user interface (GUI) and the command interpreter (that is, the bash shell), for example, are both GNU software programs. By the way, the *shell* is the command-interpreter application that accepts the commands you type and then runs programs in response to those commands. If you rebuild the kernel or develop software, you do so with the GNU C and C++ *compiler* (which is part of the GNU software that accompanies Linux). If you edit text files with the ed or emacs editor, again, you're using a GNU software package. The list goes on and on.

TECHNICAL
STUFF

Table 1-2 lists some well-known GNU software packages that come with most Linux distributions. Depending on your interests, you may never need to use many of these packages, but knowing what they are in case you ever do need them is a good idea.

GUIs and applications

Face it — typing cryptic Linux commands on a terminal is boring. For average users, using the system through a *graphical user interface* (GUI, pronounced "GOO-ee") — one that gives you icons to click and windows to open — is much easier. This case is where the X Window System, or *X*, comes to the rescue.

X is kind of like Microsoft Windows, but the underlying details of how X works are different from those of Windows. X provides the basic features of displaying windows onscreen, but unlike Microsoft Windows, it doesn't come with any specific look or feel for graphical applications. That look and feel come from GUIs such as GNOME and KDE's Plasma, which use the X Window System.

Most Linux distributions come with the X Window System in the form of XFree86 or X.Org X11, which are implementations of the X Window System for 80x86 systems. XFree86 and X.Org X11 work with a wide variety of video cards available for today's PCs.

TECHNICAL
STUFF

Until early 2004, XFree86 from the XFree86 Project (www.xfree86.org) was the most commonly used X Window System implementation for x86 systems. Around version 4.4, however, some changes in the XFree86 licensing terms caused concerns for many Linux and Unix vendors, who felt that the licensing terms were no longer compatible with the GNU GPL. In January 2004, several vendors formed the X.Org Foundation (www.x.org) to promote continued development of an open-source X Window System and graphical desktop. The first release of X.Org X11 uses the same code that was used by XFree86 4.4, up until the time when the XFree86 license changes precipitated the creation of the X.Org Foundation.

TABLE 1-2   ## Well-Known GNU Software Packages

Software Package	Description
autoconf	Generates shell scripts that automatically configure source-code packages
automake	Generates Makefile.in files for use with autoconf
bash	The default shell (command interpreter) in Linux
bc	An interactive calculator with arbitrary-precision numbers
Binutils	A package that includes several utilities for working with binary files: ar, as, gasp, gprof, ld, nm, objcopy, objdump, ranlib, readelf, size, strings, and strip
Coreutils	A package that combines three individual packages called Fileutils, Shellutils, and Textutils and that implements utilities such as chgrp, chmod, chown, cp, dd, df, dir, dircolors, du, install, ln, ls, mkdir, mkfifo, mknod, mv, rm, rmdir, sync, touch, vdir, basename, chroot, date, dirname, echo, env, expr, factor, false, groups, hostname, id, logname, nice, nohup, pathchk, printenv, printf, pwd, seq, sleep, stty, su, tee, test, true, tty, uname, uptime, users, who, whoami, yes, cut, join, nl, split, tail, and wc
cpio	Copies file archives to and from disk or to another part of the file system
diff	Compares files, showing line-by-line changes in several formats
ed	A line-oriented text editor
emacs	An extensible, customizable, full-screen text editor and computing environment
Findutils	A package that includes the find, locate, and xargs utilities
finger	A utility program designed to enable users on the Internet to get information about one another
gawk	The GNU Project's implementation of the awk programming language
gcc	Compilers for C, C++, Objective-C, and other languages
gdb	Source-level debugger for C, C++, and FORTRAN
gdbm	A replacement for the traditional dbm and ndbm database libraries
gettext	A set of utilities that enables software maintainers to *internationalize* (make the software work with different languages such as English, French, and Spanish) a software package's user messages
ghostscript	An interpreter for the PostScript and Portable Document Format (PDF) languages
ghostview	An X Window System application that makes ghostscript accessible from the GUI, enabling users to view PostScript or PDF files in a window

(continued)

TABLE 1-2 *(continued)*

Software Package	Description
The GIMP	The GNU Image Manipulation Program, an Adobe Photoshop–like image-processing program
GNOME	A GUI for a wide variety of tasks that a Linux user may perform
GNUchess	A chess game
GNU C Library	For use with all Linux programs
Gnumeric	A graphical spreadsheet (similar to Microsoft Excel) that works in GNOME
grep package	Includes the `grep`, `egrep`, and `fgrep` commands, which are used to find lines that match a specified text pattern
`groff`	A document formatting system similar to `troff`
`gtk+`	A GUI toolkit for the X Window System (used to develop GNOME applications)
`gzip`	A GNU utility for compressing and decompressing files
`indent`	Formats C source code by indenting it in one of several styles
`less`	A page-by-page display program similar to `more` but with additional capabilities
`libpng`	A library for image files in Portable Network Graphics (PNG) format
`m4`	An implementation of the traditional Unix macro processor
`make`	A utility that determines which files of a large software package need to be recompiled and issues the commands to recompile them
`ncurses`	A package for displaying and updating text on text-only terminals
`patch`	A GNU version of Larry Wall's program to take the output of `diff` and apply those differences to an original file to generate the modified version
`rcs`	Revision Control System, used for version control and management of source files in software projects
`sed`	A stream-oriented version of the ed text editor
Sharutils	A package that includes `shar` (used to make shell archives out of many files) and `unshar` (to unpack these shell archives)
`tar`	A tape-archiving program that includes *multivolume support* — the capability to archive *sparse files* (files with big chunks of data that are all zeros), handle compression and decompression, and create remote archives — and other special features for incremental and full backups
`texinfo`	A set of utilities that generates printed manuals, plain ASCII text, and online hypertext documentation (called `info`), and enables users to view and read online `info` documents
`time`	A utility that reports the user, system, and actual time that a process uses

As for the GUI, Linux distributions include one or two powerful GUI desktops: *KDE* (K Desktop Environment) and *GNOME* (GNU Object Model Environment). If both GNOME and KDE are installed on a PC, you can choose which desktop you want to use as the default or switch between the two. KDE and GNOME provide desktops similar to those of Microsoft Windows and the macOS. GNOME also comes with the Nautilus graphical shell, which makes finding files, running applications, and configuring your Linux system easy. With GNOME or KDE, you can begin using your Linux workstation without having to know cryptic Linux commands. If you ever need to use those commands directly, however, all you have to do is open a terminal window and type the commands at the prompt.

Linux also comes with many graphical applications. One of the most noteworthy programs is *the GIMP* (GNU Image Manipulation Program), a program for working with photos and other images. The GIMP's capabilities are on a par with those of Adobe Photoshop.

Although Linux used to lack in providing common productivity software such as word processing, spreadsheet, and database applications, this situation has changed. Linux now has no shortage of Linux office applications that are compatible with Microsoft Office and other productivity suites.

Networks

Linux comes with everything you need to use the system on networks to exchange data with other systems. On networks, computers that exchange data must follow well-defined rules, or *protocols*. A *network protocol* is a method that the sender and receiver agree on for exchanging data across a network. Such a protocol is similar to the rules you might follow when you're having a polite conversation with someone at a party. You typically start by saying hello, exchanging names, and then taking turns talking. That's about the same way network protocols work. The two computers use the same protocol to send bits and bytes back and forth across the network.

One of the best-known (and most popular) network protocols is Transmission Control Protocol/Internet Protocol (TCP/IP). TCP/IP is the protocol of choice on the Internet — the "network of networks" that spans the globe. Linux supports the TCP/IP protocol and any network applications that use TCP/IP.

Internet servers

Some popular network applications are designed to deliver information from one system to another. When you send electronic mail (email) or visit websites by using a web browser, you use these network applications (also called *Internet services*). Here are some common Internet services:

- **Electronic mail** (email), which you use to send messages to any other person on the Internet by using addresses such as joe@someplace.com

- **World Wide Web** (or, simply, the web), which you browse by using a web browser

- **File transfer utilities,** which you can use to upload and download files

- **Remote login, which** you use to connect to and work with another computer (the remote computer) on the Internet, assuming that you have the username and password required to access that remote computer

Any Linux PC can offer these Internet services. To do so, the PC must be connected to the Internet, and it must run special server software called *Internet servers*. Each server uses a specific protocol for transferring information. Here are some common Internet servers that you find in Linux:

- sendmail is a mail server for exchanging email messages between systems by using SMTP (Simple Mail Transfer Protocol).

- Apache httpd is the web server for sending documents from one system to another by using HTTP (Hypertext Transfer Protocol).

- vsftpd is the server for transferring files between computers on the Internet by using FTP (File Transfer Protocol).

- in.telnetd allows a user on one system to log in to another system on the Internet by using the Telnet protocol.

- sshd allows a user on one system to log in securely to another system on the Internet by using the SSH (Secure Shell) protocol.

Software development

Linux is particularly well suited to software development. Straight out the box, it's chock-full of software-development tools, such as the compiler and libraries of code needed to build programs. If you happen to know Unix and the C programming language, you'll feel right at home programming in Linux.

As far as the development environment goes, Linux has the same basic tools (such as an editor, a compiler, and a debugger) that you might use on other Unix workstations, such as those from IBM, Sun Microsystems, and HP.

TIP

If you work by day on one of these Unix workstations, you can use a Linux PC in the evening at home to duplicate that development environment at a fraction of the cost. Then you can either complete work projects at home or devote your time to software that you write for fun and to share on the Internet.

STUFF PROGRAMMERS WANT TO KNOW ABOUT LINUX

These features make Linux a productive software-development environment:

- **GNU C compiler (gcc):** Compiles ANSI-standard C programs.

- **GNU C++ compiler (g++):** Supports ANSI-standard C++ features.

- **GNU compiler for Java (gcj):** Compiles programs written in the Java programming language.

- **GNU make utility:** Enables you to compile and link large programs.

- **GNU debugger (gdb):** Enables you to step through your program to find problems and determine where and how a program failed. (The failed program's memory image is saved in the core file; gdb can examine this file.)

- **GNU profiling utility (gprof):** Enables you to determine the degree to which a piece of software uses your computer's processor time.

- **Subversion, Concurrent Versions System (CVS), and Revision Control System (RCS):** Maintain version information and controls access to the source files so that two programmers don't inadvertently modify the same source file at the same time.

- **GNU emacs editor:** Prepares source files and even launches a compile-link process to build the program.

- **Perl:** Enables you to write scripts to accomplish a specific task, tying together many smaller programs with Linux commands.

- **Tool Command Language and its graphical toolkit (Tcl/Tk):** Enable you to build graphical applications rapidly.

- **Python:** Enables you to write code in an interpreted programming language comparable to Perl and Tcl. (The Fedora Core installation program, called anaconda, is written in Python, for example.)

- **Dynamically linked, shared libraries:** Allow your actual program files to be much smaller because all the library code that several programs may need is shared, with only one copy loaded in the system's memory.

Online documentation

As you become more adept at using Linux, you may want to look up information quickly — without having to turn the pages of (ahem) this great book, for example. Luckily, Linux comes with enough online information to jog your memory in those situations when you vaguely recall a command's name but can't remember the syntax you're supposed to type.

If you use Linux commands, you can view the manual page — commonly referred to as the *man page* — for a command by using the man command. (You do have to remember that command to access online help.)

You can also get help from the GUI desktops. Both GNOME and KDE desktops come with help viewers to view online help information. Most distributions include a help option on the desktop menu or a help icon on the desktop that you can use to get online help. Then you can browse the help information by clicking the links in the initial help window. Figure 1-1 shows a typical help window from Ubuntu's desktop.

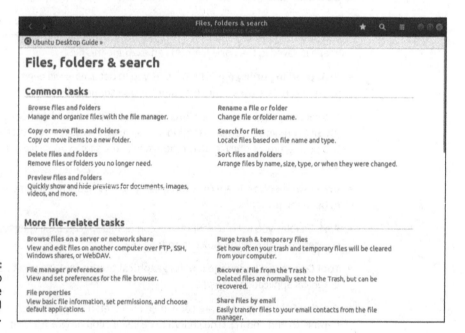

FIGURE 1-1:
Online help is available from the GUI desktop.

Managing Your PC with Linux

TIP

As an operating system, Linux acts as the intermediary through which you — as the "lord of the system" — manage all the hardware. The hardware includes the system box, the monitor, the keyboard, the mouse, and anything else connected to the system box. The catch-all term *peripheral* refers to any equipment attached to the system. If you use a laptop computer, all your hardware is packaged into the laptop.

Inside that system box is the system's brain: the microprocessor (Intel Pentium 4, for example), also called the CPU, which performs the instructions contained in a computer program. When the microprocessor runs a computer program, that program's instructions are stored in the memory, or *RAM* (random-access memory). RAM means that any part of the memory can be accessed randomly, in any order.

The system box has another crucial component: the hard drive (or hard disk, as it's sometimes called). The hard drive is the permanent storage space for computer programs and data; it's permanent in the sense that the contents don't disappear when you power off the PC. The hard drive is organized into files, which are in turn organized in a hierarchical fashion into directories and subdirectories (somewhat like papers organized in folders inside the drawers of a file cabinet).

To keep a Linux system running properly, you (or someone else) must make sure that the hardware is working properly and that the files are backed up regularly. There's also the matter of *security*, making sure that only legitimate people can access and use the system. These tasks are called *system administration*.

If you use Linux at a big facility with many computers, a full-time system administrator probably takes care of all system-administration tasks. On the other hand, if you run Linux on a home PC, you *are* the system administrator. Don't let the thought frighten you. You don't have to know any magic incantations or prepare cryptic configuration files to be a system administrator. Most Linux distributions include many graphical tools that make system administration a point-and-click job, just like running any other application.

Distribution media

Some Linux distributions come on a single DVD-ROM or require you to create it from files downloaded from a site. After installation, the Linux kernel and all the applications are stored on your hard drive, which is where your PC looks first when you tell it to do something.

Typically, the hard drive is prepared to use Linux during the installation process. After that, you usually leave the hard drive alone except to back up the data stored there or (occasionally) to install and update applications.

Using USB drives or DVD-ROMs in Linux is easy. While you're logged in at the GNOME or KDE desktop, just pop a DVD into the drive or a thumb drive into the USB port, and the system should automatically detect the media. Depending on the Linux distribution, a DVD/CD-ROM icon appears on the desktop, or a file manager opens and displays the contents of the DVD/CD-ROM. If all else fails, you can type a simple mount command to associate the media with a directory on your system. The process of accessing the files on a device from Linux is called *mounting* the CD or the DVD.

Peripheral devices

Anything connected to your PC is a peripheral device, as are some components (such as sound cards) that are installed inside the system box. You can configure and manage these peripheral devices in Linux.

One common peripheral is a printer, typically hooked up to the USB (Universal Serial Bus) or parallel port of your PC. (Many distributions come with a graphical printer configuration tool that you can use to configure the printer.)

Another peripheral device that needs configuration is the sound card. Most Linux distributions detect and configure sound cards, just as Windows does. If Linux can't detect the sound card correctly, you may have to run a text mode or graphical tool to configure the sound card.

Linux configures other peripheral devices, such as the mouse and keyboard, at the time of installation. You can pretty much leave them alone after installation.

Nowadays, PCs come with the USB interface; many devices, including printers and scanners, plug into a PC's USB port.

TIP

One nice feature of USB devices is that you can plug them into the USB port and unplug them at any time; the device doesn't have to be connected when you power up the system. These devices are called *hot-plug* because you can plug in a device when the system is *hot,* meaning while it's running. Linux supports many hot-plug USB devices. When you plug a device into the USB port, Linux loads the correct driver and makes the device available to applications.

File systems and sharing

The entire organization of directories and files is the *file system.* You can manage the file system by using Linux. When you browse the files from the GNOME or KDE graphical desktop, you work with the familiar folder icons.

REMEMBER

A key task in caring for a file system is backing up important files. In Linux, you can use the tar program to archive one or more directories on a USB drive or on other media. You can even back up files on a tape (if you have a tape drive). If you have a CD or DVD burner, you can also burn a CD or DVD with the files you want to back up or save for posterity.

Linux can share parts of the file system with other systems on a network. You can use the Network File System (NFS) to share files across the network, for example. To a user on the system, the remote system's files appear to be in a directory on the local system.

Linux also comes with the Samba package, which supports file sharing with Microsoft Windows systems. Samba makes a Linux system work just like a Windows file or print server. You can also access shared folders on other Windows systems on your network.

Network

Now that most PCs are linked in a local-area network (LAN) or connected to the Internet, you need to manage your connection to the network as well. Linux comes with a network configuration tool to set up the LAN. For connecting to the Internet with a modem, there's usually a GUI Internet dial-up tool.

If, like many users, you connect to the Internet with a DSL or cable modem, you need a PC with an Ethernet card that connects to the cable or DSL modem. You also have to set up a LAN and configure the Ethernet card. Fortunately, these steps typically are part of Linux installation. If you want to do the configurations later, you can by using a GUI network configuration tool.

Linux also includes tools for configuring a *firewall,* which is a protective buffer that helps keep your system relatively secure from anyone trying to snoop over your Internet connection. You can configure the firewall by using iptables commands or by running a GUI firewall-configuration tool.

Getting Started

Based on my experience in exploring new subjects, I prescribe a four-step process to get started with Linux (and with *Linux All-in-One For Dummies*):

1. **Install Linux on your PC (as shown in Book 1, which is this one).**

2. **Configure Linux so that everything works to your liking (as shown in Book 1).**

3. **Explore the GUI desktops and the applications (as shown in Book 2).**

4. **Find out the details of specific subjects, such as Internet servers (as shown in Book 4).**

In the rest of this chapter, I explain this prescription a bit more.

Step 1: Install

Microsoft Windows usually comes installed on your new PC, but Linux usually doesn't, so your first task is getting Linux on your PC. Although some vendors now offer Linux preinstalled, that situation is still a rarity.

After you overcome the initial human fear of the unknown, I'll bet that you find Linux fairly easy to install. But where do you *get* it in the first place? The good news is that it's easy to find online. Book 1 shows you how to install Linux step by step.

WARNING

A typical complete Linux distribution is *huge,* but if you have good bandwidth, Linux is free to download. You can visit the Linux Online website at https://www. linux.org, for example, and click the Download button.

Step 2: Configure

When you finish installing Linux, the next step is configuring individual system components (such as the sound card and the printer) and tweaking any needed settings. Book 1 shows how to configure the nooks and crannies of Linux.

TIP

If you aren't getting a graphical login screen, the X Window System may not have been configured correctly during installation. You have to fix the X configuration file for the GUI to work.

You may want to configure your GUI desktop of choice: GNOME or KDE (or both). Each desktop has configuration tools, which you can use to adjust the look and feel of the desktop (background, title fonts, or even the entire color scheme). Book 2 shows you how to make your desktop even more your own.

When you're through with configuration, all the hardware on your system and the applications should run to your liking.

Step 3: Explore

With a properly configured Linux PC at your disposal, you're ready to explore Linux itself. You can begin the process from the GUI desktop — GNOME or KDE — that you see after logging in. Look at the GUI desktops and the folders and files that make up the Linux file system, as discussed in Book 2. You can also try the applications from the desktop. You find office and multimedia applications and Internet applications to explore.

Also try the shell: Open a terminal window and type some Linux commands in that window. You can also explore the text editors that work in text mode, as covered in Book 2. Knowing how to edit text files without the GUI, just in case the GUI isn't available, is a good idea. At least you won't be helpless.

Step 4: Find out more

After you explore the Linux landscape and know what's what, you can dig deeper and find out more about specific subject areas. You may be interested in setting up Internet servers, for example. Then you can find out the details on setting up individual servers, such as sendmail for email, and Apache for a web server as covered in Book 4.

You can find out about areas such as security, scripting, and system administration in Books 5, 6, and 7.

You can expect this step to go on and on, of course, even after you have your system running the way you want it — for now. After all, learning is a lifelong journey.

Bon voyage!

» Checking the hardware

» Reserving hard drive space for Linux

» Trying the Ubuntu Live CD

» Installing Linux on an external drive

Chapter **2**

Installing Linux

Most of the PCs sold today come with Microsoft Windows preinstalled on them instead of Linux. Although this arrangement makes computers easier for the masses to use out of the box, it means that if you want to use Linux, you usually have to install it yourself.

You may feel a tad worried about installing a new operating system on your PC because the process is a bit like brain surgery — or like grafting a new brain, because you can install Linux in addition to Microsoft Windows. When you install two operating systems, you can choose to start one or the other when you power up the PC. The biggest headache in adding Linux to a PC with Windows is creating a new disk partition, which means setting aside a part of the hard drive for Linux. The rest of the installation is routine — a matter of following the instructions. If you want to try any of the Live media versions, you don't have to do any disk partitioning; just boot your PC from the Live DVD/CD/flash drive. But first, take a deep breath and exhale slooowwwly. You have nothing to worry about.

Following the Installation Steps

Installing any Linux distribution involves several steps, and I walk you through them briefly, without details. Then you can follow the detailed steps for the specific distributions and install what you want.

**DISTRIBUTION
SPECIFIC**

Some Linux distributions require you to have quite a bit of information about your PC's hardware on hand before installation. If you plan to install Debian, gather information about your PC and its peripheral components before starting the installation. Luckily, most Linux installation programs can detect and work with most PC peripherals. Nevertheless, it's a good idea to figure out your PC's hardware so that you can troubleshoot in case something goes wrong with the installation.

The very first step is burning the media for your distribution. You can burn DVDs or CDs on any system that has an appropriate burner. (You must have a DVD burner if you want to burn a DVD, but a DVD burner can burn both CDs and DVDs.) Typically, if you already have a Windows PC with a CD/DVD burner, you can simply use that system to burn the CDs.

REMEMBER

The second step is making sure that your PC can boot from the drive where the media will be. Most new PCs can boot directly from the DVD/CD drive, but some PCs may require your intervention. Typically, the PC may be set to boot from the hard drive before the DVD/CD drive, and you have to get into Setup to change the order of boot devices.

To set up a PC to boot from the DVD drive, you have to go into Setup as the PC powers up. The exact steps for entering Setup and setting the boot device vary from one PC to the next, but typically, they involve pressing a key, such as F2. When the PC powers up, a brief message tells you what key to press to enter Setup. When you're in Setup, you can designate the DVD/CD drive as the boot device. After your PC is set up to boot from the DVD/CD drive, simply put the DVD or CD in the DVD/CD drive and then restart your PC.

**DISTRIBUTION
SPECIFIC**

If you plan to try a Live CD distribution, the third step is booting your PC from the Live CD or DVD. Otherwise the third step is making room for Linux on your PC's hard drive. If you're running Microsoft Windows, this step can be easy or hard, depending on whether you want to replace Windows with Linux or to keep both Windows and a Linux distribution.

If you want to install Linux without removing (or disturbing) Windows, remember that your existing operating system uses the entire hard drive. You have to *partition* (divide) the hard drive so that Windows can live in one part of it and Linux can live in the other. Partitioning can be a scary step because you run the risk of clearing the hard drive and wiping out whatever is on the drive. Therefore, *always* make a backup of your system before undertaking any significant changes.

To set aside space on your hard drive that the Linux installation program can use, you should use a partitioning program to help you create the partition. If your PC runs Windows 10 or an older version of Windows, you may want to invest in a commercial hard drive partitioning product. On the other hand, you can repartition your PC's hard drive by using a GUI (graphical user interface) tool called QTParted, which comes with Knoppix and several other distributions.

DISTRIBUTION SPECIFIC

Note that the installers for some Linux distributions, such as openSUSE, can automatically create partitions for Linux by reducing the size of a Windows partition. In that case, you don't need to use a tool such as QTParted to shrink the existing Windows partition on your hard drive.

After you set aside a hard drive partition for Linux, you can boot the PC from the selected distribution's CD and start the Linux installation. Quite a few steps occur during installation, and they vary from one distribution to another. When you've come this far, it should be smooth sailing. Just go through the installation screens, and you'll be finished in an hour or two. Most installers, such as the openSUSE interface, display a GUI and guide you through all the steps.

One key step during installation involves partitioning the hard drive again, but this time, you simply use the extra partition you created previously.

After a few configuration steps, such as setting up the network and the time zone, select the software packages to install and then let the installer complete the remaining installation chores. Some distributions make the process even easier; they do away with the software-selection step and install a default set of software packages instead.

At the end of the installation, reboot the PC. Rebooting is sometimes required before the automatic configuration can run.

When Linux runs for the first time, you get a chance to perform some more configuration steps and install additional software packages.

Checking Your PC's Hardware

If you're concerned that your PC may not be able to run Linux, here are some of the key components of your PC that you need to consider before you start the Linux installation:

>> **DVD drive:** You must have a DVD drive (either DVD-ROM or DVD burner), and the PC must be able to boot from that drive.

The exact model doesn't matter. What does matter is how the DVD drive connects to the PC. Most new PCs have DVD drives that connect to the hard drive controller (*IDE*, for Integrated Drive Electronics, or *ATA*, for AT Attachment). If you add an external DVD drive, it most likely connects to the USB port. Any IDE/ATA or USB DVD drive works in Linux.

>> **Hard drives:** Any IDE disk drive works in Linux. Another type of hard drive controller is SCSI (Small Computer System Interface), which Linux also supports. To comfortably install and play with Linux, you need about 5GB of hard drive space. On the other hand, to try the Live CD versions of Linux, you don't need any space on the hard drive.

>> **Keyboard:** All keyboards work with Linux and the X Window System.

>> **Monitor:** The kind of monitor isn't particularly critical except that it must be capable of displaying the screen resolutions that the video card uses. The screen resolution is expressed in terms of the number of picture elements (*pixels*) horizontally and vertically (such as 1024 x 768). The installer can detect most modern monitors. If the installer doesn't detect your monitor, you can select a generic monitor type with a specific resolution (such as 1024 x 768). You can also specify the monitor by its make and model, which you can find on the back of the monitor.

>> **Mouse:** The installation program can detect the mouse. All types of mouse (such as PS/2 or USB) work with Linux and the X Window System.

>> **Network card:** Although not all PCs have network cards, these days it's rare to find one that doesn't have one. As long as your PC has a network card, the installer probably can detect and use the card, whether it's Wi-Fi or wired. If you have problems, try to find the network card's make and model so that you can search online for information about whether Linux supports that card.

>> **Processor:** The processor speed, expressed in MHz (megahertz) or GHz (gigahertz), isn't important as long as it's over 700 MHz; most processors made in the past few years have speeds well above that. As a general rule, the faster the better. Linux can run on other Intel-compatible processors, such as AMD and VIA processors.

>> **RAM:** *RAM* is the amount of memory your system has. As with processing speed, the more RAM, the better. You need a minimum of 512MB to install both Linux and the X Window System. With some distributions, the minimum amount is higher, and you'll want still more memory to be able to run a GUI desktop comfortably.

>> **SCSI controller:** Some high-performance PCs and legacy workstations have SCSI controllers that connect disk drives and other peripherals to a PC. If your PC happens to have a SCSI controller, you may want to find out the make and model of the controller.

>> **Sound card:** If your PC has a sound card, and you want to have sound in Linux, you have to make sure that the card is compatible. You can configure the sound card after successfully installing Linux.

>> **Video card:** Linux works fine with all video cards (also known as *display adapters*) in text mode, but if you want the GUI, you need a video card that works with the X Window System. The installer can detect a supported video card and configure the X Window System correctly. If the installer can't detect your video card, it helps to know the make and model of the card.

>> **Printer:** You need to know the make and model of any printer that you plan to use in Linux.

TIP

Many distributions, such as Debian GNU/Linux, work on any hardware that's compatible with the Linux kernel.

DISTRIBUTION
SPECIFIC

To check whether your PC's hardware is compatible with individual distributions, visit that vendor's site to check its hardware-compatibility list.

Setting Aside Space for Linux

In a typical Windows PC, Windows is sitting on one big partition, taking over the entire hard drive. You want to shrink that partition to create room for Linux. During Linux installation, the installation program uses the free space for the Linux partitions.

DISTRIBUTION
SPECIFIC

To try any of the Live CD distributions, such as Ubuntu, you don't have to repartition your hard drive. Just boot your PC from the Live CD. The installers can shrink a Windows partition nondestructively, so you don't need to perform the repartitioning step beforehand. If you plan to install Fedora, Debian, or any other Linux distribution on the hard drive, you have to repartition your hard drive. If you want to resize the disk partition under Windows, you can use a commercial product, or you can boot a Linux distribution and then use GParted (the partition editor) to resize the Windows partitions. GParted can resize NTFS (NT File System) partitions, which all recent versions of Windows use.

WARNING

When you resize the disk partition, you always risk losing all the data on the hard drive. Therefore, before you resize hard drive partitions with a disk-partitioning tool, *back up your hard drive.* After making your backup — and before you do *anything* to the partitions — please make sure that you can restore your files from the backup.

After Ubuntu boots and the GUI desktop appears, follow these steps to reduce the size of the Windows partition:

1. **Choose System➪Administration➪GParted from the Ubuntu desktop.**

   The GParted window appears, and the tool displays the drives that it finds on your PC. The first hard drive appears with the device name /dev/sda; the second one appears as /dev/sdb, and so on.

2. **Select the hard drive in the list of devices on the right side of the GParted window.**

3. **In the list of partitions, select the partition that you want to resize.**

   This partition is normally the largest partition. For Windows 10, Windows 8, and other recent versions, the partition type is ntfs, as shown in the Type column in the list of partitions. In a typical new PC, you may see two partitions: a small fat16 partition and a large ntfs partition.

4. **Choose GParted➪Resize/Move.**

   The Resize partition dialog box appears.

5. **Set the new size of the partition and then click Resize/Move.**

   You should choose a size that gives you 4GB or more free space after the partition. The size of the free space appears in the dialog box's Free Space After field.

6. **When you've specified all changes that you want to make, click Apply to begin the operation.**

7. **When the warning appears, click Apply.**

   All pending operations are performed, the partition is changed, and you have free space after the Windows partition.

After you create free space on the hard drive for Linux, you can proceed to install the Linux distribution of your choice.

Trying a Live CD

Before you install anything, you'll find it worthwhile to try a Live CD or bootable USB version. In addition to getting a feel for a Linux desktop, you usually can perform a few additional preinstallation chores.

To start Ubuntu, for example, boot your PC from the Live CD. A menu appears, allowing you to enter various options to control the boot process or check your system to see whether it meets hardware requirements. You should choose the default option of booting Ubuntu (automatically performed if you don't make a choice before the menu times out in 30 seconds).

A few minutes later, you see the GNOME GUI desktop, which Ubuntu uses, and you can start exploring Ubuntu. If you click the Examples folder, you find several things that Ubuntu can do. You can also choose System⇨Administration⇨GParted to reconfigure the hard drive.

When you finish using Ubuntu, choose System⇨Quit. When Ubuntu shuts down, remove the DVD, and press Enter. Should you decide that you want to install Ubuntu, click the Install icon on the desktop to begin that process.

Installing Linux on a Flash Drive

I was a fan of Live CD versions of Linux distributions for a while, but no more. I liked Live CDs because they let me create cheap media that I could distribute to students and users. This practice allowed them to enjoy the Linux experience on their own machines without installing the operating system, changing what they were comfortable with, or risking harm. In addition, this user group could quickly change from Fedora to Ubuntu to openSUSE and more. My biggest dislikes of the Live CD distributions were their incredibly slowness and inability to save configuration changes easily. Given these substantial issues, I've been seeking a better solution. Fortunately, I've found it: bootable USB distributions.

Bootable USB distributions have been around for some time but have had weaknesses that previously prevented me from embracing them. Newer ones, however, such as Fedora Media Writer (https://github.com/MartinBriza/MediaWriter) have simplified the creation method so that most users can walk through unescorted. The installation process is nondestructive, allowing you to keep existing files on the USB drive, and retaining changes (data persistence) is straightforward.

In the rest of this chapter, I show you how to create a bootable flash drive and use it in your own setting.

Creating the bootable flash drive

Although you can create a bootable flash drive by using command-line methods in Linux, the simplest technique uses Windows. (I realize that it may sound like heresy to suggest making a Linux boot medium from Windows, but most users who are interested in a Live USB implementation of Linux probably run Windows.) Follow these steps to create a bootable flash drive:

1. **Download the bootable program you wish to use.**

2. **Install the program and run it.**

3. **In the Target Device section, select the flash drive.**

   The flash drive may appear with a name such as TravelDrive.

4. **Choose where the image (the ISO file) will come from.**

   If you have a slow Internet connection, you can have one Live CD from which you pull the ISO file. If you have a faster Internet connection, use the Download option to access a current ISO file.

5. **Set the Persistent Storage amount, if prompted to do so.**

   Persistent storage is the amount of storage space allocated to the installation that is always available. I suggest using a value of at least 300MB. (I don't know why the default is 0MB.)

6. **Click the Create Live USB button, and sit back to watch the progress.**

   Be prepared to wait ten minutes for the process to complete. Two folders are usually created on the drive: syslinux (less than 7MB and responsible for the booting) and LiveOS (the size of which depends on your storage setting).

7. **Close the application, and test the new bootable drive.**

Troubleshooting the workstation

I experimented with several flash drives and failed to encounter a problem with any as long as 1GB of free space remained after installation. Smaller drives (2GB or less) are often factory-formatted with FAT (file allocation table), and larger ones are formatted with FAT32; formatting didn't make any difference in installation or usability that I could ascertain.

You must be sure that the workstation settings allow the machine to boot from USB, which typically requires reconfiguring the BIOS. To do so, follow these steps:

1. **Reboot the workstation, and press the key that takes you to the BIOS configuration.**

   Usually, this key is F12 or DEL; sometimes, it's F1 or F2.

2. **Open the Boot menu, and choose the setting Boot USB Devices First (or something similar).**

On some computers, the flash drive is hidden in the hard drive section of the boot BIOS. In this case, choose Boot⇨Hard Drives; change the primary hard drive to the storage media; and then make sure that the USB is the first choice listed under Boot Device. If the option to boot from USB is Enable/Disable, choose Enable; go to the order of boot devices; and move the USB selection above the hard drive selection.

3. **Save your changes, and exit the BIOS configuration.**

At this point, the workstation continues with the reboot and (if your USB drive is plugged in) should boot Fedora.

If you get the single-line entry Boot Error and nothing else happens, update the system BIOS per the manufacturer's instructions.

Working daily with the new drive

When your system boots, the Fedora environment loads much more quickly than it loads with Live CDs. The USB drive displays the new folders created on it, and other devices can be accessed as usual. The Install to Hard Drive icon remains on the desktop, allowing for a quick permanent transition to Fedora should you decide to do so.

An Internet connection isn't required to use the operating system, but I strongly recommend having one, because most users will want to download additional programs that allow them to test the operating system's functionality further.

Congratulations! You can start using Linux.

» Configuring the X Window System

» Resolving installation problems

» Setting up your printers

» Managing your DVDs and CD-ROMs

» Installing additional software packages

Chapter **3**

Troubleshooting and Configuring Linux

During the installation of Linux, the installer attempts to detect key hardware components, such as the network card and any installed peripherals. According to what it detects, the installer takes you through a sequence of installation steps. If the installer can't detect the network card, for example, it usually skips the network configuration step. This omission is okay if you don't in fact have a network card, but if you do have one and the installer mistakenly insists that you don't, you have an installation problem on your hands.

Another installation problem can occur when you restart the PC and see a text terminal instead of the graphical login screen. This error means that something is wrong with the X Window System configuration.

In addition, the Linux installation typically doesn't include configuration procedures for every piece of hardware on your PC system. Most installations don't set up printers during installation, for example.

In this chapter, I show you some ways to troubleshoot installation problems. You find out how to configure X Window System to start with a graphical user interface (GUI) screen and how to configure a printer.

You may also have to install additional software packages, so this chapter walks you through how to install packages in different formats, such as Red Hat Package Manager (RPM) and Debian package — the two formats in which most Linux software is distributed.

Using Text Mode Installation

Most Linux installers attempt to use the X Window System (X) to display the graphical installation screens. If the installer fails to detect a video card, for example, X doesn't start. If (for this or any other reason) the installer fails to start X, you can always fall back on text mode installation. Then you can specify the video card manually or configure X later by using a separate configuration program. You can also configure X by editing its text configuration file.

Table 3-1 lists how you can get to the text mode installation screen. Typically, the text mode installation sequence is similar to that of the graphical installation outlined in Chapter 2 of this minibook. You respond to the prompts and perform the installation.

TABLE 3-1   **Text Mode Installation in Some Linux Distributions**

Distribution	How to Get to the Text Mode Installer
Debian	Runs in text mode by default.
Fedora	Type **text** at the boot : prompt after you start the PC from the Fedora CD or DVD.
Knoppix	Start Knoppix in text mode by typing **knoppix 2** at the boot : prompt (because Knoppix is a Live distribution, you don't have to install it).
SUSE	At the first installation screen, press F3, use the arrow keys to select the text mode option, and then press Enter.
Ubuntu	Runs in text mode by default.

Troubleshooting X

Every time I installed Linux on older PCs, the GUI installation worked fine during installation, but then the graphical login screen didn't appear when I rebooted the PC for the first time after installation. Instead, I ended up with a text login screen or a black screen with a small X in the middle, or the boot process seemed to hang with a gray screen. If this problem happens to you, here's how you can troubleshoot it:

1. Press Ctrl+Alt+Delete to reboot the PC.

The PC starts to boot. You get to a screen where GRUB (GRand Unified Bootloader) prompts you for the operating system to boot. (If the distribution uses LILO as the bootloader, you get a text prompt.)

2. For GRUB, press the A key to add an option that tells the Linux kernel to boot to a prompt; for LILO, skip this step.

The GRUB bootloader displays a command line for the Linux kernel and prompts you to add what you want.

3. For GRUB, type a space followed by the word single **and press Enter; for LILO, type** linux single **and press Enter.**

The Linux kernel boots in single-user mode and displays a prompt that ends in a pound sign like the following:

```
#
```

Now you're ready to configure X.

X uses a configuration file (XF86Config-4 or xorg.conf, depending on the distribution) to figure out your display card, your monitor, and the kind of screen resolution you want. The Linux installer prepares the configuration file, but sometimes, the configuration isn't correct.

To create a working configuration file quickly, follow these steps:

1. Type the following command:

```
X -configure
```

The X server runs and creates a configuration file. The screen goes blank; then the X server exits after displaying some messages. In Fedora, the last line of the message says the following:

```
To test the server, run 'X -config ///etc/xorg.conf.new'
```

2. Use a text editor such as vi **to edit the** ///etc/xorg.conf.new **file, and insert the following line after the line** Section "Files":

```
FontPath "unix/:7100"
```

In Fedora, you must also change /dev/mouse to /dev/input/mice.

3. **Type** xfs & **to start the X font server.**

4. **Try the new configuration file by typing the following line:**

```
X -config ///etc/xorg.conf.new
```

If you see a blank screen with an X-shape cursor, the configuration file is working fine.

5. **Press Ctrl+Alt+Backspace to kill the X server.**

6. **Copy the new configuration file to the** /etc/X11 **directory with the following command:**

```
cp ///etc/xorg.conf.new /etc/X11/xorg.conf
```

7. **Reboot the PC by pressing Ctrl+Alt+Delete or typing** reboot.

If all goes well, you should get the graphical login screen.

TIP

The X configuration file created by using the -configure option of the X server doesn't display at the best resolution. To fine-tune the configuration file, you have to run a utility to adjust the display settings after you reboot the system. Which utility you use depends on the Linux distribution, but most distributions include a utility that enables you to configure the video card, monitor, and display settings through a GUI.

Resolving Other Installation Problems

I'm sure that I haven't exhausted all the installation problems lurking out there. No one can. So many components in Intel x86 PCs exist that Murphy's Law practically requires there to be some combination of hardware that the installation program can't handle. In this section, I list a few known problems. For other problems, I advise you to go to Google Groups (https://groups.google.com) and type some of the symptoms of the trouble. Assuming that others are running into similar problems, you can get some indication of how to troubleshoot your way out of your particular predicament.

Using Knoppix boot commands

The Knoppix Live CD can be a great troubleshooting tool because Knoppix is good at detecting hardware and can be run directly from the boot medium (CD/DVD/USB).

TIP

If you have trouble starting Knoppix, try entering Knoppix boot commands at the boot: prompt. If Knoppix seems to hang when trying to detect a SCSI card, for example, you can disable SCSI probing by typing **knoppix noscsi** at the boot: prompt. Or, if you want the X server to load the *nv module* (for graphics cards based on the NVIDIA chipset), you can type **knoppix xmodule=nv** at the boot: prompt.

Table 3-2 lists some commonly used Knoppix boot commands.

TABLE 3-2 **Some Common Knoppix Boot Commands**

Boot Command	What It Does
expert	Starts in *expert mode,* which enables the user to interactively set up and configure Knoppix.
failsafe	Boots without attempting to detect hardware (except for the bare minimum needed to start Linux).
fb1280x1024	Uses fixed framebuffer graphics at the specified resolution. (Specify the resolution you want, such as 1024 x 768 or 800 x 600.)
knoppix 1	Starts Knoppix in run level 1 (single-user mode), which you can use to perform rescue operations.
knoppix 2	Starts at run level 2, which provides a text-mode shell prompt only.
knoppix acpi=off	Disables ACPI (Advanced Configuration and Power Interface).
knoppix atapicd	Uses the ATAPI CD-ROM interface instead of emulating a SCSI interface for IDE CD-ROM drives.
knoppix desktop=*wmname*	Uses the specified Window Manager instead of the default KDE desktop=*wmname* (where *wmname* is fluxbox, icewm, kde, larswm, twm, wmaker, or xfce).
knoppix dma	Enables direct memory access (DMA) for all IDE drives.
knoppix floppyconfig	Runs the shell script named knoppix.sh from a floppy. (The shell script contains Linux commands that you want to run.)
knoppix fromhd=/dev/hda1	Boots from a previously copied image of Live CD that's in the specified hard drive partition.
knoppix hsync=80	Uses an 80 kHz horizontal refresh rate for X. (Enter the horizontal refresh rate you want X to use.)
knoppix lang=*xx*	Sets the keyboard language as specified by the two-letter code *xx* (where *xx* is cn = Simplified Chinese, de = German, da = Danish, es = Spanish, fr = French, it = Italian, nl = Dutch, pl = Polish, ru = Russian, sk = Slovak, tr = Turkish, tw = Traditional Chinese, or us = U.S. English).

(continued)

Troubleshooting and Configuring Linux

TABLE 3-2 *(continued)*

Boot Command	What It Does
knoppix mem=256M	Specifies that the PC has the stated amount of memory (in megabytes).
knoppix myconf=/dev/hda1	Runs the shell script knoppix.sh from the /dev/hda1 partition. (Enter the partition name where you have the knoppix.sh file.)
knoppix myconf=scan	Causes Knoppix to search for the file named knoppix.sh, scan, and execute the commands in that file, if it exists.
knoppix noeject	Doesn't eject the Live CD after you halt Knoppix.
knoppix noprompt	Doesn't prompt you to remove the Live CD after you halt Knoppix.
knoppix nowheel	Forces the PS/2 protocol for a PS/2 mouse or touchpad (as opposed to the mouse being detected automatically).
knoppix no*xxx*	Causes Knoppix to skip specific parts of the hardware detection (where *xxx* identifies the hardware or server that shouldn't be probed: apic = Advanced Programmable Interrupt Controller, agp = Accelerated Graphics Port, apm = Advanced Power Management, audio = sound card, ddc = Display Data Channel, dhcp = Dynamic Host Configuration Protocol, fstab = file system table, firewire = IEEE 1394 high-speed serial bus, pcmcia = PC Card, scsi = Small Computer System Interface, swap = hard drive space used for virtual memory, usb = Universal Serial Bus).
knoppix pci=bios	Uses BIOS directly for bad PCI controllers.
knoppix pnpbios=off	Skips the plug-and-play (PnP) BIOS initialization.
knoppix screen=*resolution*	Sets the screen resolution in pixels (where *resolution* is the resolution you want, such as 1024x768, 800x600, 640x480, and so on).
knoppix testcd	Checks the data integrity of the Live CD by using the MD5 sum.
knoppix tohd=/dev/hda1	Copies the Live CD to the specified hard drive partition and runs from there (requires 1GB of free space on the partition). A performance boost can be obtained by changing tohd to toram and utilizing RAM.
knoppix toram	Copies the Live CD to RAM (memory) and runs from there (requires 1GB of RAM).
knoppix vga=ext	Uses a 50-line text mode display.
knoppix vsync=60	Uses a vertical refresh rate of 60 Hz for X. (Enter the vertical refresh rate you want X to use.)
knoppix wheelmouse	Enables the IMPS/2 protocol for wheel mice.
knoppix xmodule=*modname*	Causes the X server to load the module specified by *modname* so that X works on your video card (where *modname* is ati, fbdev, i810, mga, nv, radeon, savage, svga, or s3).
knoppix xserver=*progname*	Starts the X server specified by *progname* (where *progname* is XFree86 or XF86_SVGA).

TIP

When you want to issue multiple Knoppix boot commands, simply combine them in a single line. To specify that you want to skip the SCSI autodetection, turn off ACPI, use the U.S. keyboard, use a wheel mouse, and require the X server to load the nv module, enter the following at the boot: prompt:

```
knoppix noscsi acpi=off lang=us wheelmouse xmodule=nv
```

Handling the fatal signal 11 error

During installation, some people get a fatal signal 11 error message, which stops the process cold. This error usually happens past the initial boot screen as the installer is starting its GUI or text interface. The most likely cause of a signal 11 error during installation is a hardware error related to memory or the cache associated with the CPU (microprocessor).

TECHNICAL STUFF

A signal 11, or SIGSEGV (short for Segment Violation Signal), error can occur in Linux applications. A *segment violation* occurs when a process tries to access a memory location that it's not supposed to access. The operating system catches the problem before it happens and stops the offending process by sending it a signal 11. During installation, a signal 11 means that the installer made an error while accessing memory and that the most likely reason is a hardware problem. A commonly suggested cure for the signal 11 problem is to turn off the CPU cache in the BIOS. To do so, you have to enter Setup while the PC boots (by pressing a function key, such as F2) and turn off the CPU cache from the BIOS Setup menu.

If the problem is due to a hardware error in memory (in other words, the result of bad memory chips), you can try swapping the memory modules around in their slots. You might also consider replacing an existing memory module with another memory module if you have one handy.

You can read more about the signal 11 problem at www.bitwizard.nl/sig11.

Getting around the PC reboot problem

On some PCs, when you press Enter at the boot prompt, the initial Linux kernel loads and immediately reboots the PC. This situation could be due to a bad implementation of ACPI in the PC's BIOS. To bypass the problem, type **linux acpi=off** at the boot prompt to turn off ACPI. If that method doesn't work, consult Table 3-3 for other boot options to try.

TABLE 3-3   Some Linux Boot Options

Boot Option	What It Does
allowcddma	Enables DMA for CD/DVD drive.
apic	Works around a bug commonly encountered in the Intel 440GX chipset BIOS and executes only with the installation program kernel.
acpi=off	Disables ACPI in case problems with it occur.
dd	Prompts for a driver disk during the installation of Red Hat Linux.
display=IP_address:0	Causes the installer GUI to appear on the remote system identified by the IP address. (Make sure that you run the command xhost +*hostname* on the remote system, where *hostname* is the host where you run the installer.)
driverdisk	Prompts for a driver disk during installation of Red Hat Linux.
enforcing=0	Turns off Security Enhanced Linux (SELinux) mandatory access control.
expert	Enables you to partition removable media and prompts for a driver disk.
ide=nodma	Disables DMA on all IDE devices and can be useful when you're having IDE-related problems.
ks	Configures the Ethernet card using DHCP and runs a kickstart installation by using a kickstart file from an NFS server identified by the boot server parameters provided by the DHCP server.
ks=*kickstartfile*	Runs a kickstart installation by using the kickstart file, specified by *kickstartfile*. (The idea behind kickstart is to create a text file with all the installation options and then kickstart the installation by booting and providing the kickstart file as input.)
lowres	Forces the installer GUI to run at a lower resolution (640 x 480).
mediacheck	Prompts you to check the integrity of the CD image (also called the ISO image). The image is checked by computing the MD5 checksum and comparing that with the official Fedora value. Checking a CD-ROM can take a few minutes.
mem=*xxx*M	Overrides the amount of memory that the kernel detects on the PC. (Some older machines could detect only 16MB of memory, and on some new machines, the video card may use a portion of the main memory.) Make sure to replace *xxx* with the number representing the megabytes of memory on your PC.
nmi_watchdog=1	Enables the built-in kernel deadlock detector that makes use of Non-Maskable Interrupt (NMI).
noapic	Prevents the kernel from using the Advanced Programmable Interrupt Controller (APIC) chip. (You can use this command on motherboards known to have a bad APIC.)
nofirewire	Doesn't load support for FireWire.

Boot Option	What It Does
noht	Disables *hyperthreading*, which is a feature that enables a single processor to act as multiple virtual processors at the hardware level.
nomce	Disables self-diagnosis checks performed on the CPU by using Machine Check Exception (MCE). On some machines, these checks are performed too often and need to be disabled.
nomount	Doesn't automatically mount any installed Linux partitions in rescue mode.
nopass	Doesn't pass the keyboard and mouse information to stage 2 of the installation program.
nopcmcia	Ignores any PCMCIA controllers in the system.
noprobe	Disables automatic hardware detection, and prompts the user for information about SCSI and network hardware installed on the PC. You can pass parameters to modules by using this approach.
noshell	Disables shell access on virtual console 2 (the one you get by pressing Ctrl+Alt+F2) during installation.
nousb	Disables the loading of USB support during the installation. (Booting without USB support may be useful if the installation program hangs early in the process.)
nousbstorage	Disables the loading of the usbstorage module in the installation program's loader. This option may help with device ordering on SCSI systems.
reboot=b	Changes the way that the kernel tries to reboot the PC so that it can reboot even if the kernel hangs during system shutdown.
pci=noacpi	Causes the kernel to not use ACPI to route interrupt requests.
pci=biosirq	Causes the kernel to use BIOS settings to route interrupt requests (IRQs).
rescue	Starts the kernel in rescue mode, where you get a shell prompt and can try to fix problems.
resolution=*HHHxVVV*	Causes the installer GUI to run in the specified video mode (where *HHH* and *VVV* are standard resolution numbers, such as 640x480, 800x600, or 1024x768).
selinux=0	Disables the SELinux kernel extensions.
serial	Turns on serial console support during installation.
skipddc	Skips the Display Data Channel (DDC) probe of monitors. (This option is useful if probing causes problems.)
vnc	Starts a VNC (Virtual Network Computing) server so that you can control the GUI installer from another networked system that runs a VNC client.

Troubleshooting and Configuring Linux

Using Linux kernel boot options

When you boot the PC for Linux installation from the DVD or the first CD-ROM, you get a text screen with the boot: prompt. Typically, you press Enter at that prompt or do nothing, and installation begins shortly. You can specify a variety of options at the boot: prompt, however. The options control various aspects of the Linux kernel startup, such as disabling support for troublesome hardware or starting the X server with a specific X driver module. Some of these boot options can be helpful in bypassing problems that you may encounter during installation.

To use these boot options, you typically type **linux** followed by the boot options. To perform text mode installation and tell the kernel that your PC has 512MB of memory, you type the following at the boot: prompt:

```
linux text mem=512M
```

Consult Table 3-3 earlier in this chapter for a brief summary of some of the Linux boot options. You can use these commands to turn certain features on or off.

TIP

Although I mention these Linux kernel boot commands in the context of troubleshooting installation problems, you can use many of these commands any time you boot a PC with any Linux distribution and want to turn specific features on or off.

Setting Up Printers

In most Linux distributions, you can set up printers only after you install the distribution. The following sections outline the printer configuration steps for Ubuntu and are similar for all distributions.

To set up a printer, follow these steps:

1. **From the desktop, choose Settings⇨Devices⇨Printers.**

If you're not logged in as root, the printer configuration tool often prompts you for the root password. The printer configuration tool, shown in Figure 3-1, is called system-config-printer.

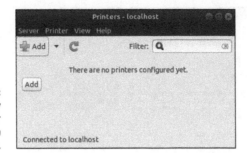

FIGURE 3-1:
The primary
printer
configuration
interface.

2. **Click the Add button to configure a new printer.**

If the device can be identified, it appears in the list. If the device can't be identified, you can still continue with the installation and manually add the drivers and configuration data needed. Figure 3-2 shows that the Epson Stylus printer is being connected to the serial port.

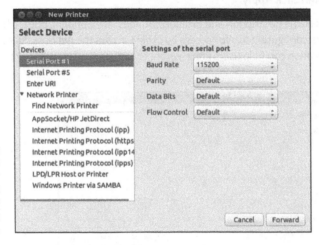

FIGURE 3-2:
You can install
a local printer
or a network
printer by
using the same
interface.

3. **Click Forward to continue.**

The system searches for drivers and offers choices based on what it thinks you're installing.

In the following example, the host is connecting to a local printer.

4. **Select the appropriate driver (see Figure 3-3) and then click Forward.**

Troubleshooting and
Configuring Linux

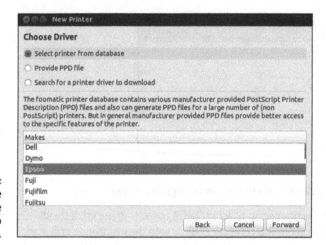

5. **Enter the printer name and description variables (see Figure 3-4), and then click Apply.**

    Both the description and location variables are optional, but are helpful if you are configuring this for access by others across the network. Identifying the location can help users know where to pick up the reports they print.

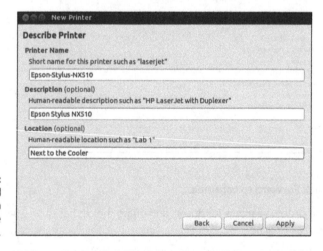

6. **Print a test page to make sure that everything is working as it should.**

    Make any modifications to the settings as needed, using the configuration options, which are shown in Figure 3-5.

7. **When the printer is configured as it should be, exit the printer configuration tool.**

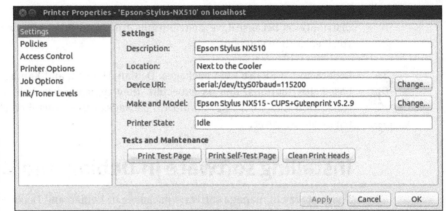

FIGURE 3-5:
Edit the configuration with the printer configuration tool.

Managing DVDs, CD-ROMs, and Flash Drives

The GUI desktop makes using DVDs, CD-ROMs, and flash drives in Linux easy. Just place the external media in the drive, and an icon appears on the desktop. Then you can access the media by double-clicking the icon on the desktop.

In some Linux distributions, the GUI automatically opens the contents of the media in a file-manager window soon after you insert the CD or DVD in the drive. To access the files and folders, simply double-click the icons that appear in the GUI file manager window.

If you see an icon for the drive, right-click that icon for a context menu. From that menu, you can eject the media when you're finished.

Installing Other Software

The exact steps for installing software depend on the type of package in which the software is distributed. Most Linux software comes in an RPM file or a Debian package file. The RPM files have an .rpm extension, and the Debian packages have a .deb extension.

Most distributions provide GUI installers to ease the process of installing new software packages. In this section, I provide a quick overview of adding software that applies to most distributions. (You don't want to add software to Live distributions because Live distributions run from ROM and/or media that start fresh each time you boot.)

REMEMBER

Fedora and SUSE use RPM packages. Debian, Ubuntu, and Xandros are all Debian-based distributions, and as expected, they typically use Debian packages (also called DEB files). Both RPM and DEB packages can be installed in any Linux distribution, however.

Installing software in Debian and Ubuntu

The best way to manage software packages in Debian and Debian-based distributions, such as Ubuntu, is to use the Advanced Packaging Tool (APT), which you usually control through the apt-get command.

When you install Debian, one of the last steps is configuring the sources for APT. The APT sources are the Internet servers (both FTP and web) where APT looks for software packages to download and install on your system. Assuming that APT is properly configured and that your system has a high-speed Internet connection, you can begin installing any package by typing the following command in a terminal window:

```
apt-get install pkgname
```

pkgname is the name of the package that you want to install. If you don't know the package name, start by typing the following command in the terminal window:

```
apt-cache search keyword
```

keyword is related to the package you want to install. To search for a package that has the word *screenshot* in its description and also contains the word *KDE*, type the following. (I use grep to search the output for occurrences of the text *KDE*.)

```
apt-cache search screenshot | grep KDE
```

This command prints the following line as the result:

```
ksnapshot - Screenshot application for KDE
```

This line shows that the ksnapshot package is what you need. If this package isn't yet installed, you could install it by typing the following command:

```
apt-get install ksnapshot
```

That, in a nutshell, is how you can use the command-line tools to look for and install packages in Debian.

DISTRIBUTION SPECIFIC

Debian and older versions of Ubuntu also come with a GUI package installer for APT called Synaptic Package Manager, whose use is intuitive:

>> **Debian:** Depending upon your version, you choose Applications⇨System Tools⇨Synaptic Package Manager from the GNOME desktop or Desktop⇨ Administration⇨Synaptic Package Manager.

>> **Ubuntu:** In old versions (pre 11.10), choose Select System⇨ Administration⇨ Synaptic Package Manager. When prompted for a password in Ubuntu, enter your normal user password, because Ubuntu has no root user. In newer versions, you can download it with the following command:

```
sudo apt-get install synaptic
```

When Synaptic Package Manager starts, it displays a Quick Introduction dialog box that tells you briefly how to mark packages for installation, upgrade, or removal and how to get to the menu to perform these actions. After reading the introduction, click Close to get rid of that dialog box and access Synaptic Package Manager.

Alternatively, you can use the Software & Updates tool, shown in Figure 3-6, to manage your software. Click the Other Software tab to get started.

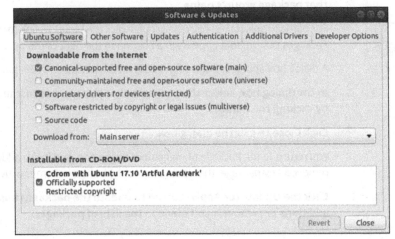

FIGURE 3-6:
Software & Updates.

From here, you can choose to specify any software you want to download and install through APT, as shown in Figure 3-7.

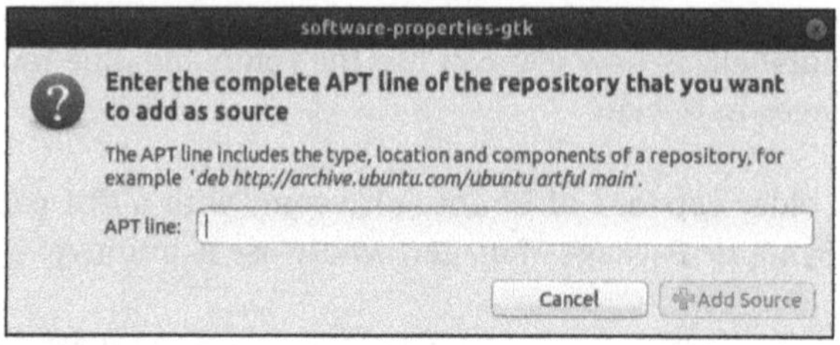

FIGURE 3-7: Specify what software to download and install.

Installing software in Fedora

Most Fedora software comes in the form of RPM files. An RPM (Red Hat Package Manager) file is a single package that contains all the files and configuration information needed to install a software product.

From the GNOME desktop, you use the Software utility, which is a graphical utility for installing and uninstalling RPMs. Follow these steps:

1. **Choose System⇨Administration⇨Software.**

If you're not logged in as root, a dialog box prompts you for the root password. The Software app starts and gathers information about the status of packages installed on your system. After it sorts through the information about all the installed packages, the utility displays the Package Manager dialog box, which contains a list of all the packages.

2. **To install an uninstalled package group, select the check box to the left of that package group's name.**

TIP

For partially uninstalled package groups, click the Details link (or the Optional Packages button) that appears in a column to the right of the package name.

A dialog box appears, displaying details on the packages in the package group.

3. **In the dialog box, select the packages that you want to install or remove by clicking the names.**

4. **Click Close to exit the dialog box.**

You return to the Package Management dialog box, and if you added or removed any package, the Update (or Apply) button becomes active.

5. **Click the Update (or Apply) button to update the packages based on any additions or removals you made in the lists of packages.**

Installing software in SUSE

In SUSE, follow these steps to install or remove software:

1. **From the main menu, choose YaST to start the YaST Control Center.**

The YaST Control Center displays categories of tasks on the left side and specific tasks for that category on the right side.

2. **Click the Software category on the left side so that the right side shows the options for software.**

3. **Click the Software Management icon on the right side.**

YaST displays a new window where you can search for software packages.

4. **Search for a package by name or select a package by browsing available packages.**

To search for a package by name, type a keyword in the Search field in the top-left corner of the window and then click Search. YaST displays the matching packages on the right side of the window. To browse for packages, click Filter in the top-left corner, choose Package Groups from the drop-down menu, and click a group to see the list of individual packages in that group.

5. **Click the Accept button in the bottom-right corner to begin installing selected packages.**

YaST checks for *dependencies* — if a package requires other packages to install correctly — before installing packages. If you want to view what changes would occur when you click Accept, click Filter and select Installation Summary.

Chapter **4**

Trying Out Linux

Y ou're sitting in front of your PC, about to turn it on. You know that the PC has Linux installed. (Maybe you did the installing yourself, but who's keeping track?) You're wondering what to expect when you turn it on and what you do afterward. Not to worry. If you're using Linux for the first time, this chapter shows you how to log in, check out the graphical desktops, try some cryptic Linux commands, and (finally) shut down the PC.

If you're trying one of the Live distributions, all you have to do is boot from the bootable media (flash drive/DVD/CD), as explained in Book 1, Chapter 2, and you can try that distribution without installing or overwriting your existing operating system.

For those of you who already know something about Linux, flip through this chapter to see whether anything looks new. You never know what you may not know!

Starting Linux

When you turn on the PC, it goes through the normal power-up sequence and loads the bootloader, which is GRUB or LILO, depending on your Linux distribution and what you select during installation. The *bootloader* (once known as the bootstrap loader) is a tiny computer program that loads the rest of the operating system from the hard drive into the computer's memory. The entire process of starting a computer is called *booting*.

For Live distributions, the bootloader typically is ISOLINUX, a bootloader designed to work from an ISO 9660 CD-ROM.

The LILO and GRUB bootloaders display a graphical screen with the names of the operating systems that the bootloader can load. If your PC has Windows and Linux, you see both names listed, and you can use the up- and down-arrow keys to select the operating system you want to use. If the PC is set up to load Linux by default, wait a few seconds, and the bootloader starts Linux. To be more precise, the bootloader loads the *Linux kernel* — the core of the Linux operating system — into the PC's memory.

Other bootloaders, such as ISOLINUX, may display a text boot: prompt at which you can type boot commands to load specific operating systems and to pass options to whichever operating system you load.

While the Linux kernel starts, you see a long list of opening messages, often referred to as the *boot messages*. (You can see these messages at any time by typing the command **dmesg** in a terminal window.) These messages include the names of the devices that Linux detects. One of the first lines in the boot messages reads

```
Calibrating delay loop ... 4997.12 BogoMIPS
(lpj=2498560)
```

BogoMIPS is Linux jargon (explained in this section in a handy sidebar) for a mea-sure of time. The number that precedes BogoMIPS depends on your PC's processor speed. The kernel uses the BogoMIPS measurement when it has to wait a small amount of time for some event to occur (such as getting a response back from a disk controller when it's ready).

After the boot messages appear, some Linux distributions switch to a graphical boot screen that shows information about the progress of system startup. When you boot some Linux distributions for the first time after installation, you get a configuration program that guides you through some configuration steps, such as setting the date and time and adding user accounts. To complete such first-time configuration steps, all you have to do is enter the requested information.

After Linux boots, you typically get a graphical login screen. For some distribu-tions, such as Knoppix, you get the desktop without having to log in as a user. On other Live distributions, you have to log in.

Figure 4-1 shows the Ubuntu desktop after I booted a PC from the Ubuntu Live dis-tribution and had an extra flash drive plugged in (appearing on the desktop as HP v125w). For some distributions, you may be logged in automatically. For other dis-tributions, a graphical login screen appears, asking you to authenticate by entering the username and password given during (or at any time after) installation.

FIGURE 4-1:
The Ubuntu
Live desktop.

Every distribution uses the root username, which happens to be the *superuser* (the administrator account). Whether you install Linux yourself or someone installs it for you, you need to know the root password. Without it, you can't do many of the tasks necessary to find out how Linux works.

WARNING

You shouldn't normally log in as root. When you log in as root, you could accidentally damage your system because you can do anything when you're root. Always log in as a normal user. When you need to perform any task as root, type **su -** in a terminal window and then enter the root password.

**DISTRIBUTION
SPECIFIC**

In Ubuntu, you define only a normal user account; Ubuntu doesn't give you the opportunity to define a root user account. Whenever you want to perform any tasks that require you to be root, you have to use the sudo command (an abbreviation for *superuser do*). The default password for root is the one you gave during the installation of the operating system.

To log in as user spiderman, for example, type **spiderman** in the first text field, and press Enter. (Move the cursor to the login dialog box before you begin typing.) Then type spiderman's password and press Enter. You see the initial graphical user interface (GUI). What you get depends on your choice of GUI: GNOME or KDE. If someone made the choice for you, don't worry; GNOME and KDE are both quite good and versatile.

Chapters 1 and 2 in Book 2 explore the GUI desktops — first GNOME and then KDE. This section focuses on the command line, which is the only interface you'll have access to if you experience problems loading a graphical desktop.

Trying Out Linux

WHAT ARE BogoMIPS AND LPJ?

When Linux boots, you get a message that says Calibrating delay loop ... 4997.12 BogoMIPS (lpj=2498560), with some number before BogoMIPS. BogoMIPS is one of those words that confounds new Linux users, but it's just jargon with a simple meaning.

BogoMIPS is Linus's invention (yes, the same Linus Torvalds who started Linux), and it means *bogus MIPS*. As you may know, *MIPS* is an acronym for *millions of instructions per second* — a measure of how fast your computer runs programs. Unfortunately, MIPS isn't a very good measure of performance; the MIPS measurements of different types of computers are difficult to compare accurately. BogoMIPS is a way to measure the computer's speed that's independent of the exact processor type. Linux uses the BogoMIPS number to calibrate a *delay loop,* in which the computer keeps running some useless instructions until a specified amount of time passes. The reason for killing valuable processor time this way is to wait for some slowpoke device to get ready for work.

Oh ... about *LPJ* — it's a recent term that stands for *loops per jiffy,* and it's another measure of time delay used by the kernel. The Linux kernel considers time in increments of jiffies, and a *jiffy* is defined as the time period equal to 1 second divided by the value of a kernel variable named HZ. In other words, HZ jiffies are in each second.

Playing with the Shell

Linux is basically Unix, and Unix just doesn't feel like Unix unless you can type cryptic commands in a text terminal. Although GNOME and KDE do a lot to bring you into the world of windows, icons, mouse, and pointer (affectionately known as *WIMP*), sometimes, you're stuck with nothing but a plain-text screen with a prompt that looks something like this (when you log in as edulaney):

```
edulaney@linux:/etc>
```

You see the text screen most often when something is wrong with the X Window System, which is the machinery that runs the windows and menus that you normally see. In those cases, you have to work with the shell and know some cryptic Linux commands.

You can prepare for unexpected encounters with the shell by trying some Linux commands in a terminal window while you're in the GNOME or KDE GUI. After you get the hang of using the terminal, you might even keep a terminal window open so you can use one of those cryptic commands, simply because using a command is faster than pointing and clicking. Those two-letter commands do pack some punch!

Starting the bash shell

Simply put, the *shell* is the Linux *command interpreter* — a program that reads what you type, interprets that text as a command, and does what the command is supposed to do.

Before you start playing with the shell, open a terminal window. In either GNOME or KDE, the panel typically includes an icon that looks like a monitor. When you click that icon, you see a window with a prompt, like the one shown in Figure 4-2. That window is a terminal window, and it works like an old-fashioned terminal. A shell program is running and ready to accept any text that you type. Type text and press Enter, and something happens (depending on what you typed).

FIGURE 4-2:
The terminal window awaits your input.

TIP

If the GNOME or KDE panel on your desktop doesn't seem to have an icon that starts a terminal or shell window, search the Main menu hierarchy; you should be able to find an item labeled Console or Terminal. Choosing that item should open a terminal window.

The prompt that you see depends on the shell that runs in that terminal window. The default Linux shell is bash (which stands for *Bourne-Again Shell)*.

bash understands a host of standard Linux commands, which you can use to look at files, go from one directory to another, see what programs are running (and who else is logged in), and do a whole lot more.

In addition to the Linux commands, bash can run any program stored in an executable file. bash can also execute *shell scripts* — text files that contain Linux commands.

Understanding shell commands

Because a shell interprets what you type, knowing how the shell figures out the text that you enter is important. All shell commands have this general format:

```
command option1 option2 ... optionN
```

Such a single line of commands is commonly called a *command line*. On a command line, you enter a command followed by one or more optional parameters (or *arguments*). Such command-line options (or arguments) help you specify what you want the command to do.

One basic rule is that you have to use a space or a tab to separate the command from the options and to separate options from one another. If you want to use an option that contains embedded spaces, you have to put that option within quotation marks. To search for two words of text in the password file, for example, enter the following grep command. (grep is one of those cryptic commands used to search for text in files.)

```
grep "WWW daemon" /etc/passwd
```

When grep prints the line with those words, it looks like the following. (What you see on your system may differ from what I show.)

```
wwwrun:x:30:8:WWW daemon apache:/var/lib/wwwrun:/bin/false
```

If you created a user account in your name, go ahead and type the grep command with your name as an argument, but remember to enclose the name in quotes if it includes spaces.

Trying a few Linux commands

While you have the terminal window open, try a few Linux commands just for fun. I'll guide you through some examples to give you a feel for what you can do at the shell prompt.

To see how long the Linux PC has been up since you last powered it up, type the following. (*Note:* I show the typed command in bold, followed by the output from that command.)

```
uptime
12:06:34 up 59 days, 16:23, 4 users, load average: 0.56, 0.55, 0.37
```

The part up 59 days, 16:23 tells you that this particular PC has been up for nearly two months. Hmmm . . . can Windows do that?

To see what version of Linux kernel your system is running, use the uname command:

```
uname -srv
```

This code runs the uname command with three options: -s, -r, and -v (which can be combined as -srv, as this example shows). The -s option causes uname to print the name of the kernel, -r prints the kernel release number, and -v prints the kernel version number. The command generates the following output on one of my Linux systems:

```
Linux 4.13..0-16-generic #19-Ubuntu SMP Wed Oct 11 18:35:14 UTC 2017
```

In this case, the system is running Linux kernel version 4.13.0.

To read a file, use the more command. Type **more /etc/passwd** to read the /etc/ passwd file, for example. The resulting output looks similar to the following:

```
root:x:0:0:root:/root:/bin/bash
bin:x:1:1:bin:/bin:/bin/bash
daemon:x:2:2:Daemon:/sbin:/bin/bash
lp:x:4:7:Printing daemon:/var/spool/lpd:/bin/bash
mail:x:8:12:Mailer daemon:/var/spool/clientmqueue:/bin/false
news:x:9:13:News system:/etc/news:/bin/bash
uucp:x:10:14:Unix-to-Unix Copy system:/etc/uucp:/bin/bash
... lines deleted ...
```

To see a list of all the programs currently running on the system, use the ps command, like this:

```
ps ax
```

The ps command takes many options, which you can provide without the usual dash prefix. This example uses the a and x options. The a option lists all processes that you're running, and the x option displays the rest of the processes. The result is that ps ax prints a list of all processes running on the system, as shown in the following sample output of the ps ax command:

```
PID TTY STAT TIME COMMAND
   1 ?  S  0:01 init [5]
   2 ?  SN 0:00 [ksoftirqd/0]
   3 ?  S< 0:00 [events/0]
   4 ?  S< 0:00 [khelper]
   9 ?  S< 0:00 [kthread]
  22 ?  S< 0:00 [kblockd/0]
  58 ?  S  0:00 [kapmd]
  79 ?  S  0:00 [pdflush]
  80 ?  S  0:00 [pdflush]
  82 ?  S< 0:00 [aio/0]
... lines deleted ...
5325 ?  Ss 0:00 /opt/kde3/bin/kdm
5502 ?  S  0:12 /usr/X11R6/bin/X -br -nolisten tcp :0 vt7 -auth /var/lib/xdm/
     authdir/authfiles/A:0-p1AOrt
5503 ?  S  0:00 -:0
6187 ?  Ss 0:00 /sbin/portmap
6358 ?  Ss 0:00 /bin/sh /usr/X11R6/bin/kde
6566 ?  Ss 0:00 /usr/sbin/cupsd
6577 ?  Ssl 0:00 /usr/sbin/nscd
... lines deleted ...
```

It's amazing how many programs can run on a system even when only you are logged in as a user, isn't it?

As you can guess, you can do everything from a shell prompt, but the procedure does take some getting used to.

Shutting Down

When you're ready to shut down Linux, you must do so in an orderly manner. Even if you're the sole user of a Linux PC, several other programs usually run in the background. Also, operating systems such as Linux try to optimize the way that they write data to the hard drive. Because hard-drive access is relatively slow (compared with the time needed to access memory locations), data generally is held in memory and written to the hard drive in large chunks. Therefore, if you simply turn off the power, you run the risk that some files won't be updated properly.

Any user can shut down the system from the desktop or from the graphical login screen without even being logged in, although some distributions, such as Debian, prompt for the root password. Typically, you should look for a Log Out option on the main menu or submenus. When you choose this option, a Log Out dialog box appears, providing options for logging out immediately or waiting 60 seconds. More detailed menu options can include rebooting or halting the system in addition to simply logging out. To shut down the system, choose Shutdown and then click OK. The system shuts down in an orderly manner.

If the logout menu doesn't have a shutdown option, first log out and then select Shutdown on the graphical login screen. You can also shut down a Linux computer from a terminal with the command init 0. This method is sometimes required if you're running the operating system within a virtual software manager such as VMware.

While the system shuts down, you see messages about processes shutting down. You may be surprised by how many processes there are even when no one is explicitly running any programs on the system. If your system doesn't automatically power off on shutdown, you can turn off the power manually.

WARNING

Shutting down or rebooting the system may *not* require root access, so it's important to make sure that physical access to the console is protected adequately. You don't want just anyone to be able to simply walk up to the console and shut down your system.

TIP

You don't always need to shut down when you're finished with a session; instead, you may choose to log out. To log out of KDE, choose Main Menu⇨Logout. You can also right-click an empty area of the desktop and choose Logout from the contextual menu that appears. To log out from GNOME, choose System⇨Log Out. Click OK when a dialog box asks whether you really want to log out. (In some GNOME desktop distributions, the logout menu option is the second or third menu button from the left on the top panel.)

Trying Out Linux

2

Linux Desktops

Contents at a Glance

CHAPTER 1: **GNOME and Its Derivatives** 69
Getting to Know the GNOME Desktop 70
Understanding the GNOME Panels. 72
Looking at Unity. 73
Looking at Cinnamon 73
Looking at MATE 74

CHAPTER 2: **The KDE Plasma Desktop** 75
Getting to Know the Plasma Desktop. 75
Understanding the Plasma Panel 78
Configuring the Plasma Bottom Panel. 81
Configuring the Plasma Desktop. 81

CHAPTER 3: **Commanding the Shell** 83
Opening Terminal Windows and Virtual Consoles 83
Using the bash Shell 84
Discovering and Using Linux Commands 92
Writing Shell Scripts 102

CHAPTER 4: **Navigating the Linux File System** 105
Understanding the Linux File System. 105
Navigating the File System with Linux Commands. 110

CHAPTER 5: **Introducing Linux Applications** 123
Taking Stock of Linux Applications 124
Introducing Office Applications and Tools. 124
Checking out Multimedia Applications. 129
Using Graphics and Imaging Apps 133

CHAPTER 6: **Using Text Editors** 137
Using GUI Text Editors 137
Text Editing with ed and vi. 140

» **Understanding the GNOME panels**

» **Looking at Unity**

» **Exploring Cinnamon**

» **Finding a MATE**

Chapter **1**

GNOME and Its Derivatives

I n the days of old, Linux distributions used to come with one or both of two popular graphical user interfaces (GUIs): GNOME and KDE. GNOME and KDE are like Microsoft Windows but unique in one respect: Unlike Microsoft Windows, Linux lets you choose your GUI. If you don't like GNOME, you can use KDE; if you don't like KDE, you can use GNOME. When both GUIs are installed, you can switch between the two in a matter of seconds. Try doing that in Microsoft Windows!

Today, that choice of GUI is often still the case, with a few big exceptions: GNOME has given birth to several variants, and KDE has a few choices (most notably Plasma). GNOME is widely used, but you'll find that some distributions include desktops such as Unity, Cinnamon, and MATE. When you encounter these desktops, just know that they started as GNOME and were altered to fit some specific purposes. The desktops have the same basic structure; I walk you through them in this chapter.

REMEMBER

GNOME and KDE were developed independently of Linux, and they run on Unix operating systems other than Linux. You also have the option to install GUIs such as FVWM and Xfce in Linux. Visit https://www.freedesktop.org/wiki/Desktops to see a list of other X desktops (desktops that run on the X Window System).

This chapter explores the major features of GNOME and its variants; Book 2, Chapter 2 does the same for KDE. The best way to figure out these GUIs is to start using them. No matter which GUI you decide to use, all GUI applications — whether they're based on GNOME or KDE — run on all GUI desktops. In other words, you can run KDE applications under GNOME, and vice versa. The only hurdle is that GNOME and KDE applications may not be installed by default.

DISTRIBUTION SPECIFIC

Each Linux distribution typically installs one GUI by default. Each distribution also customizes that GUI to create a desktop that's unique to the distribution. For this reason, there may be subtle, minor differences between what you see in your distribution and what I describe in this chapter.

Getting to Know the GNOME Desktop

The initial desktop for GNOME looks like that of any other popular GUI, such as Microsoft Windows or the macOS desktop. Figure 1-1 shows a typical GNOME desktop.

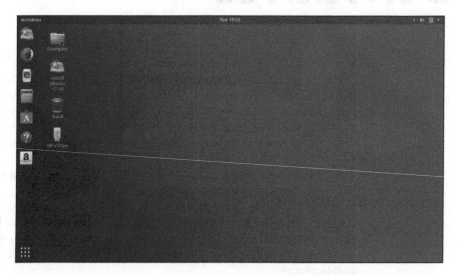

FIGURE 1-1:
A clean GNOME desktop in Ubuntu.

If you're running the Live distribution, you won't see some icons that would be present if that operating system was installed. When the system is installed, the desktop initially shows icons for your computer, your home folder, and the trash can for deleted files. Unlike some other distributions, Fedora strives for a minimum number of desktop icons and has a clean look.

The GNOME desktop displays a contextual menu when you right-click an object or any part of the desktop. Depending on where you right-click, the menu may offer the following choices:

» **New Folder:** Creates a new folder in a directory

» **Properties:** Shows the properties, including permissions, associated with a file or folder

» **Open:** Opens a folder or file

» **Compress:** Reduces the size of the file

» **Make Link:** Creates a shortcut

Figure 1-2 shows the contextual menus in a typical GNOME folder. If any menu options have a right-pointing arrow, other menus appear when you put the mouse pointer over the arrow.

FIGURE 1-2: Standard menu choices in GNOME for a folder.

Many items on this contextual menu are the same no matter what icon you click, but right-clicking certain icons (such as the Trash icon) produces a somewhat different menu. For the Trash icon, the icon contextual menu typically provides an option that permanently deletes the items in the trash. (You get a chance to say yes or no.)

TIP

I'll bet that you see a pattern here: the right click. No matter where you are in a GUI desktop, *always right-click before you pick.* You're bound to find something useful when you right-click!

Understanding the GNOME Panels

The GNOME desktop has panels, and each panel is like the Windows taskbar. The top panel has menu choices on the left, a time display in the center, and icons for common choices on the right. Between the left menu and the time, the panel shows any applications you've started (or that were automatically started for you).

The top panel

The top panel is the long bar that stretches across the top of the GNOME desktop. Figure 1-3 shows a typical view of the GNOME top panel.

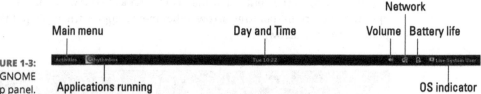

FIGURE 1-3:
The GNOME
top panel.

The panel is a parking place for icons. Some icons start programs when you click them; others show status (such as what programs are running) as well as information such as date and time.

The desktop

After you choose Activities, the leftmost area of the desktop in GNOME shows the applications that can be opened in a panel that you can think of as the *Main Menu*. The Main Menu panel, like the Start button in Microsoft Windows, is where you typically find all your applications, organized into submenus.

In the case of the Live distribution versions, the default icons on this main menu (also known as the Favorites menu) usually include the following features:

>> Firefox web browser

>> Rhythmbox

>> Software

>> Help

>> Shortcut to your files

>> Shortcut to your documents

>> Install icon

>> Link to your recent applications

You can click any icon to start the application associated with it, or right-click to start it in a new window or remove it from the menu.

The bottom panel

In addition to the top panel, GNOME includes a bottom panel. It doesn't appear onscreen by default (unlike the arrangement in KDE) if you don't turn it on, but you can use it to find important information. Figure 1-4 is an example of this panel, showing three important notifications from the system and a link to a USB drive.

FIGURE 1-4:
The bottom
panel in
GNOME.

Looking at Unity

Just as there are differences among Windows desktops from Windows 7 to Windows 10, the GNOME desktop has variations. The first of these variations is Unity. Unity was created by Canonical and Mark Shuttleworth (respectively, the organization behind and the head of Ubuntu). With it, the same clean desktop look of GNOME prevails. What differs is that the makers of Unity strive to make it as easy as possible for a user with no previous knowledge to use, which makes it ideal for netbooks as well as desktops.

One of the biggest plusses of this desktop is the fact that Unity is touch-ready.

Looking at Cinnamon

The Cinnamon desktop looks much the way that GNOME used to look several versions ago and is popular with Linux Mint. Cinnamon looks similar to the Windows of the Windows XP era.

The leftmost icon on the bottom panel is the *Main Menu* button. The Main Menu button, like the Start button in Microsoft Windows, is where you typically find all your applications, organized into submenus. Click the Main Menu button to bring up the first-level menu; then mouse over any menu item containing an arrow to bring up the next-level menu, and so on. You can go through a menu hierarchy and make choices from the final menu.

In addition to having the standard choices associated with the Main Menu appear on the bottom panel, the bottom panel of Cinnamon offers the following additional commands:

>> **Show Desktop:** Hides (but doesn't close) all windows and displays the desktop

>> **Firefox Web Browser:** Accesses the web quickly

>> **Terminal:** Opens a terminal window

>> **Files:** Displays your files

>> **Open Windows:** Jumps back and forth among any open windows

>> **Active Icons:** Performs tasks such as ejecting drives, adjusting volume, and viewing battery life

Looking at MATE

Much like Cinnamon, the MATE desktop is often associated with Linux Mint; the two look very much alike.

As in life, so in Linux: Which desktop you choose to use is as much a matter of preference as the car you drive, the cologne you wear, or the outfit you buy. It's important that you're comfortable with the interface you regularly interact with and learn to use it as best you can.

Chapter **2**

The KDE Plasma Desktop

As mentioned in Book 2, Chapter 1, Linux distributions come with one (or both) of two popular graphical user interfaces (GUIs): GNOME (or one or more of its variants) and KDE's Plasma. When both interfaces are installed, you can switch between the two in a matter of seconds. If you don't like GNOME, you can use Plasma; if you don't like Plasma, you can use GNOME.

This chapter explores the major features of Plasma, just as Book 2, Chapter 1 examines GNOME. I strongly encourage you to try both GUIs before you decide which one you're more comfortable using.

REMEMBER

You can run Plasma applications under GNOME, and vice versa. Several installation procedures allow you to choose to install whichever of the two interfaces you want to use. Installing only one interface by default allows for quicker, easier setup and installation; you can always go back and install the other interface later.

DISTRIBUTION SPECIFIC

Each distribution customizes the desktop, so there may be subtle, minor differences between what you see in your distribution and what I describe in this chapter.

Getting to Know the Plasma Desktop

A few years ago, the KDE desktop was known simply as KDE, in the same way that GNOME's is known as GNOME. Over time, however, the organization behind KDE began to be responsible for more and more things in addition to the desktop.

This situation led to confusion when someone referenced KDE; it wasn't clear whether he or she was talking about the desktop or something altogether different that the organization oversaw. To lessen the confusion, KDE decided to name the desktop Plasma.

Although the attempt to lessen the confusion is admirable, the term can still be befuddling, because many people in the industry continue to refer to the desktop by its old name. For purposes of being clear, know that KDE, KDE Plasma, and Plasma are typical references to the desktop now offered by KDE.

The initial desktop for Plasma looks like that of any other popular GUI, such as Microsoft Windows desktop or the macOS X desktop. Figure 2-1 shows a typical Plasma desktop.

TECHNICAL STUFF

KDE stands for the *K Desktop Environment*. The KDE project started in October 1996 with the intent to develop a common GUI for Unix systems that use the X Window System. The first beta version of KDE was released a year later, in October 1997. KDE version 1.0 was released in July 1998. In July 2014, KDE split into three divisions: KDE Plasma (what I focus on here), KDE Frameworks, and KDE Applications.

Figure 2-1 is from a netbook, which strives for a minimum number of desktop icons. Depending on your distribution, you may see a few other features. Along the bottom of the desktop is often the *panel,* which is like the top and bottom bars of the Windows taskbar. The panel has buttons on the left (shortcuts to various programs), a set of buttons to the available desktops, a task area, a time display, and (to the right) icons that provide volume control and access to Plasma's Clipboard manager, Klipper. In the middle of the panel are buttons for any applications that you started (or that were automatically started for you).

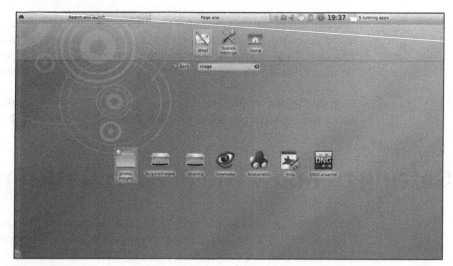

FIGURE 2-1:
A clean
Plasma
desktop.

76   BOOK 2 Linux Desktops

Desktop contextual menus

The Plasma desktop displays a contextual menu when you right-click a clear area of the desktop. The contextual menu includes a submenu that offers the following options (with slight variations among distributions):

>> Run Command

>> Lock Screen

>> Leave (exits the desktop)

>> Desktop Settings (sets such onscreen features as wallpaper)

Figure 2-2 shows the desktop contextual menu on a typical Plasma desktop.

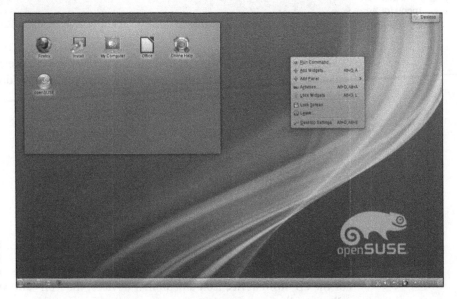

FIGURE 2-2: The contextual menu in Plasma.

Icon contextual menus

Right-clicking any icon in Plasma displays another menu, as shown in Figure 2-3. Many items on this contextual menu are the same no matter what icon you click, but right-clicking certain icons (such as the CD-ROM device icon) produces a somewhat different menu.

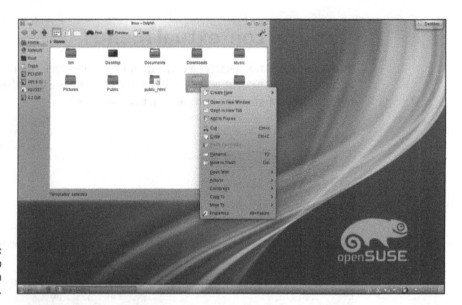

Desktop menu options with a right-pointing arrow have other menus that appear when you put the mouse pointer over the arrow. You can perform the following typical tasks from icon contextual menus:

>> Open a folder in a file manager.

>> Open a file with an application that you choose.

>> Cut or copy.

>> Rename the icon.

>> Move the icon to the trash.

>> View the properties of that icon.

For the CD-ROM device icon and similar devices, the icon contextual menu typically provides an option that ejects the media.

TIP

No matter where you are on a GUI desktop, *always right-click before you pick.* You're bound to find something useful when you right-click!

Understanding the Plasma Panel

The *panel* is the long bar that stretches across the bottom of the desktop. Figure 2-4 shows a typical view of the Plasma panel.

The panel is a parking place for icons. Some icons start programs when you click them; others show status (such as what programs are running) as well as information such as the date and time.

TIP

If you move the mouse pointer on top of an icon, a Help balloon pops up, giving you a helpful hint about the icon.

The Main Menu button

The leftmost icon on the Plasma panel is the *Main Menu* button. (Documentation calls the Main Menu button the *Application Starter*.) Like the Start button in Microsoft Windows, the Main Menu button is where you typically find all your applications, organized into submenus. The Main Menu button is often labeled K, although the letter can be changed by the distribution.

Click the Main Menu button to see the first-level menu; then mouse over any menu item with an arrow to bring up the next-level menu, and so on. You can go through a menu hierarchy and make choices from the final menu.

The KickOff application launcher allows you to access frequently used applications more quickly than navigating the traditional menu hierarchy. In most desktops, clicking the Main Menu button to open KickOff presents the following top-level categories:

>> **Favorites:** Easy access to frequently used applications and documents. To add a file to your Favorites quickly, right-click it and choose Add to Favorites from the contextual menu.

>> **Applications:** The applications and tools installed on your system. Click a subcategory with a right-pointing arrow to open more options.

>> **Computer:** Access to hard drives and removable memory devices, as well as the trash.

>> **Recently Used:** A chronological display of recently opened documents and applications.

>> **Leave:** Options to log out, restart, shut down the computer, and more.

On the Applications tab, you find the following menu subcategories (and probably a few more, depending on which distribution you are using):

>> **Games:** A menu of games (and a lot of them, at that) such as arcade, board, and card games

>> **Graphics:** Programs such as Flickr, KolourPaint, and KSnapshot (used to take the screen shots in this chapter)

>> **Internet:** Internet applications, such as a web browser, an email reader, and an instant messenger

>> **Multimedia:** Multimedia applications such as a CD player, a sound mixer, a sound recorder, and volume control

>> **Office:** Office applications such as the LibreOffice.org Office suite (which includes the Writer word processor, the Calc spreadsheet, the Impress slide presentation program, and the Draw drawing program)

>> **System:** The utilities needed for system configuration

>> **Utilities:** Additional miscellaneous utilities that Plasma can use, including text-to-speech tools, a personal alarm scheduler, and a screen magnifier

REMEMBER

Three additional Plasma menu choices — Administration, Settings, and System — may be present and can help you configure almost anything you need. These options aren't present in every distribution, as those distributions opt for their own interface to accomplish those tasks.

In each distribution, the main menu and KickOff have different categories but the same menu organization, so you usually should be able to find what you need.

Panel icons

In addition to the Main Menu button, the Plasma panel has several icons (shown in Figure 2-4). You can identify any icon by moving your cursor over it and reading the pop-up description that appears. The most common icons are as follows:

>> **Desktop Pager:** Navigates among workspaces or virtual desktops.

>> **Open Windows:** Displays all open windows.

>> **Active Window:** Switches to another running application or window.

- **Network Connection:** Displays information about current wired or wireless connections.

- **Volume:** Displays a volume control bar that you can use to change the sound's volume by dragging a slider.

- **Notifications and Jobs:** Shows the progress of current jobs such as file transfers or printing documents.

- **Time:** Displays the time. Clicking the icon displays a calendar that shows the current date.

- **Panel Toolbox:** Adjusts size, location, and controls for the panel.

Configuring the Plasma Bottom Panel

For all the power inherent in the Plasma panel, it also has a great deal of flexibility. If you right-click a blank spot on the panel, a contextual menu appears. You use this menu to add items to and remove items from the panel. You can even create an additional panel, which allows you to configure your desktop to look and work as much like GNOME as you want it to.

The most powerful menu choice is Panel Options. Choosing Panel Options ⇨ Panel Settings ⇨ More Settings displays a utility that allows you to place the panel in a location other than its default location along the bottom, adjust the alignment of the panel, automatically hide the panel, select whether windows appear in front of or behind the panel, and more.

Configuring the Plasma Desktop

After right-clicking an empty spot of the desktop, you can choose Desktop Settings from the contextual menu. This option displays the configuration tool, which allows you to configure such items as the background and special mouse actions that perform helpful functions on the desktop.

For more thorough desktop configurations, choose Main Menu ⇨ Configure Desktop to display the configuration options that set the screen size, adjust settings for multiple desktops, change the screen saver, and adjust desktop effects. These settings are organized in categories, such as Common Appearance and Behavior,

Workspace Appearance and Behavior, Network Connectivity, and Hardware. Click an item to view the subcategories for that item; click one of the subcategory items to change it. After making a change, click the Apply button to enact the change. If you don't like the result, you can often click Reset to go back to the original setting.

TIP

Depending on your distribution, you may also want to use downloadable programs such as SAX2 for desktop configuration. SAX2 (https://en.opensuse.org/Archive:SaX2) is an open-source program that simplifies configuration.

Chapter **3**

Commanding the Shell

S ometimes, things don't work perfectly, and problems pop up. What do you
do if, because of those problems, the graphical user interface (GUI) desktop
stops responding to your mouse clicks? What do you do if the GUI won't start
at all? All is not lost: You can still tell your Linux system what to do, but you have
to do so by typing commands in a text screen. In these situations, you work with
the shell — the Linux command interpreter. This chapter introduces the bash
shell, the default shell in most Linux distributions.

After you figure out how to work with the shell, you may even begin to like the
simplicity and power of the Linux commands. Then, even if you're a GUI afi-
cionado, someday soon you may find yourself firing up a terminal window and
making the system sing and dance with two- or three-letter commands strung
together by strange punctuation characters. (Hey, I can dream, can't I?)

Opening Terminal Windows and Virtual Consoles

First things first. If you're working in a GUI desktop, such as GNOME or KDE,
where do you type commands for the shell? Good question.

The easiest way to get to the shell is to open a *terminal* (also called *console*) window. The GNOME and KDE GUIs in most distributions include an icon (or a Main Menu option) to open a terminal window. Click that icon or choose the menu option to get a terminal window. If you don't see such an icon in GNOME, choose Applications⇨Accessories⇨Terminal. Now you can type commands to your heart's content.

If, for some reason, the GUI seems to be *hung* (you click and type, but nothing happens), you can turn to the virtual consoles. (The physical console is the monitor-and-keyboard combination.) Virtual consoles enable you to switch among several text consoles, even though you have only one physical console. Whether or not you're running a GUI, you can use different text consoles to type different commands.

To get to the first virtual console from the GNOME or KDE desktop, press Ctrl+Alt+F1; then press Ctrl+Alt+F2 for the second virtual console, and so on. Each virtual console is a text screen where you can log in and type Linux commands to perform various tasks. When you're finished, type **exit** to log out.

TIP

You can use up to six virtual consoles. In most distributions, the seventh console is used for the GUI desktop. To get back to the GUI desktop, press Ctrl+Alt+F7.

Using the bash Shell

If you've used MS-DOS, you may be familiar with COMMAND.COM, the DOS command interpreter. That program displays the infamous C:\> prompt. In Windows, you can see this prompt if you open a command window. (To open a command window in Microsoft Windows, choose Start⇨Run, type **command** in the text box, and then click OK.)

Linux comes with a command interpreter that resembles COMMAND.COM in DOS, but it can do a whole lot more. The Linux command interpreter is called a *shell*.

The default shell in many Linux distributions is bash. When you open a terminal window or log in at a text console, the bash shell is what prompts you for commands. Then, when you type a command, the shell executes your command.

TECHNICAL
STUFF

Just as multiple GUIs (GNOME or KDE) are available for Linux, you have a choice of shells other than bash. Some people prefer the C shell, for example. You can easily change your default shell by using the chsh command.

In addition to executing the standard Linux commands, bash can execute any computer program. Type the name of an application (the name usually is more cryptic than what you see on GNOME or KDE menus) at the shell prompt, and the shell starts that application.

Understanding the syntax of shell commands

Because a shell interprets what you type, knowing how the shell processes the text you enter is important. All shell commands have the following general format (but some commands have no options):

```
command [option1] [option2] ... [optionN]
```

Issuing such a command is a process commonly referred to as a *command line*. On a command line, you enter a command, followed by zero or more options (or *arguments*). These strings of options — the *command-line options* (or command-line arguments) — modify the way the command works so that you can get it to do specific tasks.

The shell uses a blank space or a tab to distinguish between the command and options, so you must use a space or a tab to separate the command from the options and the options from one another.

If an option contains spaces, you put that option inside quotation marks. To search for my name in the password file, for example, enter the following grep command (grep is used for searching for text in files):

```
grep "Emmett Dulaney" /etc/passwd
```

When grep prints the line with my name, it looks like this:

```
edulaney:x:1000:100:Emmett Dulaney:/home/edulaney:/bin/bash
```

If you create a user account with your username, type the grep command with your username as an argument to look for that username in the /etc/passwd file.

TECHNICAL STUFF

In the output from the grep command, you see the name of the shell (/bin/bash) following the last colon (:). Because the bash shell is an executable file, it resides in the /bin directory; you must provide the full path to it.

The number of command-line options and their format depend on the actual command. Typically, these options look like -X, where X is a single character.

You can use the -1 option with the ls command, for example. The command lists the contents of a directory, and the option provides additional details. Here's a result of typing **ls -l** in a user's home directory:

```
total 0
drwxr-xr-x 2 edulaney users 48 2018-09-08 21:11 bin
drwx------ 2 edulaney users 320 2018-09-08 21:16 Desktop
drwx------ 2 edulaney users 80 2018-09-08 21:11 Documents
drwxr-xr-x 2 edulaney users 80 2018-09-08 21:11 public_html
drwxr-xr-x 2 edulaney users 464 2018-09-17 18:21 sdump
```

If a command is too long to fit on a single line, you can press the backslash key (\) followed by Enter and then continue typing the command on the next line. Type the following command, pressing Enter after each line:

```
cat \
/etc/passwd
```

The cat command displays the contents of the /etc/passwd file.

You can *concatenate* (string together) several shorter commands on a single line by separating the commands with semicolons (;). The command

```
cd; ls -1; pwd
```

changes the current directory to your home directory, lists the contents of that directory, and then shows the name of that directory.

Combining shell commands

You can combine simple shell commands to create a more sophisticated command. Suppose that you want to find out whether a device file named sbpcd resides in your system's /dev directory, because some documentation says that you need that device file for your CD-ROM drive. You can use the ls /dev command to get a directory listing of the /dev directory and then browse it to see whether that listing contains sbpcd.

Unfortunately, the /dev directory has a great many entries, so you may find it hard to find any item with sbpcd in its name. You can combine the ls command with grep, however, and come up with a command line that does exactly what you want. Here's that command line:

```
ls /dev | grep sbpcd
```

The shell sends the output of the ls command (the directory listing) to the grep command, which searches for the string sbpcd. That vertical bar (|) is known as a *pipe* because it acts as a conduit (think of a water pipe) between the two programs. The output of the first command is fed into the input of the second one.

Controlling command input and output

Most Linux commands have a common feature: They always read from the *standard input* (usually, the keyboard) and write to the *standard output* (usually, the screen). Error messages are sent to the *standard error* (usually, to the screen as well). These three devices are often referred to as stdin, stdout, and stderr.

You can make a command get its input from a file and then send its output to another file. Just so you know, the highfalutin term for this feature is *input and output (I/O) redirection*.

Table 3-1 shows the syntax of common I/O redirection commands, and the next few sections explain how to use some of these commands.

TABLE 3-1 **Common Standard I/O Redirections**

Task	Command Syntax
Send stdout to a file.	*command > file*
Send stderr to file.	*command 2> file*
Send stdout and stderr to file.	*command > file 2>&1*
Read stdin from a file.	*command < file*
Read stdin from file.in and send stdout to file.out.	*command < file.in > file.out*
Append stdout to the end of a file.	*command >> file*
Append stderr to the end of a file.	*command 2>> file*
Append stdout and stderr to the end of a file.	*command >> file 2>&1*
Read stdin from the keyboard until the character c.	*command <<c*
Pipe stdout to command2.	*command	command2*
Pipe stdout and stderr to command2.	*command 2>&1	command2*

Getting command input from a file

If you want a command to get its instructions by reading from a file, you can redirect the standard input to come from that file instead of from the keyboard. The command

```
sort < /etc/passwd
```

displays a sorted list of the lines in the /etc/passwd file. In this case, the less-than sign (<) redirects stdin so that the sort command reads its input from the /etc/passwd file.

Saving command output in a file

To save the output of a command in a file, redirect the standard output to a file. Type **cd** to change to your home directory and then type the following command:

```
grep typedef /usr/include/* > typedef.out
```

This command searches all files in the /usr/include directory for the occurrence of the text typedef and then saves the output in a file called typedef.out. The greater-than sign (>) redirects stdout to a file. This command also illustrates another feature of bash: When you use an asterisk (*), bash replaces the asterisk with a list of all filenames in the specified directory. Therefore, /usr/include/* means all the files in the /usr/include directory.

If you want to append a command's output to the end of an existing file instead of saving the output in a new file, use two greater-than signs (>>), like this:

```
command >> filename
```

Another interesting way to send stdout to a file is to use the cat command to prepare small text files quickly. Suppose that you want to create a new text file to store lines of text you type until you type **ZZ** and press Enter. Here's how you can accomplish that task:

```
cat <<ZZ > input.txt
```

After you type this command, you can keep typing lines and then type **ZZ** on a line when you finish. Everything you type is saved in the file input.txt.

Saving error messages in a file

Sometimes, when you type a command, it generates a lot of error messages that scroll by so fast that you can't tell what's going on. One way to see all the error messages is to save them in a file so that you can see what the heck happened. You can do that by redirecting stderr to a file.

Type the following command:

```
find / -name COPYING -print 2> finderr
```

This command looks through the file system for files named COPYING and saves all the error messages (if any) in the finderr file. The number 2 followed by the greater-than sign (2>) redirects stderr to a file.

TIP

If you want to discard the error messages instead of saving them in a file, use /dev/null as the filename, like this:

```
find / -name COPYING -print 2> /dev/null
```

TECHNICAL
STUFF

That /dev/null is a special file (often called the *bit bucket* and sometimes glorified as the *Great Bit Bucket in the Sky)* that simply discards whatever it receives. Now you know what it means when you hear a phrase such as "Your mail probably ended up in the bit bucket."

Typing less with automatic command completion

Many commands take a filename as an argument. To view the contents of the /etc/modprobe.conf text file, for example, type the following command:

```
cat /etc/modprobe.conf
```

The cat command displays the /etc/modprobe.conf file. For any command that takes a filename as an argument, you can use a bash feature to avoid having to type the entire filename. You have to type only enough characters to uniquely identify the file in its directory.

To see an example, type **cat /etc/mod**, but don't press Enter; press Tab instead. bash automatically completes the filename, so the command becomes cat /etc/modprobe.conf. Then press Enter to run the command.

TIP

Whenever you type a filename, press Tab after the first few characters of the filename. bash probably can complete the filename so that you don't have to type the entire name. If you don't enter enough characters to uniquely identify the file, bash beeps. Type a few more characters and then press Tab again.

Going wild with asterisks and question marks

You have another way to avoid typing long filenames. (After all, making less work for users is why we use computers, isn't it?)

This particular trick involves using the asterisk (*) and question mark (?). These special characters are *wildcards* because they match zero or more characters in a line of text.

If you know MS-DOS, you may have used commands such as COPY *.* A: to copy all files from the current directory to the A: drive. bash accepts similar wildcards in filenames. As you might expect, bash provides many more wildcard options than the MS-DOS command interpreter does. Newer computers (particularly notebook computers and especially netbooks) don't have A and B drives anymore, of course, which deprives an entire generation of the fun of trying to copy a large file to floppy disks!

You can use three types of wildcards in bash:

>> **Asterisk (*):** Matches zero or more characters in a filename. The asterisk denotes all files in a directory.

>> **Question mark (?):** Matches any single character. If you type **test?**, bash matches any five-character text that begins with *test*.

>> **Set of characters in brackets:** Matches any single character from that set. The string [aB], for example, matches only files named a or B. The string [aB]*, though, matches any filename that starts with a or B.

Wildcards are handy when you want to do something to many files. To copy all the files from the /media/cdrom directory to the current directory, for example, type the following:

```
cp /media/cdrom/* .
```

bash replaces the wildcard character * with the names of all the files in the /media/cdrom directory. The period at the end of the command represents the current directory.

You can use the asterisk with other parts of a filename to select a more specific group of files. Suppose that you want to use the grep command to search for the text typedef struct in all files of the /usr/include directory that meet the following criteria:

>> The filename starts with s.

>> The filename ends with .h.

The wildcard specification s*.h denotes all filenames that meet these criteria. Thus, you can perform the search with the following command:

```
grep "typedef struct" /usr/include/s*.h
```

The string contains a space that you want the grep command to find, so you have to enclose that string in quotation marks. That way, bash doesn't try to interpret each word in that text as a separate command-line argument.

The question mark (?) matches a single character. Suppose that you have four files in the current directory: image1.pcx, image2.pcx, image3.pcx, and image4.pcx. To copy these files to the /personal/calendar directory, use the following command:

```
cp image?.pcx /personal/calendar
```

bash replaces the single question mark with any single character and copies the four files to /personal/calendar.

The third wildcard format — [...] — matches a single character from a specific set of characters enclosed in square brackets. You may want to combine this format with other wildcards to narrow the matching filenames to a smaller set. To see a list of all filenames in the /etc/X11/xdm directory that start with x or X, type the following command:

```
ls /etc/X11/xdm/[xX]*
```

Repeating previously typed commands

To make repeating long commands easy for you, bash stores up to 500 old commands as part of a *command history* (a list of old commands). To see the command history, type **history**. bash displays a numbered list of the old commands, including those that you entered during previous logins.

If the command list is too long, you can limit the number of old commands that you want to see. To see only the 10 most recent commands, type this command:

```
history 10
```

To repeat a command from the list that the history command shows, type an exclamation point (!), followed by that command's number. To repeat command number 3, for example, type **!3**.

You can repeat a command without knowing its command number. Suppose that you typed more /usr/lib/X11/xdm/xdm-config a few minutes ago, and now you want to look at that file again. To repeat the previous more command, type the following:

```
!more
```

Often, you want to repeat the last command that you typed, perhaps with a slight change. You may have displayed the contents of the directory by using the ls -l command, for example. To repeat that command, type two exclamation points, as follows:

```
!!
```

Sometimes, you want to repeat the previous command but add extra arguments to it. Suppose that ls -l shows too many files. Repeat that command, but pipe the output through the more command as follows:

```
!! | more
```

bash replaces the two exclamation points with the previous command and appends | more to that command.

TIP

Here's the easiest way to recall previous commands: Press the up-arrow key. bash keeps going backward through the history of commands you typed. To move forward in the command history, press the down-arrow key.

Discovering and Using Linux Commands

You type Linux commands at the shell prompt. By *Linux commands*, I mean some of the commands that the bash shell understands as well as the command-line utilities that come with Linux. In this section, I introduce a few major categories of Linux commands.

I can't cover every single Linux command in this chapter, but I want to give you a feel for the breadth of the commands by showing you common Linux commands. Table 3-2 lists common Linux commands by category. Before you start memorizing any Linux commands, browse this table.

TABLE 3-2   **Essential Linux Commands**

Command Name	Action
Finding help and abbreviations	
apropos	Finds online manual pages for a specified keyword.
info	Displays online help information about a specified command.
man	Displays online help information.
whatis	Searches for complete words only and finds the online manual pages.
alias	Defines an abbreviation for a long command.
type	Shows the type and location of a command.
unalias	Deletes an abbreviation defined with alias.
Managing files and directories	
cd	Changes the current directory.
chmod	Changes file permissions.
chown	Changes the file owner and group.
cp	Copies files.
ln	Creates symbolic links to files and directories.
ls	Displays the contents of a directory.
mkdir	Creates a directory.
mv	Renames a file and moves the file from one directory to another.
rm	Deletes files.
rmdir	Deletes directories.
pwd	Displays the current directory.
touch	Updates a file's time stamp.
Finding files	
find	Finds files based on specified criteria, such as name and size.
locate	Finds files by using a periodically updated filename database. (The database is created by the updatedb program.)

(continued)

TABLE 3-2 *(continued)*

Command Name	Action
whereis	Finds files based in the typical directories where *executable* (also known as *binary*) files are located.
which	Finds files in the directories listed in the PATH environment variable.
Processing files	
cat	Displays a file in standard output (can be used to concatenate several files into one big file).
cut	Extracts specified sections from each line of text in a file.
dd	Copies blocks of data from one file to another (used to copy data from devices).
diff	Compares two text files and finds any differences.
expand	Converts all tabs to spaces.
file	Displays the type of data in a file.
fold	Wraps each line of text to fit a specified width.
grep	Searches for regular expressions in a text file.
less	Displays a text file one page at a time. (Go backward by pressing **b**.)
lpr	Prints files.
more	Displays a text file one page at a time. (Goes forward only).
nl	Numbers all nonblank lines in a text file and prints the lines to standard output.
paste	Concatenates corresponding lines from several files.
patch	Updates a text file by using the differences between the original and revised copies of the file.
sed	Copies a file to standard output while applying specified editing commands.
sort	Sorts lines in a text file.
split	Breaks up a file into several smaller files with specified sizes.
tac	Reverses a file (last line first and so on).
tail	Displays the last few lines of a file.
tr	Substitutes one group of characters for another throughout a file.
uniq	Eliminates duplicate lines from a text file.

Command Name	Action
wc	Counts the number of lines, words, and characters in a text file.
zcat	Displays a compressed file (after decompressing).
zless	Displays a compressed file one page at a time. (Go backward by pressing **b**.)
zmore	Displays a compressed file one page at a time.
Archiving and compressing files	
compress	Compresses files.
cpio	Copies files to and from an archive.
gunzip	Decompresses files compressed with GNU Zip (gzip).
gzip	Compresses files by using GNU Zip.
tar	Creates an archive of files in one or more directories (originally meant for archiving on tape).
uncompress	Decompresses files compressed with compress.
Managing files	
bg	Runs an interrupted process in the background.
fg	Runs a process in the foreground.
free	Displays the amount of free and used memory in the system.
halt	Shuts down Linux and halts the computer.
kill	Sends a signal to a process (usually to terminate the process).
ldd	Displays the shared libraries needed to run a program.
nice	Runs a process with a lower priority (referred to as nice mode).
ps	Displays a list of running processes.
printenv	Displays the current environment variables.
pstree	Shows parent–child process relationships.
reboot	Stops Linux and then restarts the computer.
shutdown	Shuts down Linux.
top	Displays a list of most processor- and memory-intensive processes.
uname	Displays information about the system and the Linux kernel.

(continued)

TABLE 3-2 *(continued)*

Command Name	Action
Managing users	
chsh	Changes the shell (command interpreter).
groups	Prints the list of groups that include a specified user.
id	Displays the user and group ID for a specified username.
passwd	Changes the password.
su	Starts a new shell as another user. (The other user is assumed to be root when the command is invoked without any argument.)
Managing the file system	
df	Summarizes free and available space in all mounted storage devices.
du	Displays disk-use information.
fdformat	Formats a floppy disk.
fdisk	Partitions a hard drive.
fsck	Checks and repairs a file system.
mkfs	Creates a new file system.
mknod	Creates a device file.
mkswap	Creates a swap space for Linux in a file or a hard drive partition.
mount	Mounts a device (such as a CD-ROM) on a directory in the file system.
swapoff	Deactivates a swap space.
swapon	Activates a swap space.
sync	Writes *buffered* (saved in memory) data to files.
tty	Displays the device name for the current terminal.
umount	Unmounts a device from the file system.
Displaying dates and times	
cal	Displays a calendar for a specified month or year.
date	Displays the current date and time or sets a new date and time.

Becoming root (superuser)

When you want to do anything that requires a high privilege level, such as administering your system, you must become root. Normally, you log in as a regular user with your everyday username. When you need the privileges of the superuser, though, use the following command to become root:

```
su -
```

That command is su followed by a space and the minus sign (or hyphen). The shell prompts you for the root password. Type the password and press Enter.

When you finish whatever you want to do as root (and you have the privilege to do anything as root), type **exit** to return to your normal username.

TECHNICAL STUFF

Instead of becoming root by using the su - command, you can type **sudo** followed by the command that you want to run as root. In Ubuntu, you must use the sudo command because you don't get to set up a root user when you install Ubuntu. If you're listed as an authorized user in the /etc/sudoers file, sudo executes the command as though you were logged in as root. Type **man sudoers** to read more about the /etc/sudoers file.

Managing processes

Every time the shell executes a command that you type, it starts a process. The shell itself is a process, as are any scripts or programs that the shell runs.

Use the ps ax command to see a list of processes. When you type **ps ax**, bash shows you the current set of processes. Here are a few lines of output that appeared when I typed **ps ax --cols 132**. (I include the –cols 132 option to ensure that you see each command in its entirety.)

```
PID TTY STAT TIME COMMAND
1   ?    S    0:01 init [5]
2   ?    SN   0:00 [ksoftirqd/0]
3   ?    S<   0:00 [events/0]
4   ?    S<   0:00 [khelper]
9   ?    S<   0:00 [kthread]
19  ?    S<   0:00 [kacpid]
75  ?    S<   0:00 [kblockd/0]
115 ?    S    0:00 [pdflush]
116 ?    S    0:01 [pdflush]
118 ?    S<   0:00 [aio/0]
117 ?    S    0:00 [kswapd0]
711 ?    S    0:00 [kseriod]
```

```
1075 ?  S<   0:00 [reiserfs/0]
2086 ?  S    0:00 [kjournald]
2239 ?  S<s  0:00 /sbin/udevd -d
... lines deleted ...
6374 ?  S    1:51 /usr/X11R6/bin/X :0 -audit 0 -auth /var/lib/gdm/:0.Xauth
     -nolisten tcp vt7
6460 ?  Ss   0:02 /opt/gnome/bin/gdmgreeter
6671 ?  Ss   0:00 sshd: edulaney [priv]
6675 ?  S    0:00 sshd: edulaney@pts/0
6676 pts/0 Ss 0:00 -bash
6712 pts/0 S 0:00 vsftpd
14702 ? S    0:00 pickup -l -t fifo -u
14752 pts/0 R+ 0:00 ps ax --cols 132
```

In this listing, the first column has the heading PID and shows a number for each process. *PID* stands for *process ID* (identification), which is a sequential number assigned by the Linux kernel. If you look through the output of the ps ax command, you see that the init command is the first process and has a PID of 1. For that reason, init is called the mother of all processes.

The COMMAND column shows the command that created each process, and the TIME column shows the cumulative processor time used by the process. The STAT column shows the state of a process: S means that the process is sleeping, and R means that it's running. The symbols following the status letter have further meanings. < indicates a high-priority process, and + means that the process is running in the foreground. The TTY column shows the terminal, if any, associated with the process.

The process ID, or process number, is useful when you have to forcibly stop an errant process. Look at the output of the ps ax command, and note the PID of the offending process. Then use the kill command with that process number to stop the process. To stop process number 8550, start by typing the following command:

```
kill 8550
```

If the process doesn't stop after 5 seconds, repeat the command. The next step in stopping a stubborn process is typing **kill -INT***pid*, where *pid* is the process number. If that command doesn't work, try the following command as a last resort:

```
kill -9 8550
```

The -9 option sends signal number 9 to the process. Signal number 9 is the KILL signal, which should cause the process to exit. You could also type this command as **kill -KILL***pid*, where *pid* is the process ID.

Working with date and time

You can use the date command to display the current date and time or set a new date and time. Type **date** at the shell prompt, and you get a result like the following:

```
Fri Mar 16 15:10:07 EST 2018
```

As you see, issuing the date command alone displays the current date and time.

To set the date, log in as root and then type **date** followed by the date and time in the MMDDhhmmYYYY format, where each character is a digit. To set the date and time to December 31, 2018, and 9:30 p.m., type

```
date 123121302018
```

The MMDDhhmmYYYY date and time format is similar to the 24-hour military clock and has the following meaning:

>> MM is a two-digit number for the month (01 through 12).

>> DD is a two-digit number for the day of the month (01 through 31).

>> hh is a two-digit hour in 24-hour format (00 is midnight, and 23 is 11 p.m.).

>> mm is a two-digit number for the minute (00 through 59).

>> YYYY is the four-digit year (such as 2018).

The other interesting date-related command is cal. If you type **cal** without any options, it prints a calendar for the current month. If you type **cal** followed by a number, cal treats the number as the year and prints the calendar for that year. To view the calendar for a specific month in a specific year, provide the month number (1 = January, 2 = February, and so on) followed by the year. If you type **cal 4 2018**, you get the calendar for April 2018, as follows:

```
April 2018
Su Mo Tu We Th Fr Sa
1  2  3  4  5  6  7
8  9 10 11 12 13 14
15 16 17 18 19 20 21
22 23 24 25 26 27 28
29 30
```

Processing files

You can search a text file with grep and view a text file, a screen at a time, with more. To search for my username in the /etc/passwd file, use

```
grep edulaney /etc/passwd
```

To view the /etc/inittab file a screen at a time, type

```
more /etc/inittab
```

As each screen pauses, press the spacebar to go to the next page.

Many more Linux commands work on files, mostly on text files, but some commands also work on any file. The following sections describe a few file-processing tools.

Counting words and lines in a text file

I'm always curious about the sizes of files. For text files, the number of characters is the size of the file in bytes (because each character takes up 1 byte of storage space). What about words and the number of lines, though?

The Linux wc command comes to the rescue. The wc command displays the total number of lines, words, and characters in a text file. Type **wc /etc/inittab**, and you see output similar to the following:

```
97 395 2926 /etc/inittab
```

In this case, wc reports that 97 lines, 395 words, and 2,926 characters are in the /etc/inittab file. If you want to see the number of lines in a file, use the −l option, and type **wc −l /etc/inittab**. The resulting output should be similar to the following:

```
97 /etc/inittab
```

As you can see, with the −l option, wc simply displays the line count.

If you don't specify a filename, the wc command expects input from the standard input. You can use the pipe feature (|) of the shell to feed the output of another command to wc, which can be handy sometimes.

TIP

Suppose that you want a rough count of the processes running on your system. You can get a list of all processes with the ps ax command, but instead of counting lines manually, pipe the output of ps to wc to get a rough count automatically:

```
ps ax | wc -l
86
```

Here, the ps command produces 86 lines of output. Because the first line shows the headings for the tabular columns, you can estimate that about 85 processes are running on your system. (This count probably includes the processes used to run the ps and wc commands as well.)

Sorting text files

You can sort the lines in a text file by using the sort command. To see how the sort command works, first type **more /etc/passwd** to see the current contents of the /etc/passwd file. Then type **sort /etc/passwd** to see the lines sorted alphabetically. If you want to sort a file and save the sorted version in another file, you must use the bash shell's output redirection feature, like this:

```
sort /etc/passwd > ~/sorted.text
```

This command sorts the lines in the /etc/passwd file and saves the output in a file named sorted.text in your home directory.

Substituting or deleting characters from a file

Another interesting command is tr, which substitutes one group of characters for another (or deletes a selected character) throughout a file. Suppose that you have to occasionally use MS-DOS text files on your Linux system. Although you may expect to use a text file on any system without any problems, you find one catch: DOS uses a carriage return followed by a line feed to mark the end of each line, whereas Linux uses only a line feed.

TIP

On your Linux system, you can get rid of the extra carriage returns in the DOS text file by using the tr command with the -d option. Essentially, to convert the DOS text file named filename.dos to a Linux text file named filename.linux, type the following:

```
tr -d '\015' < filename.dos > filename.linux
```

In this command, '\015' denotes the code for the carriage-return character in octal notation.

Splitting a file into several smaller files

The split command is handy for those times when you want to copy a file, but the file is too large to send as one email attachment. You can use the split command to break the file into smaller files.

By default, split puts 1,000 lines into each file. The new split files are named by groups of letters: aa, ab, ac, and so on. You can specify a prefix for the filenames. To split a large file called hugefile.tar into smaller files, use split as follows:

```
split -b 9999k hugefile.tar part.
```

This command splits the hugefile.tar file into 9999KB chunks. The command creates files named part.aa, part.ab, part.ac, and so on.

To recombine the split files into a single file, use the cat command as follows:

```
cat part.?? > hugefile.tar
```

In this case, the two question marks (??) match any two-character extension in the filename. In other words, the filename part.?? matches all filenames, such as part.12, part.aa, part.ab, and part.2b.

Writing Shell Scripts

If you've ever used MS-DOS, you may remember MS-DOS *batch files*, which are text files with MS-DOS commands. Similarly, *shell scripts* are text files with a bunch of shell commands.

If you aren't a programmer, you may feel apprehensive about programming, but shell programming can be as simple as storing a few commands in a file. Right now, you may not be up to writing complex shell scripts, but you can certainly try a simple shell script.

To try your hand at a little shell programming, type the following text at the shell prompt exactly as shown, and press Ctrl+D when you finish:

```
cd
cat > simple
#!/bin/sh
echo "This script's name is: $0"
echo Argument 1: $1
echo Argument 2: $2
```

Press Ctrl+D.

The cd command changes the current directory to your home directory — the default for cd if you do not specify an option. Then the cat command displays the next line and any other lines you type before pressing Ctrl+D. In this case, you use › simple to send the output to a file named simple. After you press Ctrl+D, the cat command ends, and you see the shell prompt again. You created a file named simple that contains the following shell script:

```
#!/bin/sh
echo "This script's name is: $0"
echo Argument 1: $1
echo Argument 2: $2
```

The first line causes Linux to run the bash shell program (of the name /bin/bash). Then the shell reads the rest of the lines in the script.

Just as most Linux commands accept command-line options, a bash script accepts command-line options. Inside the script, you can refer to the options as $1, $2, and so on. The special name $0 refers to the name of the script itself.

To run this shell script, first make the file executable (that is, turn it into a program) with the following command:

```
chmod +x simple
```

Type **./simple one two** to run the script, which displays the following output:

```
This script's name is: ./simple
Argument 1: one
Argument 2: two
```

The ./ prefix in the script's name indicates that the simple file is in the current directory.

This script prints the script's name and the first two command-line options that the user types after the script's name.

Next, try running the script with a few arguments, as follows:

```
./simple "This is one argument" second-argument third
This script's name is: ./simple
Argument 1: This is one argument
Argument 2: second-argument
```

The shell treats the entire string in the double quotation marks as a single argument. Otherwise, the shell uses spaces to separate arguments on the command line.

Most useful shell scripts are more complicated than this simple script, but this exercise gives you a rough idea of how to write shell scripts. In the first two chapters of Book 7, I explore this a bit further.

REMEMBER

Place Linux commands in a file and use the chmod command to make the file executable. Voilà — you've created a shell script.

» Navigating the system with Linux
  commands

» Understanding file permissions

» Manipulating files and directories
  with Linux commands

Chapter **4**

Navigating the Linux File System

To use files and directories well, you need to understand the concept of a hierarchical file system. Even if you use the graphical user interface (GUI) file managers (addressed in Book 2, Chapter 5) to access files and folders (folders are also called *directories*), you can benefit from a lay of the land of the file system.

This chapter introduces the Linux file system and shows you how to work with files and directories by using several Linux commands.

Understanding the Linux File System

Like any other operating system, Linux organizes information in files and directories. A *directory* is a special file that can contain other files and directories. Because a directory can contain other directories, this method of organizing files gives rise to a hierarchical structure. This hierarchical organization of files is the *file system*.

The Linux file system gives you a unified view of all storage on your PC. The file system has a single root directory, indicated by a forward slash (/). Within the root directory is a hierarchy of files and directories. Parts of the file system can reside on different physical media, such as a hard drive, an external drive, and a CD-ROM. Figure 4-1 illustrates the concept of the Linux file system (which is the same in any Linux system) and shows how it spans multiple physical devices.

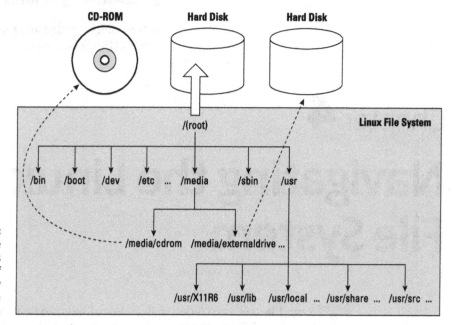

FIGURE 4-1:
The Linux file system provides a unified view of storage that may span multiple storage devices.

If you're familiar with other operating systems, such as Windows, you may find something missing in the Linux file system: drive letters. All disk drives and CD-ROM drives are part of a single file system.

REMEMBER

In Linux, you can have long filenames (up to 256 characters), and filenames are case-sensitive. Often, filenames have multiple extensions, such as `sample.tar.Z`. Unix filenames can take many forms, such as the following: `index.html`, `Makefile`, `binutils-2.15.92.0.2-5.i386.rpm`, `vsftpd_2.0.3-1_i386.deb`, `.bash_profile`, and `httpd_src.tar.gz`.

To locate a file, you need more than just the filename. You also need information about the directory hierarchy. The extended filename, showing the full hierarchy of directories leading to the file, is the *pathname*. As the name implies, it's the path to the file through the maze of the file system. Figure 4-2 shows a typical pathname for a file in Linux.

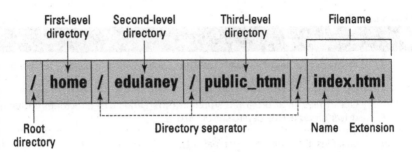

FIGURE 4-2:
The path for
the file shows
the sequence
of directories
leading up to
the file.

As Figure 4-2 shows, the pathname has the following parts:

» **The root directory,** indicated by a forward slash (/).

» **The directory hierarchy,** with each directory name separated from the previous one by a forward slash (/). A / appears after the last directory name.

» **The filename,** with a name and one or more optional extensions. (A period appears before each extension.)

The Linux file system has a well-defined set of top-level directories, and some of these directories have specific purposes. Finding your way around the file system is easier if you know the purpose of these directories. You also become adept at guessing where to look for specific types of files when you face a new situation. Table 4-1 briefly describes the top-level directories in the Linux file system.

TABLE 4-1   **Top-Level Directories in the Linux File System**

Directory	Contains
/	Base of the file system. All files and directories are contained logically in the root, or /, directory, regardless of their physical locations.
/bin	Executable programs that are part of the Linux operating system. Many Linux commands — such as cat, cp, ls, more, and tar — are in /bin.
/boot	Linux kernel and other files that the LILO and GRUB boot managers need. The kernel and other files can be anywhere, but placing them in the /boot directory is customary.
/dev	Special files that represent devices attached to the system.
/etc	Most system configuration files and the initialization scripts (in the /etc/rc.d subdirectory).

(continued)

Navigating the Linux
File System

TABLE 4-1 *(continued)*

Directory	Contains
/home	Home directories of all users. User edulaney's home directory, for example, is /home/edulaney.
/lib	Library files for all programs stored in /sbin and /bin directories (including the loadable driver modules) needed to start Linux.
/lost+found	Lost files. Every disk partition has a lost+found directory.
/media	The /media/cdrom or /media/cdrom0 directory is for mounting the CD/DVD-ROM drive. If you have a CD/DVD recorder, you find a /media/cdrecorder directory instead of /media/cdrom and may also find /media/DVD. /media is used for mounting file systems on removable media, such as CD/DVD-ROM drives, flash drives, external drives, floppy disks, and Zip drives. If you have a very old machine that still has a floppy drive on it, the /media/floppy directory also exists for mounting floppy disks.
/mnt	Temporarily mounted file systems.
/opt	Storage for large application software packages. Some distributions install the LibreOffice.org Office suite in the /opt directory, for example.
/proc	Various information about the processes running in the Linux system.
/root	Home directory for the root user.
/sbin	Executable files representing commands typically used for system administration tasks and used by the root user. Commands such as halt and shutdown reside in the /sbin directory.
/srv	Data for services (such as web and FTP) offered by this system.
/sys	Information about the devices, as seen by the Linux kernel.
/tmp	Temporary directory that any user can use as a *scratch* directory, meaning that the contents of this directory are considered to be unimportant and usually are deleted every time the system boots.
/usr	Subdirectories for many important programs, such as the X Window System (in the /usr/X11R6 directory) and the online manual. (Table 4-2 shows some of the standard subdirectories in /usr.)
/var	Various system files (such as logs), as well as directories for holding other information, such as files for the web server and anonymous FTP server.

The /usr and /var directories also contain standard subdirectories. Table 4-2 lists the important subdirectories in /usr. Table 4-3 shows a similar breakdown for the /var directory.

TABLE 4-2   **Important /usr Subdirectories**

Subdirectory	Description
/usr/bin	Executable files for many more Linux commands, including utility programs that are commonly available in Linux but aren't part of the core Linux operating system.
/usr/games	Some old Linux games.
/usr/include	Header files (filenames ending in .h) for the C and C++ programming languages and the X11 header files in the /usr/include/X11 directory and the Linux kernel header files in the /usr/include/linux directory.
/usr/lib	Libraries for C and C++ programming languages and many other libraries, such as database libraries and graphical toolkit libraries.
/usr/local	Local files. The /usr/local/bin directory, for example, is supposed to be the location for any executable program developed on your system.
/usr/sbin	Many administrative commands, such as commands for email and networking.
/usr/share	Shared data, such as default configuration files and images for many applications. /usr/share/gnome contains various shared files for the GNOME desktop, for example, and /usr/share/doc has the documentation files for many Linux applications (such as the bash shell, the Sawfish window manager, and the GIMP image processing program).
/usr/share/man	Online manual (which you can read by using the man command).
/usr/src	Source code for the Linux kernel (the core operating system).

TABLE 4-3   **Important /var Subdirectories**

Subdirectory	Contains
/var/cache	Storage area for cached data for applications.
/var/lib	Information relating to the current state of applications.
/var/lock	Locked files that ensure that a resource is used by only one application.
/var/log	Log files organized into subdirectories. The syslogd server stores its log files in /var/log, with the exact content of the files depending on the syslogd configuration file /etc/syslog.conf. /var/log/messages is the main system log file, for example; /var/log/secure contains log messages from secure services (such as sshd and xinetd), and /var/log/maillog contains the log of mail messages.
/var/mail	User mailbox files.
/var/opt	Variable data for packages stored in the /opt directory.

(continued)

TABLE 4-3 *(continued)*

Subdirectory	Contains
/var/run	Data describing the system since the time it was booted.
/var/spool	Data that's waiting for some kind of processing.
/var/tmp	Temporary files preserved between system reboots.
/var/yp	Network Information Service (NIS) database files.

Navigating the File System with Linux Commands

Although GUI file managers such as Nautilus (in GNOME) or Konqueror (in KDE) are easy to use, you can use them only if you have a working GUI desktop. Sometimes, you don't have a graphical environment in which to run a graphical file manager. You may be logged in through a text terminal, or X may not be working on your system. In those situations, you have to rely on Linux commands to work with files and directories. You can always use Linux commands, even in the graphical environment; all you have to do is open a terminal window and type the Linux commands.

In this section, I briefly describe some Linux commands for moving around the Linux file system.

Commands for directory navigation

In Linux, when you log in as root, your home directory is /root. For other users, the home directory usually is in the /home directory. My home directory (when I log in as edulaney) is /home/edulaney. This information is stored in the /etc/passwd file. By default, only you have permission to save files in your home directory, and only you can create subdirectories in your home directory to further organize your files.

Linux supports the concept of a *current* directory, which is the directory on which all file and directory commands operate. After you log in, for example, your current directory is the home directory. To see the current directory, type the pwd command.

To change the current directory, use the cd command. To change the current directory to /usr/lib, type the following:

```
cd /usr/lib
```

Then, to change the directory to the cups subdirectory in /usr/lib, type this command:

```
cd cups
```

Now if you use the pwd command, that command shows /usr/lib/cups as the current directory.

These two examples show that you can refer to a directory's name in two ways:

>> **Absolute pathname:** An example is /usr/lib, which is an exact directory in the directory tree. Think of the absolute pathname as being the complete mailing address for a package that the postal service will deliver to your next-door neighbor.

>> **Relative directory name:** An example is cups, which represents the cups subdirectory of the current directory, whatever that may be. Think of the relative directory name as giving the postal carrier directions from your house to the one next door so that the carrier can deliver the package.

If I type cd cups in /usr/lib, the current directory changes to /usr/lib/cups. If I type the same command in /home/edulaney, the shell tries to change the current directory to /home/edulaney/cups.

TIP

Use the cd command without any arguments to change the current directory back to your home directory. No matter where you are, typing cd at the shell prompt brings you back home!

TECHNICAL STUFF

The tilde character (~) refers to your home directory. Thus, you can change the current directory to your home directory by using the command cd ~. You can refer to another user's home directory by appending that user's name to the tilde. cd ~superman, for example, changes the current directory to the home directory of superman.

TIP

Wait — there's more. A single dot (.) and two dots (..) — often cleverly referred to as *dot-dot* — also have special meanings. A single dot (.) indicates the current directory, whereas two dots (..) indicate the parent directory. If the current directory is /usr/share, you go one level up to /usr by typing the following:

```
cd ..
```

Commands for directory listings and permissions

You can get a directory listing by using the ls command. By default, the ls command without options displays the contents of the current directory in a compact, multicolumn format. Type the next two commands to see the contents of the /etc/X11 directory:

```
cd /etc/X11
ls
```

The output looks like this, with some items in different colors on the console:

```
X Xsession.d cursors rgb.txt xkb
XF86Config-4 Xsession.options default-display-manager rstart xserver
Xresources Xwrapper.config fonts sysconfig xsm
Xsession app-defaults gdm xinit
```

From this listing, without the colors, you can't tell whether an entry is a file or a directory. To tell the directories and files apart, use the –F option with ls, like this:

```
ls -F
```

This time, the output gives you some more clues about the file types:

```
X@ Xsession.d/ cursors/ rgb.txt xkb/
XF86Config-4 Xsession.options default-display-manager rstart/ xserver/
Xresources/ Xwrapper.config fonts/ sysconfig/ xsm/
Xsession* app-defaults/ gdm@ xinit/
```

The output from ls –F shows the directory names with a slash (/) appended to them. Plain filenames appear as is. The at sign (@) appended to a filename (notice the file named X, for example) indicates that this file is a link to another file. In other words, this filename simply refers to another file; it's a shortcut. An asterisk (*) is appended to executable files. (Xsession, for example, is an executable file.) The shell can run any executable file.

You can see even more detailed information about the files and directories with the –1 option:

```
ls -1
```

For the `/etc/X11` directory, typical output from `ls -l` looks like the following:

```
total 84
lrwxrwxrwx 1 root root    20 Jul 15 20:32 X -> /usr/bin/X11/XFree86
-rw-r--r-- 1 root root 2878 Jul 16 14:50 XF86Config-4
drwxr-xr-x 2 root root 4096 Jul 15 20:32 Xresources
-rwxr-xr-x 1 root root 3456 Jun 1  01:59 Xsession
drwxr-xr-x 2 root root 4096 Jul 15 20:34 Xsession.d
-rw-r--r-- 1 root root 217  Jun 1  01:59 Xsession.options
-rw------- 1 root root 771  Jul 15 20:32 Xwrapper.config
drwxr-xr-x 2 root root 4096 Jul 15 20:35 app-defaults
... lines deleted ...
```

This listing shows considerable information about every directory entry, each of which can be a file or another directory. Looking at a line from the right column to the left, you see that the rightmost column shows the name of the directory entry. The date and time before the name show when the last modifications to that file were made. To the left of the date and time is the size of the file, in bytes.

The file's group and owner appear to the left of the column that shows the file size. The next number to the left indicates the number of links to the file. (A *link* is like a shortcut in Windows.) Finally, the leftmost column shows the file's permission settings, which determine who can read, write, or execute the file.

The first letter has a special meaning, as the following list shows:

>> `l`: The file is a *symbolic link* to another file. In other words, it's a shortcut to something else.

>> `d`: The file is a directory. It appears as a folder in a GUI.

>> `- (hyphen)`: The file is normal. By *normal,* I mean that it isn't a directory, a link, or anything else odd. Most of the items on your system are normal files.

>> `b`: The file represents a block device, such as a disk drive.

>> `c`: The file represents a character device, such as a serial port or a terminal.

After that first letter, the leftmost column shows a sequence of nine characters, which appears as `rwxrwxrwx` when each letter is present. Each letter indicates a specific permission. A hyphen (–) in place of a letter indicates no permission for a specific operation on the file. Think of these nine letters as being three groups of three letters (`rwx`), interpreted as follows:

>> **Leftmost `rwx` group:** Controls the read, write, and execute permission of the file's owner. In other words, if you see `rwx` in this position, the file's owner can read (`r`), write (`w`), and execute (`x`) the file. A hyphen in the place of a letter

indicates no permission. Thus, the string `rw-` means that the owner has read and write permission but not execute permission. Although executable programs (including shell programs) typically have execute permission, directories treat execute permission as being equivalent to *use* permission. A user must have execute permission on a directory before he or she can open and read the contents of the directory.

>> **Middle `rwx` group:** Controls the read, write, and execute permission of any user belonging to that file's group.

>> **Rightmost `rwx` group:** Controls the read, write, and execute permission of all other users (collectively thought of as *the world*).

Thus, a file with the permission setting `rwx------` is accessible only to the file's owner, whereas the permission setting `rwxr--r--` makes the file readable by the world.

An interesting feature of the `ls` command is that it doesn't list any file whose name begins with a period. To see these files, you must use the `ls` command with the –a option, as follows:

```
ls -a
```

Try this command in your home directory and then compare the result with what you see when you don't use the –a option:

1. **Type** cd **to change to your home directory.**

2. **Type** ls -F **to see the files and directories in your home directory.**

3. **Type** ls -aF **to see everything, including hidden files.**

TIP

Most Linux commands take single-character options, each with a hyphen as a prefix. When you want to use several options, type a hyphen and *concatenate* (string together) the option letters, one after another. Thus, `ls -al` is equivalent to `ls -a -l` as well as to `ls -l -a`.

Commands for changing permissions and ownerships

You may need to change a file's permission settings to protect it from others. Use the chmod command to change the permission settings of a file or a directory.

To use chmod effectively, you have to specify the permission settings. A good way is to concatenate letters from the columns of Table 4-4 in the order shown (Who/Action/Permission).

TABLE 4-4 **Letter Codes for File Permissions**

Who	Action	Permission
u (user)	+ (add)	r (read)
g (group)	– (remove)	w (write)
o (others)	= (assign)	x (execute)
a (all)	s (set user ID)	

TECHNICAL STUFF

You use only the single character from each column; the text in parentheses is for explanation only.

To give everyone read access to all files in a directory, pick a (for *all*) from the first column, + (for *add*) from the second column, and r (for *read*) from the third column to come up with the permission setting a+r. Then use the set of options with chmod, like this:

```
chmod a+r *.
```

On the other hand, to permit everyone to execute one specific file, type

```
chmod a+x filename
```

TIP

Suppose that you want to protect a file named mystuff. You can make it accessible to no one but you if you type the following commands, in this order:

```
chmod a-rwx mystuff
chmod u+rw mystuff
```

The first command turns off all permissions for everyone, and the second command turns on the read and write permissions for the owner (you). Type **ls -l** to verify that the change took place. (You see a permission setting of –rw-------.)

Sometimes, you have to change a file's user or group ownership for everything to work correctly. Suppose that you're instructed (by a manual, what else?) to create a directory named cups and give it the ownership of user ID lp and group ID sys. How do you do it?

Well, you can log in as root and create the cups directory with the command mkdir:

```
mkdir cups
```

If you check the file's details with the ls -l command, you see that the user and group ownership is root root.

TIP

To change the owner, use the chown command. To change the ownership of the cups directory to user ID lp and group ID sys, type

```
chown lp.sys cups
```

Commands for working with files

To copy files from one directory to another, use the cp command. If you want to copy a file to the current directory but retain the original name, use a period (.) as the second argument of the cp command. Thus, the following command copies the Xresources file from the /etc/X11 directory to the current directory (denoted by a single period):

```
cp /etc/X11/Xresources .
```

The cp command makes a new copy of a file and leaves the original intact.

TIP

If you want to copy the entire contents of a directory — including all subdirectories and their contents — to another directory, use the command cp -ar sourcedir destdir. (This command copies everything in the sourcedir directory to destdir.) To copy all files from the /etc/X11 directory to the current directory, type the following command:

```
cp -ar /etc/X11 .
```

TIP

To move a file to a new location, use the mv command. The original copy is gone, and a new copy appears at the destination. You can use mv to rename a file. If you want to change the name of today.list to old.list, use the mv command, as follows:

```
mv today.list old.list
```

On the other hand, if you want to move the today.list file to a subdirectory named saved, use this command:

```
mv today.list saved
```

An interesting feature of mv is that you can use it to move entire directories (with all their subdirectories and files) to a new location. If you have a directory named data that contains many files and subdirectories, you can move that entire directory structure to old_data by using the following command:

```
mv data old_data
```

To delete files, use the rm command. To delete a file named old.list, type the following command:

```
rm old.list
```

WARNING

Be careful with the rm command, especially when you log in as root. You can inadvertently delete important files with rm.

Commands for working with directories

To organize files in your home directory, you have to create new directories. Use the mkdir command to create a directory. To create a directory named images in the current directory, type the following:

```
mkdir images
```

After you create the directory, you can use the cd images command to change to that directory.

TIP

You can create an entire directory tree by using the –p option with the mkdir command. Suppose that your system has a /usr/src directory, and you want to create the directory tree /usr/src/book/java/examples/applets. To create this directory hierarchy, type the following command:

```
mkdir -p /usr/src/book/java/examples/applets
```

When you no longer need a directory, use the rmdir command to delete it.

REMEMBER

You can delete a directory only when the directory is empty.

To remove an empty directory tree, you can use the –p option, like this:

```
rmdir -p /usr/src/book/java/examples/applets
```

This command removes the empty parent directories of applets. The command stops when it encounters a directory that's not empty.

Commands for finding files

The find command is useful for locating files (and directories) that meet your search criteria.

When I began using Unix many years ago (Berkeley Unix in the early 1980s), I was confounded by the find command. I stayed with one basic syntax of find for a long time before graduating to more complex forms. The basic syntax that I discovered first was for finding a file anywhere in the file system. Here's how it goes: Suppose that you want to find any file or directory with a name that starts with gnome. Type the following find command to find these files:

```
find / -name "gnome*" -print
```

If you're not logged in as root, you may get a bunch of error messages. If these error messages annoy you, modify the command as follows, and the error messages are history (or, as Unix aficionados say, sent to the bit bucket):

```
find / -name "gnome*" -print 2> /dev/null
```

This command tells find to start looking at the root directory (/) to look for filenames that match gnome* and to display the full pathname of any matching file. The last part (2> /dev/null) simply sends the error messages to a special file that's the equivalent of simply ignoring them.

You can use variations of this simple form of find to locate a file in any directory, as well as any subdirectories contained in the directory. If you forget where in your home directory you've stored all files named report* (names that start with *report*), you can search for the files by using the following command:

```
find ~ -name "report*" -print
```

When you become comfortable with this syntax of find, you can use other options of find. To find only specific types of files (such as directories), use the type option. The following command displays all top-level directory names in your Linux system:

```
find / -type d -maxdepth 1 -print
```

You probably don't have to use the complex forms of find in a typical Linux system, but if you ever need to, you can look up the rest of the find options by using the following command:

```
man find
```

TIP

An easy way to find all files that match a name is to use the `locate` command, which searches a periodically updated database of files on your system. Here's a typical output that I get when I type **locate Xresources** on a Debian system (the output may differ based on your distribution):

```
/etc/X11/Xresources
/etc/X11/Xresources/xbase-clients
/etc/X11/Xresources/xfree86-common
```

DISTRIBUTION SPECIFIC

The `locate` command isn't installed by default in some Linux distributions. To install it, open the Add/Remove Software application for your distribution, and search for `locate`. Then select the package from the search results and click Accept to install it.

Commands for mounting and unmounting

Suppose that you want to access files on a DVD-ROM when you're logged in at a text console (with no GUI to help you). To do so, first mount the DVD-ROM drive's file system on a specific directory in the Linux file system.

DISTRIBUTION SPECIFIC

Start by looking at the `/etc/fstab` file for clues to the name of the CD-ROM device. Some Linux distributions use the device name `/dev/cdrom` to refer to CD/DVD-ROM drives, whereas others use device names such as `/dev/hdc`, `/dev/cdroms/cdrom0`, or `/dev/cdrecorder` (for a DVD/CD-R drive). The entry in `/etc/fstab` file also tells you the directory where that distribution expects the CD/DVD to be mounted. Some distributions use `/media/cdrom` as the mount point, and others use `/media/cdrom0` or `/media/cdrecorder`.

TIP

It's customary to use `cdrom` to mean both a CD-ROM and a DVD-ROM.

Log in as `root` (or type **su -** to become `root`), insert the DVD-ROM into the DVD drive, and then type the following command:

```
mount /dev/hdc /media/cdrom0
```

This command mounts the file system on the device named `/dev/hdc` (an IDE DVD/CD-ROM drive) on the `/media/cdrom0` directory (which is also called the *mount point*) in the Linux file system.

After the `mount` command successfully completes its task, you can access the files on the DVD-ROM by referring to the `/media/cdrom0` directory as the top-level directory of the disc. In other words, to see the contents of the DVD-ROM, type

```
ls -F /media/cdrom0
```

When you finish using the DVD-ROM, and before you eject it from the drive, you have to unmount the disc drive with the following command:

```
umount /dev/hdc
```

You can mount devices on any empty directory on the file system, but each distribution has customary locations with directories meant for mounting devices. Some distributions use directories in /mnt, for example, whereas others use the /media directory for the mount points.

Commands for checking disk-space use

You can use two simple commands — df and du — to check the disk-space use on your system. The df command shows you a summary of disk-space use for all mounted devices. When I type **df** on a PC with many mounted storage devices, here's what I get as output:

```
Filesystem 1K-blocks Used Available Use% Mounted on
/dev/hdb6 28249372 2377292 25872080 9% /
tmpfs 383968 12 383956 1% /dev/shm
/dev/hda5 5766924 1422232 4051744 26% /ubuntu/boot
/dev/hda7 6258100 2989200 2951004 51% /debian/boot
/dev/hda9 5766924 1422232 4051744 26% /ubuntu
/dev/hda10 5766924 1872992 3600984 35% /mepis
/dev/hda11 6258100 2989200 2951004 51% /debian
/dev/hda2 16087676 10593364 5494312 66% /windows/C
/dev/hdb1 107426620 9613028 97813592 9% /windows/D
```

This table lists the device, total kilobytes of storage, how much of that memory is in use, how much memory is available, the percentage of memory that's being used, and the mount point.

To see the output of df in a more readable format, type **df -h**. The output follows:

```
Filesystem Size Used Avail Use% Mounted on
/dev/hdb6   27G  2.3G  25G   9%  /
tmpfs      375M  12K 375M   1%  /dev/shm
/dev/hda5  5.5G  1.4G 3.9G  26%  /ubuntu/boot
/dev/hda7  6.0G  2.9G 2.9G  51%  /debian/boot
/dev/hda9  5.5G  1.4G 3.9G  26%  /ubuntu
/dev/hda10 5.5G  1.8G 3.5G  35%  /mepis
/dev/hda11 6.0G  2.9G 2.9G  51%  /debian
/dev/hda2   16G  11G5.3G   66%  /windows/C
/dev/hdb1  103G  9.2G 94G   9%  /windows/D
```

If you compare this output with the output of the plain df (the preceding listing), you see that df -h prints the sizes with terms such as M for megabytes and G for gigabytes. These terms are easier to understand than 1K-blocks.

The other command, du, is useful for finding out how much space a directory takes up. Type **du /etc/X11** to view the contents of all the directories in the /etc/ X11 directory, for example. (This directory contains X Window System configuration files.) You see the following:

```
12 /etc/X11/Xresources
36 /etc/X11/Xsession.d
272 /etc/X11/app-defaults
20 /etc/X11/cursors
12 /etc/X11/xinit
... lines deleted ...
12 /etc/X11/fonts/misc
8 /etc/X11/fonts/100dpi
8 /etc/X11/fonts/75dpi
8 /etc/X11/fonts/Speedo
8 /etc/X11/fonts/Type1
48 /etc/X11/fonts
2896 /etc/X11
```

Each directory name is preceded by a number, which tells you the number of kilobytes of disk space used by that directory. Thus, the /etc/X11 directory uses 2896KB (or about 2.9MB) of disk space. If you simply want the total disk space used by a directory (including all the files and subdirectories contained in that directory), use the –s option, as follows:

```
du -s /etc/X11
2896 /etc/X11
```

The –s option causes du to print only the summary information for the entire directory.

TIP

Just as df -h prints the disk-space information in megabytes and gigabytes, you can use the du -h command to view the output of du in more readable form. Here's how I combine it with the –s option to see the space that I'm using in my home directory (/home/edulaney):

```
du -sh /home/edulaney
645M /home/edulaney
```

» Trying out the office applications

» Playing with multimedia

» Working with images

Chapter **5**

Introducing Linux Applications

Most Linux distributions come with a fair number of applications to meet diverse computing needs, as you can see simply by looking at the menus in the graphical user interface (GUI) desktops. Often, more than one application of the same type exists, though only one may be installed by default. Most distributions come with the LibreOffice office application suite, which provides a word processor, spreadsheet, presentation software, and more. You have many choices of DVD players and multimedia players, plus games, utility programs, and useful tools such as scanners and digital camera applications. Some commercial distributions come with commercial office suites as well.

DISTRIBUTION SPECIFIC

When it comes to playing *multimedia* (audio and video in various formats, such as MP3, MP4, and QuickTime), freely available Linux distributions rarely come with the appropriate decoders because of licensing restrictions; the multimedia application runs but cannot play the MP3 file or the DVD movie because it lacks a decoder. Commercial distributions usually come with some of these decoders.

This chapter offers an overview of some Linux applications. After you read about these applications, you can explore them further and have them at your disposal when needed. This chapter also introduces the GUI file managers, which allow you to browse and manipulate individual files.

Taking Stock of Linux Applications

A list of all the Linux applications available could take up much of this book. A major application almost always has a website where you can get more information about it. Each Linux distribution comes with many applications and utilities; this chapter is a brief sample of what is available.

Typically, as you install a Linux distribution, you must select specific groups of applications to install. The exact list of applications on your Linux system depends on the choices you make during the installation.

It's easy to install missing applications in Debian (and Debian-based distributions, such as Ubuntu) as long as you have a connection to the Internet. You can see whether an application exists by using the `apt-cache search` command and then installing the application with the corresponding `apt-get install` command. This ease of installing (or upgrading) software is why Debian users swear by `apt-get`, even though it's a command-line tool.

Introducing Office Applications and Tools

Word processors, spreadsheets, presentation software, calendars, and calculators are office-suite staples. Most Linux distributions come with the LibreOffice suite of office applications and tools, which you can try one by one and see which one takes your fancy. Each application is fairly intuitive to use. Although some nuances of the user interface may be new to you, you'll become comfortable with the interface after using it a few times. This section briefly introduces the following applications, as well as some other commercially available office applications for Linux:

>> **LibreOffice Suite:** A Microsoft Office–like office suite with the Writer word processor, the Calc spreadsheet program, the Impress presentation program, the Draw drawing and illustration application, and the Math mathematical-formula editor

>> **Kontact:** A personal information management application in KDE

>> **Calculators:** A GNOME calculator and KDE calculator

>> **Aspell:** A spelling checker

LibreOffice.org office suite

LibreOffice.org is not only a website, but also an office suite similar to major office suites such as Microsoft Office. Its main components are the Writer word processor, the Calc spreadsheet, and the Impress presentation program.

You can easily start LibreOffice.org — either the overall suite or an individual application — from most GUI desktops by clicking a panel icon or by making a choice from the main menu. In Ubuntu, you can click a desktop icon to open the initial window of the LibreOffice.org suite. You can create new documents or open existing documents (which can be Microsoft Office files as well) from the main window.

Writer

Choosing File⇨New⇨Text Document in any LibreOffice.org window starts LibreOffice.org Writer with a blank document in its main window. Using Writer is simple; if you're familiar with Microsoft Word, you should have no trouble finding your way around Writer. You can type text in the blank document, format text, and save text.

You can also open documents that you've prepared with Microsoft Word on a Windows machine. Figure 5-1 shows a Microsoft Word document open in Libre-Office Writer.

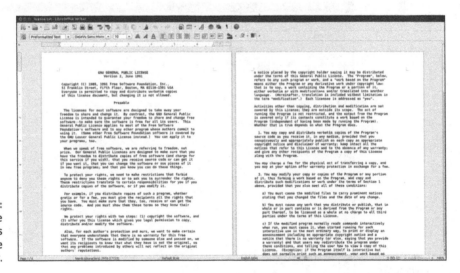

FIGURE 5-1:
You can prepare documents in LibreOffice Writer.

When you save a document, Writer saves it in LibreDocument text format by default, in a file with the .odt extension.

If you need to share Writer documents with Microsoft Word, you can save the documents in several formats, including Microsoft Word and Rich Text (.rtf) formats.

Writer is simple and intuitive to use. If you need help, choose Writer⇨Help or press F1 to bring up the Help window. Then you can click links to view specific help information about Writer.

Calc

Calc is the spreadsheet program in the LibreOffice application suite. To start Calc, choose Spreadsheet in the Office category of the main menu or choose File⇨New⇨Spreadsheet in any LibreOffice window. Calc displays its main window, which is similar to that of Windows-based spreadsheets such as Microsoft Excel. (Calc can read and write Microsoft Excel–format spreadsheet files.)

You use Calc the same way that you use Microsoft Excel. You can type entries in cells, use formulas, and format the cells (specifying the type of value and the number of digits after the decimal point, for example). Figure 5-2 shows a typical spreadsheet in Calc.

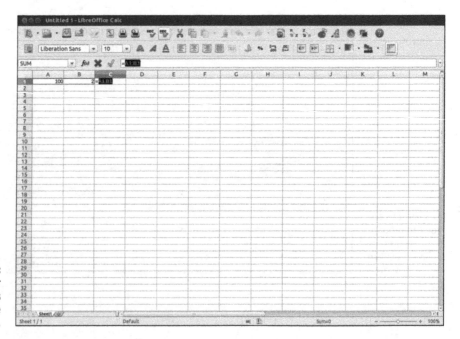

FIGURE 5-2: Prepare your spreadsheets with LibreOffice Calc.

When preparing the spreadsheet, use formulas in the same format that you would in Microsoft Excel. Use the formula SUM(D2:D6) to add the entries from cell D2 to D6, for example. To set cell D2 as the product of the entries A2 and C2, type =A2*C2 in cell D2. To find out more about the functions available in LibreOffice.org Calc, choose Help⇨LibreOffice.org Help or (in newer versions) press F1 to open the LibreOffice.org Help window. Then browse the functions by category and click a function to read more about it.

To save the spreadsheet, choose File⇨Save As. A dialog box appears, where you specify the file format, the directory location, and the name of the file. When you save a document, by default, Calc saves it in LibreDocument spreadsheet format in a file with the .ods extension. LibreOffice.org Calc can save the file in several other formats, including Microsoft Excel (.xls and .xlsx), as well as text with comma-separated values (.csv).

TIP

If you want to exchange files with Microsoft Excel, save the spreadsheet in Excel format (choosing an appropriate version), transfer that file to a Windows system, and open it in Excel.

Impress

Impress is similar to Microsoft PowerPoint; it allows you to create unique, creative slide presentations for a variety of purposes. To run Impress, choose Presentation in the Office category of the main menu or choose File⇨New⇨Presentation in any LibreOffice window.

When you first open Impress, the program prompts you for the presentation style and template. To begin working, select Empty presentation, and click Create. To open an existing document, select the appropriate option in the Presentation Wizard, click Open, and select the presentation file you want to open. You can open Microsoft PowerPoint files in Impress. Figure 5-3 shows a typical slide presentation in Impress.

The Impress window shows the first slide together with an outline view of the slides along the left side. The exact appearance depends on the document type and template you select. You can begin adding text and other graphic objects such as images, text, and lines to the slide.

To insert a new slide, choose Insert⇨Slide. A blank slide appears. Add text and graphics to that slide.

To save a presentation, choose File⇨Save. For new documents, you have to provide a filename and select the directory in which you want to save the file.

TIP

If you want to share the slides with someone who uses Microsoft PowerPoint, save the presentation in PowerPoint format.

Calendars

KDE comes with Kontact, an application that integrates existing KDE applications (such as the KMail mail reader and the KOrganizer calendar program) into a single graphical personal information manager. You can start Kontact from panel icons or the main menu. (The location of the menu entry depends on the Linux distribution.)

When Kontact starts, it usually displays a summary window with information about new email messages, upcoming scheduled events, and more. You can explore each application by clicking its icon in the left pane of the Kontact window.

To add an event or appointment for a specific date and time, select the date from the calendar, double-click the time, and type a brief description of the appointment in the New Event dialog box that appears. Click OK when you're finished.

Calculators

You have a choice of the GNOME calculator or the KDE calculator. Both calculators are scientific, so you can use them for typical scientific calculations (such as square root and inverse) as well as trigonometric functions (such as sine, cosine, and tangent).

To use the calculator, look for it in the Utilities or Accessories category of the main menu. Figure 5-4 shows the KDE calculator in SUSE.

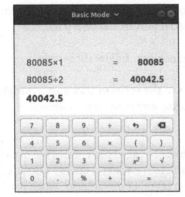

FIGURE 5-4:
Do your
calculations
in the KDE
calculator.

You can display additional buttons by choosing options from the Settings menu. Choose Settings ⇨ Statistic Buttons, for example, to show buttons that enable you to perform statistical calculations with the calculator.

Checking out Multimedia Applications

Most Linux distributions include quite a few multimedia applications — mostly multimedia audio players and CD players, but also applications for using digital cameras and burning CD-ROMs and DVDs. To play some other multimedia files (such as MPEG videos), you may have to download and install additional software on your Linux system. Here's a quick sketch of a few typical multimedia tasks and the applications you can use to perform these tasks:

>> **Using digital cameras:** Use a digital-camera tool to download photos from your digital camera in Linux or simply access the camera as a USB (universal serial bus) mass storage device.

>> **Playing audio CDs:** Use one of many audio CD players that come with Linux.

>> **Playing sound files:** Use the Rhythmbox or XMMS multimedia audio player. (You have to download some additional software to play MP3 files with Rhythmbox or XMMS.) You can also download other players from the Internet.

>> **Burning a CD or DVD:** Use a DVD or CD burner, such as K3b, to burn audio and data CDs/DVDs.

Using a digital camera

Most Linux distributions come with a digital-camera application that you can use to download pictures from digital cameras. SUSE comes with digiKam, which works with many makes and models of digital cameras. Depending on the model, the camera can connect to the serial port or the USB port.

To use digiKam with your digital camera, follow these steps:

1. **Connect your digital camera to the serial or USB port (whichever interface the camera supports), and turn on the camera.**

2. **Start digiKam.**

   Look for digiKam in the Graphics or Images submenu of the main menu. The first time you open digiKam, you're asked to specify a default location in which to store images and to set other preferences. When you finish choosing preferences, the digiKam window opens.

3. **Choose Settings ⇨ Configure digiKam.**

   A configuration dialog box appears.

4. **Click the Cameras tab of the dialog box and then click Auto Detect.**

   If your camera is supported and the camera is configured for PTP (Picture Transfer Protocol) mode, the camera is detected. If not, you can get the photos from your camera by using the alternative method described later in this section.

5. **Choose your camera model from the Camera menu.**

   A new window appears and, after a short while, displays the photos in the camera.

6. **Click the thumbnails to select the images you want to download.**

7. **Choose Camera ⇨ Download to download the images.**

   You can save these files in a folder and edit the photos in your favorite photo editor.

TIP

Don't despair if digiKam doesn't recognize your digital camera. You can still access the digital camera's storage medium (such as a compact flash card) as a USB mass storage device, provided that your camera supports USB mass storage. To access the images on your USB digital camera, follow these steps:

1. **Using the camera manual as a guide, set the camera's USB mode to Mass Storage.**

   If the camera doesn't support USB mass storage, you can't use this procedure to access the photos. If the camera supports PTP mode, you can use digiKam to download the pictures.

2. **Connect your digital camera to the USB port by using the cable that came with the camera; then turn on the camera.**

   Linux detects the camera and opens the contents of the camera in a file manager window.

3. **Click to select photos and copy them to your hard drive by dragging them into a selected folder.**

4. **Close the file manager window, disconnect the USB cable from the PC, and turn off the camera.**

Whether you're using a digital camera tool such as digiKam or accessing your camera as you would any other storage device, Linux makes it easy to get your pictures onto your computer.

Playing audio CDs

All Linux distributions come with the GNOME or KDE CD-player application. To play an audio CD, you need a sound card, and that sound card must be configured to work in Linux.

In some distributions, when you insert an audio CD into the drive, a dialog box appears and asks whether you want to play the CD with the CD player. If this dialog box doesn't appear, locate an audio CD player by choosing Applications➪Sound and Video.

The KDE CD player displays the title of the CD and the name of the current track. The CD player gets the song titles from www.freedb.org, a free, open-source CD database on the Internet. You need an active Internet connection for the CD player to download song information from the CD database. After the CD player downloads information about a particular CD, it caches that information in a local database for future use. The CD player user interface is intuitive, and you can figure it out easily. One nice feature allows you to select a track by title.

Playing sound files

You can use Rhythmbox or XMMS to open and play sound files (such as MP3 or MP4 files). Users with large MP3 music libraries usually like Rhythmbox because it helps them organize their music files. You can start Rhythmbox by choosing the music player application from the main menu in several distributions, including Debian and Fedora. When you first start Rhythmbox, it displays an assistant that prompts you for the location of your music files so that Rhythmbox can manage your music library.

After you identify the locations of music files, Rhythmbox starts and displays the library in an organized manner. Then you can select and play music.

XMMS is another music player that can play many types of sound files, including Ogg Vorbis, FLAC (Free Lossless Audio Codec, an audio file format similar to MP3), and Windows WAV.

You can start XMMS by choosing the audio player application from the main menu (look in the Multimedia or Sound & Video category). After XMMS starts, you can open a sound file (such as an MP3 file) by choosing Window Menu⇨Play File or pressing L. Then select one or more music files from the Load File dialog box, and click the Play button. XMMS starts playing the sound file.

Burning a DVD or CD

Nowadays, most GUI file managers have the capability to burn CDs. Nautilus File Manager and Xandros File Manager, for example, have built-in features for burning CDs and DVDs. Linux distributions also come with stand-alone GUI programs that enable you to burn CDs and DVDs easily. K3b is one popular CD/DVD-burning application for KDE that's available in Knoppix and SUSE.

Most CD-burning applications are simple to use. You gather the files that you want to burn to the CD or DVD and then start the burning process. For this process to work, of course, your PC must have a CD or DVD burner installed.

The top part of the K3b window lets you browse the file system to select what you want to burn onto a CD or DVD. The top-left corner shows the CD-writer device installed.

To burn a CD, choose one of the projects shown in the bottom part of the K3b window, such as New Audio CD Project or New Data DVD Project. Then add files and burn the project to the CD or DVD by choosing Project⇨Burn or pressing Ctrl+B. For an audio CD, you can drag and drop MP3 files as well as audio tracks.

REMEMBER

K3b needs the external command-line programs cdrecord and cdrdao to burn CDs. K3b also needs the growisofs program to burn DVDs.

DISTRIBUTION SPECIFIC

If you get an error message about missing cdrdao in Debian, make sure that your Debian system is connected to the Internet and then type **apt-get install cdrdao** to install it.

Using Graphics and Imaging Apps

You can use graphics and imaging applications to work with images and graphics (line drawings and shapes). Two of the most popular of these applications are

>> **The GIMP (GNU Image Manipulation Program):** A program for viewing and performing image-manipulation tasks, such as photo retouching, image composition, and image creation.

>> **Gnome Ghostview (GGv):** A graphical application capable of displaying PDFs and PostScript files.

The GIMP

The GIMP is an image-manipulation program written by Peter Mattis and Spencer Kimball and released under the GNU General Public License (GPL). Most Linux distributions come with this program, although you may have to select a package to install it. The GIMP is comparable to other image-manipulation programs, such as Adobe Photoshop and Corel Photo-Paint.

To try The GIMP, look for it in the Graphics category of the main menu. (If you can't find it in the Graphics category, choose System Settings⇨Add/Remove Software.) When you start the program, it displays a window with copyright and license information. Click the Continue button to proceed with the installation.

The next screen shows the directories to be created when you proceed with a personal installation. Installation involves creating a directory in your home directory and placing files there. This directory holds information about any changes in user preferences you may make. Click the Continue button at the bottom of the window to proceed.

Next, The GIMP creates the necessary directories, copies the necessary files to those directories, and guides you through a series of dialog boxes to complete the installation.

When installation is finished, click the Continue button. The GIMP loads any *plug-ins* — external modules that enhance its functionality — and displays a startup window that shows a message about each plug-in as it loads. Then it displays a tip of the day in a window. You can browse the tips and click the Close button to close the window. At the same time, The GIMP displays other windows, including a main navigation window; a Toolbox window (usually on the left side); a Brush Selection window; and a Layers, Channels, Paths window. The center navigation window gives you access to new images, image-editing functions, and effect filters.

The Toolbox window lets you select important image-manipulation tools quickly by clicking buttons that represent the tools you use to edit images and apply special effects. You can get pop-up help on each tool button by placing the mouse pointer over the button. Select a tool by clicking the tool's button and apply that tool's effects to an image to see what it does.

To open an image file, choose File ⇨ Open. The Load Image dialog box appears. You can change directories and select the image file that you want to open. The GIMP can read all common image file formats, such as GIF, JPEG, TIFF, PCX, BMP, PNG, and PostScript. After you select the file and click OK, The GIMP loads the image into a new window.

When you right-click an image window, a pop-up menu appears, displaying most of the options from the top toolbar.

You can do much more than just load and view images with The GIMP, but a complete discussion of its features is beyond the scope of this book. If you want to try the other features, consult *The GIMP User Manual* (GUM), available at https://www.gimp.org/docs. You can also choose Help ⇨ GIMP Online ⇨ User Manual Website to access the online documentation. (You need an Internet connection for this command to work.)

Visit https://www.gimp.org to find the latest news about The GIMP as well as links to other resources.

GNOME Ghostview

GNOME Ghostview is a graphical application for viewing and printing PostScript or PDF documents. For a long document, you can view and print selected pages. You can also view the document at various levels of magnification by zooming in or out.

To run GNOME Ghostview in Fedora, choose Graphics⇨PostScript Viewer. The GNOME Ghostview application window appears. In addition to the menu bar and toolbar along the top edge, you see a vertical divide that splits the main window into two parts.

To load and view a PostScript document in GNOME Ghostview, choose File⇨Open, or click the Open icon on the toolbar. GNOME Ghostview displays a File Selection dialog box. Use this dialog box to navigate the file system and select a PostScript file. You might select the file `tiger.ps` in the `/usr/share/ghostscript-8.64/ examples` directory, for example. (Use your system's version number of Ghostscript in place of `8.64`).

To open the selected file, click the Open File button in the File-Selection dialog box. GNOME Ghostview opens the selected file, processes its contents, and displays the output in its window.

REMEMBER

GNOME Ghostview is useful for viewing various kinds of documents in PostScript format. (These files typically have the `.ps` extension.) You can also open PDF files, which typically have `.pdf` extensions, in GNOME Ghostview.

Chapter **6**

Using Text Editors

lthough the desktop provides a beautiful graphical user interface (GUI) that's a pleasure to work in, much goes on outside that interface. Most Linux system configuration files are text files. Additionally, Linux gives you the ability to create shell scripts and interact with the operations of several programs — all by using text files.

When all is working as it should, you can edit (and even create) those files with graphical tools, but it's highly recommended that you also know how to edit them outside that interface, should a problem exist that keeps the X Window System from loading. In the interface or not, you'll be using *text editors*, which are programs designed to interact with text files.

In this chapter, I introduce you to a few text editors, both GUI and text-mode.

Using GUI Text Editors

Each of the GUI desktops — GNOME and KDE — comes with GUI text editors (text editors that have graphical user interfaces).

To use a GUI text editor, look on the main menu for text editors in an appropriate category. In the GNOME desktop, for example, choose Applications⇨Text Editor to open gedit. When you have a text editor up and running, you can open a file by clicking the Open button on the toolbar to display the Open File dialog box. You can change directories and then select the file to edit by clicking the OK button.

The GNOME text editor loads the file in its window. You can open more than one file at a time and move among files as you edit them. Figure 6-1 shows a typical session with the editor.

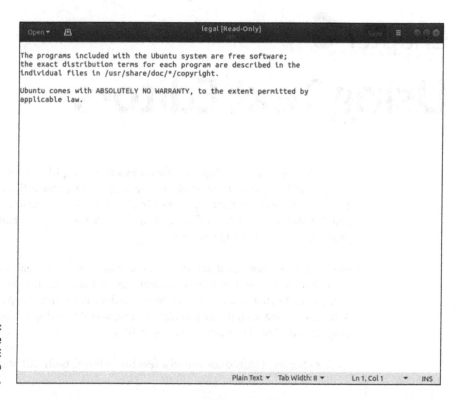

FIGURE 6-1:
You can use the GNOME text editor to edit text files.

In this case, the editor has opened legal (from the /etc directory) for editing in read-only mode. If you open a file for which you have only read permission, the text [Read-Only] is appended to the filename shown in the window title to indicate that the file is read-only, and the location of the file is displayed at the top (such as /etc). The indication that the file is read-only often appears when a regular user is opening system files that only the root user can modify. You can always make the changes you want to make and then save the file as a new file to circumvent the read-only restriction.

Within the editor, it's possible to have more than one file open at a time, as shown in Figure 6-2.

FIGURE 6-2: You can have more than one file open at the same time.

The filenames appear as tabs below the toolbar of the editor's window. You can switch among the files by clicking the tabs. The current filename appears in the last line of the window.

The rest of the text editing steps are fairly straightforward and intuitive. To enter new text, click to position the cursor, and begin typing. You can select text, copy, cut, and paste functions by clicking the buttons on the toolbar above the text-editing area.

In the KDE desktop, you can start the KDE text editor (KWrite) by choosing Applications ⇨ Accessories ⇨ Text Editor. To open a text file, choose File ⇨ Open to display a dialog box. Go to the directory of your choice, select the file to open, and click OK. KWrite opens the file and displays its contents in the window (see Figure 6-3); then you can edit the file.

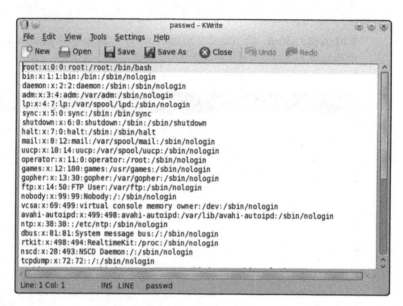

FIGURE 6-3:
You can use the KDE KWrite text editor to edit files.

Text Editing with ed and vi

GUI text editors enable you to edit text files by using the mouse and keyboard much the same way as you would in any word processor. Text-mode editors are different beasts, however; you use only the keyboard and have to type cryptic commands to perform editing tasks, such as cutting and pasting text or entering and deleting text.

Most Linux distributions come with the following two text-mode text editors:

>> ed: A line-oriented text editor

>> vi: A full-screen text editor that supports the command set of an earlier editor named ex

The ed and vi editors are cryptic compared with the graphical text editors. You should still get to know the basic editing commands of ed and vi, however, because sometimes, they're the only editors available. If Linux refuses to boot from the hard drive, for example, you may have to boot from a CD, DVD, or flash drive. In that case, you have to edit system files with the ed editor because that editor is small enough to fit on the boot medium.

In the following sections, I walk you through the basic text-editing commands of ed and vi, which aren't too hard.

Using ed

Typically, you have to use ed only when you boot a minimal version of Linux (from the medium you've set up as a boot disk, for example) and the system doesn't support full-screen mode. In all other situations, you can use the vi editor, which works in full-screen text mode.

When you use ed, you work in command or text-input mode:

>> **Command mode:** This mode is the default. In this mode, anything you type is interpreted as a command. The ed text editor has a simple command set in which each command consists of one or more characters.

>> **Text-input mode:** This mode is for typing text. You can enter text input mode with the commands a (append), c (change), and i (insert). After entering lines of text, you can leave text-input mode by entering a period (.) on a line by itself.

To practice editing a file, copy the /etc/fstab file to your home directory by issuing the following commands:

```
cd
cp /etc/fstab .
```

Now you have a file named fstab in your home directory. Type **ed -p: fstab** to begin editing a file in ed. The editor responds as follows:

```
878
:
```

This example uses the –p option to set the prompt to the colon character (:) and opens the fstab file (in the current directory, which is your home directory) for editing. The ed editor opens the file, reports the number of characters in the file (878), displays the prompt (:), and waits for a command.

REMEMBER

When you're editing with ed, make sure that you always turn on a prompt character (by using the –p option). Without the prompt, distinguishing whether ed is in text-input mode or command mode is difficult.

After ed opens a file for editing, the current line is the last line of the file. To see the current line number (the line to which ed applies your command), use the .= command, like this:

```
:.=
9
```

This output tells you that the fstab file has nine lines. (Your system's /etc/fstab file may have a different number of lines, in which case ed shows a different number.)

You can use the 1,$p command to see all lines in a file, as the following example shows:

```
:1,$p
# This file is edited by fstab-sync - see 'man fstab-sync' for details
/dev/VolGroup00/LogVol00 / ext3 defaults 1 1
LABEL=/boot /boot ext3 defaults 1 2
/dev/devpts /dev/pts devpts gid=5,mode=620 0 0
/dev/shm /dev/shm tmpfs defaults 0 0
/dev/proc /proc proc defaults 0 0
/dev/sys /sys sysfs defaults 0 0
/dev/VolGroup00/LogVol01 swap swap defaults 0 0
/dev/scd0 /media/cdrecorder auto pamconsole,exec,noauto,managed 0 0
/dev/hdc /media/cdrom auto pamconsole,exec,noauto,managed 0 0
:
```

To go to a specific line, type the line number:

```
:2
```

The editor responds by displaying that line:

```
/dev/VolGroup00/LogVol00 / ext3 defaults 1 1
:
```

Suppose that you want to delete the line that contains cdrom. To search for a string, type a slash (/) followed by the string that you want to locate:

```
:/cdrom
/dev/hdc /media/cdrom auto pamconsole,exec,noauto,managed 0 0
:
```

The editor locates the line that contains the string and then displays it. That line becomes the current line.

To delete the current line, use the d command as follows:

```
:d
:
```

To replace a string with another, use the s command. To replace cdrom with the string cd, for example, use this command:

```
:s/cdrom/cd/
:
```

To insert a line in front of the current line, use the i command:

```
:i
(type the line you want to insert)
. (type a single period to indicate you're done)
:
```

You can enter as many lines as you want. After the last line, enter a period (.) on a line by itself. That period marks the end of text-input mode, and the editor switches to command mode. In this case, you can tell that ed switches to command mode because you see the prompt (:).

When you're happy with the changes, you can write them to the file with the w command. If you want to save the changes and exit, type **wq** to perform both steps at the same time:

```
:wq
857
```

The ed editor saves the changes in the file, displays the number of saved characters, and exits. If you want to quit the editor without saving any changes, use the Q (capital Q) command.

These examples give you an idea of how to use ed commands to perform basic tasks in editing a text file. Table 6-1 lists some of the commonly used ed commands.

TABLE 6-1 ## Common ed Commands

Command	Does the Following
! command	Executes a shell command. (! pwd displays the current directory, for example.)
$	Goes to the last line in the buffer.
%	Applies a command that follows to all lines in the buffer. (%p prints all lines, for example.)
+	Goes to the next line.
+n	Goes to the nth next line (where n is a number you designate).

(continued)

TABLE 6-1 *(continued)*

Command	Does the Following
,	Applies a command that follows to all lines in the buffer. (, p prints all lines, for example.) This command is similar to %.
–	Goes to the preceding line.
–n	Goes to the *n*th previous line (where *n* is a number you designate).
.	Refers to the current line in the buffer.
/text/	Searches forward for the specified text.
;	Refers to a range of lines — the current line through the last line in the buffer.
=	Prints the line number.
?text?	Searches backward for the specified text.
^	Goes to the preceding line. (See also the – command.)
^n	Goes to the *n*th previous line (where *n* is a number you designate). (See also the –n command.)
a	Appends the current line.
c	Changes the specified lines.
d	Deletes the specified lines.
i	Inserts text before the current line.
n	Goes to line number *n* (where *n* is a number you designate).
Press Enter	Displays the next line and makes that line current.
q	Quits the editor.
Q	Quits the editor without saving changes.
r file	Reads and inserts the contents of the file after the current line.
s/old/new/	Replaces an old string with a new one.
u	Undoes the last command.
W file	Appends the contents of the buffer to the end of the specified file.
w file	Saves the buffer in the specified file. (If no file is named, it saves the buffer in the default file — the file whose contents ed is currently editing.)

Using vi

After you dabble with ed, you'll find that vi is a dream come true, even though it's still a command-line editor. The vi editor is a full-screen text editor, so you can view several lines at the same time. Most Unix systems, including Linux, come with vi. Therefore, if you know the basic features of vi, you can edit text files on almost any Unix-based system.

When vi edits a file, it reads the file into a *buffer* — a block of memory — so you can change the text in the buffer. The vi editor also uses temporary files during editing, but the original file isn't altered until you save the changes.

To start the editor, type **vi** followed by the name of the file you want to edit, like this:

```
vi /etc/fstab
```

The vi editor loads the file into memory, displays the first few lines in a text screen, and positions the cursor on the first line (see Figure 6-4).

FIGURE 6-4:
You can edit files with the vi full-screen text editor.

The last line shows the pathname of the file as well as the number of lines (2) and the number of characters (59) in the file. In this case, the text [readonly] appears after the filename because I'm opening the /etc/fstab file while I'm logged in as a normal user (which means that I don't have permission to modify the file).

Later, the last line in the vi display functions as a command entry area. The rest of the lines display the file. If the file contains fewer lines than the screen, vi displays the empty lines with a tilde (~) in the first column.

The current line is marked by the cursor, which appears as a small black rectangle. The cursor appears on top of a character.

When using vi, you work in one of three modes:

>> **Visual command mode:** This mode is the default. In this mode, anything you type is interpreted as a command that applies to the line containing the cursor. The vi commands are similar to the ed commands.

>> **Colon command mode:** You use this mode for reading or writing files, setting vi options, and quitting vi. All colon commands start with a colon (:). When you type the colon, vi positions the cursor on the last line and waits for you to type a command. The command takes effect when you press Enter.

>> **Text-input mode:** This mode is for typing text. You can enter text-input mode with the command a (insert after cursor), A (append at end of line), o (open a line below the current one), O (open a line above the current one), or i (insert after cursor). After entering lines of text, you have to press Esc to leave text-input mode and reenter visual command mode.

One problem with all these modes is that you can't easily tell the current mode that vi is in. You may begin typing only to realize that vi isn't in text-input mode, which can be frustrating.

TIP

If you want to make sure that vi is in command mode, press Esc a few times. (Pressing Esc more than once doesn't hurt.)

To view online help in vi, type **:help** while in colon command mode. When you're finished with help, type **:q** to exit the Help screen and return to the file you're editing.

The vi editor initially positions the cursor on the first character of the first line, and one of the handiest things you can know is how to move the cursor around. To get a bit of practice, try the commands shown in Table 6-2.

You can go to a specific line number at any time by using the handy colon command. To go to line 6, for example, type the following and then press Enter:

: 6

TABLE 6-2

Cursor Movement Commands in vi

Key	Moves the Cursor
↓	One line down
↑	One line up
←	One character to the left
→	One character to the right
W	One word forward
B	One word backward
Ctrl+D	Half a screen down
Ctrl+U	Half a screen up

When you type the colon, vi displays the colon on the last line of the screen. From then on, vi uses any text you type as a command. You have to press Enter to submit the command to vi. In colon command mode, vi accepts all commands that the ed editor accepts, and then some.

To search for a string, first type a slash (/). The vi editor displays the slash on the last line of the screen. Type the search string and then press Enter. The vi editor locates the string and positions the cursor at the beginning of that string. To locate the string cdrom in the file /etc/fstab, type

```
/cdrom
```

To delete the line that contains the cursor, type **dd**. The vi editor deletes that line of text and makes the next line the current one.

To begin entering text in front of the cursor, type **i**. The vi editor switches to text-input mode. Now you can enter text. When you finish entering text, press Esc to return to visual command mode.

After you finish editing the file, you can save the changes in the file with the :w command. To quit the editor without saving any changes, use the :q! command. If you want to save the changes and exit, you can use the :wq command to perform both steps at the same time. The vi editor saves the changes in the file and exits. You can also save the changes and exit the editor by pressing Shift+ZZ (that is, hold Shift down and press Z twice).

vi accepts a large number of commands in addition to the commands I just mentioned. Table 6-3 lists some commonly used vi commands, organized by task.

TABLE 6-3   **Common vi Commands**

Command	Does the Following
Insert text	
a	Inserts text after the cursor
A	Inserts text at the end of the current line
I	Inserts text at the beginning of the current line
i	Inserts text before the cursor
Delete text	
D	Deletes up to the end of the current line
dd	Deletes the current line
dG	Deletes from the current line to the end of the file
dw	Deletes the current word where the cursor presently resides
x	Deletes the character on which the cursor rests
Change text	
C	Changes up to the end of the current line
cc	Changes the current line
J	Joins the current line with the next one
rx	Replaces the character under the cursor with x (where x is any character)
Move cursor	
h or ←	Moves one character to the left
j or ↓	Moves one line down
k or ↑	Moves one line up
L	Moves to the end of the screen
l or →	Moves one character to the right
w	Moves to the beginning of the following word
b	Moves to the beginning of the previous word
Scroll text	
Ctrl+D	Scrolls forward by half a screen
Ctrl+U	Scrolls backward by half a screen

Command	Does the Following
Refresh screen	
Ctrl+L	Redraws the screen
Cut and paste text	
yy	Yanks (copies) current line to an unnamed buffer
P	Puts the yanked line above the current line
p	Puts the yanked line below the current line
Colon commands	
: ! *command*	Executes a shell command
:q	Quits the editor
:q!	Quits without saving changes
:r *filename*	Reads the file and inserts it after the current line
:w *filename*	Writes a buffer to the file
:wq	Saves changes and exits
Search text	
/*string*	Searches forward for a string
?*string*	Searches backward for a string
Miscellaneous	
u	Undoes the last command
Esc	Ends input mode and enters visual command mode
U	Undoes recent changes to the current line

3

Networking

Contents at a Glance

CHAPTER 1: Connecting to the Internet 153

Understanding the Internet 154
Deciding How to Connect to the Internet 155
Connecting with DSL 156
Connecting with a Cable Modem 162

CHAPTER 2: Setting Up a Local Area Network 167

Understanding TCP/IP 167
Setting Up an Ethernet LAN 172
Configuring TCP/IP Networking 176
Connecting Your LAN to the Internet 178

CHAPTER 3: Going Wireless 181

Understanding Wireless Ethernet Networks 181
Setting Up Wireless Hardware 184
Configuring the Wireless Access Point 185
Configuring Wireless Networking 186

CHAPTER 4: Managing the Network 191

Discovering the TCP/IP Configuration Files 191
Checking Out TCP/IP Networks 196
Configuring Networks at Boot Time 201

» **Understanding connection options**

» **Connecting to the Internet with DSL**

» **Connecting to the Internet with a cable modem**

Chapter **1**

Connecting to the Internet

Given the prevalence and popularity of the Internet, it's a safe bet to assume that you will want to connect your Linux system not only to a network but also to the largest network of all: the Internet. In this chapter, I show you how to connect to the Internet in several ways, depending on whether you have a DSL or cable modem. A tiny minority of people still connect by using a dial-up network connection, but they are few and far between these days; most users aren't comfortable with the slower performance of a dial-up connection.

Two options for connecting to the Internet — DSL and cable modem — involve attaching a special modem to an Ethernet card on your Linux system. In these cases, you have to set up Ethernet networking on your Linux system. (I explain networking in Book 3, Chapter 2.) If your machine is nothing more than a client on a network that it connects to via a mobile/Wi-Fi connection and doesn't need its own dedicated connection, things couldn't be easier; you'll simply want to skim this chapter before moving on to subsequent chapters.

Understanding the Internet

How you view the Internet depends on your perspective. Most people see the Internet in terms of the services they use. As a user, you might think of the Internet as an information-exchange medium with features such as

- » **Email:** Send email to any other user on the Internet, using addresses such as mom@home.net.

- » **Web:** Download and view documents from millions of servers throughout the Internet, connect on Facebook, search for information on Google, and so on.

- » **Information sharing:** Download software, music files, videos, and other valuable content. Reciprocally, you may provide files that users on other systems can download.

- » **Remote access:** Log in to another computer across the Internet, assuming that you have access to and permissions on that remote computer.

The techies say that the Internet is a worldwide *network of networks*. The term *internet* (without capitalization) is a shortened form of *internetworking* — the interconnection of networks. The Internet Protocol (IP) was designed with the idea of connecting many separate networks.

TECHNICAL STUFF

In terms of physical connections, the Internet is similar to a network of highways and roads. This similarity prompted the popular press to dub the Internet "the Information Superhighway." Just as the network of highways and roads includes some interstate highways, many state roads, and many more residential streets, the Internet has some very high-capacity networks (a 10-Gbps backbone can handle 10 billion bits per second) and many lower-capacity networks ranging from 56 Kbps dial-up connections to a high-speed cable connection of 100-Mbps or more. (*Kbps* is a thousand bits per second, and *Mbps* is a million bits per second.) The high-capacity network is the backbone of the Internet.

In terms of management, the Internet isn't run by a single organization; neither is it managed by any central computer. You can view the physical Internet as being a network of networks managed collectively by thousands of cooperating organizations. Yes, a collection of networks managed by *thousands* of organizations. It sounds amazing, but it works!

Deciding How to Connect to the Internet

So you want to connect your Linux workstation to the Internet, but you don't know how? Let me count the ways. Nowadays, you have some popular options for connecting homes and small offices to the Internet (whereas huge corporations and governments have many other ways to connect):

>> **Digital Subscriber Line (DSL):** Your local telephone company, as well as other telecommunications companies, may offer DSL. DSL provides a way to send high-speed digital data over a regular phone line. Typically, DSL offers data transfer rates of between 128 Kbps and 24.0 Mbps. (Usually, the higher the speed, the more you pay.) You can often download from the Internet at much higher rates than when you send data from your PC to the Internet *(upload)*. One caveat with DSL is that your home must be within a defined proximity to your local central office (the DSL provider's facility where your phone lines end up). The distance limitation varies from provider to provider. In the United States, you can check out the distance limits for many providers at www.dslreports.com/distance.

>> **Cable modem:** If the cable television company in your area offers Internet access over cable, you can use that service to hook up your Linux system to the Internet. Typically, cable modems offer higher data-transfer rates than DSL — for about the same cost — but bandwidth may be shared with other subscribers. Downloading data from the Internet via cable modem is much faster than sending data from your PC to the Internet.

DSL and cable modem services connect you to the Internet and act as your Internet service provider (ISP). In addition to improved speed over dialup, what you're paying for is an IP address and your email accounts. Table 1-1 summarizes these options and compares/contrasts them with dial-up connectivity. You can consult that table and select the type of connection that's available to you and that best suits your needs.

REMEMBER

Besides the three options shown in Table 1-1, a few less-common options may be available to you, including fiber-to-the-home (FTTH) — in the case of an office, this is known as fiber-to-the-premise (FTTP) or fiber-to-the-curb (FTTC), broadband over power lines (BPL), fixed wireless broadband (called FWB or WiMAX), and satellite Internet access (such as DIRECWAY and StarBand). If these options are available in your geographic area and you want to use one of them for Internet access, follow the specific service provider's instructions for setting up the Internet connection. Typically, satellite Internet access is available across large geographical regions (even in places that don't have phone or cable), but the initial equipment cost and monthly fees are higher than for DSL and cable.

TABLE 1-1   Comparison of Dial-up, DSL, and Cable

Feature	Dial-up	DSL	Cable
Equipment	Modem	DSL modem, Ethernet card	Cable modem, Ethernet card
Requires	Phone service and an ISP	Phone service and location within a short distance to the central office	Cable TV connection
Connection type	Dial to connect	Always on, dedicated	Always on, shared
Typical speed	56 Kbps maximum	Varies based on the type of DSL implemented and the distance from the central office	Varies by provider, but download speeds are traditionally higher than upload speeds, and higher speeds always cost more

Connecting with DSL

DSL uses your existing phone line to send digital data in addition to normal analog voice signals. (*Analog* means continuously varying, whereas digital data is represented by 1s and 0s.) The phone line goes from your home to a central office, where the line connects to the DSL provider's network. By the way, the connection from your home to the central office is called the *local loop*.

When you sign up for DSL service, the DSL provider hooks up your phone line to some special equipment at the central office. That equipment can separate the digital data from voice. From then on, your phone line can carry digital data that is directly sent to an Internet connection at the central office.

How DSL works

A special box called a *DSL modem* takes care of sending digital data from your PC to the DSL provider's central office over your phone line. Your PC can connect to the Internet with the same phone line that you use for your normal telephone calls; you can make voice calls even as the line is being used for DSL. Figure 1-1 shows a typical DSL connection to the Internet.

Your PC talks to the DSL modem through an Ethernet connection, which means that you need an Ethernet card in your Linux system.

Your PC sends digital data over the Ethernet connection to the DSL modem. The DSL modem sends the digital data at different frequencies from those used by the analog voice signals. The voice signals occupy a small portion of all the frequencies that the phone line can carry. DSL uses the higher frequencies to transfer digital data, so both voice and data can travel on the same phone line.

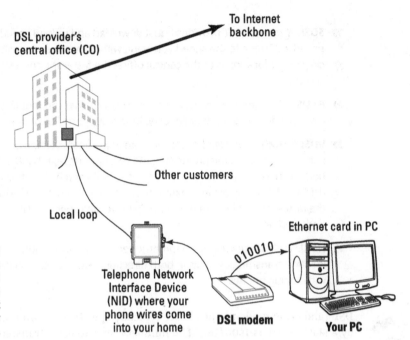

To Internet backbone

DSL provider's central office (CO)

Other customers

Local loop

Ethernet card in PC

010010

FIGURE 1-1:
DSL provides a high-speed connection to the Internet over a regular phone line.

Telephone Network Interface Device (NID) where your phone wires come into your home

DSL modem

Your PC

DSL alphabet soup: ADSL, IDSL, SDSL

WARNING

I've been using the term *DSL* as though there were only one kind of DSL, but DSL has several variants, each with different features. Take a look at a few options:

>> **ADSL:** *Asymmetric DSL* is the most common form of DSL with much higher download speeds (from the Internet to your PC) than upload speeds (from your PC to the Internet). ADSL works best when your location is within about 2 to 2.5 miles (12,000 feet) of the central office. ADSL service is priced according to the download and upload speeds you want.

A newer version, ADSL2, made some improvements in the data rate and increased the distance from the telephone exchange that the line can run. After it, ADSL2+ doubled the downstream bandwidth and kept all the features of ADSL2. Both ADSL2 and ADSL2+ are compatible with legacy ADSL equipment.

>> **IDSL:** Short for *ISDN DSL* (ISDN is an older technology called *Integrated Services Digital Network*), *IDSL* is a special type of DSL that works at distances of up to 5 miles between your phone and the central office. The downside is that IDSL averages *downstream* (from the Internet to your PC) and *upstream* (from your PC to the Internet) speeds similar to what an old-fashioned modem could do over a dial-up connection.

>> **SDSL:** *Symmetric DSL* provides equal download and upload speeds. SDSL is priced according to the speed you want, with higher speeds costing more. The closer your location is to the central office, the faster the connection you can get.

>> **RADSL:** *Rate-adaptive DSL* is a variation on ADSL that can modify its transmission speeds based on signal quality. RADSL supports line sharing.

>> **VDSL/VHDSL:** *Very-high bit-rate DSL* is an asymmetric version of DSL, and as such, it can share a telephone line. VHDSL supports high-bandwidth applications such as Voice over Internet Protocol (VoIP) and high-definition television (HDTV). VHDSL can achieve data rates up to approximately 10 Mbps, making it the fastest available form of DSL. To achieve high speeds, VHDSL uses fiber-optic cabling.

>> **HDSL:** *High-bit-rate DSL* is a symmetric version of the technology that offers identical transmission rates in both directions. HDSL doesn't allow line sharing with analog phones.

**TECHNICAL
STUFF**

DSL (and cable modem) speeds are typically specified by two numbers separated by a slash, such as 1500/384. The numbers refer to data-transfer speeds in kilobits per second (that is, thousands of bits per second, abbreviated Kbps). The first number is the download speed; the second, the upload. Thus, 1500/384 means that you can expect to download from the Internet at a maximum rate of 1,500 Kbps (or 1.5 Mbps) and upload to the Internet at 384 Kbps. If your phone line's condition isn't perfect, you may not get these maximum rates; ADSL and SDSL adjust the speeds to suit existing line conditions.

The price of DSL service depends on which variant you select. For most home users, the primary choice is ADSL (or, more accurately, the G.lite form of ADSL).

Typical DSL setup

To get DSL for your home or business, you must contact a DSL provider. You can find many DSL providers in addition to your phone company. No matter who provides the DSL service, some work has to be done at the central office — the place where your phone lines connect to the rest of the phone network. The work involves connecting your phone line to equipment that can work with the DSL modem at your home or office. Then the central office equipment and the DSL modem at your location can do whatever magic is needed to send and receive digital data over your phone line.

The distance between your home and the central office — the *loop length* — is a factor in DSL's performance. Unfortunately, the phone line can reliably carry the DSL signals over only a limited distance — typically 3 miles or less, which means that you can get DSL service only if your home (or office) is located within about 3 miles of the central office. Contact your DSL provider to verify. You may be able to check this availability on the web. Try typing into Google (www.google.com) the words **DSL availability** and then your provider's name. The search results will probably include a website where you can type your phone number to find out whether DSL is available for your home or office.

If DSL is available, you can look for types of service — ADSL versus SDSL — and pricing. The price depends on what download and upload speeds you want. Sometimes, phone companies offer a simple residential DSL (basically, the G.lite form of ADSL) with a 1500/128 speed rating, meaning that you can download at up to 1,500 Kbps and upload at 128 Kbps. These ratings are the *maximums;* your mileage may vary. Many DSL modems have other features built into them beyond just modem capabilities: NAT (network address translation) routing, multiple Ethernet ports, and even Wi-Fi capabilities are common options.

After selecting the type of DSL service and provider you want, you can place an order and have the provider install the necessary equipment at your home or office. Figure 1-2 shows a sample connection diagram for typical residential DSL service.

Here are some key points to note in Figure 1-2:

>> Connect your DSL modem's data connection to the phone jack on a wall plate.

>> Connect the DSL modem's Ethernet connection to the Ethernet card on your PC.

>> When you connect other telephones or fax machines on the same phone line, install a microfilter between the wall plate and each of these devices.

   Because the same phone line carries both voice signals and DSL data, you need the microfilter to protect the DSL data from possible interference. You can buy these filters at electronics stores or from the DSL provider.

TIP

You can protect your Linux system from intruders and, as a bonus, share the high-speed connection with other PCs in a local-area network (LAN) by using a router that can perform Network Address Translation (NAT). A NAT router translates multiple private Internet Protocol (IP) addresses from an internal LAN into a single public IP address, which allows all the internal PCs to access the Internet. The NAT router acts as a gateway between your LAN and the Internet, and it isolates your LAN from the Internet, which makes it harder for intruders to reach the systems on your LAN.

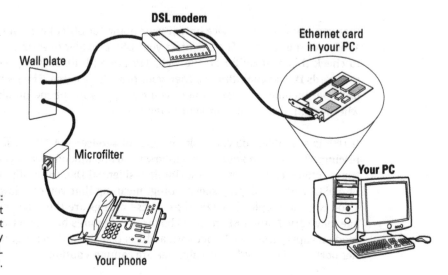

FIGURE 1-2:
You can connect
a PC's Ethernet
card directly
to the DSL
modem.

If you also want to set up a LAN, you need an Ethernet hub or switch to connect
the other PCs to the network. Figure 1-3 shows a typical setup that connects a LAN
to the Internet through a NAT router and a DSL modem.

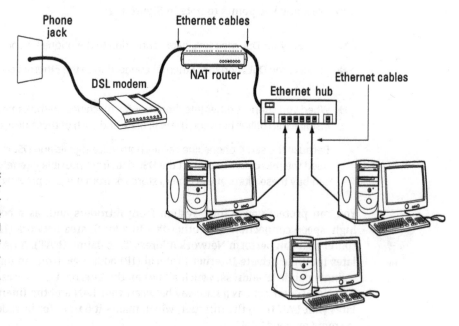

FIGURE 1-3:
A NAT router
isolates your
PC from the
Internet and
lets you share
the DSL
connection
with other
PCs in a local
area network.

Here are the points to note when setting up a connection like the one shown in Figure 1-3:

>> You need a NAT router with two Ethernet ports. (The 100BaseT and older 10BaseT ports look like large phone jacks; they're also known as *RJ-45 jacks*.) Typically, one Ethernet port is labeled *Internet* (or *External* or *WAN*, for wide-area network), and the other one is labeled *Local* or *LAN* (for local-area network).

>> You also need an Ethernet hub/switch. For a small home network, you can buy a four- or eight-port Ethernet hub. You want a hub with as many ports as the number of PCs you intend to connect to your network. For a business, you'll want to replace the hub with a switch.

>> Connect the Ethernet port of the DSL modem to the Internet port of the NAT router, using a Gigabit Ethernet cable. (These cables look like phone wires with bigger RJ-45 jacks and are often labeled *Category 6* or *Cat 6* wire.)

>> Connect the Local Ethernet port of the NAT router to one of the ports on the Ethernet hub/switch, using a Gigabit Ethernet cable.

>> Now connect each of the PCs to the Ethernet hub/switch. (To do so, you must first have an Ethernet card installed and configured in each PC.)

TIP

You can also buy a NAT router with a built-in four-port or eight-port Ethernet hub. With such a combined router and hub, you need only one box to set up a LAN and connect it to the Internet via a DSL modem. These boxes are typically sold under the name *cable/DSL router* because they work with both DSL and a cable modem.

Consult Book 3, Chapter 2 for information on how to configure networking on the Linux system so that your system can access the Internet.

REMEMBER

DSL providers typically use a protocol known as *PPP over Ethernet (PPPoE)* to establish a connection between your PC and the equipment at the provider's central office. PPPoE requires you to provide a username and password to establish the network connection over Ethernet. To set up your system for a PPPoE DSL connection, all you have to do is run a utility program that configures the system for PPPoE. You can find the utility by searching in the main menu in the GUI desktop.

DISTRIBUTION SPECIFIC

In Ubuntu, you can set up a PPPoE DSL connection by choosing System⇨Administration⇨Network Tools, clicking the modem connection, and choosing Properties. Then go through the successive screens and provide the requested account information, such as username and password.

Connecting to the Internet

Connecting with a Cable Modem

Cable TV companies also offer high-speed Internet access over the same coaxial cable that carries television signals to your home. After the cable company installs the necessary equipment at its facility to send and receive digital data over the coaxial cables, customers can sign up for cable Internet service. Then you can get high-speed Internet access over the same line that delivers cable TV signals to your home.

How a cable modem works

A box called a *cable modem* is at the heart of Internet access over the cable TV network. (See Figure 1-4.) The cable modem takes digital data from your PC's Ethernet card and puts it in an unused block of frequency. (Think of this frequency as being another TV channel, but instead of carrying pictures and sound, this channel carries digital data.)

The cable modem places *upstream data* — data that's being sent from your PC to the Internet — in a different channel from that of the *downstream* data that's coming from the Internet to your PC. By design, the speed of downstream data transfers is much higher than that of upstream transfers. The assumption is that people download far more stuff from the Internet than they upload (which is probably true for most of us).

TECHNICAL STUFF

The coaxial cable that carries all those hundreds of cable TV channels to your home is a very capable signal carrier. In particular, the coaxial cable can carry signals covering a huge range of frequencies — hundreds of megahertz (MHz). Each TV channel requires 6 MHz, and the coaxial cable can carry hundreds of such channels. The cable modem places the upstream data in a small frequency band and expects to receive the downstream data in another frequency band.

TECHNICAL STUFF

At the other end of your cable connection to the Internet is the *Cable Modem Termination System* (CMTS) — also known as the *head end* — that your cable company installs at its central facility. (Refer to Figure 1-4.) The CMTS connects the cable TV network to the Internet. It also extracts the upstream digital data sent by your cable modem (and by those of your neighbors as well) and sends it to the Internet. Further, the CMTS puts digital data into the upstream channels so that your cable modem can extract that data and provide it to your PC via the Ethernet card.

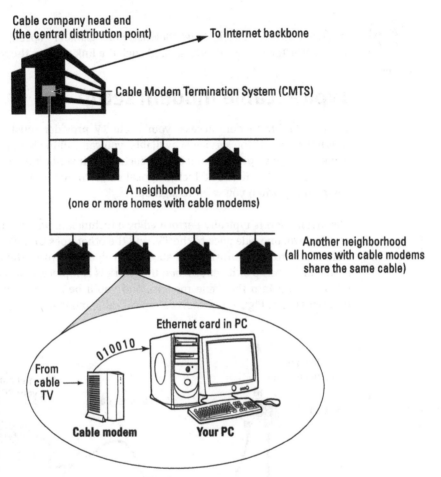

FIGURE 1-4:
Cable modems
provide high-
speed Internet
access over
the cable
TV network.

Cable modems can receive downstream data at a rate of about 150 Mbps and send data upstream at around 10 Mbps. All the cable modems in a neighborhood have the same downstream capacity, however. Each cable modem filters out — separates — the data it needs from the stream of data that the CMTS sends out. Cable modems follow a modem standard called DOCSIS, which stands for Data Over Cable Service Interface Specification. You can buy any DOCSIS 3.0-compliant modem and use it with your cable Internet service; you just call the people at the cable company and give them the modem's identifying information so that the CMTS can recognize and initialize the modem.

REMEMBER

In practice, with a cable modem, you'll most likely get downstream transfer rates of around 12 Mbps and upstream rates of 2 Mbps. These rates are maximum rates; your actual transfer rate is typically lower, depending on how many people in your neighborhood are using cable modems at the same time.

TIP

If you want to check your downstream transfer speed, go to `http://bandwidthplace.com/speedtest` and click the link to start the test.

Typical cable modem setup

To set up cable modem access, your cable TV provider must offer high-speed Internet access. If the service is available, you can call to sign up. The cable companies often have promotional offers, such as no installation fee or a reduced rate for three months. If you're lucky, a local cable company may have a promotion going on just when you want to sign up.

The installation is typically performed by a technician, who splits your incoming cable in two; one side goes to the TV, and the other goes to the cable modem. The technician provides information about the cable modem to the cable company's head end for setup at its end. When that work is complete, you can plug your PC's Ethernet card into the cable modem, and you'll be all set to enjoy high-speed Internet access. Figure 1-5 shows a typical cable modem hookup.

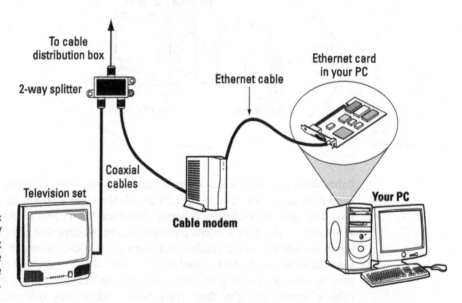

FIGURE 1-5:
The cable TV signal is split between the TV and the cable modem.

The cable modem connects to an Ethernet card in your PC. If you don't have an Ethernet card in your PC, the cable company technician often provides one.

Here are some key points to note about the cable modem setup in Figure 1-5:

>> Split the incoming cable TV signal into two parts by using a two-way splitter. (The cable company technician installs the splitter.) The two-way splitter needs to be rated for 1 GHz; otherwise, it may not let the frequencies that contain the downstream data from the Internet pass through.

>> Connect one of the video outputs from the splitter to your cable modem's F-type video connector, using a coaxial cable.

>> Connect the cable modem's Gigabit Ethernet connection to the Ethernet card on your PC.

>> Connect your TV to the other video output from the two-way splitter. When you use a cable modem to connect your Linux PC directly to the Internet, the connection is always on, so you have more of a chance that someone may try to break into the PC. Linux includes the iptables packet filtering capability, which you may want to use to protect your PC from unwanted Internet connections.

TIP

To isolate your Linux PC or LAN from the public Internet, you may want to add a NAT router between your PC and the cable modem. One of the NAT router's network interfaces connects to the Internet, and the other connects to your LAN; then the router acts as a gateway between your LAN and the Internet. As a bonus, you can even share a cable modem connection with all the tablets, phones, and PCs in your own LAN by adding an Ethernet hub. Better yet, buy a combination NAT router and switch so that you have only one box to do the entire job.

TIP

Boxes that combine NAT router and switch are typically sold under the name *cable/DSL router* because they work with both DSL and cable modem.

The NAT router translates private IP addresses into a public IP address. When connected through a NAT router, any PC in the internal LAN can access the Internet as though it had its own unique IP address. As a result, you can share a single Internet connection among many PCs — an ideal solution for a family of Net surfers!

Figure 1-6 shows a typical setup, with a cable modem connection being shared by several PCs in a LAN.

Here are the points to note when setting up a connection like the one shown in Figure 1-6:

>> You need a cable/DSL NAT router with two Ethernet ports (the port — also known as an *RJ-45 jack*, which looks like a large phone jack). Typically, one Ethernet port is labeled *Internet* (or *External* or *WAN*), and the other one is labeled *Local*.

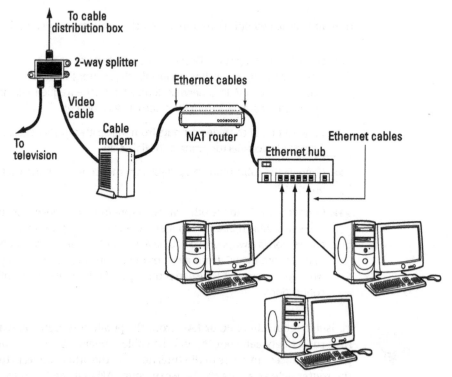

To cable
distribution box

2-way splitter

Ethernet cables

Video
cable

Cable
modem

NAT router

Ethernet cables

Ethernet hub

To
television

FIGURE 1-6:
A NAT router
isolates your
PC from the
Internet and
also lets you
share the
cable modem
connection
with other PCs
in a LAN.

>> If you plan to set up a LAN, you also need an Ethernet hub/switch. For a small home network, you can buy a four-port or eight-port Ethernet hub. You want a hub with as many ports as the number of PCs you intend to connect to your LAN.

>> Consider buying a single box that acts as both a NAT router and a hub with several Ethernet ports.

>> Connect the video cable to the video input port of the cable modem.

>> Connect the Ethernet port of the cable modem to the Internet port of the NAT router, using an Ethernet cable. (The cable looks like a phone wire except that the Ethernet cable has bigger RJ-45 jacks and is often labeled *Category 6* or *Cat 6 wire.*)

>> Connect the Local Ethernet port of the NAT router to one of the ports on the Ethernet hub, using an Ethernet cable.

>> Now connect each of the PCs to the Ethernet hub. Each PC must have an Ethernet card.

In Book 3, Chapter 2, I explain how to configure the PCs in a LAN so that all of them can access the Internet through the router.

Chapter **2**

Setting Up a Local Area Network

L inux comes with built-in support for Transmission Control Protocol/Internet Protocol (TCP/IP) networking, as do most modern operating systems from Windows to macOS. You can have TCP/IP networking over many physical interfaces, such as Ethernet cards, serial ports, and parallel ports.

Typically, you use an Ethernet network for your local area network (LAN) at your office or even your home (if you happen to have two or more systems at home), with wireless (the subject of the next chapter) gaining in popularity in most locations.

This chapter describes how to set up an Ethernet network. Even if you have a single PC, you may need to set up an Ethernet network interface so that you can connect to high-speed Internet access (via a DSL or cable modem somewhere along the way).

Understanding TCP/IP

You can understand TCP/IP networking best if you think in terms of a four-layer model, with each layer being responsible for performing a particular task. The layered model describes the flow of data between the physical connection to the network and the end-user application. Figure 2-1 shows the four-layer network model for TCP/IP.

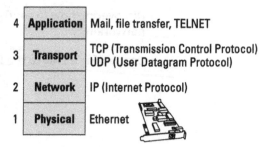

4	Application	Mail, file transfer, TELNET
3	Transport	TCP (Transmission Control Protocol) UDP (User Datagram Protocol)
2	Network	IP (Internet Protocol)
1	Physical	Ethernet

In this four-layer model, information always moves from one layer to the next. When an application sends data to another application, for example, the data goes through the layers in this order: application ➪ transport ➪ network ➪ physical. At the receiving end, the data goes up from physical ➪ network ➪ transport ➪ application.

Each layer has its own set of *protocols* — conventions — for handling and formatting the data. If you think of sending data as being something akin to sending letters through the postal service, a typical protocol is a preferred sequence of actions for a task, such as addressing an envelope (first the name, then the street address, followed by the city, state, and zip or other postal code).

These four layers, depending on what reference you look at, may have different names. If you look at the old DOD model, for example, the transport layer is called host-to-host, the network layer is called internetwork or Internet, the application layer is called process/application, and the physical layer is called network access.

Here's what the four layers do, top to bottom:

>> **Application:** Runs the applications that users use, such as email readers, file transfers, and web browsers. Application-level protocols are Simple Mail Transfer Protocol (SMTP) and Post Office Protocol (POP) for email, Hypertext Transfer Protocol (HTTP) for the web, and File Transfer Protocol (FTP) for file transfers. Application-level protocols also have a *port number* that you can think of as being an identifier for a specific application. Port 80, for example, is associated with HTTP or a web server.

>> **Transport:** Sends data from one application to another. The two most important protocols in this layer are Transmission Control Protocol (TCP) and User Datagram Protocol (UDP). TCP guarantees delivery of data; UDP just sends the data without ensuring that it actually reaches the destination.

TCP/IP AND THE INTERNET

TCP/IP has become the protocol of choice on the Internet — the network of networks that evolved from ARPANET. The U.S. government's Advanced Research Projects Agency (ARPA) initiated research in the 1970s on a new way of sending information, using packets of data sent over a network. The result was ARPANET: a national network of linked computers. Subsequently, ARPA acquired a Department of Defense prefix and became DARPA. Under the auspices of DARPA, the TCP/IP protocols emerged as a popular collection of protocols for *internetworking* — communication among networks.

TCP/IP has flourished because the protocol is *open*, which means that the technical descriptions of the protocol appear in public documents, so anyone can implement TCP/IP on specific hardware and software.

>> **Network:** Gets data packets from one network to another. If the networks are far apart, the data packets are routed from one network to the next until they reach their destinations. The primary protocol in this layer is Internet Protocol (IP).

>> **Physical:** Refers to the physical networking hardware (such as an Ethernet card or token ring card) that carries the data packets in a network.

The beauty of the layered model is that each layer takes care of only its specific task, leaving the rest to the other layers. The layers can mix and match; you can have TCP/IP network over any type of physical network medium, from Ethernet to radio waves (in a wireless network). The software is modular as well; each layer can be implemented in different modules. Typically, the transport and network layers already exist as part of the operating system, and any application can use of these layers.

TCP/IP also made great inroads because stable, working software was available. Instead of a paper description of network architecture and protocols, the TCP/IP protocols started out as working software — and who can argue with what's already working? These days, as a result, TCP/IP rules the Internet.

IP addresses

When you have many computers on a network, you need a way to identify each one uniquely. In TCP/IP networking, the address of a computer is the IP address. Because TCP/IP deals with internetworking, the address is based on the concepts of a network address and a host address. You may think of the idea of a

Setting Up a Local Area Network

network address and a host address as having to provide two addresses to identify a computer uniquely:

>> **Network address** indicates the network on which the computer is located.

>> **Host address** indicates a specific computer on that network.

The network and host addresses together constitute an *IP address,* which is a 4-byte (32-bit) value. The convention is to write each byte as a decimal value and to put a dot (.) after each number. Thus, you see network addresses such as 132.250.112.52. This way of writing IP addresses is known as *dotted-decimal* or *dotted-quad* notation.

TECHNICAL STUFF

In decimal notation, a byte (which has 8 bits) can have a value between 0 and 255. Thus, a valid IP address can use only the numbers between 0 and 255 in dotted-decimal notation.

Internet services and port numbers

The TCP/IP protocol suite has become the lingua franca of the Internet because many standard services are available on any system that supports TCP/IP. These services make the Internet tick by facilitating the transfer of mail, news, and web pages. These services go by well-known names such as the following:

>> **DHCP** (Dynamic Host Configuration Protocol) is for dynamically configuring TCP/IP network parameters on a computer. DHCP is primarily used to assign dynamic IP addresses and other networking information (such as name server, default gateway, and domain names) needed to configure TCP/IP networks. The DHCP server listens on port 67.

>> **FTP** (File Transfer Protocol) is used to transfer files between computers on the Internet. FTP uses two ports: Data is transferred on port 20, and control information is exchanged on port 21.

>> **DNS** (Domain Name System) is used to translate domain names into IP addresses. This service runs on port 53.

>> **HTTP** (Hypertext Transfer Protocol) is a protocol for sending documents from one system to another. HTTP is the underlying protocol of the World Wide Web. By default, the web server and client communicate on port 80. When combined with SSL/TLS, the protocol becomes HTTPS, and the port changes to 443.

>> **SMTP** (Simple Mail Transfer Protocol) is for exchanging email messages among systems. SMTP uses port 25 for information exchange.

TECHNICAL STUFF

WHAT ABOUT IP (IPv6)?

When the 4-byte IP address was created, the number of available addresses seemed adequate. Now, however, 4-byte addresses are running out. The Internet Engineering Task Force (IETF) recognized the potential for running out of IP addresses in 1991 and began working on the next-generation IP addressing scheme. The task force called it IPng (for Internet Protocol Next Generation) and intended for it to eventually replace the old 4-byte addressing scheme (called IPv4, for IP version 4).

Several alternative addressing schemes for IPng were proposed and debated. The final contender, with a 128-bit (16-byte) address, was dubbed IPv6 (for IP version 6). On September 18, 1995, the IETF declared the core set of IPv6 addressing protocols to be an IETF Proposed Standard. By now, many RFCs (Request for Comments) deal with various aspects of IPv6, from IPv6 over PPP for the transmission of IPv6 packets over Ethernet.

IPv6 is designed to be an evolutionary step from IPv4. The proposed standard provides direct interoperability between hosts using the older IPv4 addresses and any new IPv6 hosts. The idea is that users can upgrade their systems to use IPv6 when they want and that network operators are free to upgrade their network hardware to use IPv6 without affecting current users of IPv4. Sample implementations of IPv6 are being developed for many operating systems, including Linux. For more information about IPv6 in Linux, consult the Linux IPv6 HOWTO at `www.tldp.org/HOWTO/Linux+IPv6-HOWTO/`. For information about IPv6 in general, visit the IPv6 home page at `www.ipv6.org`.

The IPv6 128-bit addressing scheme allows for a total of 2^{128} or 340,282,366,920,938,463, 463,374,607,431,768,211,456 theoretically assignable addresses. That should last us for a while!

>> **POP3** (Post Office Protocol version 3) is used by the client to receive mail, and it uses port 110. When combined with SSL/TLS for security, the port changes to 995.

>> **IMAP** (Internet Message Access Protocol) can also be used by clients to interact with mail (in place of POP3), and it uses port 143. When combined with SSL/TLS for security, the port changes to 993.

>> **NNTP** (Network News Transfer Protocol) is for distribution of news articles in a store-and-forward fashion across the Internet. NNTP uses port 119.

>> **NetBIOS** is used by Windows for networking, and it uses several ports for the session, the most common of which is 139.

>> **SSH** (Secure Shell) is a protocol for secure remote login and other secure network services over an insecure network. SSH uses port 22.

>> **Telnet** is used when a user on one system logs in to another system on the Internet. (The user must provide a valid user ID and password to log in to the remote system.) Telnet uses port 23 by default, but the Telnet client can connect to any port.

>> **SNMP** (Simple Network Management Protocol) is for managing all types of network devices on the Internet. Like FTP, SNMP uses two ports: 161 and 162.

>> **Rendezvous Directory Service** (used by Cisco) uses port 465.

>> **TFTP** (Trivial File Transfer Protocol) is for transferring files from one system to another. (It's typically used by X terminals and diskless workstations to download boot files from another host on the network.) TFTP data transfer takes place on port 69.

>> **NFS** (Network File System) is for sharing files among computers. NFS uses Sun's Remote Procedure Call (RPC) facility, which exchanges information through port 111.

A well-known port is associated with each of these services. The TCP protocol uses each such port to locate a service on any system. (A *server process* — a special computer program running on a system — provides each service.)

Setting Up an Ethernet LAN

Ethernet is a standard way to move packets of data among two or more computers connected to a single hub, router, or switch. (You can create larger networks by connecting multiple Ethernet segments with gateways.) To set up an Ethernet LAN, you need an Ethernet card for each PC. Linux supports a wide variety of Ethernet cards for the PC.

Ethernet is a good choice for the physical data-transport mechanism for the following reasons:

>> Ethernet is a proven technology that has been in use since the early 1980s.

>> Ethernet provides good data-transfer rates — typically, 100 million bits per second (100 Mbps), although Gigabit Ethernet (1,000 Mbps) is now common.

>> Ethernet hardware is often built into PCs or can be installed at a relatively low cost. (PC Ethernet cards cost about $10 to $20.)

>> With wireless Ethernet, you can easily connect laptop PCs to your Ethernet LAN without having to run wires all over the place. (See Book 3, Chapter 3 for information on wireless Ethernet.)

How Ethernet works

What makes Ethernet tick? In essence, it's the same thing that makes any conversation work: listening and taking turns.

TECHNICAL STUFF

In an Ethernet network, all systems in a segment are connected to the same wire. A protocol is used for sending and receiving data because only one data packet can exist on the single wire at any time. An Ethernet LAN uses a data-transmission protocol known as *Carrier-Sense Multiple Access/Collision Detection* (CSMA/CD) to share the single transmission cable among all the computers. Ethernet cards in the computers follow the CSMA/CD protocol to transmit and receive Ethernet packets.

The way that the CSMA/CD protocol works is similar to the way in which you have a conversation at a party. You listen for a pause (that's sensing the carrier) and talk when no one else is speaking. If you and another person begin talking at the same time, both of you realize the problem (that's collision detection) and pause for a moment; then one of you starts speaking again. As you know from experience, everything works out.

In an Ethernet LAN, each Ethernet card checks the cable for signals; that's the carrier-sense part. If the signal level is low, the Ethernet card sends its packets on the cable; the packet contains information about the sender and the intended recipient. All Ethernet cards on the LAN listen to the signal, and the recipient receives the packet. If two cards send out a packet simultaneously, the signal level in the cable rises above a threshold, and the cards know that a collision has occurred. (Two packets have been sent out at the same time.) Both cards wait for a random amount of time before sending their packets again.

Ethernet sends data in *packets* (discrete chunks also known as *frames*). You don't have to hassle much with the innards of Ethernet packets except to note the 6-byte source and destination addresses. Each Ethernet controller has a unique 6-byte (48-bit) address at the physical layer; every packet must have one.

Setting Up a Local Area Network

WHAT IS ETHERNET?

Ethernet was invented in the early 1970s at the Xerox Palo Alto Research Center (PARC) by Robert M. Metcalfe. In the 1980s, Ethernet was standardized by the cooperative effort of three companies: Digital Equipment Corporation (DEC), Intel, and Xerox. Using the first initials of the company names, that Ethernet standard became known as the DIX standard. Later, the DIX standard was included in the 802-series standards developed by the Institute of Electrical and Electronics Engineers (IEEE). The final Ethernet specification is formally known as IEEE 802.3 CSMA/CD, but people continue to call it *Ethernet*.

Ethernet cables

Any time you hear experts talking about Ethernet, you'll also hear some bewildering terms used for the cables that carry the data. Here's a quick rundown.

The original Ethernet standard used a thick coaxial cable nearly half an inch in diameter. This wiring is called *thicknet, thickwire,* or just *thick Ethernet* although the IEEE 802.3 standard calls it *10Base5*. That designation means several things: The data-transmission rate is 10 megabits per second (10 Mbps); the transmission is *baseband* (which simply means that the cable's signal-carrying capacity is devoted to transmitting Ethernet packets only), and the total length of the cable can be no more than 500 meters. Thickwire was expensive, and the cable was rather unwieldy. Unless you're a technology-history buff, you don't have to care one whit about 10Base5 cables.

Nowadays, several other forms of Ethernet cabling are more popular, and the days of thickwire, and even thinwire, have given way to Ethernet over unshielded twisted-pair cable (UTP), known as 1xxBaseT where the xx represents the speed such as 100BaseT4, 100BaseT2, and 100BaseTX for 100-Mbps Ethernet and 1000BaseT for Gigabit Ethernet. The Electronic Industries Association/Telecommunications Industries Association (EIA/TIA) defines the following categories of shielded and unshielded twisted-pair cables:

>> **Category 1 (Cat 1):** Traditional telephone cable.

>> **Category 2 (Cat 2):** Cable certified for data transmissions up to 4 Mbps.

>> **Category 3 (Cat 3):** Cable that can carry signals up to a frequency of 16 MHz. Cat 3 was the most common type of wiring in old corporate networks, and it normally contains four pairs of wire. As network speeds pushed the 100 Mbps speed limit, Category 3 became ineffective; it's now considered to be obsolete.

» **Category 4 (Cat 4):** Cable that can carry signals up to a frequency of 20 MHz. Cat 4 wires aren't common and are now considered to be obsolete.

» **Category 5 (Cat 5):** Cable that can carry signals up to a frequency of 100 MHz. Cat 5 cables normally have four pairs of copper wire. Cat 5 UTP is the most popular cable used in new installations today. This category of cable was superseded by Category 5e (enhanced Cat 5).

» **Category 5e (Cat 5e):** Similar to Cat 5 but with improved technical parameters to mitigate communication problems. Cat 5e cables support 10BaseT, 100BaseT4, 100BaseT2, and 100BaseTX and 1000BaseT Ethernet. Nowadays, Cat 5e is the minimum acceptable wiring.

» **Category 6 (Cat 6):** Similar to Cat 5e but capable of carrying signals up to a frequency of 250 MHz. Category 6 twisted-pair uses a longitudinal separator, which separates each of the four pairs of wires. This extra construction significantly reduces the amount of crosstalk in the cable and makes the faster transfer rates possible. Cat 6 cables can support all existing Ethernet standards as well as the Gigabit Ethernet standard 1000BaseTX.

» **Category 6a (Cat 6a):** Also called augmented 6. This category offers improvements over Category 6 by offering minimum 500 MHz of bandwidth. It specifies transmission distances up to 100 meters with 10 Gbps networking speeds.

» **Category 7 (Cat 7):** The newest in wide use as of this writing. The big advantage to this cable is that shielding has been added to individual pairs and to the cable as a whole to greatly reduce crosstalk. Category 7 is rated for transmission of 600 MHz and is backward-compatible with Category 5 and Category 6. Category 7 differs from the other cables in this group in that it isn't recognized by the EIA/TIA and that it's shielded twisted-pair. (All others listed as exam objectives are unshielded.)

To set up a Gigabit Ethernet network, you need either an *Ethernet hub* — a hardware box with RJ-45 jacks. (This type of jack looks like a big telephone jack) or an *Ethernet switch* — like a hub, but smarter. You build the network by running twisted-pair wires (usually, Category 5 cables) from each PC's Ethernet card to this switch/hub. You can get an eight-port switch for about $40. Figure 2-2 shows a typical small Ethernet LAN that you might set up in a small office or your home.

When you install most the Linux distributions on a PC connected with an Ethernet card, the Linux kernel automatically detects the Ethernet card and installs the appropriate drivers. The installer also lets you set up TCP/IP networking.

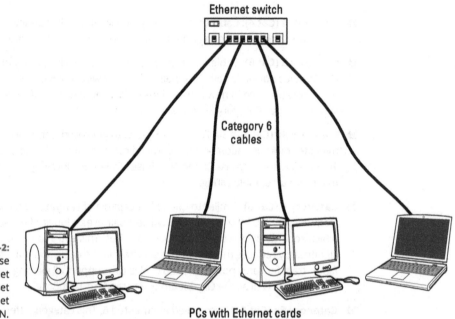

FIGURE 2-2:
You can use
an Ethernet
switch to set
up an Ethernet
LAN.

Ethernet switch

Category 6
cables

PCs with Ethernet cards

TIP

The Linux kernel loads the driver for the Ethernet card every time it boots. To verify that the Ethernet driver is loaded, type the following command in a terminal window:

```
dmesg | grep eth0
```

On one of my Linux PCs, I get the following output when I type that command:

```
eth0: RealTek RTL8139 at 0xf0e20000, 00:0c:76:f4:38:b3, IRQ 161
eth0: Identified 8139 chip type &#x2018;RTL-8101&#x2019;
eth0: link up, 100Mbps, full-duplex, lpa 0x45E1
eth0: no IPv6 routers present
```

You should see something similar showing the name of your Ethernet card and related information.

Configuring TCP/IP Networking

When you set up TCP/IP networking during Linux installation, the installation program prepares all appropriate configuration files by using the information you provide. As a result, you rarely have to configure the network manually. Most

Linux distributions, however, come with graphic user interface (GUI) tools for configuring the network devices, just in case something needs changing. For all distributions, the steps are similar.

In Ubuntu, for example, you can use the graphical network configuration tool. To start the GUI network configuration tool, choose Settings➪Network. The network configuration tool displays a dialog box, as shown in Figure 2-3. Then you can configure your network through the choices that appear in the dialog box, including settings for wired and wireless.

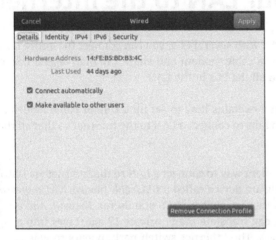

FIGURE 2-3: Move through the dialog-box choices to configure the connection.

Clicking the Security tab displays a dialog box similar to the one shown in Figure 2-4. From there, you can specify whether to use 802.1x security and what level of authentication users can use to log in.

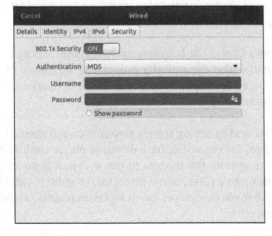

FIGURE 2-4: The Security tab allows you to configure the strength of your authentication.

Setting Up a Local Area Network

TIP

In most cases, you can set the network card so that it automatically obtains an IP address (which is the case when the Ethernet card is connected to DSL or cable modem) by using DHCP. If your network doesn't have a DHCP server (which is typically built into routers), you must specify an IP address for the network card. If you're running a private network, you may use IP addresses in the 192.168.0.0 to 192.168.255.255 range. (Other ranges of addresses are reserved for private networks, but this range suffices for most needs.)

Connecting Your LAN to the Internet

If you have a LAN with several PCs, you can connect the entire LAN to the Internet by using DSL or a cable modem and share the high-speed DSL or cable modem connection with all the PCs in the LAN.

Book 3, Chapter 1 explains how to set up a DSL or cable modem. In this section, I briefly explain how to connect a LAN to the Internet so that all the PCs can access the Internet.

The most convenient way to connect a LAN to the Internet via DSL or cable modem is to buy a hardware device called a *DSL/cable modem NAT router* with a four-port or eight-port Ethernet switch. *NAT* stands for *Network Address Translation,* and the NAT router can translate many private IP addresses into a single, externally known IP address. The Ethernet switch part appears to you as a series of RJ-45 Ethernet ports where you can connect the PCs to set up a LAN. In other words, you need only one extra box besides the DSL or cable modem.

Figure 2-5 shows how you might connect your LAN to the Internet through a NAT router with a built-in Ethernet switch. You need a DSL or cable modem hookup for this scenario to work, and you must sign up with a DSL provider (for DSL service) or with a cable provider for cable Internet service.

When you connect a LAN to the Internet, the NAT router acts as a gateway for your LAN. The NAT router also dynamically provides IP addresses to the PCs in your LAN. Therefore, on each PC, you have to set up the networking options to obtain the IP address dynamically.

If you're using DSL and incurring speeds slower than you should be (2 Mbps when it should be 5 Mbps, for example), try a different phone cord. Make sure that the phone cord that runs from the modem to the wall jack is no longer than 10 feet and doesn't go through a filter, surge protector, or splitter (which can attenuate the signal). All other phone devices (such as fax machines) should go through a filter or surge protector.

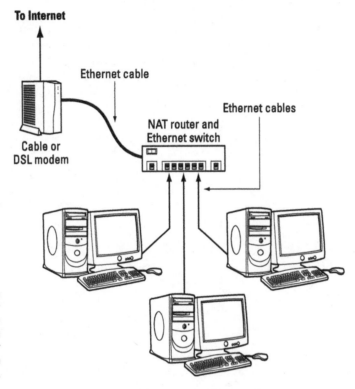

To Internet

Ethernet cable

Cable or
DSL modem

NAT router and
Ethernet switch

Ethernet cables

FIGURE 2-5:
Connect your
LAN to the
Internet through
a NAT router
with a built-in
Ethernet hub.

REMEMBER

Your LAN can mix and match all kinds of computers: Some computers may be running Linux, and others may be running Microsoft Windows or any other operating
system that supports TCP/IP. When configuring the network settings, remember
to select the option that enables Linux to automatically obtain IP address settings
and DNS information with DHCP.

» Setting up your wireless hardware

» Finding out how to configure a
wireless access point

» Configuring a wireless network

Chapter **3**

Going Wireless

I f you have laptop computers on your local-area network (LAN), or if you don't
want to run a rat's nest of wires to connect a PC to the LAN, you have the option
of using a wireless Ethernet network. In a typical scenario, you have a cable
modem or DSL connection to the Internet, and you want to connect one or more
laptops with wireless network cards to access the Internet through the cable or
DSL modem. This chapter shows you how to set up wireless networking for connecting to an Ethernet LAN and accessing the Internet.

Understanding Wireless Ethernet Networks

You've probably heard about Wi-Fi. *Wi-Fi* stands for *Wireless Fidelity* — a short-
range wireless network similar to wired Ethernet networks. Standards from an
organization known as IEEE (Institute of Electrical and Electronics Engineers)
define the technical details of how Wi-Fi networks work. Manufacturers use these
standards to build the components that you can buy to set up a wireless local-area
network (WLAN).

The standard governing Wi-Fi networks has evolved swiftly. What started as
802.11a gave birth to 802.11b, and the two combined to make up 802.11g, which
was superseded by 802.11n. But the purpose of every one of these standards was

the same: to specify how the wireless Ethernet network works at the physical layer. You don't have to fret the details of all those standards to set up a wireless network, but knowing some pertinent details is good so that you can buy the right kind of equipment for your wireless network.

The wireless Ethernet standards you'll likely encounter today have the following key characteristics:

>> **802.11b:** Operates in the 2.4 GHz radio band (2.4 GHz to 2.4835 GHz) in up to three nonoverlapping frequency bands or channels and supports a maximum bit rate of 11 Mbps per channel. One disadvantage of 802.11b is that the 2.4 GHz frequency band is crowded. Many devices (such as microwave ovens, cordless phones, medical and scientific equipment, and Bluetooth devices) work within the 2.4 GHz frequency band. Nevertheless, 802.11b is popular in corporate and home networks.

>> **802.11a:** Operates in the 5 GHz radio band (5.725 GHz to 5.850 GHz) in up to eight nonoverlapping channels and supports a maximum bit rate of 54 Mbps per channel. The 5 GHz band isn't as crowded as the 2.4 GHz band, but the 5 GHz band isn't approved for use in Europe. Products that conform to the 802.11a standard are on the market, and some wireless access points are designed to handle both 802.11a and 802.11b connections.

>> **802.11g:** Supports up to a 54 Mbps data rate in the 2.4 GHz band (the same band that 802.11b uses). 802.11g achieves the higher bit rate by using a technology called OFDM (orthogonal frequency-division multiplexing), which is also used by 802.11a. Equipment that complies with 802.11g is on the market. 802.11g has generated excitement by working in the same band as 802.11b but promising much higher data rates — and by being backward-compatible with 802.11b devices. Vendors currently offer access points that can support both the 802.11b and 802.11g connection standards.

>> **802.11n:** The goal of this standard is to significantly increase throughput in both the 2.4 GHz and the 5 GHz frequency range. The baseline goal was to reach speeds of 100 Mbps, but in theoretical conditions it can reach 600 Mbps.

>> **802.11ac:** Approved as a standard in 2014, in essence it is an extension of 802.11n but is a 5 GHz-only technology. This standard is supported on most wireless routers sold today.

In all cases, the maximum data throughput that a user sees is much less than the channel's total capacity because all users of that radio channel share this capacity. Also, the data-transfer rate decreases as the distance increases between the user's PC and the wireless access point.

To play it safe, though, go with 802.11ac, with its supported data rates five times the existing throughput and double the range of previous standards.

TIP

An 802.11g access point can communicate with older (and slower) 802.11b devices. You can also consider a MIMO (multiple-input-multiple-output) access point, which supports multiple 802.11 standards and implements techniques for getting higher throughputs and better range.

REMEMBER

To find out more about wireless Ethernet, visit www.wi-fi.org, the home page of the Wi-Fi Alliance, which is the not-for-profit international association formed in 1999 to certify interoperability of wireless LAN products based on IEEE 802.11 standards.

Understanding infrastructure and ad hoc modes

The 802.11 standard defines two modes of operation for wireless Ethernet networks: ad hoc and infrastructure. *Ad hoc* mode is simply two or more wireless Ethernet cards communicating with one another without an access point.

Infrastructure mode refers to the approach in which all the wireless Ethernet cards communicate with one another and with the wired LAN through an access point. For the discussions in this chapter, I assume that you set your wireless Ethernet card to infrastructure mode. In the configuration files, this mode is referred to as *managed.*

Understanding Wired Equivalent Privacy (WEP)

The 802.11 standard includes Wired Equivalent Privacy (WEP) for protecting wireless communications from eavesdropping. WEP relies on a 40-bit or 104-bit secret key that's shared between a mobile station (such as a laptop with a wireless Ethernet card) and an access point (also called a *base station*). The secret key is used to encrypt data packets before they're transmitted, and an integrity check is performed to ensure that packets aren't modified in transit.

The 802.11 standard doesn't explain how the shared key is established. In practice, most wireless LANs use a single key that's shared by all its mobile stations and access points. Such an approach, however, doesn't scale up very well to an environment such as a college campus, because the keys are shared with all users — and you know how it is if you share a secret with hundreds of people. For that reason, WEP typically isn't used on large wireless networks, such as the ones at universities. In such wireless networks, you have to use other security approaches, such as SSH (Secure Shell) to log in to remote systems. While once WEP was good enough to use on a home wireless network, that is no longer recommended today.

TECHNICAL STUFF

More than a decade ago, the Wi-Fi Alliance published a specification called Wi-Fi Protected Access (WPA), which replaced the existing WEP standard and improved security by making some changes. Unlike WEP, which uses fixed keys, the WPA standard uses Temporal Key Integrity Protocol (TKIP), which generates new keys for every 10 KB of data transmitted over the network and makes WPA more difficult to break. In 2004, the Wi-Fi Alliance introduced a follow-up called Wi-Fi Protected Access 2 (WPA2), the second generation of WPA security. WPA2 is based on the final IEEE 802.11i standard, which uses public key encryption with digital certificates and an authentication, authorization, and accounting RADIUS (Remote Authentication Dial-In User Service) server to provide better security for wireless Ethernet networks. WPA2 uses the Advanced Encryption Standard (AES) for data encryption. The future is looking like WPA3, which has been recently announced, and its goal of increasing security even further.

Setting Up Wireless Hardware

To set up the wireless connection, you need a wireless access point and a wireless network card in each PC. You can also set up an ad hoc wireless network among two or more PCs with wireless network cards. In this section, I focus on the scenario in which you want to set up a wireless connection to an established LAN that has a wired Internet connection through a cable modem or DSL.

In addition to the wireless access point, you need a cable modem or DSL connection to the Internet, along with a Network Access Translation (NAT) router and hub, as described in Book 3, Chapters 1 and 2. Figure 3-1 shows a typical setup for wireless Internet access through an existing cable modem or DSL connection.

As Figure 3-1 shows, the LAN has both wired and wireless PCs. In this example, a cable or DSL modem connects the LAN to the Internet through a NAT router and switch. Laptops with wireless network cards connect to the LAN through a wireless access point attached to one of the RJ-45 ports on the switch. To connect desktop PCs to this wireless network, you can use a USB wireless network card (which connects to a USB port).

TIP

If you haven't yet purchased a NAT router and hub for your cable or DSL connection, consider buying a router and hub that has a built-in wireless access point.

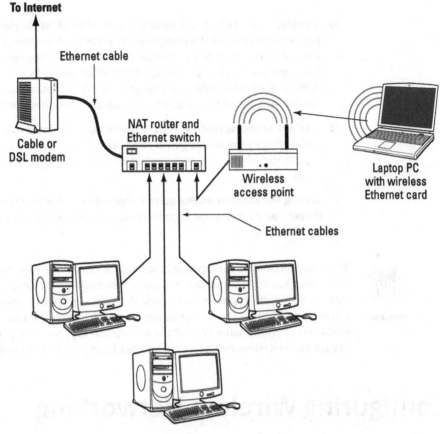

To Internet

Ethernet cable

**Cable or
DSL modem**

**NAT router and
Ethernet switch**

**Wireless
access point**

**Laptop PC
with wireless
Ethernet card**

Ethernet cables

FIGURE 3-1:
Typical
connection of
a mixed wired
and wireless
Ethernet LAN
to the Internet.

Configuring the Wireless Access Point

Configuring the wireless access point (commonly called an AP or WAP) involves
the following tasks:

- **Setting a name for the wireless network:** (The technical term for this name
is the ESSID, but WAP documentation and utilities often refer to it as SSID.)

- **Setting the frequency or channel on which the wireless access point
communicates with the wireless network cards:** The access point and the
cards must use the same channel.

- **Deciding whether to use encryption:** You usually have a number of options
and can choose to go without any encryption at all or implement one or more
levels of security.

>> **If encryption is to be used, setting the number of bits in the encryption key and the value of the encryption key:** For the encryption key, 24 bits are internal to the access point; you specify only the remaining bits. Thus, for 64-bit encryption, you specify a 40-bit key, which comes to 10 hexadecimal digits. (A *hexadecimal digit* is an integer from 0–9 or a letter from A–F.) For a 128-bit encryption key, you specify 104 bits, or 26 hexadecimal digits.

>> **Setting the access method that wireless network cards must use when connecting to the access point:** You can opt for the open-access or shared-key method. The open-access method is typical (even when encryption is used).

>> **Setting the wireless access point to operate in infrastructure (managed) mode:** You use this mode to connect wireless network cards to an existing Ethernet LAN.

REMEMBER

The exact method of configuring a wireless access point depends on the device's make and model; the vendor provides instructions for configuring the wireless access point. Typically, you work through a graphical client application on a Windows PC to do the configuration or a web-based interface for WAP. If you enable encryption, make note of the encryption key; you must specify that same key for each wireless network card on your laptop or desktop computers.

Configuring Wireless Networking

On your Linux laptop, the PCMCIA or PC Card manager recognizes the wireless network card and loads the appropriate driver for the card. Linux treats the wireless network card like another Ethernet device and assigns it a device name such as eth0 or eth1. If you already have an Ethernet card in the laptop, that card gets the eth0 device name, and the wireless PC Card becomes the eth1 device.

You do have to configure certain parameters to enable the wireless network card to communicate with the wireless access point. You have to specify the wireless network name assigned to the access point, for example, and the encryption settings must match those on the access point. Usually, you can configure everything by using a graphical network-configuration tool that's available for your Linux distribution. Just select the appropriate wireless network option and then walk through the configuration dialog boxes, such as the one shown in Figure 3-2.

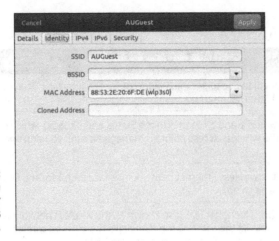

FIGURE 3-2: Configuration information for a new wireless connection.

TECHNICAL STUFF

The network-configuration tool saves your wireless network settings in a text file. The name of the text file depends on the wireless network device's name. If the wireless network device's name is eth0, the configuration is stored in the text file /etc/sysconfig/network-scripts/ifcfg-eth0. If the wireless device name is eth1, the file is /etc/sysconfig/network-scripts/ifcfg-eth1. This configuration file contains various settings for the wireless network card. Table 3-1 explains the meaning of the settings. Here is a slightly edited version of the /etc/sysconfig/network-scripts/ifcfg-eth1 file from my laptop PC:

```
IPV6INIT=no
USERCTL=no
PEERDNS=yes
TYPE=Wireless
DEVICE=eth1
HWADDR=00:02:2d:8c:f9:c4
BOOTPROTO=dhcp
ONBOOT=no
DHCP_HOSTNAME=
NAME=
ESSID='HOME'
CHANNEL=6
MODE=Managed
    RATE=auto
```

In some Linux distributions, the encryption key is stored separately. For a wireless Ethernet card whose device name is eth1, the encryption key is stored in the /etc/sysconfig/network-scripts/keys-eth1 file. Here is what this file contains for my example:

```
KEY=1fdf3fdefe
```

TABLE 3-1

Settings in Configuration File for a Wireless Ethernet Network Interface

Parameter	Meaning
BOOTPROTO	The name of the protocol to use to get the IP address for the interface. The protocol used is dhcp or bootp for an Ethernet interface.
CHANNEL	Channel number (between 1 and 14 in the United States and Canada), which must be the same as that set for the wireless access point. In managed mode, you don't need to specify the channel.
DEVICE	The device name for the wireless Ethernet network interface (eth0 for the first interface, eth1 for the second, and so on).
ESSID	Extended Service Set (ESS) Identifier (ID), also known as the wireless network name. The name is case-sensitive and must be the same as the name specified for the wireless access point. Provide the name within single quotes (for example, 'HOME').
HWADDR	The hardware address (also called the MAC address) of the wireless network card (six pairs of colon-separated hexadecimal numbers, such as 00:02:2d:8c:f9:c4). The wireless card's device driver automatically detects this address.
IPV6INIT	When set to yes, initializes IPv6 configuration for the wireless interface. Set it to no if you're not using IPv6.
MODE	The mode of operation of the wireless network card. Set it to Managed for a typical network that connects through a wireless access point.
NAME	A nickname for your wireless network. If you don't specify it, the host name is used as the nickname.
ONBOOT	Set to yes to activate the wireless interface at boot time; otherwise, set to no.
PEERDNS	Set to yes to enable the interface to modify your system's /etc/resolv.conf file to use the DNS servers obtained from the DHCP server (the same server that provides the IP address for the interface). If you set this parameter to no, the /etc/resolv.conf file is left unchanged.
RATE	Bit rate for the wireless connection, set to one of the following options: 1M, 2M, 5.5M, 11M, or auto. M means Mbps, or a million bits per second. Set it to auto to use the maximum possible transmission rate.
TYPE	Set to Wireless for a wireless network interface.
USERCTL	When set to yes, a user who isn't logged in as root can control the device. Set it to no so that only root can control the device.

TECHNICAL STUFF

The key has 10 hexadecimal digits for a 40-bit key (such as 1fdf-3fde-fe) or 26 hexadecimal digits for a 104-bit key. The keys are 64-bit and 128-bit, respectively, but the encryption algorithm automatically generates 24 bits of the key, so you need to specify only the remaining bits. The longer the key is, the more secure the encryption is.

If you ever manually edit the parameters in the wireless Ethernet configuration file, type the following command to reactivate the wireless network interface after editing the configuration file:

```
/etc/init.d/network restart
```

In SUSE Linux, use YaST to configure the wireless network. SUSE stores the wireless configuration parameters in a file whose name begins with ifcfg-wlan, followed by a number such as 0 or 1, depending on the sequence number of the wireless network interface.

The configuration file is stored in the /etc/sysconfig/network directory. Here's a typical list of wireless configuration parameters from a configuration file in SUSE Linux:

```
WIRELESS_MODE='Managed'
WIRELESS_ESSID='HOME'
WIRELESS_NICK=''
WIRELESS_RATE='auto'
WIRELESS_AUTH_MODE='open'
WIRELESS_KEY_0='0123-4567-89'
```

To check the status of the wireless network interface, type the following command:

```
iwconfig
```

Here's typical output from a laptop with a wireless Ethernet PC card. (The output should be similar in other Linux distributions.)

```
lo no wireless extensions.
eth0 no wireless extensions.
sit0 no wireless extensions.
eth1 IEEE 802.11b ESSID:"HOME" Nickname:"localhost.localdomain"
Mode:Managed Frequency:2.437 GHz Access Point: 00:30:AB:06:E2:5D
Bit Rate=11 Mb/s Sensitivity:1/3
Retry limit:4 RTS thr:off Fragment thr:off
Encryption key:1FDF-3FDE-FE Security mode:open
Power Management:off
Link Quality=51/92 Signal level=-40 dBm Noise level=-91 dBm
Rx invalid nwid:0 Rx invalid crypt:0 Rx invalid frag:27
Tx excessive retries:0 Invalid misc:0 Missed beacon:0
```

Here, the eth1 interface refers to the wireless network card. I edited the encryption key and some other parameters to hide those details, but the sample output shows you what you'd typically see when the wireless link is working.

Chapter **4**

Managing the Network

Like almost everything else in Linux, setting up Transmission Control Protocol/Internet Protocol (TCP/IP) is a matter of preparing numerous configuration files (text files that you can edit with any text editor). Most of these configuration files are in the /etc directory. The Linux installer tries to be helpful by filling in values and keeping you from needing to interact directly with each of the TCP/IP configuration files. Nevertheless, if you know the names of the files and their purposes, editing the files manually (if necessary) is often easier.

Discovering the TCP/IP Configuration Files

You can configure TCP/IP networking when you install Linux. If you want to manage the network effectively, however, you need to become familiar with the TCP/IP configuration files so that you can edit the files, if necessary. (If you want to check whether the name servers are specified correctly, for example, you have to know about the /etc/resolv.conf file, which stores the IP addresses of name servers.)

Table 4-1 summarizes the basic TCP/IP configuration files. I describe these configuration files in the next few sections.

TABLE 4-1   **Basic TCP/IP Network Configuration Files**

This File	Contains the Following
/etc/hosts	IP addresses and host names for your local network as well as any other systems that you access often
/etc/networks	Names and IP addresses of networks
/etc/host.conf	Instructions on how to translate host names into IP addresses
/etc/resolv.conf	IP addresses of name servers
/etc/hosts.allow	Instructions on which systems can access Internet services on your system
/etc/hosts.deny	Instructions on which systems must be denied access to Internet services on your system
/etc/nsswitch.conf	Instructions on how to translate host names into IP addresses

REMEMBER

A pound sign (#) in a text file indicates a comment.

/etc/hosts

The /etc/hosts text file contains a list of IP addresses and host names for your local network. In the absence of a name server, any network program on your system consults this file to determine the IP address that corresponds to a host name. Think of /etc/hosts as the local phone directory where you can look up the IP address (instead of a phone number) for a local host.

Here's the /etc/hosts file from a system, showing the IP addresses and names of other hosts on a typical LAN:

```
127.0.0.1 localhost localhost.localdomain
# Other hosts on the LAN
192.168.0.100 lnbp933
192.168.0.50 lnbp600
192.168.0.200 lnbp200
192.168.0.233 lnbp233
192.168.0.40 lnbp400
```

As the example shows, each line in the file starts with an IP address followed by the host name for that IP address. (You can have more than one host name for any given IP address.) In some distributions, such as openSUSE, the /etc/hosts file has the following: IP-Address, Fully-Qualified-Hostname, Short-Hostname. In all cases, anything after the host name (such as Short-Hostname) is taken to be an alias.

/etc/networks

/etc/networks is another text file that contains the names and IP addresses of networks. These network names are commonly used in the routing command (/sbin/route) to specify a network by its name instead of by its IP address.

Don't be alarmed if your Linux PC doesn't have the /etc/networks file. Your TCP/IP network works fine without this file. In fact, the Linux installer doesn't create a /etc/networks file.

/etc/host.conf

Linux uses a special library (collection of computer code) called the *resolver* to obtain the IP address that corresponds to a host name. The /etc/host.conf file specifies how names are *resolved* (that is, how the name gets converted to a numeric IP address). A typical /etc/host.conf file might contain the following lines:

```
order hosts, bind
multi on
```

The entries in the /etc/host.conf file tell the resolver what services to use (and in which order) to resolve names.

The order option indicates the order of services (in recent distributions, the nsswitch.conf file, discussed in a later section, performs this function). The sample entry tells the resolver to first consult the /etc/hosts file and then check the name server to resolve a name.

TECHNICAL STUFF

Use the multi option to indicate whether a host in the /etc/hosts file can have multiple IP addresses. Hosts that have more than one IP address are called *multihomed* because the presence of multiple IP addresses implies that the host has several network interfaces. (In effect, the host lives in several networks simultaneously.)

/etc/resolv.conf

The /etc/resolv.conf file is another text file used by the resolver — the library that determines the IP address for a host name. Here's a sample /etc/resolv.conf file:

```
nameserver 192.168.0.1 # dhcp: eth0
search nrockv01.md.comcast.net
```

The `nameserver` line provides the IP addresses of name servers for your domain. If you have multiple name servers, list them on separate lines. They're queried in the order in which they appear in the file.

The `search` line tells the resolver how to search for a host name. When you're trying to locate a host name `myhost`, for example, the search directive in the example causes the resolver to try `myhost.nrockv01.md.comcast.net` first, then `myhost.md.comcast.net`, and finally `myhost.comcast.net`.

REMEMBER

If you don't have a name server for your network, you can safely ignore this file. TCP/IP still works, even though you may not be able to refer to hosts by name (other than those listed in the `/etc/hosts` file).

/etc/hosts.allow

The `/etc/hosts.allow` file specifies which hosts are allowed to use the Internet services (such as Telnet and FTP) running on your system. This file is consulted before certain Internet services start. The services start only if the entries in the `hosts.allow` file imply that the requesting host is allowed to use the services.

The entries in `/etc/hosts.allow` are in *server:IP address* format, where *server* refers to the name of the program providing a specific Internet service and *IP address* identifies the host allowed to use that service. If you want all hosts in your local network (which has the network address 192.168.0.0) to access the Telnet service (provided by the `in.telnetd` program), add the following line to the `/etc/hosts.allow` file (the last octet is left off to signify all possibilities within that range):

```
in.telnetd:192.168.0.
```

If you want to let all local hosts have access to all Internet services, you can use the `ALL` keyword and rewrite the line as follows:

```
ALL:192.168.0.
```

Finally, to open all Internet services to all hosts, you can replace the IP address with `ALL`, as follows:

```
ALL:ALL
```

You can also use host names in place of IP addresses.

TIP

To find out the detailed syntax of the entries in the `/etc/hosts.allow` file, type **man hosts.allow** at the shell prompt in a terminal window.

/etc/hosts.deny

The /etc/hosts.deny file is the opposite of /etc/hosts.allow. Whereas hosts. allow specifies which hosts may access Internet services (such as Telnet and TFTP) on your system, the hosts.deny file identifies the hosts that must be denied services. The /etc/hosts.deny file is consulted if no rules in the /etc/hosts.allow file apply to the requesting host. Service is denied if the hosts.deny file has a rule that applies to the host.

The entries in /etc/hosts.deny file have the same format as those in the /etc/hosts.allow file; they're in *server:IP address* format, where *server* refers to the name of the program providing a specific Internet service and *IP address* identifies the host that must not be allowed to use that service.

If you already set up entries in the /etc/hosts.allow file to allow access to specific hosts, you can place the following line in /etc/hosts.deny to deny all other hosts access to any service on your system:

```
ALL:ALL
```

To find out the detailed syntax of the entries in the /etc/hosts.deny file, type **man hosts.deny** at the shell prompt in a terminal window.

TIP

/etc/nsswitch.conf

The /etc/nsswitch.conf file, known as the *name service switch* (NSS) file, specifies how services such as the resolver library, NIS, NIS+, and local configuration files (such as /etc/hosts and /etc/shadow) interact.

NIS and NIS+ are *network information systems* — another type of name-lookup service. Newer versions of the Linux kernel use the /etc/nsswitch.conf file to determine what takes precedence: a local configuration file, a service such as DNS (Domain Name System), or NIS.

As an example, the following hosts entry in the /etc/nsswitch.conf file says that the resolver library first tries the /etc/hosts file, then tries NIS+, and finally tries DNS:

```
hosts: files nisplus dns
```

You can find out more about the /etc/nsswitch.conf file by typing **man nsswitch.conf** in a terminal window.

TIP

Checking Out TCP/IP Networks

After you configure Ethernet and TCP/IP (whether during Linux installation or by running a network configuration tool or command later), you can use various networking applications without much problem. On the off chance that you do run into trouble, Linux includes several tools to help you monitor and diagnose problems.

Checking the network interfaces

Use the /sbin/ifconfig command, which may need to be installed in some distributions, is used to view the currently configured network interfaces. The ifconfig command is used to configure a network interface (that is, to associate an IP address with a network device). If you run ifconfig without any command-line arguments, the command displays information about current network interfaces.

This output displayed will show the loopback interface (lo) and any installed network cards as well as if they are currently active on this system. For each interface, you can see the IP address, as well as statistics on packets delivered and sent. If the Linux system has a dial-up PPP link up and running, you also see an item for the ppp0 interface in the output.

Checking the IP routing table

The other network configuration command, /sbin/route, also provides status information when you run it without a command-line argument. If you're having trouble checking a connection to another host (that you specify with an IP address), check the IP routing table to see whether a default gateway is specified. Then check the gateway's routing table to ensure that paths to an outside network appear in that routing table.

Typical output from the /sbin/route command looks like the following:

```
Kernel IP routing table
Destination Gateway      Genmask        Flags Metric Ref Use Iface
192.168.0.0 *            255.255.255.0 U      0      0   0   eth0
192.168.0.0 *            255.255.255.0 U      0      0   0   eth1
169.254.0.0 *            255.255.0.0   U      0      0   0   eth1
default     192.168.0.1 0.0.0.0        UG     0      0   0   eth0
```

As this routing table shows, the local network uses the eth0 and eth1 Ethernet interfaces, and the default gateway is the eth0 Ethernet interface. The default gateway is a routing device that handles packets addressed to any network other than the one in which the Linux system resides. In this example, packets addressed to any network address other than those beginning with 192.168.0 are sent to the gateway — 192.168.0.1. The gateway forwards those packets to other networks (assuming, of course, that the gateway is connected to another network, preferably the Internet).

Checking connectivity to a host

To check for a network connection to a specific host, use the ping command. ping is a widely used TCP/IP tool that uses a series of Internet Control Message Protocol (ICMP, pronounced *EYE-comp*) messages. ICMP provides for an echo message to which every host responds. Using the ICMP messages and replies, ping can determine whether the other system is alive and can compute the round-trip delay in communicating with that system.

The following example shows how I run ping to see whether a system on my network is alive:

```
ping 192.168.0.1
```

Here's what this command displays on my home network:

```
PING 192.168.0.1 (192.168.0.1) 56(84) bytes of data.
64 bytes from 192.168.0.1: icmp_seq=1 ttl=63 time=0.256 ms
64 bytes from 192.168.0.1: icmp_seq=2 ttl=63 time=0.267 ms
64 bytes from 192.168.0.1: icmp_seq=3 ttl=63 time=0.272 ms
64 bytes from 192.168.0.1: icmp_seq=4 ttl=63 time=0.267 ms
64 bytes from 192.168.0.1: icmp_seq=5 ttl=63 time=0.275 ms
--- 192.168.0.1 ping statistics ---
5 packets transmitted, 5 received, 0% packet loss, time 3999ms
rtt min/avg/max/mdev = 0.256/0.267/0.275/0.016 ms
```

In Linux, ping continues to run — unless you used the –c option — until you press Ctrl+C to stop it; then it displays summary statistics showing the typical time it takes to send a packet between the two systems. On some systems, ping simply reports that a remote host is alive. You can still get the timing information by using appropriate command-line arguments, however.

WARNING

The ping command relies on ICMP messages that many firewalls are configured to block. Therefore, ping may not always work and is no longer a reliable way to test network connectivity. If ping fails for a specific host, don't assume that the host is down or not connected to the network. Typically, you can use ping to check connectivity within your local-area network (LAN).

Checking network status

To check the status of the network, use the `netstat` command. This command displays the status of network connections of various types (such as TCP and UDP connections). You can view the status of the interfaces quickly by typing **netstat -i**, which results in output similar to the following:

```
Kernel Interface table
Iface MTU Met RX-OK RX-ERR RX-DRP RX-OVR TX-OK TX-ERR TX-DRP TX-OVR Flg
eth0  1500 0 613175 0      0      1      574695 0     0      0      BMRU
eth1  1500 0 4298   0      0      0      1375   1     0      0      BMRU
lo    16436 0 3255  0      0      0      3255   0     0      0      LRU
```

In this case, the output shows the current status of the loopback and Ethernet interfaces.

Table 4-2 describes the meanings of the columns.

TABLE 4-2

Meanings of Columns in the Kernel Interface Table

Column	Meaning
Iface	Name of the interface
MTU	Maximum Transmission Unit — the maximum number of bytes that a packet can contain
Met	Metric value for the interface — a number indicating distance (in terms of number of hops) that routing software uses when deciding which interface to send packets through
RX-OK, TX-OK	Number of error-free packets received (RX) or transmitted (TX)
RX-ERR, TX-ERR	Number of packets with errors
RX-DRP, TX-DRP	Number of dropped packets
RX-OVR, TX-OVR	Number of packets lost due to overflow
Flg	A = receive multicast; B = broadcast allowed; D = debugging turned on; L = loopback interface (notice the flag on lo), M = all packets received, N = trailers avoided; O = no Address Resolution Protocol (ARP) on this interface; P = point-to-point interface; R = interface is running; and U = interface is up

Another useful form of `netstat` option is –t, which shows all active TCP connections. Following is a typical result of typing **netstat -t** on one Linux PC:

```
Active Internet connections (w/o servers)
Proto Recv-Q Send-Q Local Address Foreign Address State
tcp 0 0 localhost:2654 localhost:1024 ESTABLISHED
tcp 0 0 localhost:1024 localhost:2654 ESTABLISHED
tcp 0 0 LNBNECXAN.nrockv01.:ssh 192.168.0.6:1577 ESTABLISHED
```

In this case, the output columns show the protocol (Proto), the number of bytes in the receive and transmit queues (Recv-Q, Send-Q), the local TCP port in hostname:service format (Local Address), the remote port (Foreign Address), and the state of the connection.

Type **netstat -ta** to see all TCP connections — both active and the ones your Linux system is listening to (with no connection established yet). Here's typical output from the netstat -ta command:

```
Active Internet connections (servers and established)
Proto Recv-Q Send-Q Local Address Foreign Address State
tcp 0 0 *:32769 *:* LISTEN
tcp 0 0 *:mysql *:* LISTEN
tcp 0 0 *:sunrpc *:* LISTEN
tcp 0 0 *:ftp *:* LISTEN
tcp 0 0 localhost.localdomain:ipp *:* LISTEN
tcp 0 0 *:telnet *:* LISTEN
tcp 0 0 localhost.localdomain:5335 *:* LISTEN
tcp 0 0 localhost.localdomain:smtp *:* LISTEN
tcp 0 0 192.168.0.9:45876 www.redhat.com:http ESTABLISHED
tcp 0 0 192.168.0.9:45877 www.redhat.com:http ESTABLISHED
tcp 0 0 192.168.0.9:45875 www.redhat.com:http ESTABLISHED
tcp 0 0 *:ssh *:* LISTEN
tcp 0 0 ::ffff:192.168.0.7:ssh ::ffff:192.168.0.3:4932 ESTABLISHED
```

Sniffing network packets

Sniffing network packets sounds like something illegal, doesn't it? It's nothing like that. *Sniffing* simply refers to viewing the TCP/IP network data packets. The concept is to capture all the network packets so that you can examine them later.

TIP

If you feel like sniffing TCP/IP packets, you can use tcpdump, a command-line utility that comes with Linux. As its name implies, it *dumps* (prints) the headers of TCP/IP network packets.

To use tcpdump, log in as root and type the tcpdump command in a terminal window. Typically, you want to save the output in a file and examine that file later. Otherwise, tcpdump starts spewing results that flash by in the window. To capture

1,000 packets in a file named tdout and attempt to convert the IP addresses to names, type the following command:

```
tcpdump -a -c 1000 > tdout
```

After capturing 1,000 packets, tcpdump quits. Then you can examine the output file, tdout. That file is a text file, so you can simply open it in a text editor or type **more tdout** to view the captured packets.

To whet your curiosity, here are some lines from typical output from tcpdump:

```
20:05:57.723621 arp who-has 192.168.0.1 tell
    LNBNECXAN.nrockv01.md.comcast.net
20:05:57.723843 arp reply 192.168.0.1 is-at 0:9:5b:44:78:fc
20:06:01.733633 LNBNECXAN.nrockv01.md.comcast.net.1038 > 192.168.0.6.auth: S
    536321100:536321100(0) win 5840 <mss 1460,sackOK,timestamp 7030060
    0,nop,wscale 0> (DF)
20:06:02.737022 LNBNECXAN.nrockv01.md.comcast.net.ftp > 192.168.0.6.1596:
    P 1:72 (71) ack 1 win 5840 (DF)
20:06:02.935335 192.168.0.6.1596 > LNBNECXAN.nrockv01.md.comcast.net.ftp:
    . ack 72 win 65464 (DF)
20:06:05.462481 192.168.0.6.1596 > LNBNECXAN.nrockv01.md.comcast.net.ftp:
    P 1:12 (11) ack 72 win 65464 (DF)
20:06:05.462595 LNBNECXAN.nrockv01.md.comcast.net.ftp > 192.168.0.6.1596:
    . ack 12 win 5840 (DF)
20:06:05.465344 LNBNECXAN.nrockv01.md.comcast.net.ftp > 192.168.0.6.1596:
    P 72:105(33) ack 12 win 5840 (DF)
. . . lines deleted . . .
```

The output offers some clues about what's going on, with each line showing information about one network packet. Every line starts with a time stamp followed by details on the packet (information such as where it originates and where it's going). I don't try to explain the details here, but you can type **man tcpdump** to find out some of the details (and, more important, see other ways to use tcpdump).

DISTRIBUTION SPECIFIC

If tcpdump isn't installed in Debian, type **apt-get install tcpdump** to install it.

You can use another packet sniffer called Wireshark in Linux. To find out more about Wireshark, visit www.wireshark.org.

Using GUI tools

You can check the status of your network through the graphical interfaces in several ways. One of those ways is System Monitor.

Configuring Networks at Boot Time

It makes sense to start your network automatically every time you boot the system. For that to happen, various startup scripts must contain appropriate commands. You don't have to do anything special other than configure your network (either during installation or by using the network configuration tool at a later time). If the network balks at startup, however, you can troubleshoot by checking the files I mention in this section.

DISTRIBUTION SPECIFIC

In Debian and Ubuntu, the `/etc/network/interfaces` file describes the network interfaces available on your system, and the `/sbin/ifup` command activates the interfaces when you boot the system. Here's the content of a typical `/etc/network/interfaces` file from a Debian system:

```
# This file describes the network interfaces available on your system
# and how to activate them. For more information, see interfaces(5).
# The loopback network interface
auto lo
iface lo inet loopback
# The primary network interface
auto eth0
iface eth0 inet dhcp
```

The `auto eth0` line indicates that you can bring up the Ethernet interface at initialization by using the command `ifup -a` invoked by a system startup script. The line `iface eth0 inet dhcp` identifies Ethernet as a TCP/IP network interface that's configured by Dynamic Host Configuration Protocol (DHCP).

In Fedora, the network-activation script uses a set of text files in the `/etc/sysconfig` directory to activate the network interfaces. The script checks the variables defined in the `/etc/sysconfig/network` file to decide whether to activate the network. In `/etc/sysconfig/network`, you see a line with the `NETWORKING` variable as follows:

```
NETWORKING=yes
```

The network activates only if the `NETWORKING` variable is set to `yes`. Several scripts in the `/etc/sysconfig/network-scripts` directory activate specific network interfaces. The configuration file for activating the Ethernet interface `eth0`, for example, is the file `/etc/sysconfig/network-scripts/ifcfg-eth0`. Here's what a typical `/etc/sysconfig/network-scripts/ifcfg-eth0` file contains:

```
DEVICE=eth0
BOOTPROTO=dhcp
```

```
HWADDR=00:08:74:E5:C1:06
ONBOOT=yes
TYPE=Ethernet
```

The DEVICE line provides the network device name. The BOOTPROTO variable is set to dhcp, indicating that the IP address is obtained dynamically by using DHCP. The ONBOOT variable states whether this network interface activates when Linux boots. If your PC has an Ethernet card, and you want to activate the eth0 interface at boot time, ONBOOT must be set to yes. The configuration file ifcfg-eth0 in the /etc/sysconfig/network-scripts directory works only if your PC has an Ethernet card and if the Linux kernel has detected and loaded the specific driver for that card.

DISTRIBUTION SPECIFIC

In SUSE, the network information is kept in the /etc/sysconfig/network directory in files with names beginning with ifcfg. For Ethernet interfaces, the configuration filename begins with ifcfg-eth-id- followed by the unique hardware address of the Ethernet card. Here are the key lines in a typical Ethernet configuration file:

```
BOOTPROTO='dhcp'
    STARTMODE='auto'
```

The BOOTPROTO='dhcp' line indicates that the interface is set up using DHCP, and STARTMODE='auto' means that the interface is initialized when the system boots.

Within KDE, you can start the Control Center by typing **Session Management** in the Search box and configuring the default operations for the system.

Another useful interface that can give you a quick look at whether the network is up and running is System Monitor. Although this interface offers no way to change configuration settings, it's nice to have a tool that can quickly show you the status of the system, including network status.

4

The Internet

Contents at a Glance

CHAPTER 1: Browsing the Web 205
Surfing the Web 205
Web Browsing in Linux 209

CHAPTER 2: Using FTP 217
Using Graphical FTP Clients 218
Using the Command-Line FTP Client 223

CHAPTER 3: Hosting Internet Services 229
Understanding Internet Services 229
Using the Internet Super Server 235
Running Stand-Alone Servers 239

CHAPTER 4: Managing Mail Servers 245
Installing the Mail Server 245

CHAPTER 5: Managing DNS 259
Understanding the Domain Name System (DNS) 259
Configuring DNS 266

Chapter **1**

Browsing the Web

The Internet's been around for quite a while, but it didn't reach the masses until the web came along in 1993. Before the web was created, you had to use a set of arcane Unix commands to download and use files, which was simply too complicated for most of us. With the web, however, anyone can enjoy the benefits of the Internet by using a *web browser* — a graphical application that downloads and displays web documents. A click of the mouse is all you need to go from reading a document from your company website to watching a video clip housed on a server thousands of miles away.

In this chapter, I briefly describe the web and introduce Mozilla Firefox — the primary web browser (and, for that matter, mail and newsreader, too) in most Linux distributions.

REMEMBER

Many other web browsers are available, and some are included with various distributions, but after you've used one web browser, you can easily use any other web browser.

Surfing the Web

If you've used a file server at work, you know the convenience of sharing files. You can use the word processor on your desktop to get to any document on the shared server. Now imagine a word processor that enables you to open and view a document that resides on any computer on the Internet. You can view the document in its full glory, with formatted text and graphics. If the document makes a reference to another document (possibly residing on yet another computer), you can open that linked document simply by clicking the reference. That kind of easy access to distributed documents is essentially what the web provides.

The documents have to be in a standard format, of course, so that any computer (with the appropriate web browser software) can access and interpret the document. And a standard protocol is necessary for transferring web documents from one system to another.

TECHNICAL STUFF

The standard web document format is *Hypertext Markup Language* (HTML), and the standard protocol for exchanging web documents is *Hypertext Transfer Protocol* (HTTP). HTML documents are text files and don't depend on any specific operating system, so they work on any system from Windows and Mac to any type of Unix and Linux.

REMEMBER

A *web server* is software that provides HTML documents to any client that makes the appropriate HTTP requests. A *web browser* is the client software that actually downloads an HTML document from a web server and displays the contents graphically.

Like a giant spider's web

The web is the combination of the web servers and the documents (HTML) that the servers offer. When you look at the web in this way, the web is like a giant book whose pages are scattered throughout the Internet. You use a web browser running on your computer to view the pages; the pages are connected like a giant spider's web, with the documents everywhere.

Imagine that the web pages — HTML documents — are linked by network connections that resemble a giant spider's web, so you can see why the web is called *the web*. The *World Wide* part comes from the fact that the web pages are scattered around the world.

Links and URLs

Like the pages of printed books, web pages contain text and graphics. Unlike printed books, however, web pages can include multimedia, such as video clips, sound, and links to other web pages.

The *links* in a web page are references to other web pages that you can follow to go from one page to another. The web browser typically displays these links as underlined text (in a different color) or as images. Each link is like an instruction to you — something like "For more information, please consult Chapter 4," as you might find in a book. In a web page, all you have to do is click the link; the web browser brings up the referenced page, even though that document may actually reside on a faraway computer somewhere on the Internet.

TECHNICAL STUFF

The links in a web page are referred to as *hypertext links* because when you click a link, the web browser jumps to the web page referenced by that link.

This arrangement brings up a question. In a printed book, you might ask the reader to go to a specific chapter or page in the book. How does a hypertext link indicate the location of the referenced web page? On the web, each web page has a special name, called a *Uniform Resource Locator* (URL). A URL uniquely specifies the location of a file on a computer. Figure 1-1 shows the parts of a URL.

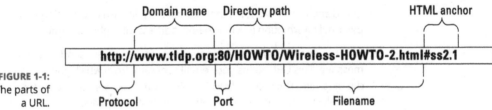

FIGURE 1-1:
The parts of a URL.

As Figure 1-1 shows, a URL has the following parts:

>> **Protocol:** Name of the protocol that the web browser uses to access the data from the file the URL specifies. In Figure 1-1, the protocol is `http://`, which means that the URL specifies the location of a web page. Here are some of the common protocol types and their meanings:

- `file://` means that the URL points to a local file. You can use this URL to view HTML files without having to connect to the Internet. The protocol `file:///var/www/html/index.html`, for example, opens the file `/var/www/html/index.html` from your Linux system.

- `ftp://` means that you can download a file by using File Transfer Protocol (FTP). The protocol `ftp://ftp.purdue.edu/pub/uns/NASA/nasa.jpg`, for example, refers to the image file `nasa.jpg` in the `/pub/uns/NASA` directory of the FTP server `ftp.purdue.edu`. If you want to access a specific user account via FTP, use a URL in the form

  ```
  ftp://username:password@ftp.somesite.com/
  ```

  with *username* and *password* embedded in the URL.

The password is in plain text and not secure.

- `http://` means that you download the file by using HTTP. This protocol is the well-known format of URLs for all websites, such as `www.amazon.com` for Amazon's home page. If the URL doesn't have a filename, the web server sends a default HTML file named `index.html`. (That filename is the default filename for the popular Unix-based Apache web servers; Microsoft Windows web servers use a different default filename.)

- `https://` specifies that you access the file through a Secure Sockets Layer (SSL) connection — a protocol designed by Netscape Communications for encrypted data transfers across the Internet. Typically, this form of URL is used when the web browser sends sensitive information (such as credit-card number, username, and password) to a web server. A URL such as

  ```
  https://some.site.com/secure/takeorder.html
  ```

  may display an HTML form that requests credit-card information and other personal information (such as name, address, and phone number).

- `mailto:` specifies an email address that you can use to send an email message. This URL opens your email program, from which you can send the message. The protocol `mailto:webmaster@someplace.com`, for example, refers to the webmaster at the host `someplace.com`.

- `news://` specifies a newsgroup that you can read by means of Network News Transfer Protocol (NNTP). The protocol

  ```
  news://news.md.comcast.giganews.com/comp.os.linux.setup
  ```

  accesses the `comp.os.linux.setup` newsgroup at the news server `news.md.comcast.giganews.com`. If you have a default news server configured for the web browser, you can omit the news server's name and use the URL `news:comp.os.linux.setup` to access the newsgroup.

>> **Domain name:** Contains the fully qualified domain name of the computer that has the file this URL specifies. You can also provide an IP address in this field. The domain name is not case-sensitive.

>> **Port:** Port number used by the protocol listed in the first part of the URL. This part of the URL is optional; all protocols have default ports. The default port for HTTP, for example, is 80. If a site configures the web server to listen to a different port, the URL has to include the port number.

>> **Directory path:** Directory path of the file referred to in the URL. For web pages, this field is the directory path of the HTML file. The directory path is case-sensitive.

>> **Filename:** Name of the file. For web pages, the filename typically ends with `.htm` or `.html`. If you omit the filename, the web server returns a default file (often named `index.html`). The filename is case-sensitive.

>> **HTML anchor:** Optional part of the URL that makes the web browser jump to a specific location in the file. If this part starts with a question mark (?) instead of a pound sign(#), the browser takes the text following the question mark to be a query. The web server returns information based on such queries.

Web servers and web browsers

The web server serves up the web pages, and the web browser downloads them and displays them to the user. That's pretty much the story with these two cooperating software packages that make the web work.

In a typical scenario, the user sits in front of a computer that's connected to the Internet and runs a web browser. When the user clicks a link or types a URL in the web browser, the browser connects to the web server and requests a document from the server. The web server sends the document (usually in HTML format) and ends the connection. The web browser interprets and displays the HTML document with text, graphics, and multimedia (if applicable).

The web browser's connection to the web server ends after the server sends the document. When the user browses through the downloaded document and clicks another hypertext link, the web browser again connects to the web server named in the hypertext link, downloads the document, ends the connection, and displays the new document. That's how the user can move from one document to another with ease.

REMEMBER

A web browser can do more than simply "talk" HTTP with the web server; web browsers can also download documents and files by using FTP, and many have integrated mail and newsreaders as well.

Web Browsing in Linux

As web pages become more interactive and complex, web browsing turns into a stimulating, engaging experience. Also, there's always the element of surprise: You can click a link and end up at unexpected web pages. Links are the most curious (and useful) aspect of the web. You can start at a page that shows today's weather, and a click later, you can be reading this week's issue of an online magazine.

Checking out web browsers for Linux

Many Linux distributions come with the Mozilla Firefox web browser. Firefox is Mozilla's improvement on its original browser, an open-source version of the venerable Netscape Communicator. Chrome, from Google, is popular as well and commonly used. Two other browsers that you might run across or consider using are

>> **Epiphany:** A GNOME web browser that uses parts of the Mozilla code to draw the web pages but has a simpler user interface than Mozilla

>> **Konqueror:** A KDE web browser that can also double as a file manager and a universal viewer

In addition to dedicated browser applications such as these, many applications are capable of downloading and displaying web pages.

DISTRIBUTION
SPECIFIC

If your distribution doesn't install Firefox by default, you can easily install it by typing **su -** to become root and then typing **apt-get install mozilla-firefox**.

Introducing Firefox's user interface

Typically, you can start Firefox by clicking an icon on the panel or by choosing Firefox from the GUI desktop's menu.

When Firefox starts, it displays a browser window with a default home page. (The main web page on a web server is the *home page.*) You can configure Firefox to use a different web page as the default home page.

Figure 1-2 shows a web page from a U.S. government website (www.irs.gov), as well as the main elements of the Firefox browser window.

TIP

Firefox supports *tabbed browsing,* which means that you can open a new tab (by pressing Ctrl+T or clicking the plus sign to the right of the last open tab) and view a web page in that tab. That way, you can view multiple web pages in a single window.

The Firefox web browser includes lots of features in its user interface, but you can master it easily. You can start with the basics to get going with Firefox and gradually expand to areas that you haven't yet explored.

Firefox toolbars

By default, the standard toolbar is hidden unless you chose to display it. If you choose to display it, then the toolbar appears, along with the options associated with the standard menus (File, Edit, and so on). You can configure what appears on the toolbar.

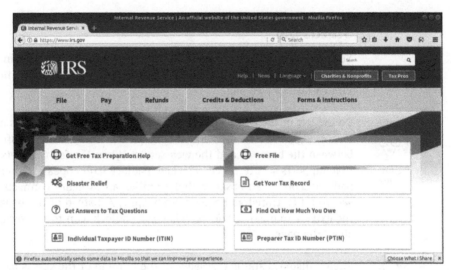

FIGURE 1-2:
The Firefox web
browser in action.

Here's what you can do with the buttons and text boxes on the Navigation toolbar, from left to right:

>> **Back:** Move to the previous web page.

>> **Location:** Show the URL of the current web page. (Type a URL in this box and press Enter to view that web page.)

>> **Show History:** Open a drop-down list of recently visited web pages.

>> **Reload:** Reload the current web page.

>> **Search:** Search by using Google (the default). You can change the default to another search engine.

>> **Bookmark:** Bookmark the page you're currently viewing. (Click the star icon at the end of the location bar.) To the right of this icon, you can view your bookmarks.

>> **Download:** See the progress of ongoing downloads or stop them.

>> **Home:** Go to the home page.

>> **Save to Pocket:** Save any article, video, or page that can display within Firefox to Pocket — a cache of sorts — and then view it later on this device or any other device.

>> **Firefox Screenshots:** Create screen shots during sessions and share them.

>> **Menu:** Open the options menu to perform tasks such as printing, opening a new private window, and configuring preferences.

Status bar

You can think of the bar along the bottom edge of the Firefox window as being the status bar, because the middle part of that area displays status information while Firefox loads a web page.

To the left of the URL, a padlock icon appears when you access a secure website. Firefox supports a secure version of HTTP that uses SSL to transfer encrypted data between the browser and the web server. When Firefox connects to a web server that supports secure HTTP, a locked-padlock icon appears. Otherwise, there's no padlock icon — an absence that signifies an insecure connection. The URL for secure HTTP transfers begins with https:// instead of the usual http:// (note the extra s in https). You can click the padlock icon to see security information about the page.

Firefox displays status messages at the left end of the status bar. You can watch the messages in this area to see what's going on. If you mouse over a link on the web page, the status bar displays the URL for that link.

Firefox menus

I haven't mentioned the Firefox menus much because you can usually get by without having to go to them (and they don't appear by default). Nevertheless, taking a quick look through the Firefox menus is worthwhile so that you know what each menu offers should you choose to display it (see Figure 1-3 for an example). Table 1-1 gives you an overview of the Firefox menus.

FIGURE 1-3:
The Firefox web browser with the menus configured to appear.

TABLE 1-1   **Firefox Menus**

Menu	Enables You to Do the Following
File	Open a file or web location, open or close a tab, send a web page or link by email, edit a web page, print the current page, and quit Firefox.
Edit	Copy and paste selections, find text in the current page, and edit your preferences.
View	Show or hide various toolbars, reload the current page, make the text larger or smaller, and view the HTML code for the page.
History	Go backward and forward in the list of pages you've visited or jump to other recently visited web pages.
Bookmarks	Bookmark a page, organize the bookmarks, and add links to the Bookmarks toolbar folder. (These links appear on the Bookmarks toolbar.)
Tools	Search the web and manage various aspects of the web page, such as themes; view information about the current page; and clear browsing history.
Help	Get online help on Firefox.

Changing your home page

Your home page is the page that Firefox loads when you start it. The default home page depends on the distribution. Often, the home page is a file from your system's hard drive. Changing the home page is easy.

First, locate the page on the web that you want to be the home page. You can get to that page any way you want. You can search with a search engine to find the page you want, type the URL in the Location text box, or even accidentally end up on a page that you want to make your home page. It doesn't matter.

When you're viewing the web page that you want to make your home page in Firefox, choose Edit➪Preferences. The Preferences page appears, as shown in Figure 1-4.

In Figure 1-4, the first set of options on the General page allows you to configure the home page. Below the text box is a Use Current Page button. Click that button to make the current page your home page. If you select this option while multiple tabs are open, the browser opens each tab with every new session.

REMEMBER

You can set a lot of other options in the Preferences pages. One set of options worth noting are those that appear in the Privacy & Security section (shown in Figure 1-5). You can use these options to configure how you want the browser to respond when it comes across a potential phishing threat or dangerous download.

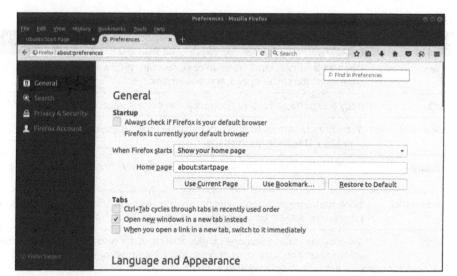

FIGURE 1-4:
Configure the Firefox browser to suit your preferences.

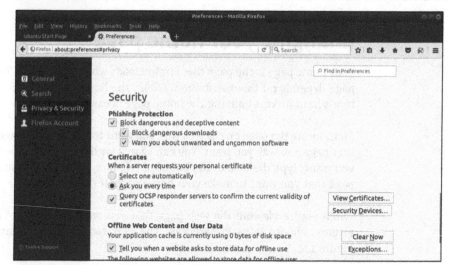

FIGURE 1-5:
In the Privacy & Security configuration settings, you can direct the browser to attempt to block dangerous and deceptive content.

Although I don't explain all the options here, click around to explore everything that you can do in this window. You can click the Use Bookmark button to select a saved URL bookmark as the home page, for example. (You have to select the bookmark from a dialog box.)

Surfing the Internet with Firefox

Where you go from the home page depends on you. All you have to do is click and see where you end up. Move your mouse around. You know when you're on a link because the mouse pointer changes to a hand with an extended index finger. Click the link, and Firefox downloads the web page referenced by that link.

How you use the web depends on what you want to do. When you get started, you may explore a lot, browsing websites and following links without any specific goal in mind (doing what you might call web window-shopping).

Another, more purposeful use of the web is to find specific information. You may want to locate all the websites that contain documents with a specified keyword, for example. For such a search, you can use one of many web search tools. Firefox's Search text box, for example, takes you to the Google Web Search page (www.google.com).

A third type of use is to visit a specific site with a known URL. When you read about a particular topic in this book, for example, you may come across a specific URL. In that case, you want to go directly to that web page.

TIP

To surf the Internet with Firefox, all you need is a starting web page. Then you can click whatever catches your fancy. Try this: Select the text in the Location text box on Firefox's Navigation toolbar, type **www.wiley.com**, and then press Enter. You go to the Wiley home page, which shows the various imprints (including the *Dummies* series) that Wiley publishes. There's your starting point. All you have to do is click, and you're on your way.

Chapter **2**

Using FTP

A s the name implies, *File Transfer Protocol* (FTP) is used to transfer files between computers. If your Internet service provider (ISP) gives you space for a personal website, you may have already used FTP to upload the files making up the website. Using an FTP client on your computer, you log in to your ISP account, provide your password, and then copy the files from your home system to the ISP's server.

You can also use FTP to download other files anonymously, such as open-source software from other computers on the Internet, in which case you don't need an account on the remote system to download files. You can simply log in by using anonymous as the username and provide your email address as the password. (Your web browser can log you in this way on your behalf, so you may not even know that the process is happening.) This type of *anonymous FTP* is great for distributing files to anyone who wants them. A hardware vendor might use anonymous FTP to provide updated device drivers to anyone who needs them, for example.

You should know that although FTP is still popular, it isn't as popular as it once was. Not long ago, email providers placed low limits on the amount of storage space client accounts were allowed to have and on the sizes of files that could be sent as attachments. Over the past few years, both of those limits have changed substantially. Although limits may still exist on attachment sizes, those limits are many times larger than they used to be, and many providers now offer unlimited storage. As these restrictions on email have eased, the use of FTP has decreased, but it's far from going away.

Linux comes with several FTP clients, both command-line clients and graphical user interface (GUI) clients. This chapter introduces a few GUI FTP clients and a command-line FTP client. It also describes the commands you use to work with remote directories.

Depending on your Linux distribution and version, you may need to install the FTP clients discussed in this chapter.

TIP

Using Graphical FTP Clients

You can use one of the following GUI FTP clients in Linux:

» **gFTP:** A graphical FTP client (www.gftp.org).

» **FileZilla:** A graphical FTP client for Linux and Windows platforms (https://filezilla-project.org).

» **Web browser:** A browser such as Firefox for anonymous FTP downloads

For uploading files, you may want to use gFTP or FileZilla because typically, you have to provide a username and password for such transfers. Web browsers work fine for anonymous downloads, which is how you typically download software from the Internet.

All three GUI FTP clients are discussed in the next three sections.

Using gFTP

Some distributions come with gFTP, a graphical FTP client, but gFTP usually isn't installed by default. In Ubuntu, you can install it with the command **sudo apt install gftp**; then enable the component called universe. In other distributions, you can download the client from www.gftp.org and install it easily.

gFTP hasn't been updated for several years, but it's still widely used, which speaks to its robustness and suitability for the job.

TECHNICAL
STUFF

After you install it, start gFTP from the main menu, from the application window, or from the desktop search feature. The gFTP window appears, as shown in Figure 2-1.

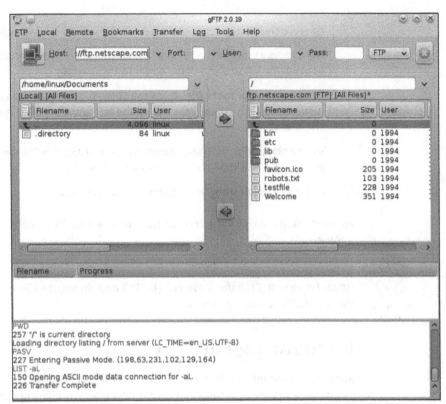

FIGURE 2-1:
The gFTP window
after opening a
connection to an
FTP server.

The gFTP window has a menu bar with menus for performing various tasks. Below the menu bar is a toolbar with buttons and text fields where you can type the name or IP address of the remote host, as well as the username and password needed to log in to the remote host. Figure 2-1 shows the gFTP window after you fill in this information and establish a connection with the remote host by clicking the button with the icon showing two computers (the leftmost one on the toolbar).

To upload or download files with gFTP, follow these steps:

1. **Enter the hostname or the IP address of the remote system in the Host field.**

   If you've used that host before, you can choose it from the drop-down menu that appears when you click the down arrow next to the Host field.

2. **Provide the username in the User field and the password in the Pass field, and then click the button with the icon showing two computers (to the left of the Host field).**

   This operation causes gFTP to connect to your chosen host and to log in with the username and password you provided. The bottom of the gFTP window shows the FTP protocol messages exchanged between the two systems.

Using FTP

3. **Observe the bottom part of the screen for any error messages.**

The directory listing of the remote system appears on the right side of the gFTP window. The left side shows the current local directory.

4. **To upload one or more files from the current system to the remote system, select the files in the list on the left and then click the right-arrow button.**

5. **To download files from the remote system, select the filenames in the list on the right and then click the left-arrow button.**

6. **When you finish transferring files, choose FTP⇨Quit.**

As these steps show, transferring files with a GUI FTP client such as gFTP is simple.

Believe it or not, gFTP isn't for FTP transfers alone. It can also transfer files by using Hypertext Transfer Protocol (HTTP) and do secure file transfers by using the Secure Shell (SSH) protocol.

Introducing FileZilla

FileZilla is another GUI FTP client for Windows and Linux. It's similar to gFTP, but its development continues (whereas development has stopped on gFTP). The two programs are similar in look and operation. You find FileZilla at `https://filezilla-project.org` (as shown in Figure 2-2). It works in all distributions and in both GNOME and KDE.

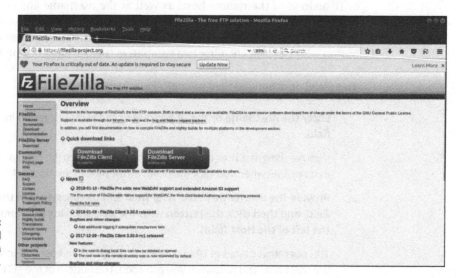

FIGURE 2-2:
Download
FileZilla from
this site.

When the main FileZilla window appears, it displays your home folder in a view similar to that of Windows Explorer. To connect to an FTP server, type the name or IP address of the remote host, along with the username and password needed to log in to the remote host. Figure 2-3 shows the FileZilla window after you fill in this information and establish a connection with the remote host.

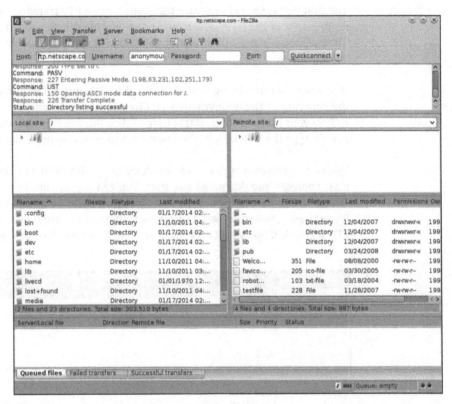

FIGURE 2-3:
FileZilla window displays the local directory and the remote FTP server's directory.

Now you can upload or download files with FileZilla just as you would with gFTP.

FTP transfers become just normal drag-and-drop file copying: Transfer files by dragging them from one system's folder and dropping them on the other system's folder.

When you finish, choose File⇨Quit.

Using a web browser as an FTP client

Any web browser can act as an FTP client, but such programs are best for anonymous FTP downloads, in which the web browser can log in by using the anonymous username and any password.

You can use the Firefox web browser as an FTP client, for example. All you have to know is how to write the URL so that the web browser can tell that you want to use FTP to download a file. The syntax of the FTP URL is

```
ftp://hostname/pathname
```

The first part (ftp://) indicates that you want an FTP transfer. The *hostname* part is the name of the FTP server (and often starts with ftp, as in ftp.wiley.com). The *pathname* is the full directory path and filename of the file that you want to download.

If you simply provide the hostname for the FTP server, the web browser displays the contents of the anonymous FTP directory. If you want to access anonymous FTP on your Linux system, start Firefox (click the web browser icon on the GNOME panel), type the FTP URL in the Location text box, and press Enter.

Figure 2-4 shows a typical FTP directory in Firefox. You can click folders to see their contents and download any files. You can access your local system by using Firefox's FTP capabilities. Type **ftp://localhost/pub/** to access the pub directory, for example. (You won't get a response from your system if you're not running an FTP server or if you've set up your firewall so that no FTP connections are allowed.)

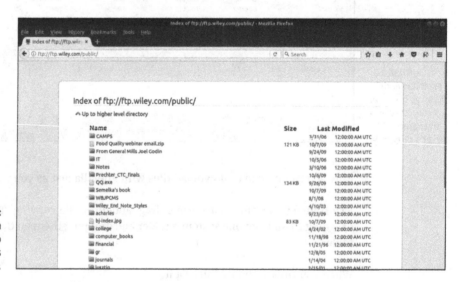

FIGURE 2-4:
You can use a web browser to download files from FTP servers.

DISTRIBUTION SPECIFIC

In Debian and Fedora, log in as root and type **/etc/init.d/vsftpd start** (in a terminal window) to start the FTP server. In SUSE, the xinetd super server controls the FTP server vsftpd. The /etc/xinetd.d/vsftpd configuration file specifies how vsftpd is started. (See Book 5, Chapter 1 for more information about xinetd configuration files.)

The same method of accessing anonymous FTP sites works if you type the host name of some other anonymous FTP server. Try typing the URL **ftp://ftp.wiley.com/**. You get the directory of the `ftp.wiley.com` server.

Using the Command-Line FTP Client

Knowing how to use FTP from the command line is a good idea. If your GUI desktop isn't working, for example, you may need to download some files to fix the problem; you can do so if you know how to use the command-line FTP client. The command-line FTP client is available in all Linux distributions, and using it isn't difficult.

The best way to figure out the command-line FTP client is to try it. The command is `ftp`, and you can try the `ftp` commands from your Linux system. You don't even need an Internet connection, because you can use the `ftp` command to connect to your own system.

Note: Your output from the `ftp` command may be different from what you see in this book because some distributions, such as Debian, use a text=mode version of gFTP as the command-line FTP client.

In the following sample FTP session, the command-line FTP client was used to log in and browse the directories on a Linux system. Here's the listing, illustrating interaction with a typical command-line FTP client:

```
ftp localhost
Connected to localhost.localdomain.
220 (vsFTPd 2.0.3)
Name (localhost:jdoe): (press Enter.)
331 Please specify the password.
Password: (enter the password for the user.)
230 Login successful.
Remote system type is Unix.
Using binary mode to transfer files.
ftp> help
Commands may be abbreviated. Commands are:
!        debug      mdir     qc        send
$        dir        mget     sendport  site
account  disconnect mkdir    put       size
append   exit       mls      pwd       status
ascii    form       mode     quit      struct
bell     get        modtime  quote     system
```

```
binary   glob      mput     recv      sunique
bye      hash      newer    reget     tenex
case     help      nmap     rstatus   tick
cd       idle      nlist    rhelp     trace
cdup     image     ntrans   rename    type
chmod    lcd       open     reset     user
close    ls        prompt   restart   umask
cr       macdef    passive  rmdir     verbose
delete   mdelete   proxy    runique   ?
ftp> help mget (to get help on a specific command.)
mget get multiple files
ftp> cd /var (This changes directory to /var.)
250 Directory successfully changed.
ftp> ls (This command lists the contents of the directory.)
227 Entering Passive Mode (127,0,0,1,38,142)
150 Here comes the directory listing.
. . . lines deleted . . .
226 Directory send OK.
ftp> bye(This command ends the session.)
```

As the listing shows, you can start the command-line FTP client by typing the command **ftp** *hostname*, where *hostname* is the name of the system you want to access. When the FTP client establishes a connection with the FTP server at the remote system, the FTP server prompts you for a username and password. After you supply the information, the FTP client displays the ftp> prompt, and you can begin typing commands to perform specific tasks. If you can't remember a specific FTP command, type **help** to view a list of commands. You can get additional help for a specific command by typing **help** *command*, where *command* is the command for which you want help.

Many FTP commands are similar to the Linux commands for navigating the file system. The command cd changes the directory, for example; pwd prints the name of the current working directory; and ls lists the contents of the current directory. Two other common commands are get, which downloads a file from the remote system to your system, and put, which uploads (sends) a file from your system to the remote host.

Table 2-1 describes some commonly used FTP commands. You don't have to type the entire FTP command. For a long command, you have to type only the first few characters — enough to identify the command uniquely. To delete a file, for example, you can type **dele**; to change the file transfer mode to binary, you can type **bin**.

TABLE 2-1 **Common FTP Commands**

Command	Description
!	Executes a shell command on the local system. !ls, for example, lists the contents of the current directory on the local system.
?	Displays a list of commands (same as help).
append	Appends a local file to a remote file.
ascii	Sets the file transfer type to ASCII (or plain text). This command is the default file transfer type.
binary	Sets the file transfer type to binary.
bye	Ends the FTP session with the remote FTP server and quits the FTP client.
cd	Changes the directory on the remote system. cd /pub/Linux, for example, changes the remote directory to /pub/Linux.
chmod	Changes the permission settings of a remote file. chmod 644 index.html, for example, changes the permission settings of the index.html file on the remote system.
close	Ends the FTP session with the FTP server and returns to the FTP client's prompt.
delete	Deletes a remote file. delete bigimage.jpg, for example, deletes that file on the remote system.
dir	Lists the contents of the current directory on the remote system.
disconnect	Ends the FTP session and returns to the FTP client's prompt. (This command is the same as close.)
get	Downloads a remote file. get junk.tar.gz junk.tgz, for example, downloads the file junk.tar.gz from the remote system and saves it as the file junk.tgz on the local system.
hash	Turns on or off the hash-mark (#) printing that shows the progress of the file transfer. When this feature is turned on, a hash mark prints onscreen for every 1,024 bytes transferred from the remote system. (This feature is the command-line version of a progress bar.)
help	Displays a list of commands.
image	Same as binary.
lcd	Changes the current directory on the local system. lcd/var/ftp/pub, for example, changes the current local directory to /var/ftp/pub.
ls	Lists the contents of the current remote directory.
mdelete	Deletes multiple files on a remote system. mdelete *.jpg, for example, deletes all remote files with names ending in .jpg in the current directory.

(continued)

Using FTP

TABLE 2-1 *(continued)*

Command	Description
mdir	Lists multiple remote files and saves the listing in a specified local file. mdir /usr/ share/doc/w* wlist, for example, saves the listing in the local file named wlist.
mget	Downloads multiple files. mget *.jpg, for example, downloads all files with names ending in .jpg. If the prompt is turned on, the FTP client asks for confirmation before downloading each file.
mkdir	Creates a directory on the remote system. mkdir images, for example, creates a directory named images in the current directory on the remote system.
mls	Same as mdir.
mput	Uploads multiple files. mput *.jpg, for example, sends all files with names ending in .jpg to the remote system. If the prompt is turned on, the FTP client asks for confirmation before sending each file.
open	Opens a connection to the FTP server on the specified host. open ftp.netscape.com, for example, connects to the FTP server on the host ftp.netscape.com.
prompt	Turns the prompt on or off. When the prompt is on, the FTP client prompts you for confirmation before downloading or uploading each file during a multiple-file transfer.
put	Sends a file to the remote system. put index.html, for example, sends the index. html file from the local system to the remote system.
pwd	Displays the full pathname of the current directory on the remote system. When you log in as a user, the initial current working directory is your home directory.
quit	Same as bye.
recv	Same as get.
rename	Renames a file on the remote system. rename old.html new.html, for example, renames the file old.html to new.html on the remote system.
rmdir	Deletes a directory on the remote system. rmdir images, for example, deletes the images directory in the current directory of the remote system.
send	Same as put.
size	Shows the size of a remote file. size bigfile.tar.gz, for example, shows the size of that remote file.
status	Shows the current status of the FTP client.
user	Sends new user information to the FTP server. User jdoe, for example, sends the username jdoe; then the FTP server prompts for the password for that username.

TIP

When downloading files from the Internet, you almost always want to transfer the files in binary mode, because the software is usually archived and compressed in binary form. (Its files aren't plain-text files.) Always use the binary command to set the mode to binary; then use the get command to download the files.

TIP

When transferring multiple files with similar names (such as image1.jpg, image2.jpg, and so on), type **prompt** to turn off prompting. (Otherwise, the FTP client asks you after each file transfer whether you want to transfer the next file.) Then type **mget** followed by the filename with a wildcard character. To download all files with names starting with image and ending with the .jpg extension, for example, type **mget image*.jpg**.

Using FTP

» **Controlling servers through inetd or xinetd**

» **Using chkconfig or update-rc.d to manage servers**

» **Using GUI utilities to configure services to start at boot time**

Chapter **3**

Hosting Internet Services

The Internet is a world of clients and servers; in other words, it's a giant network built as you would a local-area network and then scaled way beyond that. Clients make requests to servers, and servers respond to the requests. Your web browser, for example, is a client that downloads information from web servers and displays it to you. The clients and servers are computer programs that run on a wide variety of computers, of course. A Linux system is an ideal system to run different types of servers, from a web server to a Windows file and print server.

This chapter provides an overview of a typical Internet service and its client/server architecture and discusses how to manage the servers in Linux. You can use the information in this chapter to manage any server running on your Linux system.

Understanding Internet Services

Internet services are network applications designed to deliver information from one system to another. By design, each Internet service is implemented in two parts: a *server* that provides information and one or more *clients* that request information.

Such a *client/server* architecture is the most common way to build distributed information systems. The clients and servers are computer programs that run on these computers and communicate through the network. The neat part is that you can run a client at your desktop computer and access information from a server running on a computer anywhere in the world (as long as it's on the Internet).

The web itself, email, and File Transfer Protocol (FTP) are examples of Internet services that use the client/server model. When you use the web, for example, you use the web browser client to download and view web pages from the web server.

REMEMBER

Client/server architecture requires clients to communicate with the servers. That's where Transmission Control Protocol/Internet Protocol (TCP/IP) — comes in. TCP/IP provides a standard way for clients and servers to exchange packets of data. The next few sections explain how TCP/IP-based services communicate.

TCP/IP and sockets

Client/server applications such as the web and FTP use TCP/IP for data transfers between client and server. These Internet applications typically use TCP/IP communications using the Berkeley sockets interface (so named because the socket interface was introduced in Berkeley Unix around 1982). The sockets interface is nothing physical; it's computer code that a computer programmer can use to create applications that can communicate with other applications on the Internet.

REMEMBER

Even if you don't write network applications that use sockets, you may have to use or set up many network applications. Knowledge of sockets can help you understand how network-based applications work, which in turn helps you find and correct any problems with these applications.

Socket definition

Network applications use sockets to communicate over a TCP/IP network. A *socket* represents one end point of a connection. Because a socket is bidirectional, data can be sent as well as received through it. A socket has three attributes:

>> The *network address* (the IP address) of the system.

>> The *port number,* identifying the process (a *process* is a computer program running on a computer) that exchanges data through the socket.

>> The *type of socket,* identifying the protocol for data exchange.

Essentially, the IP address identifies a computer (host) on the network; the port number identifies a process (server) on the node; and the socket type determines the manner in which data is exchanged — through a connection-oriented (stream) or connectionless (datagram) protocol.

Connection-oriented protocols

The socket type indicates the protocol being used to communicate through the socket. A connection-oriented protocol works like a normal phone conversation. When you want to talk to a friend, you have to dial your friend's phone number and establish a connection before you can have a conversation. In the same way, connection-oriented data exchange requires both the sending and receiving processes to establish a connection before data exchange can begin.

In the TCP/IP protocol suite, Transmission Control Protocol (TCP) supports a connection-oriented data transfer between two processes running on two computers on the Internet. TCP provides reliable two-way data exchange between processes.

As the name TCP/IP suggests, TCP relies on Internet Protocol (IP) for delivery of packets. IP doesn't guarantee delivery of packets; neither does it deliver packets in any particular sequence. IP, however, efficiently moves packets from one network to another. TCP is responsible for arranging the packets in the proper sequence, detecting whether errors have occurred, and requesting retransmission of packets in case of an error.

TCP is useful for applications intended to exchange large amounts of data at a time. In addition, applications that need reliable data exchange use TCP. (FTP, for example, uses TCP to transfer files.)

In the sockets model, a socket that uses TCP is referred to as a *stream socket.*

Connectionless protocols

A *connectionless* data-exchange protocol doesn't require the sender and receiver to establish a connection explicitly. Using this protocol is like shouting to a friend in a crowded room; you can't be sure that your friend hears you.

In the TCP/IP protocol suite, the User Datagram Protocol (UDP) provides connectionless service for sending and receiving packets known as *datagrams.* Unlike TCP, UDP doesn't guarantee that datagrams ever reach their intended destinations. Neither does UDP ensure that datagrams are delivered in the order in which they're sent.

UDP is used by applications that exchange small amounts of data at a time and by applications that don't need the reliability and sequencing of data delivery. Simple Network Management Protocol (SNMP), for example, uses UDP to transfer data.

In the sockets model, a socket that uses UDP is referred to as a *datagram socket.*

Sockets and the client/server model

Two sockets are needed to complete a communication path. When two processes communicate, they use the client/server model to establish the connection. (Figure 3-1 illustrates the concept.) The server application listens on a specific port on the system; the server is completely identified by the IP address of the system where it runs and the port number where it listens for connections. The client initiates a connection from any available port and tries to connect to the server (identified by the IP address and port number). When the connection is established, the client and the server can exchange data according to their own protocol.

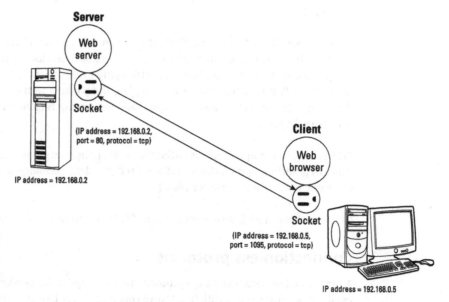

FIGURE 3-1:
Client and server
processes use
two sockets to
communicate.

The sequence of events in socket-based data exchanges depends on whether the transfer is connection-oriented (TCP) or connectionless (UDP).

For a connection-oriented data transfer using sockets, the server listens on a specific port, waiting for clients to request connection. Data transfer begins only after a connection is established.

For connectionless data transfers, the server waits for a datagram to arrive at a specified port. The client doesn't wait to establish a connection; it simply sends a datagram to the server.

Regardless of whether it's a server or a client, each application first creates a socket. Then it *associates* (binds) the socket with the local computer's IP address and a port number. The IP address identifies the machine (where the application is running), and the port number identifies the application using the socket.

REMEMBER

Servers typically listen to a well-known port number so that clients can connect to that port to access the server. For a client application, the process of binding a socket to the IP address and port is the same as that for a server, but the client can use 0 as the port number; the sockets library automatically uses an unused port number for the client.

For a connection-oriented stream socket, the communicating client and server applications have to establish a connection. The exact steps for establishing a connection depend on whether the application is a server or a client.

REMEMBER

In the client/server model, the server must be up and running before the client can run. After creating a socket and binding the socket to a port, the server application sets up a queue of connections, which determines how many clients can connect to the server. Typically, a server listens to one to five connections. The size of this so-called *listen queue*, however, is one of the parameters you can adjust (especially for a web server) to ensure that the server responds to as many clients as possible. After setting up the listen queue, the server waits for a connection from a client.

Establishing the connection from the client side is somewhat simpler. After creating a socket and binding the socket to an IP address, the client establishes a connection with the server. To make the connection, the client must know the host name or IP address of the server, as well as the port on which the server accepts connection. All Internet services have well-known standard port numbers.

TECHNICAL STUFF

After a client establishes a connection to a server via a connection-oriented stream socket, the client and server can exchange data by calling the appropriate sockets' API functions. As in a conversation between two people, the server and client alternately send and receive data; the meaning of the data depends on the message protocol that the server and clients use. Usually, a server is designed for a specific task; inherent in that design is a message protocol that the server and clients use to exchange necessary data. The web server and the web browser (client), for example, communicate by using Hypertext Transfer Protocol (HTTP).

Internet services and port numbers

The TCP/IP protocol suite is the lingua franca of the Internet because the Internet services *speak* TCP/IP. These services make the Internet tick by making possible the transfer of mail, news, and web pages. Each Internet service has its own protocol that relies on TCP/IP for the actual transfer of the information. Each service also has one or more assigned port numbers that it uses to do whatever it's designed to do. Here are some well-known Internet services and their associated protocols:

>> **DHCP (Dynamic Host Configuration Protocol):** Dynamically configures TCP/IP network parameters on a computer. DHCP is used primarily to assign dynamic IP addresses and other networking information such as name server, default gateway, and domain names that are needed to configure TCP/IP networks. The DHCP server listens on port 67.

>> **DNS (Domain Name System):** Translates URLs to IP addresses. It's typically associated with network routing and operates on port 53.

>> **FTP (File Transfer Protocol):** Transfers files between computers on the Internet. FTP uses two ports: Data is transferred on port 20, and control information is exchanged on port 21.

>> **HTTP (Hypertext Transfer Protocol):** Sends documents from one system to another. HTTP is the underlying protocol of the web. By default, the web server and client communicate on port 80.

>> **SMTP (Simple Mail Transfer Protocol):** Exchanges email messages between systems. SMTP uses port 25 for information exchange.

>> **POPv3 (Post Office Protocol version 3):** Retrieves files from the mail server. Just as SMTP exchanges email messages between systems, POP is used by clients to retrieve mail form such a server. It operates on port 110.

>> **IMAPv4 (Internet Messages Access Protocol version 4):** Reads mail from the mail server. Instead of using POP to retrieve mail, IMAP can be used to access it directly on the server by the client. It operates on port 143.

>> **SSH (Secure Shell):** Enables secure remote login and other secure network services over an insecure network. SSH uses port 22.

>> **TELNET:** Enables a user on one system to log in to another system on the Internet. (The user must provide a valid user ID and password to log in to the remote system.) Telnet uses port 23 by default, but the Telnet client can connect to any specified port.

>> **NFS (Network File System):** Shares files among computers. NFS uses Sun's Remote Procedure Call (RPC) facility, which exchanges information through port 111.

>> **NTP (Network Time Protocol):** Synchronizes the system time on a client computer with that on a server that has a more accurate clock. NTP uses port 123.

>> **SNMP (Simple Network Management Protocol):** Manages all types of network devices on the Internet. Like FTP, SNMP uses two ports: 161 and 162.

>> **TFTP (Trivial File Transfer Protocol):** Transfers files from one system to another. (It's typically used by X terminals and diskless workstations to download boot files from another host on the network.) TFTP data transfer takes place on port 69.

Each service is provided by a *server process* — a computer program that runs on a system awaiting client requests that arrive at the well-known port associated with its service. Thus, the web server expects client requests at port 80, the standard port for HTTP service.

The /etc/services text file on your Linux system stores the association between a service name and a port number (as well as a protocol). Here's a small subset of entries in the /etc/services file from a Linux system:

```
ftp-data 20/tcp
ftp 21/tcp
fsp 21/udp fspd
ssh 22/tcp # SSH Remote Login Protocol
ssh 22/udp
telnet 23/tcp
smtp 25/tcp mail
time 37/tcp timserver
time 37/udp timserver
rlp 39/udp resource # resource location
nameserver 42/tcp name # IEN 116
whois 43/tcp nicname
tacacs 49/tcp # Login Host Protocol (TACACS)
```

A quick look through the entries in the /etc/services file shows the breadth of networking services available under TCP/IP.

REMEMBER

Port number 80 is designated for web services. In other words, if you set up a web server on your system, that server listens to port 80. By the way, the Internet Assigned Numbers Authority (IANA; www.iana.org) is the organization responsible for coordinating the assignment of port numbers below 1,024.

Using the Internet Super Server

The client/server architecture of Internet services requires the server to be up and running before a client makes a request for service. It's probably a bad idea to run all the servers all the time; doing so is impractical because each server process uses system resources in the form of memory and processor time. Besides, you don't really need *all* the services up and ready at all times. Instead, run a single server that listens to all the ports and starts the appropriate server when a client request comes in. Such a server is known as an *Internet super server* because it starts various services on demand.

DISTRIBUTION SPECIFIC

The two Internet super servers are inetd and xinetd. The inetd server is the older one and is still used in Linux distributions such as Debian, Knoppix, and Ubuntu. The xinetd server is a replacement for inetd, offering improved access control and logging. The name xinetd stands for *extended* inetd. Distributions such as Fedora and SUSE use xinetd.

Using inetd

In Linux distributions that use inetd, the system starts inetd when the system boots. The inetd server reads a configuration file named /etc/inetd.conf at startup. This file tells inetd which ports to listen to and what server to start for each port. The entry in the /etc/inetd.conf file that starts Internet Message Access Protocol (IMAP) on one server looks like this:

```
imaps stream tcp nowait root /usr/sbin/tcpd /usr/sbin/imapd
```

The first item on this line, imaps, tells inetd the name of the service. inetd uses this name to look up the port number from the /etc/services file. If you type **grep imaps /etc/services**, you find that the port number of the IMAP service is 993. This specification tells inetd to listen to port 993 for FTP service requests.

The rest of the fields in the IMAP entry have the following meanings:

>> The second and third fields of the entry, stream and tcp, tell inetd that the FTP service uses a connection-oriented TCP socket to communicate with the client. For services that use the connectionless UDP sockets, these two fields are dgram and udp.

>> The fourth field, nowait, tells inetd to start a new server for each request. If this field is wait, inetd waits until the server exits before starting the server again.

>> The fifth field provides the user ID that inetd uses to run the server. In this case, the server runs the FTP server as root.

>> The sixth field specifies the program to run for this service and the last field is the argument that inetd passes to the server program. In this case, the /usr/sbin/tcpd program is provided /usr/sbin/imapd as an argument.

TECHNICAL STUFF

The `/usr/sbin/tcpd` program is an access-control facility, or a *TCP wrapper,* for Internet services. Because unnecessary Internet services are often the sources of security vulnerabilities, you may want to turn off any unneeded services or at least control access to the services. The `tcpd` program can start other services, such as FTP and Telnet, but before starting the service, `tcpd` consults the `/etc/hosts.allow` file to see whether the host requesting service is allowed that service. If nothing is in `/etc/hosts.allow` about that host, `tcpd` checks the `/etc/hosts.deny` file to see whether the service should be denied. If both files are empty, `tcpd` allows the host access to the requested service. You can place the line `ALL:ALL` in the `/etc/hosts.deny` file to deny all hosts access to any Internet services.

TIP

Browse through the `/etc/inetd.conf` file on your system to find out the kinds of services that `inetd` is set up to start. Nowadays, most `inetd` services are turned off, and many others, such as FTP, are started by stand-alone servers. In any case, if you see any services that you want to turn off, simply place a hash mark (#) at the beginning of the lines that start these services. When you make such a change in the `/etc/inetd.conf` file, type **/etc/init.d/inetd restart** to restart the `inetd` server.

Using xinetd

Linux distributions that use `xinetd` start `xinetd` when the system boots. The `xinetd` server reads a configuration file named `/etc/xinetd.conf` at startup. This file tells `xinetd` which ports to listen to and what server to start for each port. The file can contain instructions that include other configuration files. In Linux, the `/etc/xinetd.conf` file looks like the following:

```
# Simple configuration file for xinetd
#
# Set some defaults and include /etc/xinetd.d/
defaults
{
instances = 30
log_type = FILE /var/log/xinetd.log
log_on_success = HOST EXIT DURATION
log_on_failure = HOST ATTEMPT
cps = 50 10
}
includedir /etc/xinetd.d
```

Comment lines begin with the hash mark (#). The default block of attributes, enclosed in curly braces ({ ... }), specifies default values for some attributes. These default values apply to all other services in the configuration file. The `instances` attribute is set to 30, which means that no more than 30 servers can be simultaneously active for any service.

The last line in the `/etc/xinetd.conf` file uses the `includedir` directive to include all files inside the `/etc/xinetd.d` directory, excluding files that begin with a period (.). The idea is that the `/etc/xinetd.d` directory contains all service-configuration files — one file for each type of service the `xinetd` server is expected to manage. Type **ls /etc/xinetd.d** to see the `xinetd` configuration files for your system. Each file in `/etc/xinetd.d` specifies attributes for one service that `xinetd` can start.

SUSE Linux uses `xinetd` to start some services, including the `vsftpd` (Very Secure FTP daemon) server. (A *daemon* is a process that runs continuously and never dies.) Type **cat /etc/xinetd.d/vsftpd** to see the `xinetd` configuration for the `vsftpd` service. Here's a typical listing of that file on a SUSE system:

```
# default: off
# description:
# The vsftpd FTP server serves FTP connections. It uses
# normal, unencrypted usernames and passwords for authentication.
# vsftpd is designed to be secure.
service ftp
{
socket_type = stream
protocol = tcp
wait = no
user = root
server = /usr/sbin/vsftpd
        }
```

The filename (in this case, `vsftpd`) can be anything; what matters is the service name that appears next to the `service` keyword in the file. In this case, the line `service ftp` tells `xinetd` the name of the service. `xinetd` uses this name to look up the port number from the `/etc/services` file.

The attributes in `/etc/xinetd.d/vsftpd`, enclosed in curly braces ({ ... }), have the following meanings:

» The `socket_type` attribute is set to `stream`, which tells `xinetd` that the FTP service uses a connection-oriented TCP socket to communicate with the client. For services that use the connectionless UDP sockets, this attribute is set to `dgram`.

» The `wait` attribute is set to `no`, which tells `xinetd` to start a new server for each request. If this attribute is set to `yes`, `xinetd` waits until the server exits before starting the server again.

» The user attribute provides the user ID that xinetd uses to run the server. In this case, the server runs the vsftpd server as root.

» The server attribute specifies the program to run for this service. In this case, xinetd runs the /usr/sbin/vsftpd program to provide the FTP service.

Browse through the files in the /etc/xinetd.d directory on your Linux system to find out the kinds of services xinetd is set up to start. If you want to turn off any service (many services are already disabled), you can do so by editing the configuration file for that service and adding the following line inside the curly braces that enclose all attributes:

```
disable = yes
```

When you make such a change in the xinetd configuration files, you must restart the xinetd server by typing the following command:

```
/etc/init.d/xinetd restart
```

REMEMBER

Typically, you can configure services to run under xinetd or as a stand-alone service. SUSE starts the Very Secure FTP daemon (vsftpd) under the control of xinetd. Debian and Fedora, however, run vsftpd as a stand-alone server.

Running Stand-Alone Servers

Starting servers through inetd or xinetd is a smart approach but not always efficient. A web server controlled by inetd or xinetd would be started often because every time a user clicks a link on a web page, a request arrives for the web service. For such high-demand services, starting the server in a stand-alone manner is best. In stand-alone mode, the server can run as a daemon, which means that the server listens on the assigned port, and whenever a request arrives, the server handles it by making a copy of itself. In this way, the server keeps running as long as the machine is running — in theory, forever. A more efficient strategy, used for web servers, is to run multiple copies of the server and let each copy handle some of the incoming requests.

You can easily configure your Linux system to start various stand-alone servers automatically, as shown in this section.

Starting and stopping servers manually

To start a service that's not running, use the server command. If the web server (called httpd in Fedora) isn't running, you can start it by issuing a special shell script with the following command:

```
/etc/init.d/httpd start
```

That command runs the /etc/init.d/httpd script with start as the argument. If the httpd server is already running and you want to stop it, run the same command with stop as the argument, like this:

```
/etc/init.d/httpd stop
```

To stop and start a server again, just use restart as the argument:

```
/etc/init.d/httpd restart
```

You can also check the status of any service by using status as the argument:

```
/etc/init.d/httpd status
```

DISTRIBUTION SPECIFIC

In Debian, Ubuntu, and SUSE, in which the web server program is called apache2, type **/etc/init.d/apache2 start** to start the web server. In Knoppix, type **/etc/init.d/apache start**. Use the same command with arguments stop or restart to stop the web server or restart it.

What are all the services that you can start and stop? Well, the answer is in the files in the /etc/init.d directory. To get a look at it, type the following command:

```
ls /etc/init.d
```

All the files you see listed in response to this command are the services installed on your Linux system; you can start and stop them as needed. Typically, you find quite a few services listed in the /etc/init.d directory.

Starting servers automatically at boot time

You can start, stop, and restart servers manually by using the scripts in the /etc/init.d directory, but you want some of the services to start as soon as you boot the Linux system. You can configure servers to start automatically at boot time by using a graphical server-configuration utility or a command.

**DISTRIBUTION
SPECIFIC**

The command for configuring services to start automatically depends on the distribution. In Debian, Knoppix, and Ubuntu, use the `update-rc.d` command. In Fedora and SUSE, use the `systemctl` command. Both commands are explained in the following sections.

Using the systemctl command in Fedora and SUSE

Earlier versions of Fedora and SUSE favored `chkconfig`, a command-line utility for checking and updating the current setting of servers in Linux. That functionality has largely been replaced by `systemctl`, a command that is both robust and is simple to use.

Various combinations of servers are set up to start automatically at different run levels. Each *run level* represents a system configuration in which a selected set of processes runs. You're usually concerned about run levels 3 and 5, because run level 3 is for text-mode login and run level 5 is for logging in through a graphical interface.

Suppose that you want to manually start the named server. All you do is log in as `root` and type the following command at the shell prompt:

```
systmctl named start
```

If you are not root, type the following command:

```
sudo systemctl named start
```

Likewise, if you want to turn off named, you can do so with this command:

```
sudo systemctl   named stop
```

Using the update-rc.d command in Debian, Knoppix, and Ubuntu

In Debian, Knoppix, and Ubuntu, you can use the `update-rc.d` command to set up services that should start when the system boots at specific boot levels. The easiest way to set up is to use the `defaults` option in a command of the form

```
update-rc.d service defaults
```

where *service* is the name of the script file in the `/etc/init.d` directory that starts and stops the service, among other things.

When you use the defaults option, update-rc.d sets up *symbolic links* — shortcuts, in other words — to start the service in run levels 2, 3, 4, and 5 and to stop the service in run levels 0, 1, and 6. A sequence number controls the order in which each service is started. (Services with smaller sequence numbers start before those with larger sequence numbers, and the numbers typically range from 00 through 99.) If you don't explicitly specify a sequence number, update-rc.d uses a sequence number of 20 when you use the defaults option.

You can also start and stop a service at specific run levels as well as in a specific sequence. To start a service at run levels 2 and 5 at a sequence number of 85 and stop it at run levels 0, 1, and 6 at a sequence of 90, use the following command:

```
update-rc.d service start 85 2 5 . stop 90 0 1 6 .
```

Remember that *service* must be the name of a script file in the /etc/init.d directory.

TIP

If you need to stop a service from starting at system startup, type **update-rc.d –f** *service* **remove** in a terminal window, where *service* is the name of the script file in /etc/init.d that starts or stops that service.

Using a GUI service-configuration utility

If you don't like typing commands, you may be able to use a graphical user interface (GUI) tool to configure the services. Fedora and SUSE include tools such as YaST and the service-configuration utility to manage the services.

The service-configuration utility shows the names of services in a scrolling list. Each line in the list shows the name of a service with a check box in front of the name. A check mark in the box indicates that the service is selected to start at boot time for the current run level. When the dialog box first appears, many services are already selected.

You can scroll up and down the list and click the check box to select or deselect a service. If you click the check box, the check mark alternately turns on and off. Additionally, the utility shows you whether the selected service is running.

After you select all the servers you want to start when the system boots, click the Apply button on the toolbar to save the changes.

WARNING

By default, the service-configuration utility configures the selected services for the current run level. If you're selecting services from the graphical desktop, the system is in run level 5, and the services you configure are set to start at run level 5. If you want to set up the services for a different level, choose that run level from the Edit Runlevel menu.

Table 3-1 lists and describes the services. The first column shows the name of the service, which is the same as the name of the program that has to run to provide the service. You may not see all these services listed when you run the GUI service-configuration utility on your system, because the exact list of services depends on what's installed on your Linux system.

TABLE 3-1   ## Some Common Services in Linux

Service Name	Description
acpid	Listens to Advanced Configuration and Power Interface (ACPI) events from the kernel and notifies other programs when such events occur. ACPI events can occur when the kernel puts the computer into a low-power state (such as standby mode) to save energy.
apache, apache2, or httpd	Runs the Apache World Wide Web (WWW) server.
apmd	Monitors the Advanced Power Management (APM) BIOS and logs the status of electric power (AC or battery backup).
atd	Runs commands scheduled by the at and cron commands.
autofs	Automatically mounts file systems (such as when you insert a CD-ROM in the CD-ROM drive).
cron or crond	Runs user-specified programs according to a periodic schedule set by the crontab command.
gpm	Enables the use of the mouse in text-mode screens.
innd	The InterNetNews daemon, which is the Internet news server you can use to support local newsgroups on your system.
isdn	Starts and stops ISDN (Integrated Services Digital Network) services, a digital communication service over regular phone lines (enable only if you have ISDN service).
named	Translates host names into IP addresses. named is a server for the Domain Name System (DNS). You can run a copy on your system if you want.
network or networking	Enables you to activate or deactivate all network interfaces configured to start at system boot time.
nfs or nfsserver	Enables sharing of file systems specified in the /etc/exports file by using the Network File System (NFS) protocol.
nfslock	Provides file-locking capability for file systems exported using NFS protocol so that other systems running NFS can share files from your system.
pcmcia	Provides support for PCMCIA devices.

(continued)

TABLE 3-1 *(continued)*

Service Name	Description
portmap	Works with any software that relies on Remote Procedure Calls (RPC). NFS requires the portmap service.
samba, smb, or smbfs	Starts and stops the Samba smbd and nmbd services, which support LAN Manager services on a Linux system.
sendmail	Moves mail messages from one machine to another. Start this service if you want to send mail from your Linux system. If you don't plan to use your Linux system as a mail server, don't start the sendmail server, because it can slow the booting process and consume resources unnecessarily.
snmpd	Manages networks. snmpd stands for Simple Network Management Protocol daemon.
spamassassin	Runs spamd — the SpamAssassin mail filter program.
ssh or sshd	Runs the OpenSSH (Secure Shell) secure remote login facility.
syslog or syslogd	Logs various error and status messages in a log file (usually, the /var/log/messages file). This service is used by many other programs (including other services). Always run this service.
vsftpd	Transfers files by using File Transfer Protocol (FTP). vsftpd stands for Very Secure FTP daemon.
winbind	Starts and stops the Samba winbindd server, which provides a name-switch capability similar to that provided by the /etc/nsswitch.conf file.
xfs	Starts and stops the X font server.
xinetd	Starts other Internet services, such as Telnet and FTP, whenever they are needed. This server is the Internet super server, a replacement for the older inetd.
ypbind	Runs on Network Information System (NIS) clients and binds the clients to an NIS domain. You don't have to start ypbind unless you're using NIS.

Chapter **4**

Managing Mail Servers

Electronic mail (email) is one of the most popular services available on Internet hosts. Email software comes in two parts: a *mail transport agent* (MTA), which physically sends and receives mail messages, and a *mail user agent* (MUA), which reads messages and prepares new messages. While there are several ways of going about implementing this service, the two most popular currently are Postfix, which is growing in popularity, and sendmail, which has been the industry standard for years. Because of the widespread use of sendmail, this chapter describes the email service in general and shows you specifically how to configure the sendmail server on a Linux PC.

Installing the Mail Server

Depending on the choices you made during Linux installation, you may have already installed the mail server software on your system. You can choose among several mail servers, such as exim, postfix, and sendmail. I cover sendmail briefly in this chapter. If sendmail isn't installed, you can easily install it.

Using sendmail

To set up your system as a mail server, you must configure the sendmail mail transport agent properly. sendmail has the reputation of being a complex but complete mail-delivery system. Just one look at sendmail's configuration file — /etc/mail/sendmail.cf in Fedora or /etc/sendmail.cf in SUSE — can convince you that sendmail is indeed complex. Luckily, you don't have to be an expert on the sendmail configuration file. All you need is one of the predefined configuration files — such as the one installed on your system — to use sendmail.

Your system already has a working sendmail configuration file: /etc/mail/sendmail.cf. The default file assumes that you have an Internet connection and a name server. Provided that you have an Internet connection and that your system has an official domain name, you can send and receive email from your Linux PC.

TECHNICAL STUFF

To ensure that mail delivery works correctly, your system's name must match the system name that your Internet service provider (ISP) has assigned to you. Although you can give your system any host name you want, other systems can successfully deliver mail to your system only if your system's name is in the ISP's name server.

A mail-delivery test

To try the sendmail mail transfer agent, you can use the mail command to compose and send a mail message to any user account on your Linux system. As a test, compose a message and send it to yourself. Here's how to send a message with the mail command (input in boldface):

```
mail edulaney
Subject: Testing email
This is from my Linux system.
.
```

The mail command is a simple mail user agent. In the preceding example, the addressee (edulaney) is specified in the command line. The mail program prompts for a subject line. Following the subject, enter the message, and end it with a line that contains only a period. You'll be prompted for a Cc:, but leave it blank. After ending the message, the mail user agent passes the message to sendmail (the mail transport agent) for delivery to the specified address. sendmail delivers the mail message immediately. To verify the delivery of mail, type **mail** to run the mail command again and read the message.

Note: If any of your mail server software isn't properly installed, you should be prompted during this test to install any needed components and resolve the problem.

The initial `sendmail` configuration file is adequate for sending and receiving email, at least within your Linux system. External mail delivery also works, provided that your Linux system has an Internet connection and a registered domain name.

If you have an ISP account that provides your Linux system with a dynamic IP address, you have to use a mail client such as Evolution or Mozilla Mail, which contacts your ISP's mail server to deliver outbound email.

The mail-delivery mechanism

On an Internet host, the `sendmail` mail transport agent delivers mail by using Simple Mail Transfer Protocol (SMTP). SMTP-based mail transport agents listen to TCP port 25 and use a small set of text commands to exchange information with other mail transport agents. SMTP commands are simple enough that you can use them manually from a terminal to send a mail message. The `telnet` command opens a Telnet session to port 25 (the port on which `sendmail` expects SMTP commands). The `sendmail` process on the Linux system immediately replies with an announcement.

You can type **HELP** to view a list of SMTP commands. To get help on a specific command, type **HELP**_commandname_. Type **HELO localhost** to initiate a session with the host. The `sendmail` process replies with a greeting. To send the mail message, start with the `MAIL FROM:` command, which specifies the sender of the message. Next, use the `RCPT TO:` command to specify the recipient of the message. If you want to send the message to several recipients, provide each recipient's address with the `RCPT TO:` command.

To enter the mail message, use the `DATA` command. In response to the `DATA` command, `sendmail` displays an instruction that you have to end the message with a period on a line by itself. After you do so and end the message, the `sendmail` process displays a message indicating that the message is accepted for delivery. Then you can quit the `sendmail` session with the `QUIT` command.

The sendmail configuration file

You don't have to understand everything in the `sendmail` configuration file, `sendmail.cf`, but you need to know how that file is created. That way, you can make minor changes if necessary and regenerate the `sendmail.cf` file.

In SUSE, you can configure `sendmail` through the YaST Control Center. Choose System⇔Control Center (YaST). Click Network Services on the left side of the window and then click Mail Transfer Agent in the right side of the window. YaST displays a window that you can use to configure `sendmail`. First, you specify the general settings, followed by the settings for outgoing mail, and finally the settings for incoming mail. After you exit the mail configuration utility, YaST stores the mail settings in the files /etc/sysconfig/sendmail and /etc/sysconfig/mail; then it runs SuSEconfig to update the sendmail configuration file (/etc/sendmail.cf).

You can also generate the sendmail.cf file from m4 macro files — text files in which each line eventually expands to multiple lines that mean something to some program. These macro files are organized into subdirectories in the /usr/share/sendmail-cf directory in Fedora or the /usr/share/sendmail directory in SUSE. You can read the README file in that directory to find out more about the creation of sendmail configuration files.

The m4 macro processor

The m4 macro processor generates the sendmail.cf configuration file, which comes with the sendmail package in Linux. The main macro file — named sendmail.mc, generic_linux.mc, or linux.mc — is included with the sendmail package.

TECHNICAL STUFF

A *macro* is a symbolic name for code that handles some action, usually in a short-hand form that substitutes for a long string of characters. A *macro processor* such as m4 usually reads its input file and copies it to the output, processing the macros along the way. Processing a macro generally involves performing some action and generating some output. Because a macro generates a lot more text in the output than merely the macro's name, the processing of macros is referred to as *macro expansion*.

The m4 macro processor is *stream-based*, which means that it copies the input characters to the output while it's busy expanding any macros. The m4 macro processor doesn't have any concept of lines, so it copies newline characters (which mark the end of a line) to the output. In most m4 macro files, you see dnl, an m4 macro that stands for *delete through newline.* The dnl macro deletes all characters starting at the dnl up to and including the next newline character. The newline characters in the output don't cause any harm; they merely create unnecessary blank lines. The sendmail macro package uses dnl to prevent such blank lines in the output configuration file. Because dnl means to delete everything up to the end of the line, m4 macro files also use dnl as the prefix for comment lines.

To see a simple use of m4, consider the following m4 macro file, which defines two macros (hello and bye) and uses them in a form letter:

```
dnl #################################################
dnl # File: ex.m4
dnl # A simple example of m4 macros
```

```
dnl ####################################################
define('hello', 'Dear Sir/Madam')dnl
define('bye',
'Sincerely,
Customer Service')dnl
dnl Now type the letter and use the macros
hello,
This is to inform you that we received your recent inquiry.
We will respond to your question soon.
bye
```

Type this text in your favorite text editor and save it in a file named ex.m4. You can name a macro file anything you like, but using the .m4 extension for m4 macro files is customary.

Before you process the macro file by using m4, note the following key points about the example:

>> Use the dnl macro to start all the comment lines, as in the first four lines in the example.

>> End each macro definition with the dnl macro. Otherwise, when m4 processes the macro file, it produces a blank line for each macro definition.

>> Use the built-in m4 command define to define a new macro. The macro name and the value are enclosed between a pair of left and right single quotes (' ... '). Note that you can't use a plain single quote to enclose the macro name and definition.

Now process the macro file ex.m4 by typing the following command:

```
m4 ex.m4
```

m4 processes the macros and displays the following output:

```
Dear Sir/Madam,
This is to inform you that we received your recent inquiry.
We will respond to your question soon.
Sincerely,
Customer Service
```

This output reads like a typical customer-service form letter, doesn't it?

If you compare the output with the ex.m4 file, you see that m4 prints the form letter on standard output, expanding the macros hello and bye into their defined values. If you want to save the form letter in a file called `letter`, use the shell's output redirection feature, like this:

```
m4 ex.m4 > letter
```

What if you want to use the words *hello* and *bye* in the letter without expanding them? You can do so by enclosing these words in a pair of single quotes (`' ... '`). You have to do so for other predefined m4 macros, such as `define`. To use *define* as a plain word, not as a macro to expand, type **'define'**.

The sendmail macro file

The simple example in the preceding section gives you an idea of how m4 macros are defined and used to create configuration files such as the `sendmail.cf` file. You find many complex macros stored in files in the `/usr/share/sendmail-cf` directory in Fedora or the `/usr/share/sendmail` directory in SUSE. A top-level macro file (called `sendmail.mc` in Fedora and `linux.mc` in SUSE), described later in this section, brings in these macro files with the `include` macro (used to copy a file into the input stream).

DISTRIBUTION SPECIFIC

To avoid repeatedly mentioning different file and directory names for different distributions such as Fedora and SUSE, I use the file and directory names for Fedora in the following discussions. The general discussions apply to `sendmail` in all Linux distributions, but you have to replace the file and directory names with those for your specific distribution.

By defining its own set of high-level macros in files located in the `/usr/share/sendmail-cf` directory, `sendmail` essentially creates its own macro language. The `sendmail` macro files use the `.mc` extension. The primary `sendmail` macro file that you configure is `sendmail.mc`, located in the `/etc/mail` directory.

Compared with the `/etc/mail/sendmail.cf` file, the `/etc/mail/sendmail.mc` file is shorter and easier to work with. Here are some lines from the `/etc/mail/sendmail.mc` file that comes with Fedora:

```
divert(-1)dnl
dnl #
dnl # This is the sendmail macro config file for m4. If you make changes to
dnl # /etc/mail/sendmail.mc, you will need to regenerate the
dnl # /etc/mail/sendmail.cf file by confirming that the sendmail-cf package is
dnl # installed and then performing a
dnl #
dnl # /etc/mail/make
dnl #
include('/usr/share/sendmail-cf/m4/cf.m4')dnl
```

```
VERSIONID('setup for linux')dnl
OSTYPE('linux')dnl
dnl #
dnl # Do not advertise sendmail version.
dnl #
dnl define('confSMTP_LOGIN_MSG', '$j Sendmail; $b')dnl
dnl #
dnl # default logging level is 9, you might want to set it higher to
dnl # debug the configuration
dnl #
dnl define('confLOG_LEVEL', '9')dnl
dnl #
dnl # Uncomment and edit the following line if your outgoing mail needs to
dnl # be sent out through an external mail server:
dnl #
dnl define('SMART_HOST', 'smtp.your.provider')dn
. . . lines deleted . . .
dnl #
dnl MASQUERADE_AS('mydomain.com')dnl
dnl #
dnl # masquerade not just the headers, but the envelope as well
dnl #
dnl FEATURE(masquerade_envelope)dnl
dnl #
dnl # masquerade not just @mydomainalias.com, but @*.mydomainalias.com as well
dnl #
dnl FEATURE(masquerade_entire_domain)dnl
dnl #
dnl MASQUERADE_DOMAIN(localhost)dnl
dnl MASQUERADE_DOMAIN(localhost.localdomain)dnl
dnl MASQUERADE_DOMAIN(mydomainalias.com)dnl
dnl MASQUERADE_DOMAIN(mydomain.lan)dnl
MAILER(smtp)dnl
MAILER(procmail)dnl
dnl MAILER(cyrusv2)dnl
```

TIP

If you make changes to the /etc/mail/sendmail.mc file, you must generate the /etc/mail/sendmail.cf file by running the sendmail.mc file through the m4 macro processor with the following command (after logging in as root):

```
m4 /etc/mail/sendmail.mc > /etc/mail/sendmail.cf
```

The comments also tell you that you need the sendmail-cf package to process this file.

From the description of m4 macros earlier in this chapter, you see that the sendmail.mc file uses define to create new macros. You also see the liberal use of dnl to prevent too many blank lines in the output.

The other uppercase words (such as OSTYPE, FEATURE, and MAILER) are sendmail macros. These macros are defined in the .m4 files located in the subdirectories of the /usr/share/sendmail-cf directory and are incorporated into the sendmail. mc file with the following include macro:

```
include('usr/share/sendmail-cf/m4/cf.m4')dnl
```

The /usr/share/sendmail-cf/m4/cf.m4 file in turn includes the cfhead.m4 file, which includes other m4 files, and so on. The net effect is as follows: As the m4 macro processor processes the sendmail.mc file, the macro processor incorporates many m4 files from various subdirectories of /usr/share/sendmail-cf.

Here are some key points to note about the /etc/mail/sendmail.mc file:

>> VERSIONID('setup for linux') macro inserts the version information enclosed in quotes into the output.

>> OSTYPE('linux') specifies Linux as the operating system. You have to specify this macro early to ensure proper configuration.

TIP

Placing this macro right after the VERSIONID macro is customary.

>> MAILER(smtp) describes the mailer. According to instructions in the /usr/share/sendmail-cf/README file, MAILER declarations are always placed at the end of the sendmail.mc file, and MAILER(smtp) always precedes MAILER(procmail). The mailer smtp refers to the SMTP mailer.

>> FEATURE macros request various special features. FEATURE('blacklist_recipients'), for example, turns on the capability to block incoming mail for certain usernames, hosts, or addresses. The specification of what mail to allow or refuse is placed in the access database (stored in /etc/mail/access.db file). You also need the FEATURE('access_db') macro to turn on the access database.

>> MASQUERADE_AS('mydomain.com') causes sendmail to label outgoing mail as having come from the host *mydomain*.com (replace *mydomain* with your domain name). The idea is for a large organization to set up a single sendmail server that handles the mail for many subdomains and makes everything appear to come from a single domain. (Mail from many departments in a university appears to come from the university's main domain name, for example.)

>> MASQUERADE_DOMAIN(subdomain.mydomain.com) instructs sendmail to send mail from an address such as user@subdomain.mydomain.com as having originated from the same username at the domain specified by the MASQUERADE_AS macro.

The sendmail macros such as FEATURE and MAILER are described in the /usr/share/sendmail-cf/README file. Consult that file to find out more about the sendmail macros before you make changes to the sendmail.mc file.

Syntax of the sendmail.cf file

The sendmail.cf file's syntax is designed to be easy for the sendmail program to parse, because sendmail reads this file whenever it starts. Human readability wasn't a primary consideration when the file's syntax was designed. Still, with a little explanation, you can understand the control lines in sendmail.cf.

Each sendmail control line begins with a single-letter operator that defines the meaning of the rest of the line. A line that begins with a space or a tab is considered to be a continuation of the preceding line. Blank lines and lines beginning with a pound sign (#) are comments.

Often, no space appears between the single-letter operator and the arguments that follow the operator, which makes the lines even harder to understand. sendmail.cf uses the concept of a *class* — a collection of phrases. You can define a class named P and add the phrase REDIRECT to that class with the following control line:

```
CPREDIRECT
```

Because everything runs together, the command is hard to decipher. On the other hand, to define a class named Accept and set it to the values OK and RELAY, write the following:

```
C{Accept}OK RELAY
```

This command may be slightly easier to understand because the delimiters (such as the class name, Accept) are enclosed in curly braces.

Other, more recent control lines are even easier to understand. The line

```
O HelpFile=/etc/mail/helpfile
```

defines the option HelpFile as the filename /etc/mail/helpfile. That file contains help information that sendmail uses when it receives a HELP command.

Table 4-1 summarizes the one-letter control operators used in sendmail.cf. Each entry also shows an example of that operator. This table helps you understand some of the lines in sendmail.cf.

TABLE 4-1 ## Control Operators Used in sendmail.cf

Operator	Description
C	Defines a class, a variable (think of it as a set) that can contain several values. Cwlocalhost adds the name localhost to the class w.
D	Defines a macro, a name associated with a single value. DnMAILER–DAEMON defines the macro n as MAILER–DAEMON.
F	Defines a class that's been read from a file. Fw/etc/mail/local–host–names reads the names of hosts from the file /etc/mail/local–host–names and adds them to the class w.
H	Defines the format of header lines that sendmail inserts into a message. H?P?Return–Path: <$g> defines the Return–Path: field of the header.
K	Defines a map (a key-value pair database). Karith arith defines the map named arith as the compiled-in map of the same name.
M	Specifies a mailer. The following lines define the procmail mailer: Mprocmail,P=/usr/bin/procmail,F=DFMSPhnu9,S=EnvFromSMTP/HdrFromSMTP,R=EnvToSMTP/HdrFromSMTP,T=DNS/RFC822/X–Unix,A=procmail –Y –m $h $f $u.
O	Assigns a value to an option. O AliasFile=/etc/aliases defines the AliasFile option to /etc/aliases, which is the name of the sendmail alias file.
P	Defines values for the precedence field. Pjunk=–100 sets to –100 the precedence of messages marked with the header field Precedence: junk.
R	Defines a rule. (A rule has a left side and a right side; if input matches the left side, the right side replaces it. This rule is called *rewriting*.) The rewriting rule R$* ; $1 strips trailing semicolons.
S	Labels a ruleset you can start defining with subsequent R control lines. Scanonify=3 labels the next ruleset as canonify and ruleset 3.
T	Adds a username to the trusted class (class t). Troot adds root to the class of trusted users.
V	Defines the major version number of the configuration file.

Other sendmail files

The /etc/mail directory contains other files that sendmail uses. These files are referenced in the sendmail configuration file, /etc/mail/sendmail.cf in Fedora and /etc/sendmail.cf in SUSE. Here's how you can search for the /etc/mail string in the /etc/mail/sendmail.cf file in Fedora:

```
grep "\/etc\/mail" /etc/mail/sendmail.cf
```

Here's what the `grep` command displays as a result of the search on a typical Fedora system:

```
Fw/etc/mail/local-host-names
FR-o /etc/mail/relay-domains
Kmailertable hash -o /etc/mail/mailertable.db
Kvirtuser hash -o /etc/mail/virtusertable.db
Kaccess hash -T<TMPF> -o /etc/mail/access.db
#O ErrorHeader=/etc/mail/error-header
O HelpFile=/etc/mail/helpfile
O UserDatabaseSpec=/etc/mail/userdb.db
#O ServiceSwitchFile=/etc/mail/service.switch
#O DefaultAuthInfo=/etc/mail/default-auth-info
Ft/etc/mail/trusted-users
```

You can ignore the lines that begin with a hash mark or number sign (#) because `sendmail` treats those lines as comments. The other lines are `sendmail` control lines that refer to other files in the `/etc/mail` directory.

Here's what some of these `sendmail` files are supposed to contain. (Note that not all these files have to be present in your `/etc/mail` directory, and even when present, some files may be empty.)

» `/etc/mail/access`: Names or IP addresses or both of hosts allowed to send mail (useful in stopping *spam* — unwanted email).

» `/etc/mail/access.db`: Access database generated from the `/etc/mail/access` file.

» `/etc/mail/helpfile`: Help information for SMTP commands.

» `/etc/mail/local-host-names`: Names by which this host is known.

» `/etc/mail/mailertable`: Mailer table used to override how mail is routed. (The entry `comcast.net smtp:smtp.comcast.net`, for example, tells `sendmail` that mail addressed to `comcast.net` has to be sent to `smtp.comcast.net`.)

» `/etc/mail/relay-domains`: Hosts that permit relaying.

» `/etc/mail/trusted-users`: List of users allowed to send mail using other users' names without a warning.

» `/etc/mail/userdb.db`: User database file containing information about each user's login name and real name.

» `/etc/mail/virtusertable`: Database of users with virtual-domain addresses hosted on this system.

TECHNICAL STUFF

The `/etc/mail` directory sometimes contains other files — `/etc/mail/certs` and files with the `.pem` extension — that are meant for supporting Privacy Enhanced Mail (PEM) in `sendmail` by using the STARTTLS extension to SMTP. The STARTTLS extension uses TLS (more commonly known as Secure Sockets Layer [SSL]) to authenticate the sender and encrypt mail. RFC 2487 describes STARTTLS and is available at `http://ietf.org/rfc/rfc2487.txt`.

TIP

If you edit the `/etc/mail/mailertable` file, you have to type the following command before the changes take effect:

```
makemap hash /etc/mail/mailertable < /etc/mail/mailertable
```

Here's an easier way to make sure that you rebuild everything necessary after making any changes. Type the following commands while logged in as `root`:

```
cd /etc/mail
make
```

The first command changes the current directory to `/etc/mail`, and the second command runs the `make` command, which reads a file named `Makefile` in `/etc/mail` to perform the steps necessary to rebuild everything.

The .forward file

Users can redirect their own mail by placing a `.forward` file in their home directory. The `.forward` file is a plain-text file with a comma-separated list of mail addresses. Any mail sent to the user is instead forwarded to these addresses. If the `.forward` file contains a single address, all email for that user is redirected to that single email address. Suppose that a `.forward` file containing the following line is placed in the home directory of a user named `emily`:

```
ashley
```

This line causes `sendmail` to automatically send all email addressed to `emily` to the username `ashley` on the same system. User `emily` doesn't receive mail at all.

You can also forward mail to a username on another system by listing a complete email address. You can add a `.forward` file with the following line to send messages addressed to username `wilbur` to the mail address `wilbur@somewhereelse.net`:

```
wilbur@somewhereelse.net
```

To keep a copy of the message on the original system, in addition to forwarding the message to the preceding specified address, add the following line to the .forward file:

```
wilbur@somewhereelse.net, wilbur\
```

Simply append the username and end the line with a backslash (\). The backslash at the end of the line stops sendmail from repeatedly forwarding the message.

The sendmail alias file

In addition to the sendmail.cf file, sendmail consults an alias file named /etc/aliases to convert a name to an address. The location of the alias file appears in the sendmail configuration file.

Each alias typically is a shorter name for an email address. The system administrator uses the sendmail alias file to forward mail, to create a mailing list (a single alias that identifies several users), or to refer to a user by several different names. Here are some typical aliases:

```
brown: glbrown
all: jessica, isaac, alex, caleb, glbrown
```

REMEMBER

After defining any new aliases in the /etc/aliases file, you must log in as root and make the new alias active by typing the following command:

```
sendmail -bi
```

Chapter 5

Managing DNS

The *Domain Name System* (DNS) is an Internet service that converts a fully qualified domain name, such as www.debian.org, to its corresponding IP address, such as 194.109.137.218. You can think of DNS as the directory of Internet hosts; DNS is the reason why you can use easy-to-remember host names even though TCP/IP requires numeric IP addresses for data transfers. DNS is a hierarchy of distributed DNS servers. This chapter provides an overview of DNS and shows you how to set up a caching DNS server on your Linux system.

Understanding the Domain Name System (DNS)

In TCP/IP networks, each network interface (think of an Ethernet or Wi-Fi card) is identified by an IP address. Because IP addresses are hard to remember, an easy-to-remember name is assigned to the IP address, much the way that a name goes with a telephone number. Instead of having to remember that the IP address of Debian's web server is 194.109.137.218, for example, you can simply refer to that host by its name, www.debian.org. When you type **www.debian.org** as the URL in a web browser, the name www.debian.org is translated into its corresponding IP address. This process is where the concept of DNS comes in.

What is DNS?

DNS is a distributed, hierarchical database that holds information about computers on the Internet. That information includes host name, IP address, and mail-routing specifications. Because this information resides on many DNS hosts on the Internet, DNS is called a *distributed* database. The primary job of DNS is to associate host names with IP addresses and vice versa.

In ARPANET (the precursor to today's Internet), the list of host names and corresponding IP addresses was maintained in a text file named HOSTS.TXT, which was managed centrally and periodically distributed to every host on the network. As the number of hosts grew, this static host table quickly became unreasonable to maintain. DNS was proposed by Paul Mockapetris to alleviate the problems of a static host table. As formally documented in Requests for Comment (RFCs) 882 and 883 (published in November 1983; see www.faqs.org/rfcs/rfc882.html and www.faqs.org/rfcs/rfc883.html), the original DNS introduced two key concepts:

- » The use of hierarchical domain names, such as www.ee.umd.edu and https://www.debian.org.
- » The use of DNS servers throughout the Internet — a form of *distributed responsibility* — as a means of managing the host database.

Today, DNS is an Internet standard that has been updated and extended beyond its original vision. Earlier updates defined data encoding, whereas later ones focus on improving DNS security. To read these and other RFCs online, visit the RFC page of the Internet Engineering Task Force website at www.ietf.org/rfc.html.

DNS defines the following:

- » A hierarchical domain-naming system for hosts.
- » A distributed database that associates every domain name with an IP address.
- » Library routines (resolvers) that network applications can use to query the distributed DNS database. (This library is called the *resolver library*.)
- » A protocol for DNS clients and servers to exchange information about names and IP addresses.

Nowadays, all hosts on the Internet rely on DNS to access various Internet services on remote hosts. As you may know from experience, when you obtain Internet access from an Internet service provider (ISP), your ISP provides you the IP addresses of *name servers* — the DNS servers that your system accesses whenever host names are mapped to IP addresses.

If you have a small local-area network, you may decide to run a DNS server on one of the hosts or use the name servers provided by the ISP. For medium-size networks with several subnets, you can run a DNS server on each subnet to provide efficient DNS lookups. On a large corporate network, the corporate domain (such as www.microsoft.com) is further subdivided into a hierarchy of subdomains; several DNS servers may be used in each subdomain.

The following sections provide an overview of the hierarchical domain-naming convention and describe BIND — the DNS software used on most Unix systems, including Linux.

Discovering hierarchical domain names

DNS uses a hierarchical tree of domains to organize the *namespace* — the entire set of names. Each higher-level domain has authority over its lower-level subdomains. Each domain represents a distinct block of the namespace and is managed by a single administrative authority. Figure 5-1 illustrates the hierarchical organization of the DNS namespace.

FIGURE 5-1:
The DNS namespace is organized as a hierarchy.

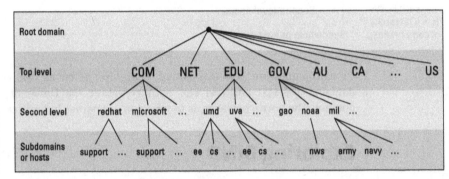

The root of the tree is called the *root domain* and is represented by a single dot (.). The top-level, or root-level, domains come next. The top-level domains are further divided into second-level domains, which in turn can be broken into further subdomains.

The top-level domains are relatively fixed and include com, net, org, edu, gov, and mil, the commonly used top-level domains in the United States. These top-level domains came about as the Internet came into widespread use in the early 1990s.

Another set of top-level domain names is for countries. These domain names use the two-letter country codes assigned by the International Organization for Standardization (ISO; www.iso.org). The top-level country code domain for the United

Managing DNS

States, for example, is us. In the United States, many local governments and organizations use the us domain. mcps.k12.md.us, for example, is the domain name of the Montgomery County Public Schools in the state of Maryland, in the United States.

To this list, you can add other generic top-level domain names that have been added since the original set. These domain names include biz (for business), name (for family names), museum, and travel, with more proposed and on the way.

The *fully qualified domain name* (FQDN) is constructed by stringing together the subdomain names, from lower-level to higher-level, using a period (.) as a separator. redhat.com is a fully qualified domain name, for example; so is ee.umd.edu. Note that each domain may also refer to a specific host computer. Figure 5-2 illustrates the components of an FQDN.

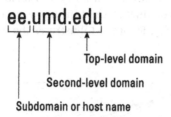

FIGURE 5-2:
Each FQDN
has a hierarchy
of components.

Top-level domain

Second-level domain

Subdomain or host name

Domain names are case-insensitive. Therefore, as far as DNS is concerned, the domains UMD.EDU and umd.edu both represent the University of Maryland's domain. The norm, however, is to type domain names in lowercase.

Exploring BIND

Most Unix systems, including Linux, come with the Berkeley Internet Name Domain (BIND) system, which is a well-known implementation of DNS. The BIND software is installed during the Linux installation as long as you select the name server when selecting the packages for installation.

DISTRIBUTION
SPECIFIC

In Debian and Ubuntu, type **dpkg -l bind*** to see whether BIND is installed. In Fedora and SUSE, type **rpm -q bind** to see whether the BIND package is installed.

In Debian and Ubuntu, type **apt-get install bind9** to install BIND. In Fedora, log in as root, mount the DVD, and type **cd /media/cdrom/Fedora/RPMS** followed by **rpm -ivh bind***. In SUSE, click Software Management in the YaST Control Center's Software category; use YaST's search facility to look for *bind*; then select the relevant packages and install them.

BIND includes three major components:

>> The named daemon (the name server), which responds to queries about host names and IP addresses.

>> A resolver library that applications can use to resolve host names into IP addresses (and vice versa).

>> Command-line DNS utility programs (DNS clients), such as dig (Domain Internet Groper) and host, that users can use to query DNS.

The next few sections describe these components of BIND. Later sections explain how to configure the resolver and the name server.

named: BIND name server

The named daemon is the name server that responds to queries about host names and IP addresses. Based on the configuration files and the local DNS database, named provides answers to queries or asks other servers and caches their responses. The named server also performs a function referred to as *zone transfer*, which involves copying data among the name servers in a domain.

The name server operates in one of three modes:

>> **Primary or master:** In this case, the name server keeps the master copy of the domain's data on disk. One primary server is for each domain or subdomain.

>> **Secondary or slave:** A secondary name server copies its domain's data from the primary server, using a zone transfer operation. You can have one or more secondary name servers for a domain.

>> **Caching:** A caching name server loads the addresses of a few authoritative servers for the root domain and gets all domain data by caching responses to queries that it has resolved by contacting other name servers. Primary and secondary servers also cache responses.

A *name server* can be authoritative or not, depending on what information it's providing. As the term implies, the response from an authoritative name server is supposed to be accurate. The primary and secondary name servers are authoritative for their own domains, but they're not authoritative for responses provided from cached information.

Caching name servers are never authoritative, because all their responses come from cached information.

REMEMBER

To run a name server on your Linux system, you have to run named with the appropriate configuration files. Later in this chapter in the "Configuring a caching name server" section, you find out about the configuration files and data files that control how the name server operates.

Resolver library

Finding an IP address for a host name is referred to as *resolving the hostname*. Network-aware applications, such as a web browser or a File Transfer Protocol (FTP) client, use a resolver library to perform the conversion from the name to an IP address. Depending on the settings in the /etc/host.conf file, the resolver library consults the /etc/hosts file or makes a DNS query to resolve a host name to its IP address. The resolver library queries the name servers listed in the /etc/resolv.conf file.

You don't have to know much about the resolver library unless you're writing network-aware applications. To run Internet services properly, all you have to know is how to configure the resolver. Later in this chapter in the "Configuring a caching name server" section, you see how to configure the server and other aspects of DNS.

DNS utility programs

You can use the DNS utility programs dig and host to try DNS interactively from the shell prompt. These utility programs are DNS clients; you can use them to query the DNS database and debug any name server set up on your system. By default, these programs query the name server listed in your system's /etc/resolv.conf file.

You can use dig (the Domain Internet Groper program) to look up IP addresses for a domain name, or vice versa. To look up the IP address of ftp.redhat.com, type

```
dig ftp.redhat.com
```

dig prints the results of the DNS query in great detail. Look in the part of the output labeled ANSWER SECTION: for the result. Here's what that section looks like for this sample query:

```
;; ANSWER SECTION:
ftp.redhat.com.  300 IN A 209.132.183.61
```

This output means that the name ftp.redhat.com refers to the IP address 209.132.183.61.

Reverse lookups (finding host names for IP addresses) are also easy with `dig`. To find the host name that corresponds to the IP address 209.132.183.61, type the following:

```
dig -x 209.132.183.61
```

Again, the answer appears in the ANSWER SECTION of the output, which, for this example, looks like this:

```
;; ANSWER SECTION:
61.132.183.209.in-addr.arpa. 600 IN PTR ftp.redhat.com.
```

In this case, the host name that corresponds to the IP address 209.132.183.61 is ftp.redhat.com.

You can also query DNS by using the `host` program, which produces output in a compact format. Here's a typical use of `host` to look up an IP address for a host name:

```
host pranksanonymous.com
```

This command generates the following output:

```
pranksanonymous.com has address 160.153.75.33
pranksanonymous.com mail is handled by 0 mail.pranksanonymous.com.
```

By default, `host` prints the IP address and any *MX record*. These records list the names of mail handlers for the specified host.

For a reverse lookup, use the `-t ptr` option along with the IP address as an argument, like this:

```
host -t ptr 160.153.75.33
```

Here's the relay from `host`:

```
33.75.153.160.in-addr.arpa domain name pointer ip-160-153-75-33.
    ip.secureserver.net.
```

In this case, `host` prints the PTR record (from the DNS database) that shows the host name that corresponds to the IP address. (PTR refers to *pointer*, and the PTR record specifies the name that corresponds to an address.)

You can also try other types of records, such as CNAME (for canonical name), as follows:

```
host -t cname www.ee.umd.edu
```

The response from host is

```
www.ee.umd.edu is an alias for ajclark.eng.umd.edu.
```

This output indicates that the *canonical name* (or alias) for www.ee.umd.edu is ajclark.eng.umd.edu.

Configuring DNS

You configure DNS by using configuration files. The exact set of files depends on whether you're running a name server and, if so, the type of name server: caching or primary. Some configuration files are needed whether you run a name server or not.

Configuring the resolver

You don't need a name server running on your system to use the DNS clients (dig and host). You can use those clients to query your domain's name server. Typically, your ISP provides this information. You have to list the IP addresses of these name servers in the /etc/resolv.conf file, which the resolver library reads to determine how to resolve host names. The format of this file is

```
domain your-domain.com
search your-domain.com
nameserver A.B.C.D
nameserver X.Y.Z.W
```

where A.B.C.D and X.Y.Z.W are the IP addresses (dot-separated numeric addresses, such as 192.168.0.1) of the primary and secondary name servers that your ISP provides.

The domain line lists the local domain name. The search line specifies the domains on which a host name is searched first. (Usually, you put your own domain in the search line.) The domain listed on the search line is appended to any hostname before the resolver library tries to resolve it. If you look for a host named mailhost, the resolver library first tries mailhost.*your-domain*.com; if that search fails, it tries `mailhost`. The search line applies to any host name that you try to access. If you're trying to access `www.redhat.com`, for example, the resolver first tries `www.redhat.com.`*your-domain*`.com` and then `www.redhat.com`.

Another important configuration file is `/etc/host.conf`. This file tells the resolver what to do when attempting to resolve a host name. A typical `/etc/host.conf` file contains the following line:

```
order hosts,bind
```

This command tells the resolver to consult the `/etc/host.conf` file first and, if the resolver doesn't find an entry there, to query the name server listed in the `/etc/resolv.conf` file. The `/etc/host.conf` file usually lists any local host names and their IP addresses. Here's a typical line from the `/etc/host.conf` file:

```
127.0.0.1 lnbp200 localhost.localdomain localhost
```

This line says that the IP address 127.0.0.1 is assigned to the host names `lnbp200`, `localhost.localdomain`, and `localhost`.

In the latest version of the Linux kernel — the one that uses GNU C Library version 2 (`glibc 2`) or later — the name service switch (NSS) file, `/etc/nsswitch.conf`, controls how services such as the resolver library, NIS, NIS+, and local files such as `/etc/hosts` and `/etc/shadow` interact. The following `hosts` entry in the `/etc/nsswitch.conf` file tells the resolver library to first try the `/etc/hosts` file, then try NIS+, and finally try DNS:

```
hosts: files nisplus dns
```

To find more about the `/etc/nsswitch.conf` file, type **man nsswitch.conf** in a terminal window.

Configuring a caching name server

A *caching name server* is a simple-but-useful name server that finds answers to host-name queries (by using other name servers) and then remembers the answer (by saving it in a cache) for the next time you need it. This caching name server can shorten the time it takes to access hosts you've = accessed recently because the answer is already in the cache.

When you install BIND, the configuration files for a caching name server are installed as well, so you can start running the caching name server without much work. This section describes the configuration files and what you have to do to start the caching name server.

The /etc/named.conf file

The first configuration file you need is /etc/named.conf. (That's the name in Fedora and SUSE; in Debian and Ubuntu, the BIND configuration file is called /etc/bind/named.conf.) The named server reads this configuration file when it starts. You already have this file if you've installed BIND. Here's an example /etc/named.conf file:

```
options {
directory "/var/named";
dump-file "/var/named/data/cache_dump.db";
statistics-file "/var/named/data/named_stats.txt";
/*
* If there is a firewall between you and name servers you want
* to talk to, you might need to uncomment the query-source
* directive below. Previous versions of BIND always asked
* questions using port 53, but BIND 8.1 uses an unprivileged
* port by default.
*/
// query-source address * port 53;
};
//
// a caching only nameserver config
//
controls {
inet 127.0.0.1 allow { localhost; } keys { rndckey; };
};
zone "." IN {
type hint;
file "named.ca";
};
zone "localdomain" IN {
type master;
file "localdomain.zone";
allow-update { none; };
};
zone "localhost" IN {
type master;
file "localhost.zone";
allow-update { none; };
};
zone "0.0.127.in-addr.arpa" IN {
type master;
file "named.local";
allow-update { none; };
};
zone "0.0.0.0.0.0.0.0.0.0.0.0.0.0.0.0.0.0.0.0.0.0.0.0.0.0.0.0.0.0.0.0.ip6.arpa" IN
{
```

```
type master;
file "named.ip6.local";
allow-update { none; };
};
zone "255.in-addr.arpa" IN {
type master;
file "named.broadcast";
allow-update { none; };
};
zone "0.in-addr.arpa" IN {
type master;
file "named.zero";
allow-update { none; };
};
include "/etc/rndc.key";
```

Comments are C-style (/* ... */) or C++-style (starts with //). The file contains block statements enclosed in curly braces ({ ... }) and terminated by a semicolon (;). A block statement in turn contains other statements, each ending with a semicolon.

This /etc/named.conf file begins with an options block statement with several option statements. The directory option statement tells named where to look for all other files that appear on lines in the configuration file. In this case, named looks for the files in the /var/named directory.

DISTRIBUTION SPECIFIC

In SUSE, the directory option in /etc/named.conf refers to the /var/lib/named directory, which means that all other BIND configuration files are in /var/lib/named. In Debian, the configuration files are explicitly specified to be in the /etc/bind directory.

TECHNICAL STUFF

The controls statement in /etc/named.conf contains security information so that the rndc command can connect to the named service at port 953 and interact with named. In this case, the controls statement contains the following line:

```
inet 127.0.0.1 allow { localhost; } keys { rndckey; };
```

This command says that rndc can connect from localhost with the key named rndc. (The file /etc/rndc.key defines the key and the encryption algorithm to be used.)

TECHNICAL STUFF

The rndc (remote name daemon control) utility is a successor to the older ndc (name daemon controller) utility used to control the named server by sending it messages over a special control channel, a Transmission Control Protocol (TCP) port where named listens for messages. The rndc utility uses a cryptographic key to authenticate itself to the named server. The named server has the same cryptographic key so that it can decode the authentication information sent by rndc.

After the options statement, the /etc/named.conf file contains several zone statements, each enclosed in curly braces and terminated by a semicolon. Each zone statement defines a zone. The first zone is named . (root zone); it's a hint zone that specifies the root name servers. (When the DNS server starts, it uses the hint zone to find a root name server and get the most recent list of root name servers.)

The next two zone statements in /etc/named.conf are master zones. (A *master zone* is the master copy of data for a domain.) The syntax for a *master zone statement* for an Internet class zone (indicated by the IN keyword) is as follows:

```
zone "zone-name" IN {
type master;
file "zone-file";
[ ... other optional statements ...]
};
```

zone-name is the name of the zone, and *zone-file* is the zone file that contains the resource records (RR) — the database entries — for that zone. The next two sections describe zone-file formats and RR formats.

Zone-file formats

The zone file typically starts with directives, each of which begins with a dollar sign ($) followed by a keyword. Two commonly used directives are $TTL and $ORIGIN.

The line

```
$TTL 86400
```

uses the $TTL directive to set the default time to live (TTL) for subsequent records with undefined TTLs. The value is in seconds, and the valid TTLs are in the range 0 to 2147483647 seconds. In this case, the directive sets the default TTL as 86400 seconds (or one day).

The $ORIGIN directive sets the domain name that's appended to any unqualified records. The following $ORIGIN directive sets the domain name to localhost:

```
$ORIGIN localhost.
```

If no $ORIGIN directive exists, the initial $ORIGIN is the same as the zone name that comes after the zone keyword in the /etc/named.conf file.

After the directives, the zone file contains one or more RRs. These records follow a specific format, which are outlined in the next section.

RR formats

You have to understand the format of the RRs before you can understand and intelligently work with zone files. Each RR has the following format (with optional fields shown in square brackets):

```
[domain] [ttl] [class] type data [;comment]
```

The fields are separated by tabs or spaces and may contain some special characters, such as @ for the domain and a semicolon (;) to indicate the start of a comment.

The first field, which must begin at the first character of the line, identifies the domain. You can use @ to use the current $ORIGIN for the domain name for this record. If you have multiple records for the same domain name, leave the first field blank.

The optional *ttl* field specifies the TTL — the duration for which the data can be cached and considered to be valid. You can specify the duration in one of the following formats:

>> *N*, where *N* is the number of seconds

>> *N*W, where *N* is the number of weeks

>> *N*D, where *N* is the number of days

>> *N*H, where *N* is the number of hours

>> *N*M, where *N* is the number of minutes

>> *N*S, where *N* is the number of seconds

The letters W, D, H, M, and S can also be lowercase. Thus, you can enter 86400 or 1D (or 1d) to indicate a duration of one day. You can also combine these letters to specify more precise durations, such as 5w6d16h to indicate 5 weeks, 6 days, and 16 hours.

The *class* field specifies the network type. The most commonly used value for this field is IN for Internet.

Next in the RR is the *type* field, which denotes the type of record (such as SOA, NS, A, or PTR). Table 5-1 lists the DNS RR types. The *data* field comes next, and its content depends on the *type* field.

Read the RRs in the zone files — at least the ones of type SOA, NS, A, PTR, and MX, which are some of the most commonly used. (You'll find the zone files in the /etc/bind directory in Debian, the /var/named directory in Fedora, and the /var/lib/named directory in SUSE.) Next is a brief description of these records, illustrating each record type through an example.

TABLE 5-1   **DNS RR Types**

Type	Name	Description
A	IPv4 to IPv6 Transition Address	Specifies the IPv6 address corresponding to a name using a format suitable for transition from IPv4 to IPv6
AAAA	IPv6 Address	Specifies the IPv6 host address corresponding to a name
AS	Address	Specifies the IP address corresponding to a host name
CERT	Digital Certificate	Holds a digital certificate
CNAME	Canonical Name	Defines the nickname or alias for a host name
DNAME	Delegation Name	Replaces the specified domain name with another name to be looked up
HINFO	Host Info	Identifies the hardware and operating system for a host
KEY	Public Key	Stores a public key associated with a DNS name
MX	Mail Exchanger	Identifies the host that accepts mail meant for a domain (used to route email)
NS	Name Server	Identifies authoritative name servers for a zone
PTR	Pointer	Specifies the name corresponding to an address (used for *reverse mapping* — converting an IP address to a host name)
RP	Responsible Person	Provides the name of a technical contact for a domain
SIG	Signature	Contains data authenticated in the secure DNS (see RFC 2535 for details)
SOA	Start of Authority	Indicates that all subsequent records are authoritative for this zone
SRV	Services	Lists well-known network services provided by the domain
TXT	Text	Includes comments and other information in the DNS database

A typical SOA record follows:

```
@ 1D IN SOA @ root (
42 ; serial
3H ; refresh -- 3 hours
15M ; retry -- 15 minutes
1W ; expiry -- 1 week
1D ) ; minimum -- 1 day
```

The first field specifies the domain as @, which means that the current domain (by default, the zone name, as shown in the /etc/named.conf file). The next field specifies a TTL of one day for this record. The class field is set to IN, which means the record is for Internet. The type field specifies the record type as SOA. The rest of the fields constitute the data for the SOA record. The data includes the name of the primary name server (in this case, @, or the current domain), the email address of the technical contact, and five times enclosed in parentheses.

The NS record specifies the authoritative name servers for a zone. A typical NS record looks like the following:

```
. 3600000 IN NS A.ROOT-SERVERS.NET.
```

In this case, the NS record lists the authoritative name server for the root zone. (Note that the name of the first field is a single period.) The TTL field specifies that the record is valid for 1,000 hours (3600000 seconds). The class is IN, for Internet; the record type is NS. The final field lists the name of the name server (A.ROOT-SERVERS.NET.), which ends with a period.

An A record specifies the address corresponding to a name. The following A record shows the address of A.ROOT-SERVERS.NET. as 198.41.0.4:

```
A.ROOT-SERVERS.NET. 3600000 A 198.41.0.4
```

In this case, the network class isn't specified because the field is optional, and the default is IN.

PTR records are used for reverse mapping — converting an address to a name. Consider the following example:

```
1 IN PTR localhost.
```

This record comes from a file for a zone named 0.0.127.in-addr.arpa. Therefore, this record says that the name associated with the address 127.0.0.1 is localhost.

An MX record specifies the name of a host that accepts mail on behalf of a specific domain. Here's a typical MX record:

```
Server7 IN MX 10 mailhub.lnbsoft.com.
```

This record says that mail addressed to the host named server7 in the current domain is sent to mailhub.lnbsoft.com. (This host is called a *mail exchanger*.) The number 10 is the preference value. In a list of multiple MX records with different preference values, the ones with lower preference values are tried first.

Armed with this bit of information about RR, you can go through the zone files for the caching name server.

The root zone file

The Internet has 13 root name servers, most of which are located in the United States. Information about the 13 root name servers is in the zone file referenced in the zone statement for the root zone in the /etc/named.conf file. (The root zone file is /var/named/named.ca in Fedora, /etc/bind/db.root in Debian and Ubuntu, and /var/lib/named/root.hint in SUSE.) The following listing shows the root zone file:

```
; This file holds the information on root name servers needed to
; initialize cache of Internet domain name servers
; (e.g. reference this file in the "cache . <file>"
; configuration file of BIND domain name servers).
;
; This file is made available by InterNIC
; under anonymous FTP as
; file /domain/named.cache
; on server FTP.INTERNIC.NET
; -OR- RS.INTERNIC.NET
;
; last update: Jan 29, 2018
; related version of root zone: 2018012900
;
;
; formerly NS.INTERNIC.NET
;
.                        3600000 IN NS A.ROOT-SERVERS.NET.
A.ROOT-SERVERS.NET.      3600000 A  198.41.0.4
;
; formerly NS1.ISI.EDU
;
.                        3600000 NS B.ROOT-SERVERS.NET.
B.ROOT-SERVERS.NET.      3600000 A  192.228.79.201
```

```
;
; formerly C.PSI.NET
;
. 3600000 NS C.ROOT-SERVERS.NET.
C.ROOT-SERVERS.NET. 3600000 A 192.33.4.12
;
; formerly TERP.UMD.EDU
;
. 3600000 NS D.ROOT-SERVERS.NET.
D.ROOT-SERVERS.NET. 3600000 A 128.8.10.90
;
; formerly NS.NASA.GOV
;
. 3600000 NS E.ROOT-SERVERS.NET.
E.ROOT-SERVERS.NET. 3600000 A 192.203.230.10
;
; formerly NS.ISC.ORG
;
. 3600000 NS F.ROOT-SERVERS.NET.
F.ROOT-SERVERS.NET. 3600000 A 192.5.5.241
;
; formerly NS.NIC.DDN.MIL
;
. 3600000 NS G.ROOT-SERVERS.NET.
G.ROOT-SERVERS.NET. 3600000 A 192.112.36.4
;
; formerly AOS.ARL.ARMY.MIL
;
. 3600000 NS H.ROOT-SERVERS.NET.
H.ROOT-SERVERS.NET. 3600000 A 128.63.2.53
;
; formerly NIC.NORDU.NET
;
. 3600000 NS I.ROOT-SERVERS.NET.
I.ROOT-SERVERS.NET. 3600000 A 192.36.148.17
;
; operated by VeriSign, Inc.
;
. 3600000 NS J.ROOT-SERVERS.NET.
J.ROOT-SERVERS.NET. 3600000 A 192.58.128.30
;
; operated by RIPE NCC
;
. 3600000 NS K.ROOT-SERVERS.NET.
K.ROOT-SERVERS.NET. 3600000 A 193.0.14.129
;
; operated by ICANN
;
```

```
.  3600000 NS L.ROOT-SERVERS.NET.
L.ROOT-SERVERS.NET. 3600000 A 198.32.64.12
;
; operated by WIDE
;
.  3600000 NS M.ROOT-SERVERS.NET.
M.ROOT-SERVERS.NET. 3600000 A 202.12.27.33
; End of File
```

This file contains NS and A RRs that specify the names of authoritative name servers and their addresses for the root zone (indicated by the . in the first field of each NS record).

The comment lines in the file begin with a semicolon. These comments give you hints about the location of the 13 root name servers. This file is a necessity for any name server because the name server has to be able to reach at least one root name server.

The localhost.zone file

The /etc/named.conf file includes a zone statement for the localhost zone that specifies the zone file as localhost.zone. That file is located in the /var/named directory in Fedora, in the /var/local/named directory in SUSE, and in /etc/bind/db.local in Debian. Here's what the localhost.zone file contains:

```
$TTL 86400
$ORIGIN localhost.
@ 1D IN SOA @ root (
42 ; serial (d. adams)
3H ; refresh
15M ; retry
1W ; expiry
1D ) ; minimum
1D IN NS @
1D IN A 127.0.0.1
```

This zone file starts with a $TTL directive that sets the default TTL to one day (86400 seconds) for subsequent records with undefined TTLs. Next, the $ORIGIN directive sets the domain name to localhost.

After these two directives, the localhost.zone file contains three RRs: an SOA record, an NS record, and an A record. The SOA and NS records specify localhost as the primary authoritative name server for the zone. The A record specifies the address of localhost as 127.0.0.1.

The zone file for reverse mapping 127.0.0.1

The third zone statement in the /etc/named.conf file specifies a reverse-mapping zone named 0.0.127.in-addr.arpa. For this zone, the zone file is /var/named/named.localhost in Fedora, /var/lib/named/127.0.0.zone in SUSE, and /etc/bind/db.127 in Debian and Ubuntu. This zone file contains the following:

```
$TTL 86400
@ IN SOA localhost. root.localhost. (
1997022700 ; Serial
28800 ; Refresh
14400 ; Retry
3600000 ; Expire
86400 ) ; Minimum
IN NS localhost.
1 IN PTR localhost.
```

The SOA and NS records specify localhost as the primary name server. The PTR record specifies localhost as the name that corresponds to the address 127.0.0.1.

TECHNICAL STUFF

The SOA record also shows root.localhost. as the email address of the technical contact for the domain. The DNS zone files use the format *user.host.* (note the ending period) format for the email address. When sending any email to the contact, you have to replace the first period with @ and remove the final period.

Caching name server: Startup and test

After you've studied the configuration files for the caching name server, you can start the name server and see it in operation.

DISTRIBUTION SPECIFIC

To start the name server, log in as root and type **/etc/init.d/named start** in Fedora and SUSE. To ensure that the named server starts every time you reboot the system, type **chkconfig -- level 35 named on** in Fedora and SUSE. In Debian and Ubuntu, type **/etc/init.d/bind9 start** to start the named server.

The named server writes diagnostic log messages in the /var/log/messages file. After you start named, you can check the log messages by opening /var/log/messages in a text editor. If no error messages are from named, you can proceed to test the name server.

REMEMBER

Before you try the caching name server, you have to specify that name server as your primary one. To do so, make sure that the first line in the /etc/resolv.conf file is the following:

```
nameserver 127.0.0.1
```

Now you can use host to test the name server. To look up the IP address of www.gao.gov by using the caching name server on localhost, type the following command:

```
host www.gao.gov localhost
```

Here's the resulting output from the host command:

```
Using domain server:
Name: localhost
Address: 127.0.0.1#53
Aliases:
www.gao.gov. has address 161.203.16.77
```

As the output shows, the host command uses localhost as the DNS server and returns the IP address of www.gao.gov. If you get similar output, the caching name server is up and running.

Configuring a primary name server

The best way to configure a primary name server is to start by configuring a caching name server (as explained in the previous sections). Then add master zones for the domains for which you want this name server to be the primary name server. Suppose that you want to define a primary name server for the server7. net domain. Here are the steps that you'd perform to configure that primary name server on a Fedora system (after logging in as root):

1. **Add the following zone statements to the** /etc/named.conf **file:**

```
zone "server7.net" IN {
type master;
file "server7.zone";
};
zone "0.168.192.in-addr.arpa" IN {
type master;
file "0.168.192.zone";
};
```

2. **Create the zone file** /var/named/server7.zone **with the following lines in it:**

```
$TTL 86400
$ORIGIN server7.net.
@ 1D IN SOA @ root.server7.net (
100 ; serial
```

```
3H ; refresh
15M ; retry
1W ; expiry
1D ) ; minimum
1D IN NS @
1D IN A 192.168.0.7
wxp IN A 192.168.0.2
```

3. **Create the zone file**/var/named/0.168.192.zone **with the following lines in it:**

```
$TTL 86400
; Remember zone name is: 0.168.192.in-addr.arpa
@ IN SOA server7.net. root.server7.net (
1 ; Serial
28800 ; Refresh
14400 ; Retry
3600000 ; Expire
86400 ) ; Minimum
IN NS server7.net.
7 IN PTR server7.net.
2 IN PTR wxp.server7.net.
```

4. **To test the new configuration, restart the** named **server with the following command:**

```
sudo systemctl restart named
```

5. **Use** dig **or** host **to query the DNS server.**

Here's how to use host to check the address of the host wxp.server7.net at the DNS server running on localhost:

```
host wxp.server7.net localhost
```

This command results in the following output:

```
Using domain server:
Name: localhost
Address: 127.0.0.1#53
Aliases:
wxp.server7.net has address 192.168.0.2
```

If you want to use dig to check the DNS server, type the following command:

```
dig @localhost wxp.server7.net
```

That @localhost part specifies the DNS server that dig contacts.

When you successfully use dig to contact a DNS server, you can get a bit fancier with what you ask that server to do. Here, for example, is the command to type to try a reverse lookup with the IP address 192.168.0.2:

```
host 192.168.0.2 localhost
```

This command displays the following output:

```
Using domain server:
Name: localhost
Address: 127.0.0.1#53
Aliases:
2.0.168.192.in-addr.arpa domain name pointer wxp.server7.net
```

5

Administration

Contents at a Glance

CHAPTER 1: **Introducing Basic System Administration** 283

Taking Stock of System Administration Tasks. 284
Becoming root 285
Understanding How Linux Boots 287
Taking Stock of Linux System Configuration Files 294
Monitoring System Performance 296
Viewing System Information with the /proc File System 302
Understanding Linux Devices 305
Managing Loadable Driver Modules. 308
Scheduling Jobs in Linux. 310
Introducing Some GUI System Administration Tools. 316

CHAPTER 2: **Managing Users and Groups** 319

Adding User Accounts. 320
Understanding the /etc/passwd File 323
Managing Groups 324
Setting Other User and Group Administration Values. 325
Exploring the User Environment. 326
Changing User and Group Ownership of Files 328

CHAPTER 3: **Managing File Systems** 331

Exploring the Linux File System. 331
Sharing Files with NFS. 339
Backing Up and Restoring Files 341
Accessing a DOS or Windows File System 348
Mounting an NTFS partition. 351

CHAPTER 4: **Working with Samba and NFS** 353

Sharing Files with NFS. 353
Setting Up a Windows Server Using Samba 357

» **Understanding the system startup process**

» **Taking stock of the system configuration files**

» **Viewing system information through the /proc file system**

» **Monitoring system performance**

» **Managing devices and scheduling jobs**

» **Using GUI system administration tools**

Chapter **1**

Introducing Basic System Administration

S ystem administration refers to whatever must be done to keep a computer system up and running. That system could be just a stand-alone client machine, a network server that an organization depends on for its livelihood, and almost anything in between the two extremes. The *system administrator* is whoever is in charge of taking care of these tasks and making the system perform as needed.

If you're running Linux at home or in a small office, you're most likely the only one who can do it; thus, you're the system administrator for your systems. Or maybe you're the system administrator for an entire local-area network (LAN) full of Linux servers running an e-commerce site. Regardless of your position or title, this chapter introduces you to some of the basic system administration procedures and shows you how to perform common tasks.

Taking Stock of System Administration Tasks

What are system administration tasks? An off-the-cuff reply is "Anything you have to do to keep the system running well." More accurately, though, a system administrator's duties include

- » **Adding and removing user accounts:** You have to add new user accounts and remove unnecessary user accounts. If a user forgets the password, you have to change the password.

- » **Managing the printing system:** You have to turn the print queue on or off, check the print queue's status, and delete print jobs if necessary.

- » **Installing, configuring, and upgrading the operating system and various utilities:** You have to install or upgrade parts of the Linux operating system and other software that's part of the operating system.

- » **Installing new software:** You have to install software that comes in various package formats, such as RPM or DEB. You also have to download and unpack software that comes in source-code form and then build executable programs from the source code.

- » **Managing hardware:** Sometimes, you have to add new hardware and install drivers so that the devices work properly.

- » **Making backups:** You have to back up files, whether to an optical drive, a USB memory stick, a network server, an external hard drive, or tape.

- » **Mounting and unmounting file systems:** When you want to access the files on a DVD drive, for example, you have to mount that DVD's file system on one of the directories in your Linux file system. You may also have to mount such things as CD-ROMs or even old floppy disks from the archive closet that were created in both Linux format and DOS format.

- » **Automating tasks:** You have to schedule Linux tasks to take place automatically (at specific times) or periodically (at regular intervals).

- » **Monitoring the system's performance:** You may want to keep an eye on system performance to see where the processor is spending most of its time and to see the amount of free and used memory in the system.

- » **Starting and shutting down the system:** Although starting the system typically involves nothing more than powering up the PC, you do have to take some care when you shut down your Linux system. If your system is set up for a graphical login screen, you can perform the shutdown operation by choosing a menu item from the login screen. Otherwise, use the shutdown command to stop all programs before turning off your PC's power switch.

>> **Monitoring network status:** If you have a network presence (whether a LAN, a DSL line, or a cable modem connection), you may want to check the status of various network interfaces and make sure that your network connection is up and running.

>> **Setting up host and network security:** You have to make sure that system files are protected and that your system can defend itself against attacks over the network.

>> **Monitoring security:** You have to keep an eye on any intrusions, usually by checking the log files.

That's a long list of tasks! Not all these items are covered in this chapter, but the rest of Book 5 describes most of these tasks. The focus of this chapter is on some of the basics, such as becoming root (the superuser), describing the system configuration files, monitoring system performance, managing devices, setting up periodic jobs, and using the graphic user interface (GUI) tools.

Becoming root

You have to log in as root to perform system administration tasks. The root user is the superuser and the only account with all the privileges needed to do anything in the system.

WARNING

Common wisdom says you should *not* normally log in as root. When you're root, you can easily delete all the files with one misstep — especially when you're typing commands. You type the command rm *.html to delete all files that have the .html extension, for example. But what if you accidentally press the spacebar after the asterisk (*)? The shell takes the command to be rm * .html and — because * matches any filename — deletes everything in the current directory. This scenario seems implausible until it happens to you!

Using the su - command

If you're logged in as a normal user, how do you do any system administration chores? Well, you become root only for the time being. If you're working at a terminal window or console, type

```
su -
```

Then enter the root password in response to the prompt. From this point, you're root. Do whatever you have to do. To return to your usual self, type

```
exit
```

That's it! The process is easy and a lot safer than logging in and having an entire session as the root user.

DISTRIBUTION SPECIFIC

By the way, some distributions (such as Knoppix) have a root user but not a root password. In this case, you can become root simply by typing **su -** at the shell prompt in a terminal window. Other distributions (such as Ubuntu) don't have a root user. To perform any task that requires root privileges in Ubuntu, you must type **sudo** followed by the command and then provide your normal user password when prompted.

I address this issue in more detail in Book 6, but you can control who can use sudo through configuration files.

Recovering from a forgotten root password

To perform system administration tasks, you have to know the root password. What happens if you forget the root password? Not to worry. You can reset the root password by following these steps:

1. **Reboot the PC (select Reboot as you log out of the GUI screen) or power up as usual.**

As soon you see the graphical GRUB (GRand Unified BootLoader) bootloader screen that shows the names of the operating systems, you can boot. If your system runs the LILO (LInux Loader) bootloader, press Ctrl+X, type **linux single** at the boot: prompt, and press Enter. Then proceed to Step 4. If you don't see the graphical loader screen on reboot, it may not be installed (which can occasionally occur when you choose to install from a Live CD). In this case, I recommend that you reinstall from the CD.

2. **If you have more than one operating system installed, press the arrow key to select Linux as your operating system and then press the A key.**

GRUB prompts you for commands to add to its default boot command.

3. **Press the spacebar, type** single, **and press Enter.**

Linux starts as usual but runs in a single-user mode that doesn't require you to log in. After Linux starts, you see a command-line prompt similar to the following:

```
sh-3.00#
```

4. **Type the** passwd **command to change the** root **password as follows:**

```
sh-3.00# passwd
Changing password for user root.
New password:
```

5. **Type the new** root **password that you want to use (it doesn't appear onscreen) and then press Enter.**

   Linux asks for the password again, like this:

```
Retype new password:
```

6. **Type the password again, and press Enter.**

   If you enter the same password both times, the passwd command changes the root password.

7. **Type** reboot, **and press Enter to reboot the PC.**

   After Linux starts, it displays the familiar login screen. Now you can log in as root with the new password.

For SUSE Linux, make these changes:

» In Step 3, type **single init=/bin/sh** (instead of **single**), and before proceeding to Step 4, type **mount / -n -0 remount,rw** at the command-line prompt.

» Perform Steps 4 through 6 to change the root password; then type **mount / -n -o remount,ro** before continuing to Step 7 and rebooting the PC.

WARNING

Make sure that your Linux PC is *physically* secure. As these steps show, anyone who can physically access your Linux PC can simply reboot, set a new root password, and do whatever he or she wants with the system. Another way to protect against resetting the password is to set a GRUB password, which causes GRUB to require a valid password before it boots Linux. After that, of course, you must remember to enter the GRUB password every time you boot your system.

Understanding How Linux Boots

Knowing the sequence in which Linux starts processes as it boots is important. You can use this knowledge to start and stop services, such as the web server and Network File System (NFS). The next few sections provide an overview of how Linux boots and starts the initial set of processes. These sections also familiarize you with the shell scripts that start various services on a Linux system.

Understanding the init process

When Linux boots, it loads and runs the core operating-system program from the hard drive. The core operating system is designed to run other programs. A process named `init` starts the initial set of processes on your Linux system.

To see the processes currently running on the system, type

```
ps ax | more
```

You get an output listing that starts like this:

```
PID TTY STAT TIME COMMAND
1   ?    S  0:22 init [2]
```

The first column, with the heading *PID*, shows a number for each process. *PID* stands for process ID (identification) — a sequential number assigned by the Linux kernel. The first entry in the process list, with a PID of 1, is the `init` process. This entry starts all other processes in your Linux system, which is why `init` is sometimes referred to as the mother of all processes.

What the `init` process starts depends on

>> **The run level,** an identifier that identifies a system configuration in which only a selected group of processes can exist.

>> **The contents of the** `/etc/inittab` **file,** a text file that specifies which processes to start at different run levels.

>> **Shell scripts that are executed at specific run levels,** some of which are located in the `/etc/init.d` directory and subdirectories of `/etc`. (These subdirectories have names that begin with `rc`.)

DISTRIBUTION SPECIFIC

Most Linux distributions use seven run levels: 0 through 6. The meaning of the run levels differs from one distribution to another. Table 1-1 shows the meanings of the run levels and points out some of the actions specific to Fedora, Debian, SUSE, and Ubuntu.

The current run level together with the contents of the `/etc/inittab` file control which processes `init` starts in Linux. The default run level is 2 in Debian and Ubuntu. In Fedora and SUSE, run level 3 is used for text-mode login screens, and run level 5 is used for the graphical login screen. You can change the default run level by editing a line in the `/etc/inittab` file.

TABLE 1-1   **Run Levels in Linux**

Run Level	Meaning
0	Shut down the system.
1	Run in single-user stand-alone mode. (No one else can log in; you work at the text console.)
2	Run in multiuser mode. (Debian and Ubuntu use run level 2 as the default run level.)
3	Run in full multiuser mode (for text-mode login in Fedora and SUSE).
4	Run in full multiuser mode (unused in Fedora and SUSE).
5	Run in full multiuser mode (the default run level with graphical login in Fedora and SUSE).
6	Reboot the system.

To check the current run level, type the following command in a terminal window:

```
/sbin/runlevel
```

In Debian, the `runlevel` command prints an output like this:

```
N 2
```

The first character of the output shows the previous run level (N means no previous run level), and the second character shows the current run level (2). In this case, the system started at run level 2. If you're in a GUI desktop in Fedora, the `runlevel` command should show 5 as the current run level.

Examining the /etc/inittab file

The `/etc/inittab` file is the key to understanding the processes that `init` starts at various run levels. You can look at the contents of the file by using the `more` command, as follows:

```
more /etc/inittab
```

REMEMBER

To see the contents of the `/etc/inittab` file with the `more` command, you don't have to log in as `root`.

To interpret the contents of the /etc/inittab file, follow these steps:

1. **Look for the line that contains the phrase** initdefault.

   Here's that line from the /etc/inittab file in a Debian system:

   ```
   id:2:initdefault:
   ```

   That line shows the default run level (in this case, 2).

2. **Find all the lines that specify what** init **runs at run level 2.**

   Look for a line that has a 2 between the first two colons (:). Here's a relevant line in Debian:

   ```
   12:2:wait:/etc/init.d/rc 2
   ```

   This line specifies that init executes the file /etc/init.d/rc with 2 as an argument.

If you look at the file /etc/init.d/rc in a Debian system, you find that it's a shell script. You can study this file to see how it starts various processes for run levels 1 through 5.

TECHNICAL STUFF

Each entry in the /etc/inittab file tells init what to do at one or more run levels; you simply list all run levels at which the process runs. Each inittab entry has four fields, separated by colons, in the following format:

```
id:runlevels:action:process
```

Table 1-2 shows what each field means.

TABLE 1-2   **Fields in Each inittab Entry**

Field	Meaning
id	A unique one- or two-character identifier. The init process uses this field internally. You can use any identifier you want as long as you don't use the same identifier on more than one line.
runlevels	A sequence of zero or more characters, each denoting a run level. For example, if the runlevels field is 12345, that entry applies to each of the run levels (1 through 5). This field is ignored if the action field is set to sysinit, boot, or bootwait.
action	What the init process will do with this entry. If this field is initdefault, for example, init interprets the runlevels field as the default run level. If this field is set to wait, init starts the program or script specified in the process field and waits until that process exits.
process	Name of the script or program that init starts. Some settings of the action field require no process field. When the action field is initdefault, for example, there's no need for a process field.

Trying a new run level with the init command

To try a new run level, you don't have to change the default run level in the /etc/inittab file. If you log in as root, you can change the run level (and, consequently, the processes that run in Linux) by typing **init** followed by the run level.

To put the system in single-user mode, for example, type the following:

```
init 1
```

Thus, if you want to try run level 3 without changing the default run level in the /etc/inittab file, enter the following command at the shell prompt:

```
init 3
```

The system ends all current processes and enters run level 3. By default, the init command waits 20 seconds before stopping all current processes and starting the new processes for run level 3.

TIP

To switch to run level 3 immediately, type the command init -t0 3. The number after the -t option indicates the number of seconds init waits before changing the run level.

You can also use the telinit command, which is simply a symbolic link (a shortcut) to init. If you make changes in the /etc/inittab file and want init to reload its configuration file, use the command telinit q.

Understanding the Linux startup scripts

The init process runs several scripts at system startup. In the following discussions, a Debian system is used as an example, but the basic sequence is similar in other distributions; only the names and locations of the scripts may vary.

DISTRIBUTION SPECIFIC

If you look at the /etc/inittab file in a Debian system, you find the following lines near the beginning of the file:

```
# Boot-time system configuration/initialization script.
  si::sysinit:/etc/init.d/rcS
```

The first line is a comment line. The second line causes init to run the /etc/init.d/rcS script, which is the first Linux startup script that init runs in a Debian system. The rcS script performs many initialization tasks, such as mounting the file systems, setting the clock, configuring the keyboard layout, starting the net-work, and loading many other driver modules. The rcS script performs these initialization tasks by calling many other scripts and reading configuration files located in the /etc/rcS.d directory.

After executing the /etc/init.d/rcS script, the init process runs the /etc/init.d/rc script with the run level as an argument. For run level 2, the following line in /etc/inittab specifies what init executes:

```
l2:2:wait:/etc/init.d/rc 2
```

This example says that init executes the command /etc/init.d/rc 2 and waits until that command completes.

The /etc/init.d/rc script is somewhat complicated. Here's how it works:

>> It executes scripts in a directory corresponding to the run level. For example, for run level 2, the /etc/init.d/rc script runs the scripts in the /etc/rc2.d directory.

>> In the directory that corresponds with the run level, /etc/init.d/rc looks for all files that begin with K and executes each of them with the stop argument, which kills any currently running processes. Then it locates all files that begin with S and executes each file with a start argument, which starts the processes needed for the specified run level.

To see what happens if the script is executed at run level 2, type the following command:

```
ls -l /etc/rc2.d
```

In the resulting listing, the K scripts — the files whose names begin with K — stop (or *kill*) servers, whereas the S scripts start servers. The /etc/init.d/rc script executes these files in the order in which they appear in the directory listing.

Manually starting and stopping servers

In Linux, the server startup scripts reside in the /etc/init.d directory. You can manually invoke scripts in this directory to start, stop, or restart specific processes — usually, servers. To stop the FTP server, for example (the server program is vsftpd), type the following command:

```
/etc/init.d/vsftpd stop
```

If vsftpd is already running, and you want to restart it, type the following command:

```
/etc/init.d/vsftpd restart
```

You can enhance your system administration skills by familiarizing yourself with the scripts in the /etc/init.d directory. To see that directory's listing, type the following command:

```
ls /etc/init.d
```

The script names give you some clue about which server the scripts can start and stop. The samba script, for example, starts and stops the processes required for Samba Windows networking services. At your leisure, you may want to study some of these scripts to see what they do. You don't have to understand all the shell programming; the comments help you discover the purpose of each script.

Automatically starting servers at system startup

You want some servers to start automatically every time you boot the system. The exact commands to configure the servers vary from one distribution to another.

DISTRIBUTION SPECIFIC

In Fedora and SUSE, use the chkconfig command to set up a server to start whenever the system boots into a specific run level. If you start the Secure Shell (SSH) server, for example, you want the sshd server to start whenever the system starts. You can make that startup happen by using the chkconfig command. To set sshd to start whenever the system boots into run level 3, 4, or 5, type the following command (while logged in as root):

```
chkconfig --level 345 sshd on
```

DISTRIBUTION SPECIFIC

In Fedora and SUSE, you can also use the chkconfig command to check which servers are turned on or off. To see the complete list of all servers for all run levels, type the following command:

```
chkconfig --list
```

DISTRIBUTION SPECIFIC

In Debian and Ubuntu, you can use the update-rc.d command to enable a server to start automatically at system startup. To set sshd to start automatically at the default run levels, for example, type **update-rc.d sshd defaults** in a terminal window while logged in as root. You can also specify the exact run levels and the sequence number (the order in which each server starts). To find out more about the update-rc.d command, type **man update-rc.d** in a terminal window.

Taking Stock of Linux System Configuration Files

Linux includes a host of configuration files. All these files share text files that you can edit with any text editor. To edit these configuration files, you must log in as root. Table 1-3 lists some of the most popular configuration files and briefly describes them. This table gives you an idea of what types of configuration files a system administrator has to work with. In many cases, Linux includes GUI utility programs for setting up many of these configuration files.

TABLE 1-3   Some Linux Configuration Files

Configuration File	Description
/boot/grub	Location of files for the GRUB bootloader.
/boot/grub/menu.lst	Configuration file for the boot menu that GRUB displays before it boots your system.
/boot/System.map	Map of the Linux kernel (this file maps the kernel addresses into names of functions and variables).
/boot/vmlinuz	The Linux kernel (the operating system's core).
/etc/apache2/ httpd.conf	Configuration file for the Apache web server (Debian).
/etc/apt/ sources.list	Configuration file that lists the sources — FTP or websites or CD-ROM — from which the Advanced Packaging Tool (APT) obtains packages (Debian and Ubuntu).
/etc/at.allow	Usernames of users allowed to use the at command to schedule jobs for later execution.
/etc/at.deny	Usernames of users forbidden to use the at command.
/etc/bashrc	Systemwide functions and aliases for the bash shell (Fedora).
/etc/bash.bashrc	Systemwide functions and aliases for the bash shell (Debian, SUSE, and Ubuntu).
/etc/cups/ cupsd.conf	Printer configuration file for the Common Unix Printing System (CUPS) scheduler.

Configuration File	Description
/etc/fonts	Directory with font configuration files. (In particular, you can put local font configuration settings in the file /etc/fonts/local.conf.)
/etc/fstab	Information about file systems available for mounting and where each file system is to be mounted.
/etc/group	Information about groups.
/etc/grub.conf	The configuration for the GRUB bootloader in Fedora and SUSE.
/etc/hosts	List of IP numbers and their corresponding host names.
/etc/hosts.allow	Hosts allowed to access Internet services on this system.
/etc/hosts.deny	Hosts forbidden to access Internet services on this system.
/etc/httpd/conf/ httpd.conf	Configuration file for the Apache web server (Fedora).
/etc/init.d	Directory with scripts to start and stop various servers.
/etc/init.d/rcS	Linux initialization script in Debian, SUSE, and Ubuntu.
/etc/inittab	Configuration file used by the init process that starts all the other processes.
/etc/issue	File containing a message to be printed before displaying the text mode login prompt (usually, the distribution name and the version number).
/etc/lilo.conf	The configuration for the Linux Loader (LILO) — one of the bootloaders that can load the operating system from disk (present only if you use the LILO bootloader).
/etc/login.defs	Default information for creating user accounts, used by the useradd command.
/etc/modprobe.conf	Configuration file for loadable kernel modules, used by the modprobe command (Fedora and SUSE).
/etc/modules.conf	Configuration file for loadable modules (Debian).
/etc/mtab	Information about currently mounted file systems.
/etc/passwd	Information about all user accounts. (Actual passwords are stored in /etc/shadow.)
/etc/profile	Systemwide environment and startup file for the bash shell.
/etc/profile.d	Directory containing script files (with names that end in .sh) that the /etc/profile script executes.
/etc/rc.d/ rc.sysinit	Linux initialization script in Fedora.

(continued)

TABLE 1-3 *(continued)*

Configuration File	Description
/etc/shadow	Secure file with encrypted passwords for all user accounts (can be read only by root).
/etc/shells	List of all the shells on the system that the user can use.
/etc/skel	Directory that holds initial versions of files such as .bash_profile that copy to a new user's home directory.
/etc/sysconfig	Linux configuration files (Fedora and SUSE).
/etc/sysctl.conf	Configuration file with kernel parameters that are read in and set by sysctl at system startup.
/etc/termcap	Database of terminal capabilities and options (Fedora and SUSE).
/etc/udev	Directory containing configuration files for udev — the program that allows you to dynamically name hot-pluggable devices and create device files in the /dev directory.
/etc/X11	Directory with configuration files for the X Window System (X11) and various display managers, such as gdm and xdm.
/etc/X11/xorg.conf	Configuration file for X.Org X11 — the X Window System (Fedora, Ubuntu, and SUSE).
/etc/xinetd.conf	Configuration for the xinetd daemon that starts Internet services on demand.
/etc/yum.conf	Configuration for the Yum package updater and installer (Fedora).
/var/log/apache2	Web-server access and error logs (Debian).
/var/log/cron	Log file with messages from the cron process that runs scheduled jobs.
/var/log/boot.msg	File with boot messages (SUSE).
/var/log/dmesg	File with boot messages (Debian, Fedora, and Ubuntu).
/var/log/httpd	Web-server access and error logs (Fedora).
/var/log/messages	System log.

Monitoring System Performance

When you're the system administrator, you must keep an eye on how well your Linux system is performing. You can monitor the overall performance of your system by looking at information such as

- » Central processing unit (CPU) usage
- » Physical memory usage
- » Virtual memory (swap-space) usage
- » Hard drive usage

Linux comes with utilities that you can use to monitor these performance parameters. The following sections introduce a few of these utilities and show you how to understand the information presented by said utilities.

Using the top utility

To view the top CPU processes — the ones that use most of the CPU time — you can use the text mode top utility. To start that utility, type **top** in a terminal window (or text console). The top utility displays a text screen listing the current processes, arranged in the order of CPU usage, along with various other information, such as memory and swap-space usage. Figure 1-1 shows typical output from the top utility.

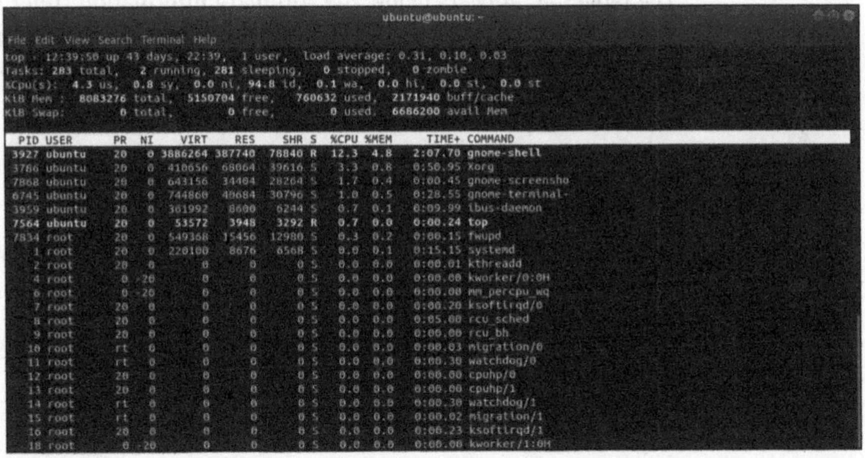

FIGURE 1-1:
You can see the top CPU processes by using the top utility.

The top utility updates the display every 5 seconds. If you keep top running in a window, you can continually monitor the status of your Linux system. To quit top, press Q, press Ctrl+C, or close the terminal window.

The first five lines of the output screen (refer to Figure 1-1) provide summary information about the system, as follows:

» The first line shows the current time, how long the system has been up, how many users are logged in, and three *load averages* — the average number of processes ready to run during the past 1, 5, and 15 minutes.

» The second line lists the total number of processes/tasks and the status of these processes.

» The third line shows CPU usage — what percentage of CPU time is used by user processes, what percentage by system (kernel) processes, and the percentage of time during which the CPU is idle.

» The fourth line shows how the physical memory is being used — the total amount, how much is used, how much is free, and how much is allocated to buffers (for reading from the hard drive, for example).

» The fifth line shows how the virtual memory (or swap space) is being used — the total amount of swap space, how much is used, how much is free, and how much is being cached.

The table that appears below the summary information (refer to Figure 1-1) lists information about the current processes, arranged in decreasing order by amount of CPU time used. Table 1-4 summarizes the meanings of the column headings in the table that top displays.

Using the uptime command

You can use the uptime command to get a summary of the system's state. Just type the command like this:

```
uptime
```

It displays output similar to the following:

```
15:03:21 up 32 days, 57 min, 3 users, load average: 0.13, 0.23, 0.27
```

This output shows the current time, how long the system has been up, the number of users, and (finally) the three load averages — the average number of processes that were ready to run in the past 1, 5, and 15 minutes. Load averages greater than 1 imply that many processes are competing for CPU time simultaneously.

The load averages give you an indication of how busy the system is.

TABLE 1-4   **Column Headings in top Utility's Output**

Heading	Meaning
PID	Process ID of the process.
USER	Username under which the process is running.
PR	Priority of the process.
NI	Nice value of the process. The value ranges from –20 (highest priority) to 19 (lowest priority), and the default is 0. (The *nice value* represents the relative priority of the process: The higher the value, the lower the priority and the nicer the process, because it yields to other processes.)
VIRT	Total amount of virtual memory used by the process, in kilobytes.
RES	Total physical memory used by a task (typically shown in kilobytes, but an m suffix indicates megabytes).
SHR	Amount of shared memory used by the process.
S	State of the process (S for sleeping, D for uninterruptible sleep, R for running, Z for zombies — processes that should be dead but are still running — and T for stopped).
%CPU	Percentage of CPU time used since the last screen update.
%MEM	Percentage of physical memory used by the process.
TIME+	Total CPU time the process has used since it started.
COMMAND	Shortened form of the command that started the process.

Using the vmstat utility

You can get summary information about the overall system usage with the vmstat utility. To view system usage information averaged over 5-second intervals, type the following command (the second argument indicates the total number of lines of output vmstat displays):

```
vmstat 5 8
```

You see output similar to the following listing:

```
procs -----------memory---------- ---swap-- -----io---- --system-- ----cpu----
 r  b   swpd   free   buff  cache   si   so    bi    bo   in   cs us sy id wa
 0  0  31324   4016  18568 136004    1    1    17    16    8  110 33  4 61  1
 0  1  31324   2520  15348 139692    0    0  7798   199 1157  377  8  8  6 78
 1  0  31324   1584  12936 141480    0   19  5784   105 1099  437 12  5  0 82
 2  0  31324   1928  13004 137136    7    0  1586   138 1104  561 43  6  0 51
 3  1  31324   1484  13148 132064    0    0  1260    51 1080  427 50  5  0 46
```

```
0 0 31324 1804 13240 127976 0 0 1126 46 1082 782 19 5 47 30
0 0 31324 1900 13240 127976 0 0 0 0 1010 211 3 1 96 0
0 0 31324 1916 13248 127976 0 0 0 10 1015 224 3 2 95 0
```

The first line of output shows the averages since the last reboot. After that line, vmstat displays the 5-second average data seven more times, covering the next 35 seconds. The tabular output is grouped as six categories of information, indicated by the fields in the first line of output. The second line shows further details for each of the six major fields. You can interpret these fields by using Table 1-5.

TABLE 1-5   **Meaning of Fields in the vmstat Utility's Output**

Field Name	Description
procs	Number of processes and their types: r = processes waiting to run, b = processes in uninterruptible sleep, and w = processes swapped out but ready to run.
memory	Information about physical memory and swap-space usage (all numbers in kilobytes): swpd = virtual memory used, free = free physical memory, buff = memory used as buffers, and cache = virtual memory that's cached.
swap	Amount of swapping (the numbers are in kilobytes per second): si = amount of memory swapped in from disk, and so = amount of memory swapped to disk.
io	Information about input and output. (The numbers are in blocks per second, where the block size depends on the disk device.) bi = rate of blocks sent to disk, and bo = rate of blocks received from disk.
system	Information about the system: in = number of interrupts per second (including clock interrupts), and cs = number of context switches per second — how many times the kernel changed which process was running.
cpu	Percentages of CPU time used: us = percentage of CPU time used by user processes, sy = percentage of CPU time used by system processes, id = percentage of time CPU is idle, and wa = time spent waiting for input or output (I/O).

TECHNICAL STUFF

In the vmstat utility's output, high values in the si and so fields indicate too much swapping. (*Swapping* refers to the copying of information between physical memory and the virtual memory on the hard drive.) High numbers in the bi and bo fields indicate too much disk activity.

Checking disk performance and disk usage

Linux comes with the /sbin/hdparm program to control IDE or ATAPI hard drives, which are common on PCs. One feature of the hdparm program allows you to use the –t option to determine the rate at which data is read from the disk into a buffer in memory. Here's the result of typing **/sbin/hdparm -t /dev/hda** on one system:

```
/dev/hda:
 Timing buffered disk reads: 178 MB in 3.03 seconds = 58.81 MB/sec
```

The command requires the IDE drive's device name (/dev/hda for the first hard drive and /dev/hdb for the second hard drive) as an argument. If you have an IDE hard drive, you can try this command to see how fast data is read from your system's disk drive.

To display the space available in the currently mounted file systems, use the df command. If you want a more readable output from df, type the following command:

```
df -h
```

Here's typical output from this command:

```
Filesystem Size Used Avail Use% Mounted on
/dev/hda5 7.1G 3.9G 2.9G 59% /
/dev/hda3 99M 18M 77M 19% /boot
none 125M 0 125M 0% /dev/shm
/dev/scd0 2.6G 0 100% /media/cdrecorder
```

As this example shows, the –h option causes the df command to display the sizes in gigabytes (G) and megabytes (M).

To check the disk space being used by a specific directory, use the du command. You can specify the –h option to view the output in kilobytes (K) and megabytes (M), as shown in the following example:

```
du -h /var/log
```

Here's typical output from that command:

```
152K /var/log/cups
4.0K /var/log/vbox
4.0K /var/log/httpd
508K /var/log/gdm
4.0K /var/log/samba
8.0K /var/log/mail
4.0K /var/log/news/OLD
8.0K /var/log/news
4.0K /var/log/squid
2.2M /var/log
```

The du command displays the disk space used by each directory, and the last line shows the total disk space used by that directory. If you want to see only the total space used by a directory, use the –s option. Type **du -sh /home** to see the space used by the /home directory, for example. The command produces output that looks like this:

```
89M  /home
```

Viewing System Information with the /proc File System

Your Linux system has a special /proc file system. You can find out many things about your system from this file system. In fact, you can even change kernel parameters through the /proc file system (just by writing to a file in that file system), thereby modifying the system's behavior.

The /proc file system isn't a real directory on the hard drive but a collection of data structures in memory, managed by the Linux kernel, that appears to you as a set of directories and files. The purpose of /proc (also called the *process file system*) is to give you access to information about the Linux kernel, as well as help you find out about all processes currently running on your system.

You can access the /proc file system just as you access any other directory, but you have to know the meaning of various files to interpret the information. Typically, you use the cat or more command to view the contents of a file in /proc. The file's contents provide information about some aspect of the system.

As with any directory, start by looking at a detailed directory listing of /proc. To do so, log in as root and type **ls -l /proc** in a terminal window. In the output, the first set of directories (indicated by the letter d at the beginning of the line) represents the processes currently running on your system. Each directory that corresponds to a process has the process ID (a number) as its name.

WARNING

Notice also a very large file named /proc/kcore; that file represents the *entire* physical memory of your system. Although /proc/kcore appears in the listing as a huge file, no single physical file occupies that much space on your hard drive, so don't try to remove the file to reclaim disk space.

Several files and directories in /proc contain interesting information about your Linux PC. The /proc/cpuinfo file, for example, lists the key characteristics of your system, such as processor type and floating-point processor information. You can view the processor information by typing **cat /proc/cpuinfo**. Here's what appears when cat /proc/cpuinfo is run on a sample system:

```
processor : 0
vendor_id : GenuineIntel
cpu family : 6
model : 42
model name : Intel(R) Core(TM)i5-2410M CPU 2.30GHz
stepping : 7
cpu MHz : 2294.764
cache size : 3072 KB
phsical id : 0
siblings : 4
core id : 0
cpu cores : 2
apicid : 0
initial apicid : 0
fpu : yes
fpu_exception : yes
cpuid level : 13
wp : yes
flags : fpu vme de pse tsc msr pae mce cx8 apic sep mtrr pge mca
   cmov pat pse36 clflush dts acpi mmx fxsr sse sse2 ss ht tm pbe
   pni monitor ds_cpl cid
bogomips : 4589.52
```

This output is from an Intel Core i5-2410M system (2.30 GHz x 4). The listing shows many interesting characteristics of the processor. The last line in the /proc/cpuinfo file shows the BogoMIPS for the processor, as computed by the Linux kernel when it boots. (BogoMIPS is something that Linux uses internally to time-delay loops.)

Table 1-6 summarizes some of the files in the /proc file system that provide information about your Linux system. You can view some of these files on your system to see what they contain but note that not all files shown in Table 1-6 are present on your system. The specific contents of the /proc file system depend on the kernel configuration and the driver modules that are loaded (which in turn depend on your PC's hardware configuration).

TIP

You can navigate the /proc file system just as you'd work with any other directories and files in Linux. Use the more or cat command to view the contents of a file.

Introducing Basic
System Administration

TABLE 1-6   Some Files and Directories in /proc

File Name	Content
/proc/acpi	Information about Advanced Configuration and Power Interface (ACPI) — an industry-standard interface for configuration and power management on laptops, desktops, and servers.
/proc/bus	Directory with bus-specific information for each bus type, such as PCI.
/proc/cmdline	The command line used to start the Linux kernel (such as ro root=LABEL=/ rhgb).
/proc/cpuinfo	Information about the CPU (the microprocessor).
/proc/devices	Available block and character devices in your system.
/proc/dma	Information about DMA (direct memory access) channels that are used.
/proc/driver/rtc	Information about the PC's real-time clock (RTC).
/proc/filesystems	List of supported file systems.
/proc/ide	Directory containing information about IDE devices.
/proc/interrupts	Information about interrupt request (IRQ) numbers and how they're used.
/proc/ioports	Information about input/output (I/O) port addresses and how they're used.
/proc/kcore	Image of the physical memory.
/proc/kmsg	Kernel messages.
/proc/loadavg	Load average (average number of processes waiting to run in the past 1, 5, and 15 minutes).
/proc/locks	Current kernel locks (used to ensure that multiple processes don't write to a file at the same time).
/proc/meminfo	Information about physical memory and swap-space usage.
/proc/misc	Miscellaneous information.
/proc/modules	List of loaded driver modules.
/proc/mounts	List of mounted file systems.
/proc/net	Directory with many subdirectories that contain information about networking.
/proc/partitions	List of partitions known to the Linux kernel.
/proc/pci	Information about PCI devices found on the system.
/proc/scsi	Directory with information about SCSI devices found on the system (present only if you have a SCSI device).

File Name	Content
/proc/stat	Overall statistics about the system.
/proc/swaps	Information about the swap space and how much is used.
/proc/sys	Directory with information about the system. You can change kernel parameters by writing to files in this directory. (Using this method to tune system performance requires expertise to do properly.)
/proc/uptime	Information about how long the system has been up.
/proc/version	Kernel version number.

Understanding Linux Devices

Linux treats all devices as files and uses a device just as it uses a file — opens it, writes data to it, reads data from it, and closes it when finished. This ability to treat every device as a file is possible because of *device drivers*, which are special programs that control a particular type of hardware. When the kernel writes data to the device, the device driver does whatever is appropriate for that device. When the kernel writes data to the DVD drive, for example, the DVD device driver puts that data on the physical medium of the DVD disk.

Thus, the device driver isolates the device-specific code from the rest of the kernel and makes a device look like a file. Any application can access a device by opening the file specific to that device.

Device files

Applications can access a device as though it were a file. These files, called *device files*, appear in the /dev directory in the Linux file system.

If you use the ls command to look at the list of files in the /dev directory, you see several thousand files. These files don't mean that your system has several thousand devices. The /dev directory has files for all possible types of devices, which is why the number of device files is so large.

How does the kernel know which device driver to use when an application opens a specific device file? The answer is in two numbers called the *major* and *minor device numbers*. Each device file is mapped to a specific device driver through these numbers.

To see an example of the major and minor device numbers, type the following command in a terminal window:

```
ls -l /dev/hda
```

You see a line of output similar to the following:

```
brw-rw---- 1 root disk 3, 0 Aug 16 14:50 /dev/hda
```

In this line, the major and minor device numbers appear just before the date. In this case, the major device number is 3, and the minor device number is 0. The kernel selects the device driver for this device file by using the major device number.

You don't have to know much about device files and device numbers except to be aware of their existence.

TECHNICAL STUFF

In case you're curious, all the major and minor numbers for devices are assigned according to device type. The Linux Assigned Names And Numbers Authority (LANANA) assigns these numbers. You can see the current device list at www.lanana.org/docs/device-list/devices-2.6+.txt.

Block devices

The first letter in the listing of a device file also provides an important clue. For the /dev/hda device, the first letter is b, which indicates that /dev/hda is a *block device* — one that can accept or provide data in chunks (typically, 512 bytes or 1KB). By the way, /dev/hda refers to the first IDE hard drive on your system (the C: drive in Windows). Hard drives and CD-ROM drives are examples of block devices.

Character devices

If the first letter in the listing of a device file is c, the device is a *character device* — one that can receive and send data one character (1 byte) at a time. The serial port and parallel ports, for example, are character devices. To see the specific listing of a character device, type the following command in a terminal window:

```
ls -l /dev/ttyS0
```

The listing of this device is similar to the following:

```
crw-rw---- 1 root uucp 4, 64 Aug 16 14:50 /dev/ttyS0
```

Note that the first letter is c because /dev/ttyS0 — the first serial port — is a character device.

Network devices

Network devices that enable your system to interact with a network — such as Ethernet and dial-up Point-to-Point Protocol (PPP) connections — are special because they need no file to correspond to the device. Instead, the kernel uses a special name for the device. Ethernet devices, for example, are named eth0 for the first Ethernet card, eth1 for the second one, and so on. PPP connections are named ppp0, ppp1, and so on.

Because network devices aren't mapped to device files, no files corresponding to these devices are in the /dev directory.

Persistent device naming with udev

Starting with the Linux kernel 2.6, a new approach for handling devices was added, based on the following features:

>> **sysfs:** The kernel provides the sysfs file system, which is mounted on the / sys directory of the file system. The sysfs file system displays all the devices in the system as well as lots of information about each device, including the location of the device on the bus, attributes such as name and serial number, and the major and minor numbers of the device.

>> **/sbin/hotplug:** This program is called whenever a device is added or removed and can do whatever is necessary to handle the device.

>> **/sbin/udev:** This program takes care of dynamically named devices based on device characteristics such as serial number, device number on a bus, or a user-assigned name based on a set of rules that are set through the text file / etc/udev/udev.rules.

REMEMBER

The udev program's configuration file is /etc/udev/udev.conf. Based on settings in that configuration file, udev creates device nodes automatically in the directory specified by the udev_root parameter. To manage the device nodes in the /dev directory, for example, udev_root should be defined in /etc/udev/udev.conf as follows:

```
udev_root="/dev/"
```

Managing Loadable Driver Modules

To use any device, the Linux kernel must contain the driver. If the driver code is linked into the kernel as a *monolithic* program (a program in the form of a single large file), adding a new driver means rebuilding the kernel with the new driver code. Rebuilding the kernel means that you have to reboot the PC with the new kernel before you can use the new device driver. Luckily, the Linux kernel uses a modular design that does away with rebooting hassles. Linux device drivers can be created in the form of modules that the kernel can load and unload without having to restart the PC.

TECHNICAL STUFF

Driver modules are one type of a broader category of software modules called *loadable kernel modules.* Other types of kernel modules include code that can support new types of file systems, modules for network protocols, and modules that interpret different formats of executable files.

Loading and unloading modules

You can manage the loadable device driver modules by using a set of commands. You have to log in as root to use some of these commands. Table 1-7 summarizes a few common module commands.

If you have to use any of these commands, log in as root or type **su -** in a terminal window to become root.

TABLE 1-7   Commands to Manage Kernel Modules

This Command	Does the Following
insmod	Inserts a module into the kernel.
rmmod	Removes a module from the kernel.
depmod	Determines interdependencies among modules.
ksyms	Displays a list of symbols along with the name of the module that defines the symbol.
lsmod	Lists all currently loaded modules.
modinfo	Displays information about a kernel module.
modprobe	Inserts or removes a module or a set of modules intelligently. (If module A requires B, for example, modprobe automatically loads B when asked to load A.)

To see what modules are currently loaded, type **lsmod**. You see a long list of modules. The list that you see depends on the types of devices installed on your system.

The list displayed by `lsmod` includes all types of Linux kernel modules, not just device drivers. If you use the Ext3 file system, you typically find two modules — jbd and ext3 — that are part of the Ext3 file system (the latest file system for Linux).

REMEMBER

Another commonly used module command is `modprobe`. Use `modprobe` when you need to manually load or remove one or more modules. The best thing about `modprobe` is that you don't need to worry if a module requires other modules to work. The `modprobe` command automatically loads any other module needed by a module. To manually load the sound driver, use the command

```
modprobe snd-card-0
```

This command causes `modprobe` to load everything needed to make sound work.

TIP

You can use `modprobe` with the `-r` option to remove modules. To remove the sound modules, use the following command:

```
modprobe -r snd-card-0
```

This command gets rid of all the modules that the `modprobe snd-card-0` command loaded.

Understanding the /etc/modprobe.d files

How does the `modprobe` command know that it needs to load the `snd-intel8x0` driver module? The answer's in the configuration files beneath the `/etc/modprobe.d` directory. The files there, all ending in the extension `.conf`, contain instructions that tell `modprobe` what it should load when it load a module.

To view the contents of a particular configuration file, type

```
cat /etc/modprobe.d/xxx.conf
```

Where xxx is the name of the configuration file that you want to view.

Scheduling Jobs in Linux

As a system administrator, you may have to run some programs automatically at regular intervals or execute one or more commands at a specified time in the future. Your Linux system includes the facilities to schedule jobs to run at any future date or time you want. You can also set up the system to perform a task periodically or just once. Here are some typical tasks you can perform by scheduling jobs on your Linux system:

>> Back up the files in the middle of the night.

>> Download large files in the early morning when the system isn't busy.

>> Send yourself messages as reminders of meetings.

>> Analyze system logs periodically and look for any abnormal activities.

You can set up these jobs by using the at command or the crontab facility of Linux. The next few sections introduce these job-scheduling features of Linux.

Scheduling one-time jobs

If you want to run one or more commands at a later time, you can use the at command. The atd *daemon* — a program designed to process jobs submitted with at — runs your commands at the specified time and mails the output to you.

REMEMBER

Before you try the at command, you need to know that the following configuration files control which users can schedule tasks by using the at command:

>> /etc/at.allow contains the names of the users who may use the at command to submit jobs.

>> /etc/at.deny contains the names of users who are not allowed to use the at command to submit jobs.

If these files aren't present, or if you find an empty /etc/at.deny file, any user can submit jobs by using the at command. The default in Linux is an empty /etc/at.deny file; when this default is in place, anyone can use the at command. If you don't want some users to use at, simply list their usernames in the /etc/at.deny file.

To use at to schedule a one-time job for execution at a later time, follow these steps:

1. **Run the at command with the date or time when you want your commands to be executed.**

   When you press Enter, the at> prompt appears, as follows:

   ```
   at 21:30
   at>
   ```

   This method is the simplest way to indicate the time when you want to execute one or more commands; simply specify the time in a 24-hour format. In this case, you want to execute the commands at 9:30 tonight (or tomorrow, if it's already past 9:30 p.m.). You can, however, specify the execution time in many ways. (See Table 1-8 for examples.)

TABLE 1-8   **Formats for the at Command for the Time of Execution**

Command	When the Job Will Run
at now	Immediately
at now + 15 minutes	15 minutes from the current time
at now + 4 hours	4 hours from the current time
at now + 7 days	7 days from the current time
at noon	At noon today (or tomorrow, if it's already past noon)
at now next hour	Exactly 60 minutes from now
at now next day	At the same time tomorrow
at 17:00 tomorrow	At 5:00 p.m. tomorrow
at 4:45pm	At 4:45 p.m. today (or tomorrow, if it's already past 4:45 p.m.)
at 3:00 Dec 28, 2018	At 3:00 a.m. on December 28, 2018

2. **At the at> prompt, type the commands you want to execute as though you were typing at the shell prompt.**

   After each command, press Enter and continue with the next command.

3. **When you finish entering the commands you want to execute, press Ctrl+D to indicate the end.**

Here's an example that shows how to execute the ps command at a future time:

```
at> ps
at> <EOT>
job 1 at 2018-12-28 21:30
```

After you press Ctrl+D, the at command responds with the <EOT> message, a job number, and the date and time when the job will execute.

After you enter one or more jobs, you can view the current list of scheduled jobs with the atq command. The output of this command looks similar to the following:

```
4 2018-12-28 03:00 a root
5 2018-10-26 21:57 a root
6 2018-10-26 16:45 a root
```

The first field in each line shows the job number — the same number that the at command displays when you submit the job. The next field shows the year, month, day, and time of execution. The last field shows the jobs pending in the a queue and the username.

If you want to cancel a job, use the atrm command to remove that job from the queue. When you're removing a job with the atrm command, refer to the job by its number, as follows:

```
atrm 4
```

This command deletes job 4 scheduled for 3:00 a.m. on December 28, 2018.

TIP

When a job executes, the output is mailed to you. Type **mail** at a terminal window to read your mail and to view the output from your jobs.

Scheduling recurring jobs

Although at is good for running commands at a specific time, it's not useful for running a program automatically at repeated intervals. You have to use crontab to schedule such recurring jobs, such as if you want to back up your files to tape at midnight every evening.

You schedule recurring jobs by placing job information in a file with a specific format and submitting this file with the crontab command. The cron daemon — crond — checks the job information every minute and executes the recurring jobs at the specified times. Because the cron daemon processes recurring jobs, such jobs are also referred to as *cron jobs*.

Any output from a cron job is mailed to the user who submits the job. (In the submitted job-information file, you can specify a different recipient for the mailed output.)

Two configuration files control who can schedule cron jobs by using crontab:

» /etc/cron.allow contains the names of the users who are allowed to use the crontab command to submit jobs.

» /etc/cron.deny contains the names of users who are not allowed to use the crontab command to submit jobs.

If the /etc/cron.allow file exists, only users listed in this file can schedule cron jobs. If only the /etc/cron.deny file exists, users listed in this file can't schedule cron jobs. If neither file exists, the default Linux setup enables any user to submit cron jobs.

To submit a cron job, follow these steps:

1. **Prepare a shell script (or an executable program in any programming language) that can perform the recurring task you want to perform.**

You can skip this step if you want to execute an existing program periodically.

2. **Prepare a text file with information about the times when you want the shell script or program (from Step 1) to execute; then submit this file by using crontab.**

You can submit several recurring jobs with a single file. Each line with timing information about a job has a standard format, with six fields. The first five fields specify when the job runs, and the sixth and subsequent fields constitute the command that runs. Here's a line that executes the my job shell script in a user's home directory at 5 minutes past midnight each day:

```
5 0 * * * $HOME/myjob
```

Table 1-9 shows the meaning of the first five fields. *Note:* An asterisk (*) means all possible values for that field. Also, an entry in any of the first five fields can be a single number, a comma-separated list of numbers, a pair of numbers separated by a hyphen (indicating a range of numbers), or an asterisk.

If the text file `jobinfo` (in the current directory) contains the job information, submit this information to `crontab` with the following command:

```
crontab jobinfo
```

That's it! You're set with the `cron` job. From now on, the `cron` job runs at regular intervals (as specified in the job-information file), and you receive mail messages with the output from the job.

To verify that the job is indeed scheduled, type the following command:

```
crontab -l
```

The output of the `crontab -l` command shows the `cron` jobs currently installed in your name. To remove your `cron` jobs, type **crontab -r**.

If you log in as `root`, you can also set up, examine, and remove `cron` jobs for any user. To set up `cron` jobs for a user, use this command:

```
crontab _u username filename
```

Here, *username* is the user for whom you install the `cron` jobs, and *filename* is the file that contains information about the jobs.

TABLE 1-9   ## Format for the Time of Execution in crontab Files

Field Number	Meaning of Field	Acceptable Range of Values*
1	Minute	0–59
2	Hour of the day	0–23
3	Day of the month	0–31
4	Month	1–12 (1 means January, 2 means February, and so on) or the names of months using the first three letters — Jan, Feb, Mar, Apr, May, Jun, Jul, Aug, Sep, Oct, Nov, Dec
5	Day of the week	0–6 (0 means Sunday, 1 means Monday, and so on) or the three-letter abbreviations of weekdays — Sun, Mon, Tue, Wed, Thu, Fri, Sat

An asterisk in a field means all possible values for that field. If an asterisk is in the third field, for example, the job is executed every day.

Use the following form of the `crontab` command to view the `cron` jobs for a user:

```
crontab _u username -l
```

To remove a user's cron jobs, use the following command:

```
crontab -u username -r
```

Note: The cron daemon also executes the cron jobs listed in the systemwide cron job file /etc/crontab. Here's a typical /etc/crontab file from a Linux system (type **cat /etc/crontab** to view the file):

```
SHELL=/bin/bash
PATH=/sbin:/bin:/usr/sbin:/usr/bin
MAILTO=root
HOME=/
# run-parts
01 * * * * root run-parts /etc/cron.hourly
02 4 * * * root run-parts /etc/cron.daily
22 4 * * 0 root run-parts /etc/cron.weekly
42 4 1 * * root run-parts /etc/cron.monthly
```

The first four lines set up several environment variables for the jobs listed in this file. The MAILTO environment variable specifies the user who receives the mail message with the output from the cron jobs in this file.

The line that begins with # is a comment line. The four lines following the run-parts comment execute the run-parts shell script (located in the /usr/bin directory) at various times with the name of a specific directory as argument. Each argument to run-parts — /etc/cron.hourly, /etc/cron.daily, /etc/cron.weekly, and /etc/cron.monthly — is a directory. Essentially, run-parts executes all scripts located in the directory that you provide as an argument.

Table 1-10 lists the directories where you can find these scripts and when they execute. You have to look at the scripts in these directories to know what executes at these intervals.

TABLE 1-10

Script Directories for cron Jobs

Directory Name	Script Executes
/etc/cron.hourly	Every hour
/etc/cron.daily	Each day
/etc/cron.weekly	Weekly
/etc/cron.monthly	Once each month

Introducing Some GUI System Administration Tools

Each Linux distribution comes with GUI tools for performing system administration tasks. The GUI tools prompt you for input and then run the necessary Linux commands to perform the task. Although slight differences exist among them, the tools have become more uniform as time has passed.

Figure 1-2 shows the System Monitor utility in Ubuntu with the File Systems tab selected. You can also choose Processes (shown in Figure 1-3) to kill a process, stop it, change priority, and so on.

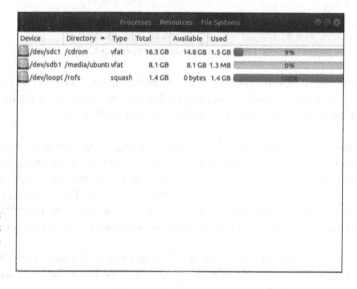

FIGURE 1-2:
The File Systems tab in System Monitor within Ubuntu.

A graphical look at the current state of the system is available on the Resources tab (shown in Figure 1-4); you can change nothing here other that colors used to represent each item. In this case, a quick look at the resources shows no network activity at all; therefore, connectivity should be the first thing you investigate if you're troubleshooting the client.

As I mention earlier in this chapter, some distributions have more inclusive tools than others. Whereas Ubuntu has Settings (shown in Figure 1-5), for example, SUSE has the YaST Control Center. Aside from the fact that YaST has more options, the interfaces are very similar.

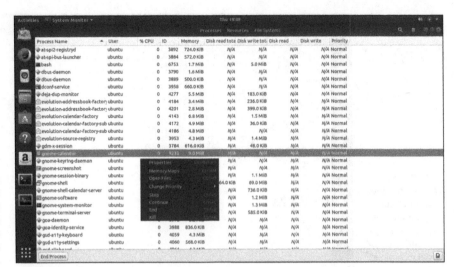

FIGURE 1-3:
The options available on the Processes tab of System Monitor within Ubuntu.

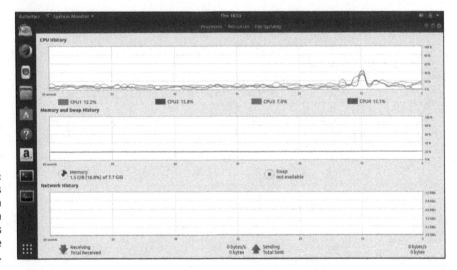

FIGURE 1-4:
The Resources tab of System Monitor within Ubuntu shows the current state of the system.

As you can see from Figure 1-5, the GUI tool is truly meant to be a one-stop-shopping spot for all your system administration chores.

Most Linux distributions include GUI utilities that perform system administration chores. If you use any of these GUI utilities to perform a task that requires you to be root, the utility typically pops up a dialog box that prompts you for the root password (except in Ubuntu, in which the GUI tools prompt for your normal user password). Just type the password and press Enter. If you don't want to use the utility, click Cancel.

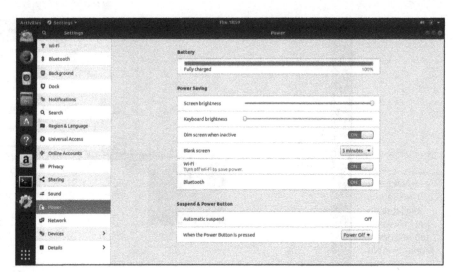

FIGURE 1-5:
The Settings tool
within Ubuntu
shows most
system settings
and lets you
make changes.

» Managing your groups

» Working in the user environment

» Changing user and group ownerships of files and directories

» Managing a user account with a GUI user manager and commands

Chapter **2**

Managing Users and Groups

inux is a multiuser system, so it has many user accounts. Even if you've set up a test machine and you're the only user using that system, you'll have a host of system user accounts. Most of these accounts aren't for people to use; they're for running specific programs, because many servers require a unique username and group name. The FTP server, for example, runs under the username `ftp`.

User accounts can belong to one or more groups. Typically, each username has a corresponding private group name. By default, each user belongs to that corresponding private group, but you can define other groups for the purpose of providing access to specific files and directories based on group membership.

User and group ownerships of files ensure that only the right people (or the right processes) can access certain files and directories. Managing the user and group accounts is a typical task in system administration. It's not hard to do this part of the job, given the tools that come with Linux, as you discover in this chapter.

Adding User Accounts

You get the chance to add user accounts when you boot your system for the first time after installing Linux. Typically (depending on your distribution), the root account is the only one that has to be created/configured during installation. If you don't add other user accounts when you start the system for the first time, you can add new users later by using a graphical user interface (GUI) user account manager or the useradd command.

REMEMBER

Creating user accounts besides root is always a good idea. Even if you're the only user of the system, logging in as a less privileged user is good practice, because that way, you can't damage any important system files inadvertently. If necessary, you can type **su -** to log in as root and then perform any system administration tasks.

Managing user accounts by using a GUI user manager

Most Linux distributions come with a GUI tool for managing user accounts. You can use that GUI tool to add user accounts. The tool displays a list of current user accounts and has an Add button for adding users. For the purposes of illustration, Figure 2-1 shows the Add User interface from Settings in Ubuntu.

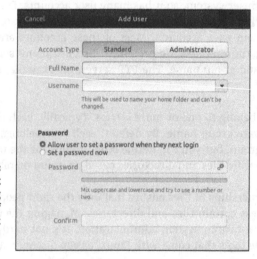

FIGURE 2-1: In Ubuntu, start by choosing which type of user you want to add; then fill in the details.

The basic steps, regardless of the specific GUI tool, are as follows:

1. **Click the Add User button.**

   A dialog box prompts you for information about the username and password variables for the new user account.

2. **Enter the requested information.**

   The GUI tool takes care of adding the new user account.

3. **(Optional) In some distributions, you can click one of the other tabs for the user to configure additional information.**

   Where available, the Details tab allows you to override the defaults for the home directory, shell, and ID information.

   The Password Settings tab, when present, allows you to override the defaults for the password configuration. Plug-Ins can be used for some parameters but are often used for *quota configuration* (such as size limits on files and the number of inodes that can be created):

   - *Soft limits* warn the user.

   - *Hard limits* stop the user.

TIP

The tabs other than User Data are used to override the system defaults. If you want to change the system defaults, change the variables in the User and Group Administration interface.

In most distributions, the tool you use to add users is called User and Group Management because it can configure two types of accounts: Users and Groups. Selecting Groups instead of Users allows you to add groups to /etc/group.

To add a new user account, click the Add button and then enter the information requested in the New Local User window. Fill in the requested information (including any add-ins, such as for group quotas) and then click the OK button.

You can add more user or group accounts, if you like. When you finish, click the OK button to create any new accounts you've added; then you exit automatically.

By default, all local users are placed in a group named users. Sometimes, you want a user to be in another group as well so that the user can access the files owned by that group. Adding a user to another group is easy. To add the username kdulaney to the group called wheel (a group of those allowed to become other users by using the sudo command), type the following command in a terminal window:

```
usermod -G wheel kdulaney
```

TIP

To remove a user account, click the username in the list of user accounts and then click the Remove or the Delete button.

Managing user accounts by using commands

If you're working from a text console, you can create a new user account by using the `useradd` command. Follow these steps to add an account for a new user:

1. **Log in as** root.

   If you're not already logged in as root, type **su -** to become root.

2. **Type the following** useradd **command with the** –c **option to create the account and add a comment:**

   ```
   /usr/sbin/useradd -c "Kristin Dulaney" kdulaney
   ```

3. **Set the password by using the** passwd **command, as follows:**

   ```
   passwd kdulaney
   ```

   You're prompted for the password twice. If you type a password that someone can easily guess, the passwd program scolds you and suggests that you use a more difficult password.

TECHNICAL STUFF

The `useradd` command consults the following configuration files to obtain default information about various parameters for the new user account:

» **/etc/default/useradd:** Specifies the default shell (`/bin/bash`) and the default home directory location (`/home`)

» **/etc/login.defs:** Provides systemwide defaults for automatic group and user IDs, as well as password-expiration parameters

» **/etc/skel:** Contains the default files that `useradd` creates in the user's home directory

Examine these files with the `cat` or `more` command to see what they contain.

REMEMBER

You can delete a user account by using the `userdel` command. Simply type **/usr/sbin/userdel** *username* at the command prompt, where *username* is the name of the user you want to remove. To wipe out that user's home directory as well, type **userdel –r** *username*.

To modify any information in a user account, use the usermod command. For user kdulaney to have root as the primary group, type the following:

```
usermod -g root kdulaney
```

To find out more about the useradd, userdel, and usermod commands, type **man useradd**, **man userdel**, or **man usermod**, respectively, in a terminal window.

TIP

Understanding the /etc/passwd File

The /etc/passwd file is a list of all user accounts. It's a text file, and any user can read it; no special privileges are needed. Each line in /etc/passwd has seven fields, separated by colons (:).

Here's a typical entry from the /etc/passwd file:

```
kdulaney:x:1000:1000:Kristin Dulaney,,,,:/home/kdulaney:/bin/bash
```

As the example shows, the format of each line in /etc/passwd looks like this:

```
username:password:UID:GID:GECOS:homedir:shell
```

Table 2-1 explains the meaning of the seven fields in each /etc/passwd entry.

TABLE 2-1   **Fields in the /etc/passwd File**

This Field	Contains
username	An alphanumeric username, usually eight characters long and unique. (Linux allows usernames to be longer than eight characters, but some other operating systems don't.)
password	When present, a 13-character encrypted password. (An *empty field* means that no password is required to access the account. An x means that the password is stored in the /etc/shadow file, which is more secure.)
UID	A unique number that serves as the user identifier. (root has a UID of 0, and usually, UIDs from 1 to 100 are reserved for nonhuman users such as servers; keeping the UID value to less than 32,767 is best.)
GID	The default group ID of the group to which the user belongs. (GID 0 is for group root; other groups are defined in /etc/group; and users can be, and usually are, in more than one group at a time.)

(continued)

TABLE 2-1 *(continued)*

This Field	Contains
GECOS	Optional personal information about the user. (The `finger` command uses this field; *GECOS* stands for General Electric Comprehensive Operating System, a long-forgotten operating system that's immortalized by the name of this field in /etc/passwd.). The value here is often the user's human name.
`homedir`	The name of the user's home directory.
`shell`	The command interpreter (`shell`), such as bash (`/bin/bash`), which executes when this user logs in.

Managing Groups

A *group* is something to which users belong. A group has a name and an identification number (ID). After a group is defined, users can belong to one or more of these groups.

You can find all the existing groups listed in /etc/group. Here's the line that defines the group named wheel:

```
wheel:x:10:root,kdulaney
```

As this example shows, each line in /etc/group has the following format, with four fields separated by colons:

```
groupname:password:GID:membership
```

Table 2-2 explains the meaning of the four fields in a group definition.

TABLE 2-2   **Meaning of Fields in /etc/group File**

Field Name	Meaning
groupname	The name of the group (such as wheel)
password	The group password. (An x means that the password is stored in the /etc/shadow file.)
GID	The numerical group ID (such as 10).
membership	A comma-separated list of usernames that belong to this group (such as root,kdulaney).

If you want to create a new group, you can simply use the groupadd command. To add a group called class with an automatically selected group ID, type the following command in a terminal window (you have to be logged in as root):

```
groupadd class
```

Then you can add users to this group with the usermod command. To add the user kdulaney to the group named class, type the following commands:

```
usermod -G class kdulaney
```

If you want to remove a group, use the groupdel command. To remove a group named class, type

```
groupdel class
```

Setting Other User and Group Administration Values

One of the easiest ways to administer users and groups is to make certain that you have the default values set to what you want them to be.

You should follow the concept of least privilege. The goal of least privilege, as the name implies, is to give users the minimal privileges needed to do their jobs — nothing more. By limiting users to only what they need, you leave little room for security to be an issue.

Often, you can set global password values and options so that users are prevented from using passwords that can be found in a dictionary, that are names, or that use common words. You can also set a minimum password length.

Seriously consider the possible encryption methods:

>> DES is the default encryption method in many distributions, and although it works in almost any environment, it limits passwords to eight characters or fewer.

>> MD5 lets you use longer passwords and is supported by all newer distributions, but it can be a problem if you need to interact with older systems.

>> SHA-512 (usually, the other choice offered) is a strong hash method is not compatible with many systems.

Exploring the User Environment

When you log in as a user, you get a set of environment variables that controls many aspects of what you see and do on your Linux system. If you want to see your current environment, type the following command in a terminal window:

```
env
```

(By the way, the `printenv` command also displays the environment, but `env` is shorter.)

The `env` command prints a long list of lines. The collection of lines is the current environment; each line defines an environment variable. The `env` command displays this typical line:

```
HOSTNAME=localhost.localdomain
```

This line defines the environment variable `HOSTNAME` as `localhost.localdomain`.

An *environment variable* is nothing more than a name associated with a string. Here is an example of how the environment variable named PATH may be defined for a normal user:

```
PATH=/usr/local/bin:/bin:/usr/bin:/usr/local/sbin:/usr/&#x2028;sbin:/sbin
```

The string to the right of the equal sign (=) is the value of the `PATH` environment variable. By convention, the `PATH` environment variable is a sequence of directory names, with names separated by colons (:).

Each environment variable has a specific purpose. When the shell has to search for a file, for example, it simply searches the directories listed in the `PATH` environment variable in the order of their appearance. Therefore, if two programs have the same name, the shell executes the one that it finds first.

In a fashion similar to the shell's use of the `PATH` environment variable, an editor such as `vi` uses the value of the `TERM` environment variable to figure out how to display the file you edit with `vi`. To see the current setting of `TERM`, type the following command at the shell prompt:

```
echo $TERM
```

If you type this command in a terminal window, the output is as follows:

```
xterm
```

To define an environment variable in bash, use the following syntax:

```
export NAME=Value
```

Here, *NAME* denotes the name of the environment variable, and *Value* is the string representing its value. Therefore, you set TERM to the value xterm by using the following command:

```
export TERM=xterm
```

TIP

After you define an environment variable, you can change its value simply by specifying the new value with the syntax NAME=*new-value*. To change the definition of TERM to vt100, for example, type **TERM=vt100** at the shell prompt.

With an environment variable such as PATH, you typically want to append a new directory name to the existing definition rather than define the PATH from scratch. If you download and install the fictional XYZ 5 Development Kit, you have to add the location of the XYZ binaries to PATH. Here's how you accomplish that task:

```
export PATH=$PATH:/usr/xyz/xyz.5.0/bin
```

This command appends the string :/usr/xyz/xyz.5.0/bin to the current definition of the PATH environment variable. The net effect is to add /usr/xyz/xyz.5.0/bin to the list of directories in PATH.

Note: You also can write this export command as follows:

```
export PATH=${PATH}:/usr/xyz/xyz.5.0/bin
```

After you type that command, you can access programs in the /usr/xyz/xyz.5.0/bin directory that the interpreter can execute.

PATH and TERM are only two of several common environment variables. Table 2-3 lists some of the environment variables for a typical Linux user.

TABLE 2-3 **Typical Environment Variables in Linux**

Environment Variable	Contents
DISPLAY	The name of the display on which the X Window System displays output (typically set to :0.0)
HOME	Your home directory
HOSTNAME	The host name of your system
LOGNAME	Your login name
MAIL	The location of your mail directory
PATH	The list of directories in which the shell looks for programs
SHELL	Your shell (SHELL=/bin/bash for bash)
TERM	The type of terminal

Changing User and Group Ownership of Files

In Linux, each file or directory has two types of owners: a user and a group. In other words, a user and group own each file and directory. The user and group ownerships can control who can access a file or directory.

To view the owner of a file or directory, use the ls -l command to see the detailed listing of a directory. Here's a typical file's information:

```
-rw-rw-r-- 1 kdulaney kdulaney 40909 Aug 16 20:37

    composer.txt
```

In this example, the first set of characters shows the file's permission setting — who can read, write, or execute the file. The third and fourth fields (in this example, kdulaney kdulaney) indicate the user and group owner of the file. Each user has a private group that has the same name as the username. Thus, most files appear to show the username twice when you list user and group ownership.

As a system administrator, you may decide to change the group ownership of a file to a common group. Suppose that you want to change the group ownership of the `composer.txt` file to the `class` group. To do so, log in as `root` and then type the following command:

```
chgrp class composer.txt
```

This `chgrp` command changes the group ownership of `composer.txt` to `class`.

You can use the `chown` command to change the user owner. The command has the following format:

```
chown username filename
```

To change the user ownership of a file named `sample.jpg` to `kdulaney`, type

```
chown kdulaney sample.jpg
```

The `chown` command can change both the user and group owner at the same time. To change the user owner to `kdulaney` and the group owner to `class`, type

```
chown kdulaney.class composer.txt
```

In other words, you simply append the group name to the username with a period in between the two values.

» **Sharing Files through NFS**

» **Performing file backup and restoration**

» **Mounting the NTFS file system**

» **Accessing MS-DOS files**

Chapter **3**

Managing File Systems

A *file system* refers to the organization of files and directories. As a system administrator, you have to perform certain operations to manage file systems on various storage media. You have to know, for example, how to *mount* — add a file system on a storage medium by attaching it to the overall Linux file system. You also have to back up important data and restore files from a backup. Other file-system operations include sharing files with the Network File System (NFS) and accessing MS-DOS files. This chapter shows you how to perform all file-system management tasks.

Exploring the Linux File System

Whether you are studying for the Linux-related certification exams or just trying to understand the working of Linux more, it is important to know that the files and directories in your PC store information in an organized manner, just like paper filing systems. When you store information on paper, you typically put several pages in a folder and then store the folder in a file cabinet. If you have many folders, you probably have some sort of filing system. You might label each folder's tab and then arrange them alphabetically in the file cabinet, for example. You might have several file cabinets, each with lots of drawers, which in turn contain folders full of pages.

Operating systems such as Linux organize information in your computer in a manner similar to your paper filing system. Linux uses a file system to organize all information in your computer. The storage media aren't a metal file cabinet and paper, of course. Instead, Linux stores information on devices such as hard drives, USB drives, and DVD drives.

To draw an analogy between your computer's file system and a paper filing system, think of a disk drive as being the file cabinet. The drawers in the file cabinet correspond to the directories in the file system. The folders in each drawer are also directories — because a directory in a computer file system can contain other directories. You can think of files as being the pages inside the folder — where the actual information is stored. Figure 3-1 illustrates the analogy between a file cabinet and the Linux file system.

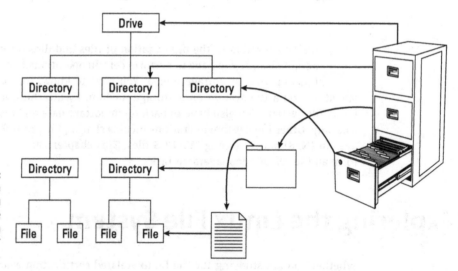

The Linux file system has a hierarchical structure. Directories can contain other directories, which in turn contain individual files.

Everything in your Linux system is organized in files and directories. To access and use documents and programs on your system, you have to be familiar with the file system.

Understanding the file-system hierarchy

For basic administration and for exam study alike, know that the Linux file system is organized like a tree, with a root directory from which all other directories branch out. When you write a complete pathname, the root directory is represented by a single slash (/). Then there's a hierarchy of files and directories. Parts of the file system can be on different physical drives or in different hard drive partitions.

Linux uses a standard directory hierarchy. Figure 3-2 shows some of the standard parts of the Linux file system. You can create new directories anywhere in this structure.

FIGURE 3-2:
The Linux file system uses a standard directory hierarchy similar to this one.

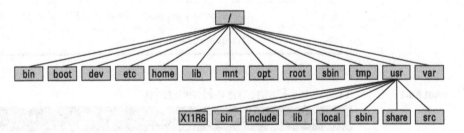

Write the name of any file or directory by concatenating the names of directories that identify where that file or directory is and by using the forward slash (/) as a separator. In Figure 3-2, the usr directory at the top level is written as /usr because the root directory (/) contains usr. On the other hand, the X11R6 directory is inside the usr directory, which is inside the root directory (/). Therefore, the X11R6 directory is uniquely identified by the name /usr/X11R6. This type of full name is a *pathname* because the name identifies the path you take from the root directory to reach a file. Thus, /usr/X11R6 is a pathname.

Each of the standard directories in the Linux file system has a specific purpose. Table 3-1, Table 3-2, and Table 3-3 summarize these directories.

TABLE 3-1

Standard Directories in Linux File System

Directory	Used to Store
/bin	Executable files for user commands (for use by all users)
/boot	Files needed by the bootloader to load the Linux kernel
/dev	Device files
/etc	Host-specific system configuration files
/home	User home directories
/lib	Shared libraries and kernel modules
/media	Mount point for removable media
/mnt	Mount point for a temporarily mounted file system
/opt	Add-on application software packages
/root	Home directory for the root user
/sbin	Utilities for system administration
/srv	Data for services (such as web and FTP) offered by this system
/tmp	Temporary files

TABLE 3-2

The /usr Directory Hierarchy

Directory	Secondary Directory Hierarchy
/usr/bin	Most user commands
/usr/games	Many games install here though they are not technically required to do so other than for historic reasons
/usr/include	Directory for *include files* — files that are inserted into source code of applications by using various directives — used in developing Linux applications
/usr/lib	Libraries used by software packages and for programming
/usr/libexec	Libraries for applications
/usr/local	Any local software
/usr/sbin	Nonessential system administrator utilities
/usr/share	Shared data that doesn't depend on the system architecture (whether the system is an Intel PC or a Sun SPARC workstation)
/usr/src	Source code

TABLE 3-3

The /var Directory Hierarchy

Directory	Variable Data
/var/cache	Cached data for applications
/var/crash	Dump files from kernel crashes
/var/lib	Information relating to the current state of applications
/var/lock	Lock files to ensure that a resource is used by one application only
/var/log	Log files organized into subdirectories
/var/mail	User mailbox files
/var/opt	Variable data for packages stored in the /opt directory
/var/run	Data describing the system since it was booted
/var/spool	Data that's waiting for some kind of processing
/var/tmp	Temporary files preserved between system reboots
/var/yp	Network Information Service (NIS) database files

TECHNICAL STUFF

OVERVIEW OF FHS

The Filesystem Hierarchy Standard (FHS) specifies the organization of files and directories in Unix-like operating systems, such as Linux. FHS defines a standard set of directories and their intended use. The FHS, if faithfully adopted by all Linux distributions, should help improve the interoperability of applications, system administration tools, development tools, and scripts across all Linux distributions. FHS even helps the system documentation (as well as books like this one) because the same description of the file system applies to all Linux distributions. Version 3.0 of FHS is the latest version, as of this writing; it was released on June 3, 2015.

FHS is part of the Linux Standard Base (see https://wiki.linuxfoundation.org/lsb/start): a set of binary standards aimed at reducing variations among the Linux distributions and promoting portability of applications. As of this writing, the most current Base is 5.0. To find out more about the Linux Standard Base, check out the home page at https://wiki.linuxfoundation.org/lsb/start.

Mounting a device on the file system

The storage devices that you use in Linux contain Linux file systems and it is good to know this for daily work, but necessary to know this for exam study. Each device has its own local file system, consisting of a hierarchy of directories. Before you can access the files on a device, you have to attach the device's directory hierarchy to the tree that represents the overall Linux file system.

Mounting is the operation you perform to cause the file system on a physical storage device (a hard drive partition or a CD-ROM) to appear as part of the Linux file system. Figure 3-3 illustrates the concept of mounting.

Figure 3-3 shows each device with a name that begins with /dev. In the figure, /dev/cdrom is the first DVD/CD-ROM drive. Physical devices are mounted at specific mount points on the Linux file system. The DVD/CD-ROM drive, /dev/cdrom, is mounted on /media/cdrom in the file system. After the CD-ROM is mounted in this way, the Fedora directory on a CD-ROM or DVD-ROM appears as /media/cdrom/Fedora in the Linux file system.

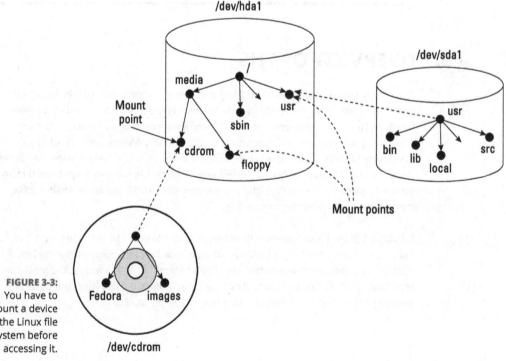

FIGURE 3-3:
You have to mount a device on the Linux file system before accessing it.

You can use the `mount` command to manually mount a device on the Linux file system at a specified directory. That directory is the *mount point.* To mount the DVD/CD-ROM drive at the `/media/cdrom` directory, type the following command (after logging in as `root`):

```
mount /dev/cdrom /media/cdrom
```

The `mount` command reports an error if the DVD/CD-ROM device is already mounted or if no CD or DVD is in the drive. Otherwise, the `mount` operation succeeds, and you can access the contents of the DVD or CD through the `/media/cdrom` directory.

REMEMBER

You can use any directory as the mount point. If you mount a device on a non-empty directory, however, you can't access the files in that directory until you unmount the device by using the `umount` command. Therefore, always use an empty directory as the mount point.

TIP

To unmount a device when you no longer need it, use the `umount` command. For a DVD/CD-ROM device with the device name `/dev/cdrom`, type the following command to unmount the device:

```
umount /dev/cdrom
```

The `umount` command succeeds as long as no one is using the DVD/CD-ROM. If you get an error when trying to unmount the DVD/CD-ROM, check to see whether the current working directory is on the DVD or CD. If you're currently working in one of the DVD/CD-ROM's directories, that also qualifies as a use of the DVD/CD-ROM.

Examining the /etc/fstab file

The `mount` command has the following general format:

```
mount device-name mount-point
```

REMEMBER

You can mount by specifying only the CD-ROM device name or the *mount-point* name, provided that the `/etc/fstab` file contains an entry for the CD-ROM mount point. That entry specifies the CD-ROM device name and the file-system type. That's why you can mount the CD-ROM with a shorter `mount` command.

In Debian, you can mount the CD-ROM by typing one of the following commands:

```
mount /dev/cdrom
mount /media/cdrom
```

The /etc/fstab file is a *configuration file* — a text file containing information that the mount and umount commands use. Each line in the /etc/fstab file provides information about a device and its mount point in the Linux file system. Essentially, the /etc/fstab file associates various mount points within the file system with specific devices, which enables the mount command to work from the command line with only the mount point or the device as argument.

Here's a /etc/fstab file from a SUSE system. (The file has a similar format in other Linux distributions.)

```
/dev/hda7 /boot ext3 acl,user_xattr 1 2
/dev/hda6 /data1 auto noauto,user 0 0
/dev/hda9 /data2 auto noauto,user 0 0
/dev/hda10 /data3 auto noauto,user 0 0
/dev/hda5 /data4 auto noauto,user 0 0
/dev/hda2 /windows/C ntfs ro,users,gid=users,umask=0002,nls=utf8 0 0
/dev/hda8 swap swap pri=42 0 0
devpts /dev/pts devpts mode=0620,gid=5 0 0
proc /proc proc defaults 0 0
usbfs /proc/bus/usb usbfs noauto 0 0
sysfs /sys sysfs noauto 0 0
/dev/cdrecorder /media/cdrecorder subfs fs=cdfss,ro,procuid,nosuid,nodev,exec,
    iocharset=utf8 0 0
```

The first field on each line shows a device name, such as a hard drive partition. The second field is the mount point, and the third field indicates the type of file system on the device. You can ignore the last three fields for now.

This /etc/fstab file shows that the /dev/hda8 device functions as a swap device for virtual memory, which is why both the mount point and the file-system type are set to swap.

The Linux operating system uses the contents of the /etc/fstab file to mount various file systems automatically. During Linux startup, the init process executes a shell script that runs the mount -a command. That command reads the /etc/fstab file and mounts all listed file systems (except those with the noauto option). The third field on each line of /etc/fstab specifies the type of file system on that device, and the fourth field shows a comma-separated list of options that the mount command uses when mounting that device on the file system. Typically, you find the defaults option in this field. The defaults option implies (among other things) that the device mounts at boot time, that only the root user can mount the device, and that the device mounts for both reading and writing. If the options include noauto, the device doesn't mount automatically when the system boots.

DISTRIBUTION SPECIFIC

In Fedora, you often find the managed option in the fourth field of /etc/fstab entries. The managed option indicates that the line was added to the fstab file by the HAL (hardware abstraction layer) daemon, which runs the fstab-sync command to add entries in the /etc/fstab file for each removable drive that it detects. You typically find that the entries for DVD/CD-ROM drive(s) (/dev/hdc in most systems) have the managed option in the fourth field.

Sharing Files with NFS

Sharing files through the NFS is simple and involves two basic steps:

>> On the NFS server, export one or more directories by listing them in the /etc/exports file and by running the /usr/sbin/exportfs command. In addition, you must run the NFS server.

>> On each client system, use the mount command to mount the directories the server has exported.

DISTRIBUTION SPECIFIC

How you start the NFS server depends on the Linux distribution. If a graphic user interface (GUI) sysadmin tool is available, you can start the NFS server from that tool. Otherwise, you can type a command in a terminal window to start the NFS server:

>> In Debian, you can type **invoke-rc.d nfs-kernel-server start** and **invoke-rc.d nfs-common start** to start the NFS server.

>> In Fedora, type **service nfs start**.

>> To start the NFS server in SUSE, you can use the YaST Control Center. From the main menu, choose the Kickoff Application Launcher⇨YaST⇨System⇨System Services (run level).

The only problem in using NFS is that each client system must support it. Most PCs don't come with NFS, which means that you have to buy NFS software separately if you want to use NFS to share files. If, however, all systems on your local-area network (LAN) run Linux or other variants of Unix with built-in NFS support, using NFS makes sense.

WARNING

NFS has security vulnerabilities. Therefore, don't set up NFS on systems that are directly connected to the Internet; be sure to put a firewall between them and the Internet.

The upcoming section walks you through an NFS setup, using an example of two Linux PCs on a LAN.

Exporting a file system with NFS

To export a file system with NFS, start with the server system that *exports* — makes available to the client systems — the contents of a directory. On the server, you must run the NFS service and also designate one or more file systems to be exported to the client systems.

You have to add an appropriate entry to the /etc/exports file. Suppose that you want to export the /home directory, and you want to enable the hostname LNBP75 to mount this file system for read and write operations. (You can use a host's IP address in place of the host name.) You can do so by adding the following entry to the /etc/exports file:

```
/home LNBP75(rw)
```

If you use the IP address of a host, the entry might look like this:

```
/home 192.168.1.200(rw)
```

This entry specifies that 192.168.1.200 is the IP address of the host that's allowed full access to the /home directory.

After adding the entry in the /etc/exports file, start the NFS server, using a method appropriate for your Linux distribution. In Fedora, for example, log in as root, and type the following command in a terminal window:

```
service nfs start
```

When the NFS service is up, the server side of NFS is ready. Now you can try to mount the exported file system from a client system and access the exported file system.

TIP

If you ever make any changes to the exported file systems listed in the /etc/exports file, remember to restart the NFS service. In Fedora, type **service nfs restart** in a terminal window.

Mounting an NFS file system

To access an exported NFS file system on a client system, you have to mount that file system on a *mount point* — which is, in practical terms, nothing more than a local directory. Suppose that you want to access the /home/public directory exported from the server named LNBP200 at the local directory /mnt/lnbp200 on the client system. To do so, follow these steps:

1. Log in as root, **and create the directory with the following command:**

```
mkdir /mnt/lnbp200
```

2. Type the following command to perform the mount **operation:**

```
mount lnbp200:/home/public /mnt/lnbp200
```

If you know only the IP address of the server, replace the host name (in this case, lnbp200) with the IP address.

3. Change the directory to/mnt/lnbp200 **with the command** cd /mnt/lnbp200.

Now you can view and access exported files from this directory.

TIP

To confirm that the NFS file system is indeed mounted, log in as root on the client system, and type **mount** in a terminal window. You see a line similar to the following about the NFS file system:

```
lnbp200:/home/public on /mnt/lnbp200 type nfs (rw,addr=192.168.1.200)
```

Backing Up and Restoring Files

For exam study and for administration, know that backing up and restoring files are crucial system administration tasks. If something happens to your system's hard drive, you have to rely on the backups to recover important files. The following discussion presents some backup strategies, describes several backup media, and explains how to back up and restore files by using the tape archiver (tar) program that comes with Linux. In addition, you find out how to perform incremental and automatic backups on tapes.

REMEMBER

If you have a CD burner, you can back up files also by recording them on a CD-R. Consult Book 2, Chapter 5, for information on what application you can use to burn a data CD.

Selecting a backup strategy and media

Your Linux system's hard drive contains everything you need to keep the system running, as well as other files (such as documents and databases) that keep your business running. You have to back up these files so that you can recover quickly and bring the system back to normal in case the hard drive crashes. Typically, you have to follow a strict regimen of regular backups because you can never tell when the hard drive may fail or the file system may get corrupted.

To implement such a regimen, first decide which files you want to back up, how often, and what backup storage media to use. This process is what I mean by selecting a backup strategy and backup media.

Your choice of backup strategy and backup media depends on your assessment of the risk of business disruption due to hard drive failure. Depending on how you use your Linux system, a disk failure may or may not have much effect on you.

If you use your Linux system as a learning tool (to find out more about Linux or programming), for example, all you may need are backup copies of some system files required to configure Linux. In this case, your backup strategy can be to save important system configuration files on your preferred storage media every time you change any system configuration.

On the other hand, if you use your Linux system as an office server that provides shared file storage for many users, the risk of business disruption due to disk failure is much higher. In this case, you have to back up all the files every week and back up any new or changed files every day. You can perform these backups in an automated manner (with the job-scheduling features described in Book 5, Chapter 1). Also, you probably need a backup storage medium that can store many gigabytes of data. In other words, for high-risk situations, your backup strategy has to be more elaborate and will require additional equipment (such as a high-capacity external hard drive).

Your choice of backup media depends on the amount of data you have to back up. For a small amount of data (such as system configuration files), you can use some inexpensive USB flash drives as backup media. If your PC has a great deal of data, however, you'll want to turn to high-capacity USB flash drives or other large capacity media options. To back up entire servers, use an external hard drive (which could be attached to the computer or the network) or a similar storage device.

When backing up files to these media, you have to refer to the backup device by name. You can find backup devices in the /dev directory.

Commercial backup utilities for Linux

The next section explains how to back up and restore files by using the tape archiver (`tar`) program that comes with Linux. Although you can manage backups with `tar`, several commercial backup utilities come with GUIs and other features to simplify backups. Here are some well-known commercial backup utilities for Linux:

>> **BRU:** Backup and restore utility from TOLIS Group, Inc. (www.tolisgroup.com)

>> **CA ARCserve Backup for Linux:** Data-protection technology for Linux systems from Computer Associates (www.arcserve.com)

Using the tape archiver: tar

You can use the `tar` command to archive files to a device, such as a hard drive or tape. The `tar` program creates an archive file that can contain other directories and files and (optionally) compress the archive for efficient storage. Then the archive is written to a specified device or another file. Many software packages are distributed in the form of a compressed `tar` file.

The command syntax of the `tar` program is as follows:

```
tar options destination source
```

Here, *options* usually is specified by a sequence of single letters, with each letter specifying what `tar` does; *destination* is the device name of the backup device; and *source* is a list of file or directory names denoting the files to back up.

Backing up and restoring a single-volume archive

Suppose that you want to back up the contents of the /etc/X11 directory on a hard drive. Log in as `root`, and type the following command, where *xxx* represents your drive:

```
tar zcvf /dev/xxx /etc/X11
```

The `tar` program displays a list of filenames as each file is copied to the compressed `tar` archive. In this case, the options are `zcvf`, the destination is /dev/*xxx* (the drive), and the source is the /etc/X11 directory (which implies all its subdirectories and their contents). You can use a similar `tar` command to back up files to a tape by replacing the hard drive location with that of the tape device, such as /dev/st0 for a SCSI tape drive.

Table 3-4 defines a few common `tar` options.

TABLE 3-4

Common tar Options

Option	Does the Following
c	Creates a new archive.
f	Specifies the name of the archive file or device on the next field in the command line.
M	Specifies a multivolume archive. (For more information, see the next section, "Backing up and restoring a multivolume archive.")
t	Lists the contents of the archive.
v	Displays verbose messages.
x	Extracts files from the archive.
z	Compresses the tar archive by using gzip.

To view the contents of the tar archive that you create on the drive, type the following command (replacing *xxx* with the drive device):

```
tar ztf /dev/xxx
```

You see a list of filenames (each beginning with /etc/X11) indicating what's in the backup. In this tar command, the t option lists the contents of the tar archive.

To extract the files from a tar backup, follow these steps while logged in as root:

1. **Change the directory to**/tmp **by typing this command:**

   ```
   cd /tmp
   ```

   This step is where you can practice extracting the files from the tar backup. For a real backup, change the directory to an appropriate location. (Typically, you type **cd /**.)

2. **Type the following command:**

   ```
   tar zxvf /dev/xxx
   ```

   This tar command uses the x option to extract the files from the archive stored on the device (replace *xxx* with the drive).

Now if you check the contents of the /tmp directory, you notice that the tar command creates an etc/X11 directory tree in /tmp and restores all the files from the tar archive to that directory. The tar command strips the leading / from the filenames in the archive and restores the files in the current directory. If you want to restore the /etc/X11 directory from the archive, use this command (substituting the device name for *xxx*):

```
tar zxvf /dev/xxx -C /
```

The –C option changes directories to the directory specified (in this case, the root directory of /) before doing the tar; the / at the end of the command denotes the directory where you want to restore the backup files.

You can use the tar command to create, view, and restore an archive. You can store the archive in a file or in any device you specify with a device name.

Backing up and restoring a multivolume archive

Sometimes, the capacity of a single storage medium is less than the total storage space needed to store the archive. In this case, you can use the M option for a multivolume archive, meaning that the archive can span multiple tapes. Note, however, that you can't create a compressed, multivolume archive, so you have to drop the z option.

Note: The M tells tar to create a multivolume archive. The tar command prompts you for a second media when the first one is filled. Take out the first media and insert another when you see the following prompt:

```
Prepare volume #2  and hit return:
```

When you press Enter, the tar program continues with the second media. For larger archives, the tar program continues to prompt for new media as needed.

To restore from this multivolume archive, type **cd /tmp** to change the directory to /tmp. (I use the /tmp directory for illustrative purposes, but you have to use a real directory when you restore files from archive.) Then type (replacing *xxx* with the device you're using)

```
tar xvfM /dev/xxx
```

The tar program prompts you to feed the media as necessary.

TIP

Use the du –s command to determine the amount of storage you need for archiving a directory. Type **du -s /etc** to see the total size of the /etc directory in kilobytes, for example. Here's typical output from that command:

```
35724 /etc
```

The resulting output shows that the /etc directory requires at least 35,724 kilobytes of storage space to back up.

Backing up on tapes

Although backing up on tapes is as simple as using the right device name in the tar command, you do have to know some nuances of the tape device to use it well. When you use tar to back up to the device named /dev/st0 (the first SCSI tape drive), the tape device automatically rewinds the tape when the tar program finishes copying the archive to the tape. The /dev/st0 device is called a *rewinding tape device* because it rewinds tapes by default.

If your tape can hold several gigabytes of data, you may want to write several tar archives — one after another — to the same tape. (Otherwise, much of the tape may be left empty.) If you plan to do so, your tape device can't rewind the tape after the tar program finishes. To help you with scenarios like this one, several Linux tape devices are nonrewinding. The nonrewinding SCSI tape device is called /dev/nst0. Use this device name if you want to write one archive after another on a tape.

TIP

After each archive, the nonrewinding tape device writes an end of file (EOF) marker to separate one archive from the next. Use the mt command to control the tape; you can move from one marker to the next or rewind the tape. When you finish writing several archives to a tape using the /dev/nst0 device name, for example, you can force the tape to rewind with the following command:

```
mt -f /dev/nst0 rewind
```

After rewinding the tape, you can use the following command to extract files from the first archive to the current disk directory:

```
tar xvf /dev/nst0
```

After that, you must move past the EOF marker to the next archive. To do so, use the following mt command:

```
mt -f /dev/nst0 fsf 1
```

This command positions the tape at the beginning of the next archive. Now use the tar xvf command again to read this archive.

REMEMBER

If you save multiple archives on a tape, you have to keep track of the archives yourself. The order of the archives can be hard to remember, so you may be better off simply saving one archive per tape.

Performing incremental backups

Suppose that you use tar to back up your system's hard drive on a tape. Because creating a full backup can take quite some time, you don't want to repeat this task every night. (Besides, only a small number of files may have changed during the day.) To locate the files that need backing up, you can use the find command to list all files that have changed in the past 24 hours:

```
find / -mtime -1 -type f -print
```

This command prints a list of files that have changed within the past day. The -mtime -1 option means that you want the files that were last modified less than one day ago. Now you can combine this find command with the tar command to back up only those files that have changed within the past day:

```
tar cvf /dev/st0 `find / -mtime -1 -type f -print`
```

When you place a command between single back quotes, the shell executes that command and places the output at that point in the command line. The result is that the tar program saves only the changed files in the archive. This process gives you an incremental backup of only the files that have changed since the previous day.

Performing automated backups

Book 5, Chapter 1 shows you how to use crontab to set up recurring jobs (called *cron jobs*). The Linux system performs these tasks at regular intervals. Backing up your system is a good use of the crontab facility. Suppose that your backup strategy is as follows:

» Every Sunday at 1:15 a.m., your system backs up the entire hard drive on the tape.

» Monday through Saturday, your system performs an incremental backup at 3:10 a.m. by saving only those files that have changed during the past 24 hours.

To set up this automated backup schedule, log in as root, and type the following lines in a file named backups (assuming that you're using a SCSI tape drive):

```
15 1 * * 0 tar zcvf /dev/st0 /
10 3 * * 1-6 tar zcvf /dev/st0 `find / -mtime -1 -type f -print`
```

Next, submit this job schedule by using the following crontab command:

```
crontab backups
```

Now you're set for an automated backup. All you need to do is to place a new tape in the tape drive every day. Remember also to give each tape an appropriate label.

Accessing a DOS or Windows File System

If you're using a legacy machine that you just don't want to throw out and have a really old version of Microsoft Windows installed on your hard drive, you've probably already mounted the DOS or Windows partition under Linux. If not, you can easily mount DOS or Windows partitions in Linux. Mounting makes the DOS or Windows directory hierarchy appear as part of the Linux file system.

Mounting a DOS or Windows disk partition

To mount a DOS or Windows hard drive partition or storage device in Linux, use the mount command, but include the option -t vfat to indicate the file-system type as DOS. If your DOS partition happens to be the first partition on your IDE (Integrated Drive Electronics) drive, and you want to mount it on /dosc, use the following mount command:

```
mount -t vfat /dev/hda1 /dosc
```

The -t vfat part of the mount command specifies that the device you mount — /dev/hda1 — has an MS-DOS file system. Figure 3-4 illustrates the effect of this mount command.

Figure 3-4 shows how directories in your DOS partition map to the Linux file system. What was the C:\DOS directory under DOS becomes /dosc/dos under Linux. Similarly, C:\WINDOWS is now /dosc/windows. You probably can see the pattern. To convert a DOS filename to Linux (when you mount the DOS partition on /dosc), perform the following steps:

1. Change the DOS names to lowercase.

2. Change C:\ to /dosc/.

3. Change all backslashes (\) to slashes (/).

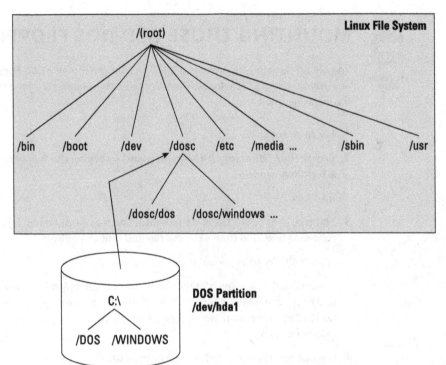

FIGURE 3-4:
Here's how
you mount a
DOS partition
on the /dosc
directory.

Mounting those ancient DOS floppy disks

Just as you mount a DOS hard drive partition on the Linux file system, you can mount a DOS floppy disk on a legacy machine. You must log in as root to mount a floppy, but you can set up your system so that any user can mount a DOS floppy disk. You also have to know the device name for the floppy drive. By default, Linux defines the following two generic floppy device names:

>> /dev/fd0 is the A drive (the first floppy drive).

>> /dev/fd1 is the B drive (the second floppy drive, if you have one).

You can use any empty directory in the file system as the mount point, but the Linux system comes with a directory, /media/floppy, specifically for mounting a floppy disk.

To mount a DOS floppy disk on the /media/floppy directory, put the floppy in the drive, and type the following command:

```
mount -t vfat /dev/fd0 /media/floppy
```

MOUNTING THOSE OLD DOS FLOPPIES

You can set up your Linux system so that any user can mount a DOS floppy. To enable any user to mount a DOS floppy in the A drive on the /a directory, for example, perform the following steps:

1. **Log in as** root.

2. **Create the/a directory (the mount point) by typing the following command in a terminal window:**

   mkdir /a

3. **Edit the/etc/fstab file in a text editor (such as** vi **or** emacs**) by inserting the following line, and then save the file and quit the editor:**

   /dev/fd0 /a vfat noauto,user 0 0

   The first field in that line is the device name of the floppy drive (/dev/fd0); the second field is the mount directory (/a); the third field shows the type of file system (vfat). The user option (which appears next to noauto) enables all users to mount DOS floppy disks.

4. **Log out and then log back in as a normal user.**

5. **To confirm that you can mount a DOS floppy as a normal user and not just as root, insert a DOS floppy into the A drive, and type the following command:**

   mount /a

   The mount operation succeeds, and you see a listing of the DOS floppy when you type the command ls /a.

6. **To unmount the DOS floppy, type** umount /a.

After you mount the floppy, you can copy files to and from the floppy by using the Linux copy command (cp). To copy the file gnome1.pcx from the current directory to the floppy, type the following:

```
cp gnome1.pcx /media/floppy
```

Similarly, to see the contents of the floppy disk, type the following:

```
ls /media/floppy
```

If you want to remove the floppy disk from the drive, first unmount the floppy drive. *Unmounting* removes the association between the floppy disk's file system and the mount point on the Linux file system. Use the `umount` command to unmount the floppy disk, like this:

```
umount /dev/fd0
```

Mounting an NTFS partition

Nowadays, most PCs come with Windows 10 or Windows 8 preinstalled on the hard drive. Both of these versions of Windows, as well as the older Windows 7, Vista, and XP, typically use the NT File System (NTFS). Linux supports read-only access to NTFS partitions, and many distributions come with the `ntfs.ko` kernel module, which is needed to access an NTFS partition.

If you've installed Linux on a Windows system and want to access files on the NTFS partition, but your distribution doesn't include the `ntfs.ko` module, you can build the kernel after enabling an NTFS module during the kernel configuration step.

After rebuilding and booting from the new kernel, log in as `root`, and type the following command to create a mount point for the NTFS partition. (In this case, you're creating a mount point in the `/mnt` directory.)

```
mkdir /mnt/windir
```

Now you can mount the NTFS partition with the following command:

```
mount /dev/hda2 /mnt/windir -t ntfs -r -o umask=0222
```

REMEMBER

If necessary, replace `/dev/hda2` with the device name for the NTFS partition on your system. On most PCs that come with Windows preinstalled, the NTFS partition is the second one (`/dev/hda2`); the first partition (`/dev/hda1`) usually is a hidden partition that holds files used for the Windows installation.

Chapter **4**

Working with Samba and NFS

I f your local-area network (LAN) is like most others, it needs the capability to share files between systems that run Linux and other systems that don't. Though this percentage may be getting smaller as Linux use grows, it's still too large to ignore. Therefore, Linux includes two prominent file-sharing services:

>> **Network File System (NFS):** For file sharing with other Unix systems (or PCs with NFS client software)

>> **Samba:** For file sharing and print sharing with Windows systems

This chapter describes how to share files by using both NFS and Samba.

Sharing Files with NFS

Sharing files through NFS is simple and involves two basic steps:

>> On the Linux system that runs the NFS server, you export (share) one or more directories by listing them in the /etc/exports file and by running the exportfs command. In addition, you must start the NFS server.

>> On each client system, you use the mount command to mount the directories that your server exported.

The only problem with using NFS is that each client system must support it. Microsoft Windows doesn't ship with NFS, so you have to buy the NFS software separately if you want to share files by using NFS. Using NFS if all systems on your LAN run Linux (or other variants of Unix with built-in NFS support) makes good sense, however.

WARNING

NFS has security vulnerabilities, so you shouldn't set up NFS on systems that are directly connected to the Internet without using the RPCSEC_GSS security that comes with NFS version 4 (NFSv4). Version 4.2 was released in November 2016; you should use it for most purposes, because it includes all the needed updates.

The next few sections walk you through NFS setup, using an example of two Linux PCs on a LAN.

Exporting a file system with NFS

Start with the server system that *exports* — makes available to the client systems — the contents of a directory. On the server, you must run the NFS service and designate one or more file systems to export.

To export a file system, you have to add an appropriate entry to the /etc/exports file. Suppose that you want to export the /home directory, and you want to enable the host named LNBP75 to mount this file system for read and write operations. You can do so by adding the following entry to the /etc/exports file:

```
/home LNBP75(rw,sync)
```

If you want to give access to all hosts on a LAN such as 192.168.0.0, you could change this line to

```
/home 192.168.0.0/24(rw,sync)
```

Every line in the /etc/exports file has this general format:

```
Directory host1(options) host2(options) ...
```

The first field is the directory being shared via NFS, followed by one or more fields that specify which hosts can mount that directory remotely and several options in parentheses. You can specify the hosts with names or IP addresses, including ranges of addresses.

The options in parentheses denote the kind of access each host is granted and how user and group IDs from the server are mapped to ID the client. (If a file is owned by root on the server, for example, what owner is that on the client?) Within the parentheses, commas separate the options. If a host is allowed both read and write access, and all IDs are to be mapped to the anonymous user (by default, the anonymous user is named nobody), the options look like this:

```
(rw,all_squash)
```

Table 4-1 shows the options you can use in the /etc/exports file. You find two types of options: general options and user ID mapping options.

TABLE 4-1 **Options in /etc/exports**

Option	Description
General Options	
secure	Allows connections only from port 1024 or lower (default)
insecure	Allows connections from port 1024 or higher
ro	Allows read-only access (default)
rw	Allows both read and write access
sync	Performs write operations (writing information to the disk) when requested (by default)
async	Performs write operations when the server is ready
no_wdelay	Performs write operations immediately
wdelay	Waits a bit to see whether related write requests arrive and then performs them together (by default)
hide	Hides an exported directory that's a subdirectory of another exported directory (by default)
no_hide	Causes a directory to not be hidden (opposite of hide)
subtree_check	Performs subtree checking, which involves checking parent directories of an exported subdirectory whenever a file is accessed (by default)
no_subtree_check	Turns off subtree checking (opposite of subtree_check)
insecure_locks	Allows insecure file locking

(continued)

TABLE 4-1 *(continued)*

Option	Description
User ID Mapping Options	
all_squash	Maps all user IDs and group IDs to the anonymous user on the client
no_all_squash	Maps remote user and group IDs to similar IDs on the client (by default)
root_squash	Maps remote root user to the anonymous user on the client (by default)
no_root_squash	Maps remote root user to the local root user
anonuid=UID	Sets the user ID of anonymous user to be used for the all_squash and root_squash options
anongid=GID	Sets the group ID of anonymous user to be used for the all_squash and root_squash options

After adding the entry in the /etc/exports file, manually export the file system by typing the following command in a terminal window:

```
exportfs -a
```

This command exports all file systems defined in the /etc/exports file.

Now you can start the NFS server processes.

DISTRIBUTION SPECIFIC

In Debian, start the NFS server by logging in as root and typing **/etc/init.d/nfs-kernel-server start** in a terminal window. In Fedora, type **/etc/init.d/nfs start**. In SUSE, type **/etc/init.d/nfsserver start**. If you want the NFS server to start when the system boots, type **update-rc.d nfs-kernel-server defaults** in Debian. In Fedora, type **chkconfig - -level 35 nfs on**. In SUSE, type **chkconfig - -level 35 nfsserver on**.

When the NFS service is up, the server side of NFS is ready. Now you can try to mount the exported file system from a client system and access the exported file system as needed.

TIP

If you ever make any changes in the exported file systems listed in the /etc/exports file, remember to restart the NFS service. To restart a service, invoke the script in the /etc/init.d directory with restart as the argument (instead of the start argument that you use to start the service).

Mounting an NFS file system

To access an exported NFS file system on a client system, you have to mount that file system on a mount point. The *mount point* is nothing more than a local directory. Suppose that you want to access the /home directory exported from the server named LNBP200 at the local directory /mnt/lnbp200 on the client system. To do so, follow these steps:

1. **Log in as** root **, and create the directory with this command:**

   ```
   mkdir /mnt/lnbp200
   ```

2. **Type the following command to mount the directory from the remote system (**LNBP200**) on the local directory**/mnt/lnbp200:

   ```
   mount lnbp200:/home /mnt/lnbp200
   ```

After completing these steps, you can view and access exported files from the local directory /mnt/lnbp200.

To confirm that the NFS file system is indeed mounted, log in as root on the client system, and type **mount** in a terminal window. You see a line similar to the following about the NFS file system:

```
lnbp200:/home/public on /mnt/lnbp200 type nfs (rw,addr=192.168.0.4)
```

TECHNICAL STUFF

NFS supports two types of mount operations: hard and soft. By default, a mount is hard, which means that if the NFS server doesn't respond, the client keeps trying to access the server indefinitely until the server responds. You can soft-mount an NFS volume by adding the –o soft option to the mount command. For a soft mount, the client returns an error if the NFS server fails to respond and doesn't retry.

Setting Up a Windows Server Using Samba

If you rely on Windows for file sharing and print sharing, you probably use Windows in your servers and clients. If so, you can still move to a Linux PC as your server without losing Windows' file-sharing and print-sharing capabilities; you can set up Linux as a Windows server. When you install Linux, you also get a chance to install the Samba software package, which performs that setup. All you have to do is select the Windows File Server package group during installation.

REMEMBER

After you install and configure Samba on your Linux PC, your client PCs — even if they're running an old Windows operating system or one of the more recent Windows versions — can access shared disks and printers on the Linux PC. To do so, they use the Common Internet File System (CIFS) protocol, the underlying protocol in Windows file and print sharing.

With the Samba package installed, you can make your Linux PC a Windows client, which means that the Linux PC can access the disks and printers that a Windows server manages. At the same time, your Linux PC can be a client to other Windows systems on the network.

The Samba software package has these major components:

» **/etc/samba/smb.conf:** The Samba configuration file that the Server Message Block (SMB) server uses.

» **/etc/samba/smbusers:** A Samba configuration file showing the Samba usernames that correspond to usernames on the local Linux PC.

» **nmbd:** The NetBIOS name server, which clients use to look up servers. (*NetBIOS* stands for *Network Basic Input/Output System* — an interface that applications use to communicate with network transports, such as TCP/IP.)

» **nmblookup:** A command that returns the IP address of a Windows PC identified by its NetBIOS name.

» **smbadduser:** A program that adds users to the SMB password file.

» **smbcacls:** A program that manipulates Windows NT access control lists on shared files.

» **smbclient:** The Windows client, which runs on Linux and allows Linux to access the files and printer on any Windows server.

» **smbcontrol:** A program that sends messages to the smbd, nmbd, or winbindd processes.

» **smbd:** The SMB server, which accepts connections from Windows clients and provides file-sharing and print-sharing services.

» **smbmount:** A program that mounts a Samba share directory on a Linux PC.

» **smbpasswd:** A program that changes the password for an SMB user.

» **smbprint:** A script that enables printing on a printer on an SMB server.

» **smbstatus:** A command that lists the current SMB connections for the local host.

» **smbtar:** A program that backs up SMB shares directly to tape drives on the Linux system.

- ➤ **smbumount:** A program that unmounts a currently mounted Samba share directory.

- ➤ **testparm:** A program that ensures that the Samba configuration file is correct.

- ➤ **winbindd:** A server that resolves names from Windows NT servers.

The following sections describe how to configure and use Samba.

Installing Samba

You may have installed Samba when you installed Linux. You can check first, and if you don't find Samba on your system, you can easily install it.

To see whether Samba is installed, type **dpkg –l samba*** in Debian and Ubuntu, or type **rpm -q samba** in Fedora and SUSE.

DISTRIBUTION SPECIFIC

In Debian and Ubuntu, type **apt-get install samba** to install Samba. In Fedora, log in as root, and type **yum install samba samba-swat.** This command installs not only samba, but also the web configuration interface SWAT (Samba Web Administration Tool). In SUSE, click Software Management in the YaST Control Center's Software category. Then use YaST's search facility to look for samba, select the relevant packages, and install them.

After installing the Samba software, you have to configure Samba before you can use it.

Configuring Samba

To set up the Windows file-sharing and print-sharing services, you can edit the configuration file manually or use a graphical user interface (GUI) tool. Using the GUI tool is much easier than editing a configuration file. Fedora and SUSE come with GUI tools for configuring the Samba server.

DISTRIBUTION SPECIFIC

In Fedora, choose System Settings⇨Advanced⇨Samba from the KDE desktop to open the Samba Server Configuration window. Enter a valid username and password at the prompt. The resulting configuration interface lets you create and edit entries in the configuration file /etc/samba/smb.conf.

DISTRIBUTION SPECIFIC

In SUSE, you can configure Samba through the YaST Control Center. Choose System⇨Control Center (YaST) from the main menu. Click Network Services on the left side of the window; then click Samba Server on the right side of the window. In the window that appears, select a workgroup name (YaST displays the name of any existing Windows workgroup on your LAN), and click Next. Then you can select the server type, enable the server, and select what you want to share. When you exit the Samba server configuration utility, YaST stores the Samba settings in configuration files in the /etc/samba directory.

After configuring Samba, type the following command in a terminal window to verify that the Samba configuration file is okay:

```
testparm
```

If the command says that it loaded the files, you're all set to go. The testparm command also displays the contents of the Samba configuration file.

TECHNICAL STUFF

Samba uses the /etc/samba/smb.conf file as its configuration file. This text file has a syntax similar to that of a legacy Microsoft Windows INI file. You can edit that file in any text editor on your Linux system. Like the old Windows INI files, the /etc/samba/smb.conf file consists of sections, with a list of parameters in each section. Each section of the smb.conf file begins with the name of the section in brackets. The section continues until the next section begins or until the file ends. Each line uses the name = value syntax to specify the value of a parameter. As with Windows INI files, comment lines begin with a semicolon (;). In the /etc/samba/smb.conf file, comments may also begin with a hash mark (#).

DISTRIBUTION SPECIFIC

To start the Samba services automatically when the system reboots, type **update-rc.d samba defaults** in Debian and Ubuntu, or type **chkconfig - -level 35 smb on** in Fedora and SUSE. To start Samba immediately, type **/etc/init.d/smb start** in Fedora and SUSE, or type **/etc/init.d/samba start** in Debian and Ubuntu.

Trying out Samba

You can now access the Samba server on the Linux system from one of the Windows systems on the LAN. Depending on which version of Windows you're using, you usually have a Network Neighborhood, Network, or Network icon/option that you can click to see the newly added server.

When you see the Samba server, you can open it by double-clicking the icon. After you enter your Samba username and password, you can access the folders and printers (if any) on the Samba share.

You can use the smbclient program to access shared directories and printers on Windows systems on the LAN and to ensure that your Linux Samba server is working.

DISCOVERING MORE ABOUT SAMBA

This chapter is only an introduction to Samba. To find out more about Samba, consult the following resources:

- To view Samba documentation online, visit www.samba.org/samba/docs/.

- Read *Using Samba,* 3rd Edition, by Gerald Carter, Jay Ts, and Robert Eckstein (O'Reilly & Associates, 2007)

You should also visit www.samba.org to keep up with the latest news on Samba development. This site also has links to resources for learning Samba.

Working with Samba and NFS

Security

Contents at a Glance

CHAPTER 1: Introducing Linux Security 365
Why Worry about Security? 366
Establishing a Security Framework 366
Securing Linux 372
Delving Into Computer Security Terminology and Tools 375
Keeping Up with Security News and Updates 379

CHAPTER 2: Securing Linux 381
Securing Passwords 382
Protecting Files and Directories 384
Encrypting and Signing Files with GnuPG 389
Monitoring System Security 396
Securing Internet Services 397
Using Secure Shell for Remote Logins 399
Setting Up Simple Firewalls 402
Security Files to Be Aware Of 411

CHAPTER 3: Vulnerability Testing and Computer Security Audits 413
Understanding Security Audits 414
Implementing a Security Test Methodology 416
Vulnerability Testing Types 424
Exploring Security Testing Tools 425

» Understanding host-related security issues

» Understanding network-related security issues

» Interpreting computer security terminology

» Keeping up with security news and updates

Chapter **1**

Introducing Linux Security

This chapter explains why you need to worry about security — and offers a high-level view of how to get a handle on security. I explain the idea of an overall security framework and discuss the two key aspects of security: host security and network security. I end the chapter introducing you to the terminology used in discussing computer security.

TIP

According to the weighting, 15 percent of the questions on the LX0-104 exam fall under the Security domain. This number should be viewed as being very conservative because so much of administration involves security. You'll find topics related to it appearing in domains such as Administrative Tasks, Essential System Services, and Networking Fundamentals. For that reason, you'll find a lot of security-relevant information in the three chapters of Book 6 and in other chapters as well.

Why Worry about Security?

In today's networked world, you have no choice but to worry about your Linux system's security. For a stand-alone system or a system used in an isolated local area network (LAN), you have to focus on protecting the system from the users and the users from one another. In other words, you don't want a user to modify or delete system files, whether intentionally or unintentionally, and you don't want a user destroying another user's files (or his own, if you can prevent it).

Because the odds are quite strong that your Linux system is connected to the Internet, you have to secure the system from unwanted accesses over the Internet. These intruders — or *crackers*, as they're commonly known — typically impersonate a user, steal or destroy information, and even deny you access to your own system. The latter attack is known as a *denial of service* (DoS) or *distributed denial of service* (DDoS) attack.

By its very nature, an Internet connection makes your system accessible to any other system on the Internet. After all, the Internet connects a huge number of networks across the globe. In fact, the client/server architecture of Internet services, such as Hypertext Transfer Protocol (HTTP) and File Transfer Protocol (FTP), rely on the wide-open network access that the Internet provides. Unfortunately, the easy accessibility to Internet services running on your system also means that anyone on the 'Net can easily access your system.

If you operate an Internet host that provides information to others, you certainly want everyone to access your system's Internet services, such as FTP and web servers. These servers often have vulnerabilities, however, that crackers may exploit to harm your system. You need to know about the potential security risks of Internet services and the precautions you can take to minimize the risk that someone will exploit the weaknesses of your FTP or web server.

You also want to protect your company's internal network from outsiders, even though your goal is to provide information to the outside world through your web or FTP server. You can protect your internal network by setting up an Internet *firewall* — a controlled-access point to the internal network — and placing the web and FTP servers on a host outside the firewall.

Establishing a Security Framework

The first step in securing your Linux system is setting up a *security policy* — a set of guidelines that states what you enable users (as well as visitors over the Internet) to do on your Linux system. The level of security you establish depends on how you use the Linux system and on how much is at risk if someone gains unauthorized access to your system.

If you're a system administrator for one or more Linux systems in an organization, you probably want to involve company management, as well as users, in setting up the security policy. Obviously, you can't create a draconian policy that blocks all access. (That policy would prevent anyone from effectively working on the system.) On the other hand, if users are creating or using data that's valuable to the organization, you must set up a policy that protects the data from disclosure to outsiders. In other words, the security policy should strike a balance between users' needs and your need to protect the system.

For a stand-alone Linux system or a home system that you occasionally connect to the Internet, the security policy can be just a list of the Internet services that you want to run on the system and the user accounts that you plan to set up on the system. For any larger organization, you probably have one or more Linux systems on a LAN connected to the Internet — preferably through a firewall. (To reiterate, a *firewall* is a device that controls the flow of Internet Protocol [IP] packets between the LAN and the Internet.) In such cases, thinking of computer security systematically (across the entire organization) is best. Figure 1-1 shows the key elements of an organizationwide framework for computer security.

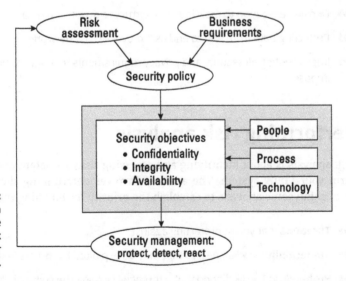

FIGURE 1-1:
Start with an organizationwide framework for computer security.

The security framework outlined in Figure 1-1 focuses on

>> Determining the business requirements for security

>> Performing risk assessments

>> Establishing a security policy

>> Implementing a cybersecurity solution that includes people, process, and technology to mitigate identified security risks

>> Continuously monitoring and managing security

The following sections discuss some of the key elements of the security framework.

Determining business requirements for security

The business requirements for security identify the computer resources and information you have to protect (including any requirements imposed by applicable laws, such as the requirement to protect the privacy of some types of data). Typical security requirements may include items such as the following:

>> Enabling access to information by authorized users.

>> Implementing business rules that specify who has access to what information.

>> Employing a strong user-authentication system.

>> Denying execution to malicious or destructive actions on data.

>> Protecting data from end to end as it moves across networks.

>> Implementing all security and privacy requirements that applicable laws impose.

Performing risk analysis

Risk analysis is about identifying and assessing risks — potential events that can harm your Linux system. The analysis involves determining the following and performing some analysis to establish the priority for handling the risks:

>> **Threats:** What you're protecting against.

>> **Vulnerabilities:** Weaknesses that may be exploited by threats (the risks).

>> **Probability:** The likelihood that a threat will exploit the vulnerability.

>> **Impact:** The effect of exploiting a specific vulnerability.

>> **Mitigation:** What to do to reduce vulnerabilities.

Typical threats

Some typical threats to your Linux system include the following:

>> **DoS attack:** The computer and network are tied up so that legitimate users can't make use of the systems. For businesses, a DoS attack can mean a loss of revenue. Because bringing a system to its knees with a single computer attack is a bit of a challenge these days, the more common tactic is to point many computers at a single site and let them do the dirty work. Although the purpose and result are the same as ever, this ganging-up is referred to as a distributed (DDoS) attack because more than one computer is attacking the host.

>> **Unauthorized access:** The computer and network are used by someone who isn't an authorized user. The unauthorized user can steal information or maliciously corrupt or destroy data. Some businesses may be hurt by the negative publicity resulting from the mere fact that an unauthorized user gained access to the system, even if the data shows no sign of explicit damage.

>> **Disclosure of information to the public:** *Disclosure* in this case means the unauthorized release of information. The disclosure of a password file, for example, enables potential attackers to figure out username and password combinations for accessing a system. Exposure of other sensitive information, such as financial and medical data, may be a potential liability for a business.

Typical vulnerabilities

The threats to your system and network come from exploitation of vulnerabilities in your organization's resources, both computer and people. Following are some common vulnerabilities:

>> People's foibles (divulging passwords, losing security cards, and so on)

>> Internal network connections (routers, switches)

>> Interconnection points (gateways [routers and firewalls] between the Internet and the internal network)

>> Third-party network providers (Internet service providers [ISPs], long-distance carriers) with looser security

>> Operating-system security holes (potential holes in Internet servers, such as those associated with sendmail, named, and bind)

>> Application security holes (known weaknesses in specific applications)

The 1-2-3 of risk analysis (probability and effect)

To perform risk analysis, assign a numeric value to the probability and effect of each potential vulnerability. To develop a workable risk analysis, do the following for each vulnerability or risk:

1. **Assign subjective ratings of low, medium, and high to the probability.**

   As the ratings suggest, low probability means a lesser chance that the vulnerability will be exploited; high probability means a greater chance.

2. **Assign similar ratings to the effect.**

   What you consider to be the effect is up to you. If the exploitation of a vulnerability would affect your business greatly, assign it a high effect rating.

3. **Assign a numeric value to the three levels — low = 1, medium = 2, and high = 3 — for both probability and effect.**

4. **Multiply the probability by the effect.**

   You can think of this product as being the *risk level*.

5. **Decide to develop protections for vulnerabilities that exceed a specific threshold for the product of probability and effect.**

   You might choose to handle all vulnerabilities that have a probability × effect value greater than 6, for example.

If you want to characterize the probability and effect with finer gradations, use a scale of, say, 1 through 5 instead of 1 through 3, and follow the same steps.

Establishing a security policy

Using risk analysis and any business requirements that you may have to address (regardless of risk level) as a foundation, you can craft a security policy for the organization. Such a security policy typically addresses high-level objectives such as ensuring the confidentiality, integrity, and availability of data and systems.

The security policy typically addresses the following areas:

>> **Authentication:** Examples include what method is used to ensure that a user is the real user, who gets access to the system, the minimum length and complexity of passwords, how often users change passwords, and how long a user can be idle before that user is logged out automatically.

>> **Authorization:** Examples include what different classes of users can do on the system and who can have the `root` password.

>> **Data protection:** Examples include what data must be protected, who has access to the data, and whether encryption is necessary for some data.

>> **Internet access:** Examples include restrictions on LAN users from accessing the Internet, what Internet services (such as web and Internet Relay Chat) users can access, whether incoming emails and attachments are scanned for viruses, whether the network has a firewall, and whether virtual private networks (VPNs) are used to connect private networks across the Internet.

>> **Internet services:** Examples include what Internet services are allowed on each Linux system; the existence of any file servers, mail servers, or web servers; what services run on each type of server; and what services, if any, run on Linux systems used as desktop workstations.

>> **Security audits:** Examples include who tests whether the security is adequate, how often security is tested, and how problems found during security testing are handled.

>> **Incident handling:** Examples include the procedures for handling any computer security incidents, who must be informed, and what information must be gathered to help with the investigation of incidents.

>> **Responsibilities:** Examples include who is responsible for maintaining security, who monitors log files and audit trails for signs of unauthorized access, and who maintains the security policy.

Implementing security solutions (mitigation)

After you analyze the risks (vulnerabilities) and develop a security policy, you must select the *mitigation approach:* how to protect against specific vulnerabilities. You develop an overall security solution based on security policy, business requirements, and available technology. This solution makes use of people, process, and technology, and includes the following:

>> Services (authentication, access control, encryption)

>> Mechanisms (username and password, firewalls)

>> Objects (hardware, software)

Because it's impossible to protect computer systems from all attacks, solutions identified through the risk management process must support three integral concepts of a holistic security program:

>> **Protection:** Provide countermeasures such as policies, procedures, and technical solutions to defend against attacks on the assets being protected.

>> **Detection:** Monitor for potential breakdowns in the protective measures that could result in security breaches.

>> **Reaction (response):** Respond to detected breaches to thwart attacks before damage occurs; often requires human involvement.

Because absolute protection from attacks is impossible to achieve, a security program that doesn't incorporate detection and reaction is incomplete.

Managing security

In addition to implementing security solutions, you also need to implement security management measures to continually monitor, detect, and respond to any security incidents.

The combination of the risk analysis, security policy, security solutions, and security management provides the overall security framework. Such a framework helps establish a common level of understanding of security concerns and a common basis for the design and implementation of security solutions.

Securing Linux

After you define a security policy, you can proceed to secure the system according to the policy. The exact steps depend on what you want to do with the system, whether the system is a server or workstation, and how many users must access the system.

To secure the Linux system, you have to handle two broad categories of security issues:

>> **Host-security issues:** These issues relate to securing the operating system and the files and directories on the system.

>> **Network-security issues:** These issues refer to the threat of attacks over the network connection.

TIP

If your host is connecting to a large network, Directory Services can become a significant issue. Directory Services security is outside the scope of this book, but you can find information about it by searching online.

Understanding the host-security issues

Here are some high-level guidelines to address host security (some of which I cover in detail in Book 6, Chapter 2):

>> When installing Linux, select only the package groups that you need for your system. Don't install unnecessary software. If your system is used as a workstation, for example, you don't have to install most of the servers (web server, news server, and so on).

>> Create initial user accounts, and make sure that all passwords are strong enough that password-cracking programs can't guess them. Linux includes tools that enforce strong passwords.

>> Set file ownerships and permissions to protect important files and directories.

>> If mandatory access-control capabilities are available, enable them. Support for this feature has been incorporated, through Security Enhanced Linux (SELinux) since kernel 2.6. The best way to think of SELinux is as a wrapper that can be placed around standard Linux to provide more security measures. AppArmor is favored over SELinux in some distributions but it serves the same purpose and offers similar features to SELinux.

>> Use the GNU Privacy Guard (GnuPG) to encrypt or decrypt files with sensitive information and to authenticate files that you download from the Internet. GnuPG comes with Linux, and you can use the gpg command to perform tasks such as encrypting or decrypting a file and digitally signing a file. (See Book 6, Chapter 2 for an explanation of digital signatures.)

>> Use file-integrity checking tools, such as Tripwire, to monitor any changes to crucial system files and directories. Visit www.tripwire.com for the commercial version.

>> Periodically check various log files for signs of any break-ins or attempted break-ins. These log files are in the /var/log directory of your system.

>> Install security updates as soon as they're available and tested. These security updates fix known vulnerabilities in Linux. Be sure to test an update on nonproduction machines before rolling it out to your production servers.

Introducing Linux
Security

TIP

You can spend a great deal of time *hardening* your server — locking down the services on it to make it as secure across the network as possible. But don't overlook the fact that someone could pick up the server and walk right out the door with it. When locking down a system, be sure that you also physically secure it with locked doors and cables where necessary.

Understanding network-security issues

The issue of security comes up as soon as you connect your organization's internal network to the Internet. You need to think of security even if you connect a single computer to the Internet, but security concerns are more pressing when an entire internal network is opened to the world.

If you're an experienced system administrator, you already know that the cost of managing an Internet presence doesn't worry corporate management; management's main concern is security. To get management's backing for the website, you have to lay out a plan to keep the corporate network secure from intruders.

You may think that you can avoid jeopardizing the internal network by connecting only external servers, such as web and FTP servers, to the Internet, but employing this simplistic approach isn't wise. This approach is like deciding not to drive because you might have an accident. Not having a network connection between your web server and your internal network also has the following drawbacks:

- » You can't use network file transfers, such as FTP, to copy documents and data from your internal network to the web server.

- » Users on the internal network can't access the corporate web server.

- » Users on the internal network don't have access to web servers on the Internet. Such a restriction makes a valuable resource — the web — inaccessible to the users in your organization.

A practical solution to this problem is to set up an Internet firewall and to put the web server on a highly secured host outside the firewall.

In addition to using a firewall, here are some steps you can take to address network security (explained further in Book 6, Chapter 2):

- » Enable only those Internet services you need on a system. In particular, don't enable services that aren't properly configured.

- » Use Secure Shell (ssh) for remote logins. Don't use the r commands, such as rlogin and rsh.

>> Secure any Internet services, such as FTP or Telnet, that you want to run on your system. You can use the TCP wrapper access-control files — /etc/ hosts.allow and /etc/hosts.deny — to secure some of these services. (See Book 6, Chapter 3 for more on the TCP wrapper.)

>> Promptly fix any known vulnerabilities of Internet services that you choose to run. Typically, you can download and install the latest security updates from your Linux distribution's online update sites.

Delving Into Computer Security Terminology and Tools

Computer books, magazine articles, and experts on computer security use some terms that you need to know to understand discussions of computer security (and to communicate effectively with security vendors).

TIP

Table 1-1 describes some commonly used computer security terms. If you're taking the LX0-104 exam, port scanning and setuid are important.

TABLE 1-1 **Common Computer Security Terminology**

Term	Description
Application gateway	A proxy service that acts as a gateway for application-level protocols, such as FTP, HTTP, NNTP, and SSH.
Authentication	The process of confirming that a user is indeed who he or she claims to be. The typical authentication method is a challenge-response method wherein the user enters a username and secret password to confirm his or her identity.
Backdoor	A security weakness that a cracker places on a host to bypass security features.
Bastion host	A highly secured computer that serves as an organization's main point of presence on the Internet. A bastion host typically resides on the perimeter network, but a *dual-homed host* (with one network interface connected to the Internet and the other to the internal network) is also a bastion host.
Buffer overflow	A security flaw in a program that enables a cracker to send an excessive amount of data to that program and to overwrite parts of the running program with code in the data being sent. The result is that the cracker can execute arbitrary code on the system and possibly gain access to the system as a privileged user. The new exec-shield feature of the Linux kernel protects against buffer overflows.

(continued)

Introducing Linux Security

TABLE 1-1 *(continued)*

Term	Description
Certificate	An electronic document that identifies an entity (such as a person, an organization, or a computer) and associates a public key with that identity. A certificate contains the certificate holder's name, a serial number, an expiration date, a copy of the certificate holder's public key, and the digital signature of the certificate authority so that a recipient can verify that the certificate is real.
Certificate authority (CA)	An organization that validates identities and issues certificates.
Confidentiality	For data, a state of being accessible to no one but authorized users (usually achieved by encryption).
Cracker	A person who breaks into (or attempts to break into) a host, often with malicious intent.
DDoS	A variant of the DoS attack that uses a coordinated attack from a distributed system of computers rather than a single source. It often uses worms to spread to — and take control of — multiple computers that can then attack the target.
Decryption	The process of transforming encrypted information into its original, intelligible form.
Digital signature	A one-way MD5 (Message Digest algorithm 5) or SHA-1 (Secure Hash Algorithm-1) hash of a message encrypted with the private key of the message originator, used to verify the integrity of a message and ensure nonrepudiation.
DMZ	Another name for the perimeter network. (DMZ originally stood for *demilitarized zone,* the buffer zone separating the warring North and South in Korea and Vietnam.)
DoS	An attack that uses so many of the resources on your computer and network that legitimate users can't access and use the system. From a single source, the attack overwhelms the target computer with messages and blocks legitimate traffic. It can prevent one system from being able to exchange data with other systems or prevent the system from using the Internet.
Dual-homed host	A computer with two network interfaces. (Think of each network as a home).
Encryption	The process of transforming information so that it's unintelligible to anyone but the intended recipient. The transformation is performed by a mathematical operation between a key and the information.
Exploit tools	Publicly available and sophisticated tools that intruders of various skill levels can use to determine vulnerabilities and gain entry into targeted systems.
Firewall	A controlled-access gateway between an organization's internal network and the Internet. A dual-homed host can be configured as a firewall.
Hash	The result when a mathematical function converts a message to a fixed-size numeric value known as a *message digest* (or *hash*). The MD5 algorithm, for example, produces a 128-bit message digest; SHA-1 generates a 160-bit message digest. The hash of a message is encrypted with the private key of the sender to produce the digital signature.

Term	Description
Host	A computer on a network that's configured to offer services to other computers on the network.
Integrity	For received data, a state of being the same as originally sent (that is, unaltered in transit).
IP spoofing	An attack in which a cracker figures out the IP address of a trusted host and then sends packets that appear to come from the trusted host. The attacker can send packets but can't see responses. But the attacker can predict the sequence of packets and essentially send commands that set up a backdoor for future break-ins.
IPSec (IP Security Protocol)	A security protocol for the network layer of the OSI networking model, designed to provide cryptographic security services for IP packets. IPSec provides encryption-based authentication, integrity, access control, and confidentiality. (For information on IPSec for Linux, visit www.ipsec-howto.org.)
Logic bombs	A form of sabotage in which a programmer inserts code that causes the program to perform a destructive action when some triggering event occurs, such as terminating the programmer's employment.
Nonrepudiation	A security feature that prevents the sender of data from being able to deny having sent the data.
Packet	A collection of bytes, assembled according to a specific protocol, that serves as the basic unit of communication on a network. On TCP/IP networks, for example, the packet may be referred to as an *IP packet* or a *TCP/IP packet.*
Packet filtering	Selective blocking of packets according to type of packet (as specified by the source and destination IP address or port).
Perimeter network	A network between the Internet and the protected internal network. The perimeter network (also known as DMZ) is where the bastion host resides.
Port scanning	A method of discovering which ports are open (in other words, which Internet services are enabled) on a system, performed by sending connection requests to the ports, one by one. This procedure is usually a precursor to further attacks; two port-scanning tools to know are nmap and netstat.
Proxy server	A server on the bastion host that enables internal clients to access external servers (and enables external clients to access servers inside the protected network). Proxy servers are available for various Internet services, such as FTP and HTTP.
Public key cryptography	An encryption method that uses a pair of keys — a private key and a public key — to encrypt and decrypt the information. Anything encrypted with the public key is decrypted only with the corresponding private key, and vice versa.
Public Key Infrastructure (PKI)	A set of standards and services that enables the use of public key cryptography and certificates in a networked environment. PKI facilitates tasks such as issuing, renewing, and revoking certificates, and generating and distributing public and private key pairs.

(continued)

Introducing Linux Security

TABLE 1-1 *(continued)*

Term	Description
Screening router	An Internet router that filters packets.
setuid program	A program that runs with the permissions of the owner regardless of who runs the program. If root owns a setuid/suid program, that program has root privileges regardless of who started the program. Crackers often exploit vulnerabilities in setuid programs to gain privileged access to a system. Similarly, sgid programs are used to run with the permissions of the group, regardless of who runs the program, and have their own similar vulnerabilities.
Sniffer	Synonymous with *packet sniffer* — a program that intercepts routed data and examines each packet in search of specified information, such as passwords transmitted in clear text.
Spyware	Any software that covertly gathers user information through the user's Internet connection and usually transmits that information in the background to someone else. Spyware can also gather information about email addresses and even passwords and credit card numbers. Spyware is similar to a Trojan horse in that users are tricked into installing spyware when they install something else.
Symmetric key encryption	An encryption method wherein the same key is used to encrypt and decrypt the information.
Threat	An event or activity, deliberate or unintentional, with the potential for causing harm to a system or network.
Trojan horse	A program that masquerades as a benign program but is really a backdoor used for attacking a system. Attackers often install a collection of Trojan horse programs that enable the attacker to freely access the system with root privileges yet hide that fact from the system administrator. Such collections of Trojan horse programs are called *rootkits*.
Virus	A self-replicating program that spreads from one computer to another by attaching itself to other programs.
Vulnerability	A flaw or weakness that may cause harm to a system or network.
War-dialing	Simple programs that dial consecutive phone numbers looking for modems.
War-driving	A method of gaining entry into wireless computer networks that uses a laptop, antennas, and a wireless network card and that involves patrolling locations to gain unauthorized access.
Worm	A self-replicating program that copies itself from one computer to another over a network.

Table 1-2 lists some commonly used computer security tools. I discuss some of these tools in other chapters, where they were related to specific topics; others are relevant only to security.

TABLE 1-2   **Common Computer Security Tools**

Tool	Description
chage	With this command, you can modify the time between required password changes (both minimum and maximum number of days), the number of days of warning to be given that a change must be made, and expiration date.
find	One of the most powerful all-around tools, this command allows you to find almost anything on machine if you can come up with the right syntax. Among the plethora of choices, you can find files created by a user, by a group, or on a certain date, with certain permissions.
lsof	An acronym for *list open files*, this utility does just that. Depending on the parameters used, you can choose to see files opened by a process or by a user.
netstat	To see the status of the network, including network connections, routing tables and statistics per interface, this tool does it all. A similar command, ss, is intended to replace much of the functionality here.
nmap	This tool is used to scan the network and create a map of what's available on it. This capability makes it an ideal tool for port scanning and security auditing.
passwd	A utility (not the file by the same name that holds user account information), with which users can change their passwords at the command line whenever necessary. Many users don't know that this utility exists, so they change their passwords when required through one of the graphical interface tools.
su	To temporarily become another user, su can be used within the current user's session. Another shell is created; upon exiting this second shell, the user goes back to the original session. This utility can be used to become the root user or any other user (provided the corresponding password is given).
sudo	Instead of creating a new session (as su requires) to perform a job with elevated privileges, sudo enables the user to just run that task with elevated privileges.
ulimit	Resource limits on shells can be set or viewed using this command to keep one user from excessively hogging system resources.
usermod	This utility can be thought of as an enhanced version of chage. It can it used to set/change password expiration parameters and to specify a default shell, lock or unlock an account, and so on.

Keeping Up with Security News and Updates

To keep up with the latest security alerts, you may want to visit one or both of the following sites on a daily basis:

» CERT Software Engineering Institute of Carnegie Mellon University at www.sei.cmu.edu/

» U.S. Computer Emergency Readiness Team (US-CERT) at www.us-cert.gov

If you prefer to receive regular security updates through email, you can also sign up for (subscribe to) various mailing lists:

- **US-CERT National Cyber Alert System:** Follow the directions at www.us-cert.gov to subscribe to this mailing list. The Cyber Alert System features four categories of security information through its mailing lists:

  - *Current Activity:* Alerts that provide technical information about vulnerabilities in various common software products.

  - *Alerts:* Alerts sent when vulnerabilities affect the general public. Each alert outlines the steps and actions that nontechnical home and corporate computer users can take to protect themselves from attacks.

  - *Bulletins:* Weekly summaries of security issues and new vulnerabilities along with patches, workarounds, and other actions that users can take to help reduce risks.

  - *Tips:* Advice on common security issues for nontechnical computer users.

- **Red Hat Security Center:** Although this site (https://access.redhat.com/security/) focuses on Red Hat, many of the vulnerabilities listed here apply to Linux as a whole.

» Protecting the system's files and directories

» Using GnuPG to encrypt and sign files

» Monitoring the security of your system

» Hardening Internet services

» Using Secure Shell for secure remote logins

» Setting up simple firewalls and enabling packet filtering

Chapter **2**

Securing Linux

To secure your Linux system, you have to pay attention to both host security and network security. The distinction between the two types of security is somewhat arbitrary, because securing the network involves securing the applications on the host that relate to what Internet services your system offers.

This chapter first examines host security and then explains how you can secure network services (mostly by not offering unnecessary services), how you can use a firewall to stop unwanted network packets from reaching your network, and how to use Secure Shell (SSH) for secure remote logins.

Host is the techie term for your Linux system, especially when you use it to provide services on a network. But the term makes sense even when you think of the computer by itself as the host for everything that runs on it: the operating system and all applications. A key aspect of computer security is securing the host.

Securing Passwords

Historically, Unix passwords are stored in the `/etc/passwd` file, which any user can read. A typical old-style `/etc/passwd` file entry for the `root` user looks like this:

```
root:t6Z7NWDK1K8sU:0:0:root:/root:/bin/bash
```

The fields are separated by colons (`:`), and the second field contains the password in encrypted form. To check whether a password is valid, the login program encrypts the plain-text password that the user enters and compares the password with the contents of the `/etc/passwd` file. If the passwords match, the user is allowed to log in.

Password-cracking programs work just like the login program except that these programs choose one word at a time from a dictionary, encrypt the word, and compare the encrypted word with the encrypted passwords in the `/etc/passwd` file for a match. To crack the passwords, the intruder needs access to the `/etc/passwd` file or to a copy of it. Often, crackers use weaknesses of various Internet servers (such as mail and FTP) to get a copy of the `/etc/passwd` file.

REMEMBER

Copies of files also exist on backup media, so be sure to store media securely, away from unauthorized eyes.

Over the years, passwords have become more secure in Linux due to several improvements, including shadow passwords and pluggable authentication modules (PAMs, described in the next two sections). You can install shadow passwords or a PAM easily while you install Linux. During Linux installation, you typically get a chance to configure the authentication. If you enable MD5 security and enable shadow passwords, you automatically enable more secure passwords within Linux and make it much more difficult for crackers to ascertain the stored values.

Shadow passwords

Obviously, leaving passwords lying around where anyone can get at them — even if the passwords are encrypted — is bad security. Instead of storing passwords in the `/etc/passwd` file (which any user capable of accessing the system can read), Linux now stores them in a shadow password file, `/etc/shadow`. Only the superuser (root) can read this file. Here's the entry for `root` in the new-style `/etc/passwd` file:

```
root:x:0:0:root:/root:/bin/bash
```

In this case, the second field contains x instead of an encrypted password. The x is the *shadow password*. The actual encrypted password is now stored in the /etc/ shadow file, where the entry for root is like this:

```
root:$1$AAAni/yN$uESHbzUpy9Cgfoo1Bf0tS0:11077:0:99999:7:-1:-1:134540356
```

The format of the /etc/shadow entries with colon-separated fields resembles the entries in the /etc/passwd file, but the meanings of most of the fields differ. The first field is still the username, and the second one is the encrypted password.

The remaining fields in each /etc/shadow entry control when the password expires. You don't have to interpret or change these entries in the /etc/shadow file. Instead, use the chage command to change the password expiration information. For starters, you can check a user's password expiration information by using the chage command with the -l option, as follows (while logged in as root):

```
chage -l root
```

This command displays expiration information, including how long the password lasts and how often you can change the password.

If you want to ensure that the user is forced to change a password at regular intervals, you can use the -M option to set the maximum number of days that a password stays valid. To make sure that user kdulaney is prompted to change the password in 90 days, for example, log in as root and type the following command:

```
chage -M 90 kdulaney
```

You can use the command for each user account to ensure that all passwords expire when appropriate and that all users choose new passwords.

Pluggable authentication modules (PAMs)

In addition to improving the password file's security by using shadow passwords, Linux improves the encryption of the passwords stored in the /etc/shadow file by using the MD5 message-digest algorithm described in RFC 1321 (www.ietf.org/ rfc/rfc1321.txt). MD5 reduces a message of any length to a 128-bit message digest (or *fingerprint*) of a document so that you can digitally sign it by encrypting it with your private key. MD5 works quite well for password encryption, too.

Another advantage of MD5 over older-style password encryption is that whereas older passwords were limited to a maximum of eight characters, new passwords encrypted with MD5 can be much longer. Longer passwords are harder to guess, even if the /etc/shadow file falls into the wrong hands.

You can tell that MD5 encryption is in effect in the /etc/shadow file. The encrypted passwords are longer, and they all sport the 1 prefix, as in the second field of the following sample entry:

```
root:$1$AAAni/yN$uESHbzUpy9Cgfoo1Bf0tS0:11077:0:99999:7:-1:-1:134540356
```

An add-on program module called a pluggable authentication module (PAM) performs the MD5 encryption. Linux PAMs provide a flexible method for authenticating users. By setting the PAM's configuration files, you can change your authentication method on the fly without modifying vital programs that verify a user's identity (such as login and passwd).

Linux uses PAM capabilities extensively. The PAMs reside in many modules; their configuration files are in the /etc/pam.d directory of your system. Check out the contents of this directory on your system by typing the following command:

```
ls /etc/pam.d
```

Each configuration file in this directory specifies how users are authenticated for a specific utility.

Protecting Files and Directories

One important aspect of securing the host is protecting important system files — and the directories that contain these files. You can protect the files through file ownership and the permission settings that control who can read, write, or (in the case of executable programs) execute the file.

The default Linux file security is controlled through the following settings for each file or directory:

>> User ownership

>> Group ownership

>> Read, write, execute permissions for the owner

>> Read, write, execute permissions for the group

>> Read, write, execute permissions for others (everyone else)

Viewing ownerships and permissions

You can see settings related to ownership and permissions for a file when you look at a detailed listing with the ls -l command. For example, in Ubuntu, type the following command to see the detailed listing of the /etc/inittab file:

```
ls -l /etc/inittab
```

The resulting listing looks something like this:

```
-rw-r--r-- 1 root root 1666 Feb 16 07:57 /etc/inittab
```

The first set of characters describes the file permissions for user, group, and others. The third and fourth fields show the user and group that own this file. In this case, user and group names are the same: root.

Changing file ownerships

You can set the user and group ownerships with the chown command. If the file /dev/hda should be owned by the user root and the group disk, you type the following command as root to set up this ownership:

```
chown root.disk /dev/hda
```

To change the group ownership alone, use the chgrp command. Here's how you can change the group ownership of a file from whatever it was earlier to the group named accounting:

```
chgrp accounting ledger.out
```

Changing file permissions

Use the chmod command to set the file permissions. To use chmod effectively, you have to specify the permission settings. One way is to concatenate one or more letters from each column of Table 2-1, in the order shown in the table (Who/Action/Permission).

To give everyone read and write access to all files in a directory, type **chmod a+rw ***. To permit everyone to execute a specific file, type **chmod a+x** *filename*.

TABLE 2-1

File Permission Codes

Who	Action	Permission
u (user)	+ (add)	r (read)
g (group)	– (remove)	w (write)
o (others)	= (assign)	x (execute)
a (all)	s (set user ID)	

Another way to specify a permission setting is to use a three-digit sequence of numbers. In a detailed listing, the read, write, and execute permission settings for the user, group, and others appear as the sequence

```
rwxrwxrwx
```

with dashes in place of letters for disallowed operations. Think of rwxrwxrwx as being three occurrences of the string rwx. Now assign the values r=4, w=2, and x=1. To get the value of the sequence rwx, simply add the values of r, w, and x. Thus, rwx = 7. With this formula, you can assign a three-digit value to any permission setting. If the user can read and write the file but everyone else can only read the file, for example, the permission setting is rw-r--r--, and the value is 644. Thus, if you want all files in a directory to be readable by everyone but writable only by the user, use the following command:

```
chmod 644 *
```

Setting default permission

What permission setting does a file get when you (or a program) create a new file? The answer is in what is known as the *user file-creation mask*, which you can see and set by using the umask command.

Type **umask**, and the command prints a number showing the current file-creation mask. For the root user, the mask is set to 022, whereas the mask for other users is 002. To see the effect of this file-creation mask and to interpret the meaning of the mask, follow these steps:

1. **Log in as** root, **and type the following command:**

```
touch junkfile
```

This command creates a file named junkfile with nothing in it.

2. **Type** ls -l junkfile **to see that file's permissions.**

You see a line similar to the following:

```
-rw-r--r-- 1 root root 0 Aug 24 10:56 junkfile
```

Interpret the numerical value of the permission setting by converting each three-letter permission in the first field (excluding the first letter) to a number between 0 and 7. For each letter that's present, the first letter gets a value of 4, the second letter is 2, and the third is 1. rw- translates to 4+2+0 (because the third letter is missing), or 6. Similarly, r-- is 4+0+0 = 4. Thus, the permission string -rw-r--r-- becomes 644.

3. **Subtract the numerical permission setting from 666.**

What you get is the umask setting. In this case, 666 - 644 results in a umask of 022. Thus, a umask of 022 results in a default permission setting of 666 - 022 = 644. When you rewrite 644 in terms of a permission string, it becomes rw-r--r--.

To set a new umask, type **umask** followed by the numerical value of the mask. Here's how you go about it:

1. **Figure out what permission settings you want for new files.**

If you want new files that can be read and written only by the owner and no one else, the permission setting looks like this:

```
rw-------
```

2. **Convert the permissions to a numerical value by using the conversion method that assigns 4 to the first field, 2 to the second, and 1 to the third.**

Thus, for files that are readable and writable only by their owner, the permission setting is 600.

3. **Subtract the desired permission setting from 666 to get the value of the mask.**

For a permission setting of 600, the mask becomes 666 - 600 = 066.

4. **Use the** umask **command to set the file-creation mask by typing** umask 066.

REMEMBER

A default umask of 022 is good for system security because it translates to files that have read and write permission for the owner and read permissions for everyone else. The bottom line is that you don't want a default umask that results in files that are writable by the whole world.

Checking for set user ID permission

Another permission setting can be a security hazard. This permission setting, called the *set user ID* (or setuid and/or suid for short), applies to executable files. When the suid permission is enabled, the file executes under the user ID of the file's owner. In other words, if an executable program is owned by root and the suid permission is set, the program runs as though root is executing it, no matter who executed the program. The suid permission means that the program can do a lot more (such as read all files, create new files, and delete files) than a normal user program can do. Another risk is that if a suid program file has a security hole, crackers can do a lot more damage through such programs than through other vulnerabilities.

You can find all suid programs with a simple find command:

```
find / -type f -perm +4000
```

You see a list of files such as the following:

```
/bin/su
/bin/ping
/bin/eject
/bin/mount
/bin/ping6
/bin/umount
/opt/kde4/bin/fileshareset
/opt/kde4/bin/artswrapper
/opt/kde4/bin/kcheckpass
&#x2026; lines deleted &#x2026;
```

Many of the programs have the suid permission because they need it, but you should check the complete list to make sure that it contains no strange suid programs (such as suid programs in a user's home directory).

If you type **ls -l /bin/su**, you see the following permission settings:

```
-rwsr-xr-x 1 root root 25756 Aug 19 17:06 /bin/su
```

The s in the owner's permission setting (-rws) tells you that the suid permission is set for the /bin/su file, which is the executable file for the su command that you can use to become root or another user.

Encrypting and Signing Files with GnuPG

Linux comes with the GNU Privacy Guard (GnuPG or GPG) encryption and authentication utility. With GnuPG, you can create your public and private key pair, encrypt files with your key, and digitally sign a message to authenticate that it's from you. If you send a digitally signed message to someone who has your public key, the recipient can verify that you signed the message.

Understanding public key encryption

The basic idea behind public key encryption is to use a pair of keys — one private and the other public — that are related but can't be used to guess one from the other. Anything encrypted with the private key can be decrypted only with the corresponding public key, and vice versa. The public key is for distribution to other people; you keep the private key in a safe place.

You can use public key encryption to communicate securely with others; Figure 2-1 illustrates the basic idea. Suppose that Alice wants to send secure messages to Bob. Each person generates public key and private key pairs, after which they exchange their public keys. When Alice wants to send a message to Bob, she encrypts the message by using Bob's public key and sends the encrypted message to him. Now the message is secure from eavesdropping, because only Bob's private key can decrypt the message, and only Bob has that key. When Bob receives the message, he uses his private key to decrypt the message and read it.

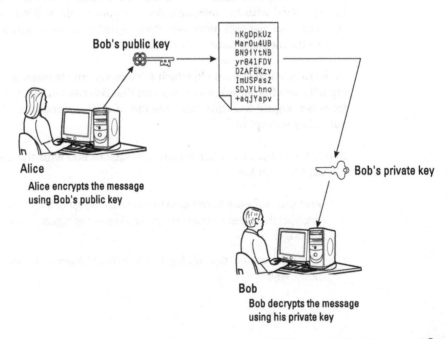

Bob's public key

```
hKgDpkUz
MarOu4UB
BN91YtNB
yr841FDV
DZAFEKzv
ImUSPasZ
SDJYLhno
+aqjYapv
```

Alice

Alice encrypts the message using Bob's public key

Bob's private key

Bob

Bob decrypts the message using his private key

FIGURE 2-1: Bob and Alice can communicate securely with public key encryption.

At this point, you might say, "Wait a minute! How does Bob know that the message really came from Alice? What if someone else uses Bob's public key and sends a message as though it came from Alice?" This situation is where digital signatures come in.

Understanding digital signatures

The purpose of digital (electronic) signatures is the same as that of pen-and-ink signatures, but how you sign digitally is different. Unlike a pen-and-ink signature, your digital signature depends on the message you're signing. The first step in creating a digital signature is applying a mathematical function to the message and reducing it to a fixed-size message digest (also called a *hash* or a *fingerprint*). No matter how big your message is, the message digest is usually 128 or 160 bits, depending on the hashing function.

The next step is applying public key encryption. Simply encrypt the message digest with your private key, and you get the digital signature for the message. Typically, the digital signature is added to the end of the message, and voilà — you get an electronically signed message.

What good does the digital signature do? Well, anyone who wants to verify that the message is indeed signed by you takes your public key and decrypts the digital signature. What that person gets is the message digest (the encrypted hash) of the message. Then he or she applies the same hash function to the message and compares the computed hash with the decrypted value. If the two match, then no one has tampered with the message. Because your public key was used to verify the signature, the message must have been signed with the private key known only to you, so the message must be from you!

In the theoretical scenario in which Alice sends private messages to Bob, Alice can digitally sign her message to make sure that Bob can tell that the message is really from her. Figure 2-2 illustrates the use of digital signatures along with normal public key encryption.

Here's how Alice sends her private message to Bob with the assurance that Bob can tell it's from her:

1. Alice uses software to compute the message digest of the message and then encrypts the digest by using her private key — her digital signature for the message.

2. Alice encrypts the message (again, using some convenient software *and* Bob's public key).

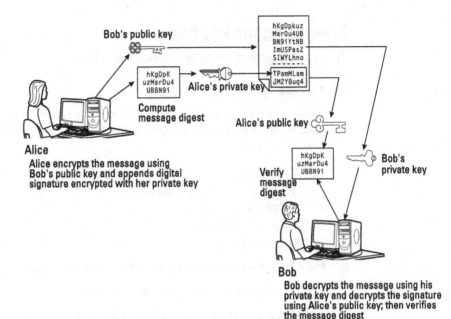

FIGURE 2-2:
Alice can digitally sign her message so that Bob can tell it's really from her.

Labels within figure:

Bob's public key

hKgDpkuz
MarOu4UB
BN91YtNB
ImUSPasZ
SIWYLhno

hKgDpK
uzMarDu4
UBBN91

Alice's private key

TPamMLam
JM2Y8uq4

Compute message digest

Alice's public key

Alice

Alice encrypts the message using Bob's public key and appends digital signature encrypted with her private key

Verify message digest

hKgDpK
uzMarDu4
UBBN91

Bob's private key

Bob

Bob decrypts the message using his private key and decrypts the signature using Alice's public key; then verifies the message digest

3. She sends both the encrypted message and the digital signature to Bob.

4. Bob decrypts the message, using his private key.

5. Bob decrypts the digital signature, using Alice's public key, which gives him the message digest.

6. Bob computes the message digest of the message and compares it with what he got by decrypting the digital signature.

7. If the two message digests match, Bob can be sure that the message really came from Alice.

Using GPG

GPG includes the tools you need to use public key encryption and digital signatures. You can figure out how to use GPG gradually as you begin using encryption. The following sections show some of the typical tasks you can perform with GPG.

Generating the key pair

The steps for generating the key pairs are as follows:

1. **Type gpg --gen-key.**

   If you're using GPG for the first time, it creates a .gnupg directory in your home directory and a file named gpg.conf in that directory. Then it asks what kind of keys you want:

   ```
   Please select what kind of key you want:
   (1) DSA and ElGamal (default)
   (2) DSA (sign only)
   (4) RSA (sign only)
   Your selection?
   ```

2. **Press Enter for the default choice, which is good enough.**

   GPG prompts you for the key size (the number of bits).

3. **Press Enter again to accept the default value of 2,048 bits.**

   GPG asks you when the keys expire. The default is to never expire.

4. **If the default is what you want (and why not?), press Enter.**

5. **When GPG asks whether you really want the keys to never expire, press the Y key to confirm.**

   GPG prompts you for your name, your email address, and a comment to make it easier to associate the key pair with your name.

6. **Type each piece of requested information, and press Enter.**

7. **When GPG gives you a chance to change the information or confirm it, confirm by typing o and pressing Enter.**

   GPG prompts you for a passphrase that protects your private key.

8. **Type a long phrase that includes lowercase and uppercase letters, numbers, and punctuation marks — the longer the better — and then press Enter.**

REMEMBER

   Be careful to choose a passphrase that you can remember easily.

   GPG generates the keys. It may ask you to perform some work on the PC so that the random-number generator can generate enough random numbers for the key-generation process.

Exchanging keys

To communicate with others, you have to give them your public key. You also have to get public keys from those who may send you a message (or when someone who might sign a file and you want to verify the signature). GPG keeps the public keys in your key ring. (The key ring is simply the public keys stored in a file, but the name sounds nice because everyone has a key ring in the real world, and these keys are keys of a sort.) To list the keys in your key ring, type

```
gpg --list-keys
```

To send your public key to someone or to place it on a website, you have to export the key to a file. The best way is to put the key in what GPG documentation calls ASCII-armored format, with a command like this:

```
gpg --armor --export kdualney@insightbb.com > kdulaneykey.asc
```

This command saves the public key in ASCII-armored format (which looks like garbled text) in the file named kdulaneykey.asc. You replace the email address with your email address (the one you used when you created the key) and replace the output filename with something different.

After you export the public key to a file, you can mail that file to others or place it on a website for use by others.

When you import a key from someone, you typically get it in ASCII-armored format as well. If you have a us-cert@us-cert.gov GPG public key in a file named uscertkey.asc (obtained from the link at www.us-cert.gov/pgp/email.html), you import it into the key ring with the following command:

```
gpg --import uscertkey.asc
```

Use the gpg --list-keys command to verify that the key is in your key ring. Here's what you might see when typing **gpg --list-keys** on the system:

```
/home/kdulaney/.gnupg/pubring.gpg
-----------------------------
pub 1024D/7B38A728 2018-08-28
uid Kristin Dulaney <kdulaney@insightbb.com>
sub 2048g/3BD6D418 2018-08-28
pub 2048R/F0E187D0 2019-09-08 [expires: 2019-10-01]
uid US-CERT Operations Key <us-cert@us-cert.gov>
```

The next step is checking the fingerprint of the new key. Type the following command to get the fingerprint of the US-CERT key:

```
gpg --fingerprint us-cert@us-cert.gov
```

GPG prints the fingerprint, as follows:

```
pub 2048R/F0E187D0 2018-09-08 [expires: 2019-10-01]
Key fingerprint = 049F E3BA 240B 4CF1 3A76 06DC 1868 49EC F0E1 87D0
uid US-CERT Operations Key <us-cert@us-cert.gov>
```

At this point, you need to verify the key fingerprint with someone at the US-CERT organization.

If you think that the key fingerprint is good, you can sign the key and validate it. Here's the command you use to sign the key:

```
gpg --sign-key us-cert@us-cert.gov
```

GPG asks for confirmation and then prompts you for your passphrase. After that, GPG signs the key.

WARNING

Because key verification and signing are potential weak links in GPG, be careful about what keys you sign. By signing a key, you say that you trust the key to be from that person or organization.

Signing a file

You may find signing files to be useful if you send a file to someone and want to assure the recipient that no one tampered with the file and that you did in fact send the file. GPG makes signing a file easy. You can compress and sign a file named message with the following command:

```
gpg -o message.sig -s message
```

To verify the signature, type

```
gpg --verify message.sig
```

To get back the original document, type

```
gpg -o message --decrypt message.sig
```

Sometimes, you don't care about keeping a message secret, but you want to sign it to indicate that the message is from you. In such a case, you can generate and append a clear-text signature with the following command:

```
gpg -o message.asc --clearsign message
```

This command appends a clear-text signature to the text message. Here's a typical clear-text signature block:

```
-----BEGIN PGP SIGNATURE-----
Version: GnuPG v1.4.2 (GNU/Linux)

iD8DBQFDEhAtaHWlHHs4pygRAhiqAJ9Qj0pPMgKVBuokDyUZaEYVsp6RIQCfaoBm
9zCwrSAG9mo2DXJvbKS3ri8=
=2uc/
-----END PGP SIGNATURE-----
```

When a message has a clear-text signature appended, you can use GPG to verify the signature with the following command:

```
gpg --verify message.asc
```

If you indeed signed the message, the last line of the output says that the signature is good.

Encrypting and decrypting documents

To encrypt a message meant for a recipient, you can use the --encrypt (or -e) GPG command. Here's how you might encrypt a message for US-CERT by using its GPG key:

```
gpg -o message.gpg -e -r us-cert@us-cert.gov message
```

The message is encrypted with the US-CERT public key (without a signature, but you can add the signature with the -s command).

When US-CERT receives the message.gpg file, the recipient must decrypt it by using US-CERT's private key. Here's the command that someone at US-CERT can use:

```
gpg -o message --decrypt message.gpg
```

Then GPG prompts for the passphrase to unlock the US-CERT private key, decrypts the message, and saves the output in the file named message.

If you want to encrypt a file that no one else has to decrypt, you can use GPG to perform symmetric encryption. In this case, you provide a passphrase to encrypt the file with the following GPG command:

```
gpg -o secret.gpg -c somefile
```

GPG prompts you for the passphrase and asks you to repeat the passphrase (to make sure that you didn't mistype anything). Then GPG encrypts the file, using a key generated from the passphrase.

To decrypt a file encrypted with a symmetric key, type

```
gpg -o myfile --decrypt secret.gpg
```

GPG prompts you for the passphrase. If you enter the correct passphrase, GPG decrypts the file and saves the output (in this example) in the file named myfile.

Monitoring System Security

Even if you secure your system, you have to monitor the log files periodically for signs of intrusion. You may want to use Tripwire (a good tool for detecting any changes made in the system files) so that you can monitor the integrity of critical system files and directories. Your Linux system probably doesn't come with the Tripwire File Integrity Manager package; you have to buy it from www.tripwire. com. After you purchase and install Tripwire, you can configure it to monitor any changes in specified system files and directories on your system.

Periodically examine the log files in the /var/log directory and its subdirectories. Many Linux applications, including some servers, write log information by using the logging capabilities of syslogd or rsyslogd. On Linux systems, the log files written by syslogd and rsyslogd reside in the /var/log directory. Make sure that only the root user can read and write these files.

REMEMBER

The syslogd configuration file is /etc/syslog.conf, and the rsyslogd configuration file (existing on many newer systems) is /etc/rsyslog.conf. The default configuration of syslogd generates the necessary log files, but if you want to examine and understand the configuration file, type **man syslog.conf** or **man rsyslog.conf** for more information.

Securing Internet Services

For an Internet-connected Linux system, or even one on a TCP/IP local-area network (LAN) that's not connected to the Internet, a significant threat is that someone could use one of many Internet services to gain access to your system. Each service — such as mail, web, and FTP — requires running a server program that responds to client requests arriving over the TCP/IP network. Some of these server programs have weaknesses that an outsider could use to log in to your system — maybe with `root` privileges. Luckily, Linux comes with some facilities that you can use to make the Internet services more secure.

WARNING

Potential intruders can employ a *port-scanning tool* — a program that attempts to establish a TCP/IP connection at a port and then looks for a response — to check which Internet servers are running on your system. Then, to gain access to your system, intruders can potentially exploit any known weaknesses of one or more services.

Turning off stand-alone services

To provide Internet services such as web, email, and FTP, your Linux system has to run server programs that listen to incoming TCP/IP network requests. Some of these servers start when your system boots, and they run all the time. Such servers are *stand-alone servers*. The web server and mail server are examples of stand-alone servers.

Another server, `xinetd`, starts other servers that are configured to work under `xinetd`. Some Linux systems use the `inetd` server instead of `xinetd` to start other servers.

Some servers can be configured to run on a stand-alone basis or under a super server such as `xinetd`. The `vsftpd` FTP server, for example, can be configured to run as a stand-alone server or to run under the control of `xinetd`.

DISTRIBUTION SPECIFIC

In Debian and Ubuntu, use the `update-rc.d` command to turn off stand-alone servers, and use the `invoke-rc.d` command to start or stop servers interactively. To get a clue about the available services, type **ls /etc/init.d**, and look at all the script files designed to turn services on or off. You have to use these filenames when you want to turn a service on or off. To turn off Samba service, for example, type **update-rc.d -f samba remove**. If the service was already running, type **invoke-rc.d samba stop** to stop the service. You can use the `invoke-rc.d` command to stop any service in a similar manner.

DISTRIBUTION SPECIFIC

In Fedora and SUSE, you can turn stand-alone servers on and off by using the `systemctl` command. You can get the names of the service scripts by typing **ls /etc/init.d**. Then you can turn off a service (such as Samba) by typing **sudo systemctl stop smb**. If the service was already running, type **/etc/init.d/smb stop** to stop the service. You can run scripts from the /etc/init.d directory with the `stop` argument to stop any service in a similar manner.

Configuring the Internet super server

In addition to stand-alone servers such as web and mail servers, the servers `inetd` and `xinetd` servers have to be configured separately. These servers are *Internet super servers* because they can start other servers on demand.

TIP

Type **ps ax | grep inetd** to see which Internet super server — `inetd` or `xinetd` — your system runs.

DISTRIBUTION SPECIFIC

Debian and Ubuntu use `inetd`, and Fedora and SUSE use `xinetd`.

The `inetd` server is configured through the /etc/inetd.conf file. You can disable a service by locating the appropriate line in that file and commenting it out by placing a pound sign (#) at the beginning of the line. After saving the configuration file, type **/etc/init.d/inetd restart** to restart the `inetd` server.

Configuring the `xinetd` server is a bit more complicated. The `xinetd` server reads a configuration file named /etc/xinetd.conf at startup. This file in turn refers to configuration files stored in the /etc/xinetd.d directory. The configuration files in /etc/xinetd.d tell `xinetd` which ports to listen to and which server to start for each port. Type **ls /etc/xinetd.d** to see a list of the files in the /etc/xinetd.d directory on your system. Each file represents a service that `xinetd` can start. To turn off any of these services, edit the file in a text editor, and add a `disable = yes` line in the file. After you make any changes in the `xinetd` configuration files, you must restart the `xinetd` server; otherwise, the changes don't take effect. To restart the `xinetd` server, type **/etc/init.d/xinetd restart**. This command stops the `xinetd` server and then starts it again. When the server restarts, it reads the configuration files, and the changes take effect.

Configuring TCP wrapper security

A common security feature of `inetd` and `xinetd` is their use of the TCP wrapper to start various services. The *TCP wrapper* is a block of code that provides an access-control facility for Internet services, acting like a protective package for your message. The TCP wrapper can start other services, such as FTP and Telnet, but before starting a service, it consults the /etc/hosts.allow file to see whether the host requesting the service is allowed to use that service. If nothing about that host appears in /etc/hosts.allow, the TCP wrapper checks the /etc/hosts.deny file to see whether it denies the service. If both files are empty, the TCP wrapper provides access to the requested service.

Here are the steps to follow to tighten access to the services that inetd or xinetd is configured to start:

1. **Use a text editor to edit the** /etc/hosts.deny **file, adding the following line to that file:**

   ```
   ALL:ALL
   ```

   This setting denies all hosts access to any Internet services on your system.

2. **Edit the** /etc/hosts.allow **file and add to it the names of hosts that can access services on your system.**

   To enable only hosts from the 192.168.1.0 network and the localhost (IP address 127.0.0.1) to access the services on your system, place the following line in the /etc/hosts.allow file:

   ```
   ALL: 192.168.1.0/255.255.255.0 127.0.0.1
   ```

3. **If you want to permit a specific remote host access to a specific Internet service, use the following syntax for a line in** /etc/hosts.allow**:**

   server_program_name: *hosts*

   Here, *server_program_name* is the name of the server program, and *hosts* is a comma-separated list of the hosts that can access the service. You may also enter *hosts* as a network address or an entire domain name, such as .mycompany.com.

Using Secure Shell for Remote Logins

Linux comes with Open Secure Shell (OpenSSH) software, a suite of programs that provides a secure replacement for the Berkeley r commands: rlogin (remote login), rsh (remote shell), and rcp (remote copy). OpenSSH uses public key cryptography to authenticate users and to encrypt communications between two hosts so that users can log in from remote systems securely and copy files securely.

This section briefly describes how to use the OpenSSH software in Linux. To find out more about OpenSSH and read the latest news about it, visit www.openssh.com or www.openssh.org.

The OpenSSH software is installed during Linux installation. Table 2-2 lists the main components of the OpenSSH software.

TABLE 2-2 **Components of the OpenSSH Software**

Component	Description
/usr/sbin/sshd	This SSH daemon must run on a host if you want users on remote systems to use the ssh client to log in securely. When a connection from the ssh client arrives, sshd performs authentication by using public key cryptography and establishes an encrypted communication link with the ssh client.
/usr/bin/ssh	Users can run this SSH client to log in to a host that is running sshd. Users can also use ssh to execute a command on another host.
/usr/bin/slogin	This component is a symbolic link to /usr/bin/ssh.
/usr/bin/scp	This secure-copy program works like rcp, but securely. The scp program uses ssh for data transfer and provides the same authentication and security as ssh.
/usr/bin/ssh-keygen	You use this program to generate the public and private key pairs that you need for the public key cryptography used in OpenSSH. The ssh-keygen program can generate key pairs for both RSA and DSA (Digital Signature Algorithm) authentication. (RSA comes from the first initials of the last names of Ron Rivest, Adi Shamir, and Leonard Adleman — the developers of the RSA algorithm.)
/etc/ssh/sshd_config	This configuration file for the sshd server specifies many parameters for sshd, including the port to listen to, the protocol to use, and the location of other files. (The two versions of SSH protocols are SSH1 and SSH2, both supported by OpenSSH.)
/etc/ssh/ssh_config	This configuration file is for the ssh client. Each user can also have an ssh configuration file named config in the .ssh subdirectory of the user's home directory.

OpenSSH uses public key encryption, in which the sender and receiver both have a pair of keys: a public key and a private key. The public keys are freely distributed, and each party knows the other's public key. The sender encrypts data by using the recipient's public key. Only the recipient's private key can decrypt the data.

To use OpenSSH, start the sshd server and then generate the host keys. Here's how:

>> If you want to support SSH-based remote logins on a host, start the sshd server on your system. Type **ps ax | grep sshd** to see whether the server is already running. If it isn't, log in as root, and turn on the SSH service.

>> Generate the host keys with the following command:

```
ssh-keygen -d -f /etc/ssh/ssh_host_key -N ''
```

> The –d flag causes the ssh–keygen program to generate DSA keys, which the SSH2 protocol uses. If you see a message saying that the file /etc/ssh/ssh_host_key already exists the key pairs were generated during Linux installation. You can use the existing file without having to regenerate the keys.

A user who wants to log in by using SSH can use an ssh command like the following

```
ssh 192.168.0.4 -l kdulaney
```

where 192.168.0.4 is the IP address of the other Linux system. Then SSH displays a message:

```
The authenticity of host '192.168.0.4 (192.168.0.4)' can't be established.
RSA key fingerprint is 7b:79:f2:dd:8c:54:00:a6:94:ec:fa:8e:7f:c9:ad:66.
Are you sure you want to continue connecting (yes/no)?
```

Type **yes**, and press Enter. SSH adds the host to its list of known hosts and prompts you for a password on the other Linux system:

```
kdulaney@192.168.0.4's password:
```

After entering the password, you have a secure login session with that system. You can also log in to this account with the following equivalent command:

```
ssh kdulaney@192.168.0.4
```

If you simply want to copy a file securely from another system on the LAN (identified by its IP address, 192.168.0.4), you can use scp like this:

```
scp 192.168.0.4:/etc/X11/xorg.conf
```

This command prompts for a password and securely copies the /etc/X11/xorg.conf file from the 192.168.0.4 host to the system from which the scp command was typed, as follows:

```
kdulaney@192.168.0.4's password: (type the password.)
xorg.conf 100% 2814 2.8KB/s 00:00
```

Setting Up Simple Firewalls

A *firewall* is a network device or host with two or more network interfaces — one connected to the protected internal network and the other connected to unprotected networks, such as the Internet. The firewall controls access to and from the protected internal network.

If you connect an internal network directly to the Internet, you have to make sure that every system on the internal network is properly secured — which can be nearly impossible, because a single careless user can render the entire internal network vulnerable.

A firewall is a single point of connection to the Internet: You can direct all your efforts toward making that firewall system a daunting barrier to unauthorized external users. Essentially, a firewall is a protective fence that keeps unwanted external data and software out and sensitive internal data and software in. (See Figure 2-3.)

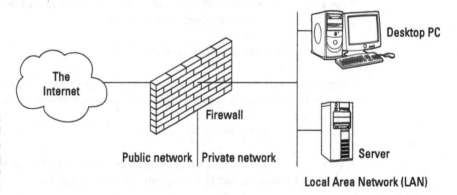

FIGURE 2-3:
A firewall protects hosts on a private network from the Internet.

The firewall runs software that examines the network packets arriving at its network interfaces and then takes appropriate action based on a set of rules. The idea is to define these rules so that they allow only authorized network traffic to flow between the two interfaces. Configuring the firewall involves setting up the rules properly. A configuration strategy is to reject all network traffic and then enable only a limited set of network packets to go through the firewall. The authorized network traffic would include the connections necessary to enable internal users to do things such as visit websites and receive electronic mail.

To be useful, a firewall must have the following general characteristics:

>> It must control the flow of packets between the Internet and the internal network.

>> It must *not* provide dynamic routing because dynamic routing tables are subject to route *spoofing* — the use of fake routes by intruders. Instead, the firewall uses static routing tables (which you can set up with the route command on Linux systems).

>> It must not allow any external user to log in as root. That way, even if the firewall system is compromised, the intruder is blocked from using root privileges from a remote login.

>> It must be kept in a physically secure location.

>> It must distinguish between packets that come from the Internet and packets that come from the internal protected network. This feature allows the firewall to reject packets that come from the Internet but have the IP address of a trusted system on the internal network.

>> It acts as the SMTP mail gateway for the internal network. Set up the sendmail software so that all outgoing mail appears to come from the firewall system.

>> Its user accounts are limited to a few user accounts for those internal users who need access to external systems. External users who need access to the internal network should use SSH for remote login (see "Using Secure Shell for Remote Logins" earlier in this chapter).

>> It keeps a log of all system activities, such as successful and unsuccessful login attempts.

>> It provides DNS name-lookup service to the outside world to resolve any host names that are known to the outside world.

>> It provides good performance so that it doesn't hinder internal users' access to specific Internet services (such as HTTP and FTP).

A firewall can take many forms. Here are three common forms of a firewall:

>> **Packet filter firewall:** This simple firewall uses a router capable of filtering (blocking or allowing) packets according to various characteristics, including the source and destination IP addresses, the network protocol (TCP or UDP), and the source and destination port numbers. Packet filter firewalls are usually placed at the outermost boundary with an untrusted network, and they form the first line of defense. An example of a packet filter firewall is a network router that employs filter rules to screen network traffic.

Packet filter firewalls are fast and flexible, but they can't prevent attacks that exploit application-specific vulnerabilities or functions. They can log only a minimal amount of information, such as source IP address, destination IP address, and traffic type. Also, they're vulnerable to attacks and exploits that take advantage of flaws within the TCP/IP protocol, such as IP address spoofing, which involves altering the address information in network packets to make them appear to come from a trusted IP address.

>> **Stateful inspection firewall:** This type of firewall keeps track of the network connections that network applications are using. When an application on an internal system uses a network connection to create a session with a remote system, a port is also opened on the internal system. This port receives network traffic from the remote system. For successful connections, packet filter firewalls must permit incoming packets from the remote system.

Opening many ports to incoming traffic creates a risk of intrusion by unauthorized users who abuse the expected conventions of network protocols such as TCP. Stateful inspection firewalls solve this problem by creating a table of outbound network connections, along with each session's corresponding internal port. Then this *state table* is used to validate any inbound packets. This stateful inspection is more secure than a packet filter because it tracks internal ports individually rather than opening all internal ports for external access.

>> **Application-proxy gateway firewall:** This firewall acts as an intermediary between internal applications that attempt to communicate with external servers such as a web server. A web proxy receives requests for external web pages from web browser clients running inside the firewall and relays them to the exterior web server as though the firewall was the requesting web client. The external web server responds to the firewall, and the firewall forwards the response to the inside client as though the firewall was the web server. No direct network connection is ever made from the inside client host to the external web server.

Application-proxy gateway firewalls have some advantages over packet filter firewalls and stateful inspection firewalls. First, application-proxy gateway firewalls examine the entire network packet rather than only the network addresses and ports, which enables these firewalls to provide more extensive logging capabilities than packet filters or stateful inspection firewalls.

Another advantage is that application-proxy gateway firewalls can authenticate users directly, whereas packet filter firewalls and stateful inspection firewalls normally authenticate users on the basis of the IP address of the system (that is, source, destination, and protocol type). Given that network addresses can be easily spoofed, the authentication capabilities of application-proxy gateway firewalls are superior to those found in packet filter and stateful inspection firewalls.

The advanced functionality of application-proxy gateway firewalls, however, results in some disadvantages compared with packet filter or stateful inspection firewalls:

- Because of the full packet awareness found in application-proxy gateways, the firewall is forced to spend significant time reading and interpreting each packet. Therefore, application-proxy gateway firewalls generally aren't well suited to high-bandwidth or real-time applications. To reduce the load on the firewall, a dedicated proxy server can be used to secure less time-sensitive services, such as email and most web traffic.

- Application-proxy gateway firewalls are often limited in terms of support for new network applications and protocols. An individual application-specific proxy agent is required for each type of network traffic that needs to go through the firewall. Most vendors of application-proxy gateways provide generic proxy agents to support undefined network protocols or applications. Those generic agents, however, tend to negate many of the strengths of the application-proxy gateway architecture; they simply allow traffic to *tunnel* through the firewall.

Most firewalls implement a combination of these firewall functionalities. Many vendors of packet filter firewalls or stateful inspection firewalls have also implemented basic application–proxy functionality to offset some of the weaknesses associated with their firewalls. In most cases, these vendors implement application proxies to provide better logging of network traffic and stronger user authentication. Nearly all major firewall vendors have introduced multiple firewall functions into their products in some manner.

TIP

In a large organization, you may also have to isolate smaller internal networks from the corporate network. You can set up such internal firewalls the same way that you set up Internet firewalls.

Using NAT

Network Address Translation (NAT) is an effective tool that enables you to hide the network addresses of an internal network behind a firewall. In essence, NAT allows an organization to use private network addresses behind a firewall while maintaining the ability to connect to external systems through the firewall.

Here are the three methods of implementing NAT:

>> **Static:** In static NAT, each internal system on the private network has a corresponding external, routable IP address associated with it. This technique is seldom used because unique IP addresses are in short supply.

>> **Hiding:** In hiding NAT, all systems behind a firewall share an external, routable IP address, and the internal systems use private IP addresses. Thus, in a hiding NAT, several systems behind a firewall still appear to be a single system.

>> **Port address translation:** With port address translation, you can place hosts behind a firewall system and still make them selectively accessible to external users.

In terms of strengths and weaknesses, each type of NAT — static, hiding, and port address translation — is applicable in certain situations. The variable is the amount of design flexibility offered by each type. Static NAT offers the most flexibility, but it's not always practical because of the shortage of IP addresses. Hiding NAT technology is seldom used because port address translation offers additional features. Port address translation tends to be the most convenient and secure solution.

Enabling packet filtering on your Linux system

The Linux kernel has built-in packet filtering software in the form of something called `netfilter`. You use the `iptables` command to set up the rules for what happens to the packets based on the IP addresses in their header and the network connection type.

TIP

To find out more about `netfilter` and `iptables`, visit the documentation section of the `netfilter` website at www.netfilter.org/documentation.

The built-in packet filtering capability is handy when you don't have a dedicated firewall between your Linux system and the Internet, such as when you connect your Linux system to the Internet through a DSL or cable modem. Essentially, you can have a packet filtering firewall inside your Linux system sitting between the kernel and the applications.

Using the security level configuration tool

Most Linux distributions, such as Fedora and SUSE, now include GUI tools to turn on a packet filtering firewall and simplify the configuration experience for the user.

In some distributions, you need to install ufw (an acronym for Uncomplicated Firewall), which lets you manage a net-filter firewall and simplify configuration. ufw serves as a front end to `iptables`, which allows you to enter commands in a terminal window directly through it. The command

```
sudo ufw enable
```

turns the firewall on, and the command

```
sudo ufw status verbose
```

displays such information as the following:

```
Status: active
```

```
Logging: on (low)
```

```
Default: deny (incoming), allow (outgoing), disabled (routed)
```

```
New profiles: skip
```

The default settings are exactly what you're looking for in most cases for a client machine: allowing outgoing traffic and denying incoming traffic.

You can allow incoming packets meant for specific Internet services such as SSH, Telnet, and FTP. If you select a network interface such as eth0 (the first Ethernet card) as trusted, all network traffic over that interface is allowed without any filtering.

DISTRIBUTION SPECIFIC

In SUSE, to set up a firewall, choose Main Menu⇨System⇨YaST. In the YaST Control Center window that appears, click Security and Users on the left side of the window and then click Firewall on the right side. YaST opens a window that you can use to configure the firewall.

You can designate network interfaces (by device name, such as eth0, ppp0, and so on) to one of three zones: internal, external, or demilitarized zone. Then, for that zone, you can specify what services (such as HTTP, FTP, and SSH) are allowed. If you have two or more network interfaces, and you use the Linux system as a gateway (a router), you can enable forwarding packets between network interfaces (a feature called *masquerading*).

You can also turn on different levels of logging, such as logging all dropped packets that attempt connection at specific ports. If you change the firewall settings, choose the Startup category and click Save Settings and Restart Firewall Now.

Using the iptables command

As I mention earlier in the chapter, the graphical user interface (GUI) firewall configuration tools are just front ends that use the iptables command to implement the firewall. If your Linux system doesn't have a GUI tool, you can use iptables directly to configure firewalling on your Linux system.

Using the `iptables` command is somewhat complex. The command uses the concept of a *chain*, which is a sequence of rules. Each rule says what to do with a packet if the header contains certain information, such as the source or destination IP address. If a rule doesn't apply, `iptables` consults the next rule in the chain. By default, there are three chains:

» **INPUT chain:** Contains the first set of rules against which packets are tested. The packets continue to the next chain only if the INPUT chain doesn't specify DROP or REJECT.

» **FORWARD chain:** Contains the rules that apply to packets attempting to pass through this system to another system (when you use your Linux system as a router between your LAN and the Internet, for example).

» **OUTPUT chain:** Includes the rules applied to packets before they're sent out (either to another network or to an application).

When an incoming packet arrives, the kernel uses `iptables` to make a routing decision based on the destination IP address of the packet. If the packet is for this server, the kernel passes the packet to the INPUT chain. If the packet satisfies all the rules in the INPUT chain, the packet is processed by local processes such as an Internet server that's listening for packets of this type.

If the kernel has IP forwarding enabled, and the packet has a destination IP address of a different network, the kernel passes the packet to the FORWARD chain. If the packet satisfies the rules in the FORWARD chain, it's sent out to the other network. If the kernel doesn't have IP forwarding enabled, and the packet's destination address isn't for this server, the packet is dropped.

If the local processing programs that receive the input packets want to send network packets out, those packets pass through the OUTPUT chain. If the OUTPUT chain accepts those packets, they're sent out to the specified destination network.

You can view the current chains, add rules to the existing chains, or create new chains of rules by using the `iptables` command, which normally requires you to be root to interact with. When you view the current chains, you can save them to a file. If you've configured nothing else, and your system has no firewall configured, typing **iptables -L** should show the following:

```
Chain INPUT (policy ACCEPT)
target prot opt source destination
Chain FORWARD (policy ACCEPT)
target prot opt source destination
Chain OUTPUT (policy ACCEPT)
target prot opt source destination
```

In this case, all three chains — INPUT, FORWARD, and OUTPUT — show the same ACCEPT policy, which means that everything is wide open.

If you're setting up a packet filter, the first thing you do is specify the packets that you want to accept. To accept packets from the 192.168.0.0 network address, add the following rule to the INPUT chain:

```
iptables -A INPUT -s 192.168.0.0/24 -j ACCEPT
```

Now add a rule to drop everything except local loopback (the lo network interface) traffic and stop all forwarding with the following commands:

```
iptables -A INPUT -i ! lo -j REJECT
iptables -A FORWARD -j REJECT
```

The first iptables command, for example, appends to the INPUT chain (-A INPUT) the rule that if the packet doesn't come from the lo interface (-i ! lo), iptables rejects the packet (-j REJECT).

Before rejecting all other packets, you may add more rules to each INPUT chain to allow specific packets in. You can select packets to accept or reject based on many parameters, such as IP addresses, protocol types (TCP, UDP), network interface, and port numbers.

You can do all sorts of specialized packet filtering with iptables. Suppose that you set up a web server and want to accept packets meant for only HTTP (port 80) and SSH services. The SSH service (port 22) is for you to securely log in and administer the server. Also suppose that the server's IP address is 192.168.0.10. Here's how you might set up the rules for this server:

```
iptables -P INPUT DROP
iptables -A INPUT -s 0/0 -d 192.168.0.10 -p tcp --dport 80 -j ACCEPT
iptables -A INPUT -s 0/0 -d 192.168.0.10 -p tcp --dport 22 -j ACCEPT
```

In this case, the first ruleset up the default policy of the INPUT chain to DROP, which means that if none of the specific rules matches, the packet is dropped. The next two rules say that packets addressed to 192.168.0.10 and meant for ports 80 and 22 are accepted.

WARNING

Don't type iptables commands from a remote login session. A rule that begins denying packets from all addresses can also stop what you type from reaching the system; in that case, you may have no way of accessing the system over the network. To avoid unpleasant surprises, always type iptables rules at the console — the keyboard and monitor connected directly to your Linux PC that's running the packet filter. If you want to delete all filtering rules in a hurry, type **iptables -F** to flush them. To change the default policy for the INPUT chain to ACCEPT, type **iptables -t filter -P INPUT ACCEPT**. This command causes iptables to accept all incoming packets by default.

Not every iptables command is discussed in this section. You can type **man iptables** to read a summary of the commands. You can also read about netfilter and iptables at https://netfilter.org/projects/iptables/index.html.

After you define the rules by using the iptables command, those rules are in memory and are gone when you reboot the system. Use the iptables-save command to store the rules in a file. You can save the rules in a file named iptables.rules by using the following command:

```
iptables-save > iptables.rules
```

Here's a listing of the iptables.rules file generated on a Fedora system:

```
# Generated by iptables-save v1.3.0 on Sun Dec 28 16:10:12 2019
*filter
:FORWARD ACCEPT [0:0]
:INPUT ACCEPT [0:0]
:OUTPUT ACCEPT [6:636]
-A FORWARD -j REJECT --reject-with icmp-port-unreachable
-A INPUT -s 192.168.0.0/255.255.255.0 -j ACCEPT
-A INPUT -i ! lo -j REJECT --reject-with icmp-port-unreachable
COMMIT
# Completed on Sun Dec 28 16:10:12 2019
```

These rules correspond to the following iptables commands used to configure the filter:

```
iptables -A INPUT -s 192.168.0.0/24 -j ACCEPT
iptables -A INPUT -i ! lo -j REJECT
iptables -A FORWARD -j REJECT
```

If you want to load these saved rules into iptables, use the following command:

```
iptables-restore < iptables.rules
```

Security Files to Be Aware Of

Table 2-3 lists 11 files, or directories, that security administrators should be aware of and able to explain.

TABLE 2-3   ## Key Security Files

File	Description
/etc/nologin	If this file exists, it denies login to all users except root. This file can be handy when maintenance needs to be done and users need to stay off the system for a period of time. Removing the file restores login capability for all users. The file can be created as a text file with any editor, or you can often use the nologin command to create it.
/etc/passwd	This file holds much of the user account information and is addressed heavily in this chapter.
/etc/shadow	When shadowing is turned on – which it almost always is – password values (hashes) are stored in this file (which is more secure) as opposed to in /etc/passwd.
/etc/xinetd.d/*	This directory can be used to store configuration files used by xinetd, the server daemon.
/etc/xinetd.conf	This file is the main configuration file used by xinetd, the server daemon.
/etc/xinetd.d/*	This directory can be used to store configuration files used by inetd, the Internet daemon. In almost all distributions, inetd has been replaced by xinetd.
/etc/inetd.conf	This file is the main configuration file used by inetd, the Internet daemon.
/etc/inittab	This file is the initial startup (initialization) table used to identify what starts and stops as the system is booted and changes run states.
/etc/init.d/*	This directory can hold configuration files that are used during the change of run states/level and referenced by the inittab file.
/etc/hosts.allow	If this file exists, it specifically lists the hosts that are allowed to network with this one. If the file doesn't exist, by default, all hosts are allowed to network with this one.
/etc/hosts.deny	If this file exists, it specifically lists the hosts that aren't allowed to network with this one. If the file doesn't exist, by default, all hosts are allowed to network with this one. The three possibilities are an allow file that identifies only hosts that can network with this one, a deny file that identifies only hosts that can't connect with this one, and neither file allows all other hosts to network with this one.

» **Learning a security test methodology**

» **Reviewing host and network security**

» **Appreciating vulnerability testing**

» **Exploring different security testing tools**

Chapter **3**

Vulnerability Testing and Computer Security Audits

When you see the term *audit*, the odds are good that you think of the kind involving taxes. In actuality, many types of audits exist, and one of them is a *computer security audit*. The purpose of a computer security audit, in its simplest form, is to test your system and network security. For larger organizations, an independent auditor (much like with the auditing of financial statements) can do the security audit. If you have only a few Linux systems or a small network, you can do the security audit as a self-assessment to figure out whether you're doing everything okay.

This chapter explains how to perform computer security audits and shows you some free tools and resources that can help you test your system's security.

Understanding Security Audits

An *audit* is an independent assessment of whatever it is you're auditing, so a *computer security audit* is an independent assessment of computer security. If someone conducts a computer security audit of your organization, he or she focuses typically on two areas:

>> **Independent verification** of whether your organization complies with its existing policies and procedures for computer security. This part is the nontechnical aspect of the security audit.

>> **Independent testing** of how effective your security controls (any hardware and software mechanisms that you use to secure the system) are. This part is the technical aspect of the security audit.

You need security audits for the same reason that you need financial audits: to verify that everything's being done the way it's supposed to be done. In public as well as private organizations, management may want to have independent security audits done to assure themselves that their security is A-OK. Regardless of your organization's size, you can always perform security audits on your own, either to prepare for independent security audits or to find whether you're doing everything correctly.

No matter whether you have independent security audits or a self-assessment, here are some of the benefits you get from security audits:

>> Periodic risk assessments that consider internal and external threats to systems and data.

>> Periodic testing of the effectiveness of security policies, security controls, and techniques.

>> Identification of any significant deficiencies in your system's security (so that you know what to fix).

>> In the case of self-assessments, preparation for any annual independent security testing that your organization may have to face.

Nontechnical aspects of security audits

The nontechnical side of computer security audits focuses on your organization-wide security framework. The audit examines how well the organization has set up and implemented its policies, plans, and procedures for computer security. Here's a list of some items to be verified:

>> Risks are periodically assessed.

>> An entitywide security program plan is in place.

>> A security program-management structure is in place.

>> Computer security responsibilities are clearly assigned.

>> Effective security-related personnel policies are in place.

>> The security program's effectiveness is monitored, and changes are made when needed.

As you might expect, the nontechnical aspects of the security audit involve reviewing documents and interviewing appropriate people to find out how the organization manages computer security. For a small organization or a home PC, expecting plans and procedures in documents is ridiculous. In those cases, simply make sure that you have some technical controls in place to secure your system and your network connection.

Technical aspects of security audits

The technical side of computer security audits focuses on testing the technical controls that secure your hosts and network. This testing involves determining the following:

>> **How well the host is secured:** Examples include whether all operating system patches are applied, file permissions are set correctly, user accounts are protected, file changes are monitored, and log files are monitored.

>> **How well the network is secured:** Examples include whether unnecessary Internet services are turned off, a firewall is installed, remote logins secured with tools such as Secure Shell (SSH), and whether Transport Control Protocol (TCP) wrapper access controls are used.

Typically, security experts use automated tools to perform these two security reviews for individual hosts and for the entire network.

Implementing a Security Test Methodology

A key element of a computer security audit is a security test that checks the technical mechanisms used to secure a host and the network. The security-test methodology follows these high-level steps:

1. **Take stock of the organization's networks, hosts, network devices (routers, switches, firewalls, and so on), and Internet connection.**

2. **If many hosts and network connections exist, determine which important hosts and network devices need to be tested.**

   The importance of a host depends on the kinds of applications it runs. A host that runs the corporate database, for example, is more important than the hosts that serve as desktop systems.

3. **Test the hosts individually.**

   Typically, this step involves logging in as a system administrator and checking various aspects of host security, from passwords to system log files.

4. **Test the network.**

   You usually perform this step by attempting to break through the network defenses from another system on the Internet. If the network has a firewall, the testing checks whether the firewall is configured correctly.

5. **Analyze the test results of both host and network tests to determine vulnerabilities and risks.**

Each type of testing (host and network) focuses on three areas of overall computer security:

» **Prevention:** Includes the mechanisms (nontechnical and technical) that help prevent attacks on the system and the network.

» **Detection:** Refers to techniques such as monitoring log files, checking file integrity, and using intrusion detection systems that detect when someone is about to break into (or has already broken into) your system.

» **Response:** Includes the steps for tasks such as reporting an incident to authorities and restoring important files from backup after a computer security incident occurs.

For host and network security, each area has some overlap. Prevention mechanisms for host security (such as good passwords and file permissions) can also provide network security, for example. Nevertheless, thinking in terms of the three areas — prevention, detection, and response — is helpful.

Some common computer vulnerabilities

Before you can think about prevention, however, you have to know the types of problems you're trying to prevent — the common security vulnerabilities. The prevention and detection steps typically depend on the specific vulnerabilities. The idea is to check whether a host or a network has the vulnerabilities that crackers exploit.

Online resources on computer vulnerabilities

Several online resources identify and categorize computer security vulnerabilities:

>> **SANS Institute** publishes a semiweekly high-level executive summary of the most important news articles that have been published on computer security during the past week. You can view past issues and sign up for the new issues at www.sans.org/newsletters/newsbites/?msc=cishp.

>> **CVE** (Common Vulnerabilities and Exposures) is a list of standardized names of vulnerabilities. For more information on CVE, see http://cve.mitre.org. Using the CVE name to describe vulnerabilities is common practice. Version 2.0 of the naming rules took place on January 1, 2018. These rules are explained in detail in the document at http://cve.mitre.org/cve/cna/ CNA_Rules_v2.0.pdf.

>> **National Vulnerability Database** is a searchable index of information on computer vulnerabilities, published by the National Institute of Standards and Technology (NIST), a U.S. government agency. You can find the database at https://nvd.nist.gov.

Typical computer vulnerabilities

Table 3-1 summarizes some common Unix and cross-platform vulnerabilities that apply to Linux.

TABLE 3-1   Some Vulnerabilities Common to Unix Systems

Vulnerability Type	Description
BIND DNS	Berkeley Internet Name Domain (BIND) is a package that implements the Domain Name System (DNS), the Internet's name service that translates a name to an IP address. Some versions of BIND have vulnerabilities.
Apache Web Server	Some Apache Web Server modules (such as mod_ssl) have known vulnerabilities. Any vulnerability in Common Gateway Interface (CGI) programs used with web servers to process interactive web pages can give attackers a way to gain access to a system.
Authentication	User accounts sometimes have no passwords or have weak passwords that are easily cracked by password-cracking programs.
CVS, Subversion	Concurrent Versions System (CVS) is a popular source-code control system used in Linux systems. Subversion is another version control system for Linux that is becoming popular. These version control systems have vulnerabilities that can enable an attacker to execute arbitrary code on the system.
sendmail	sendmail is a complex program used to transport mail messages from one system to another, and some versions of sendmail have vulnerabilities.
SNMP	Simple Network Management Protocol (SNMP) is used to remotely monitor and administer various network-connected systems ranging from routers to computers. SNMP lacks good access control, so an attacker may be able to reconfigure or shut down your system if it's running SNMP.
Open Secure Sockets Layer (OpenSSL)	Many applications, such as Apache Web Server, use OpenSSL to provide cryptographic security for a network connection. Unfortunately, some versions of OpenSSL have known vulnerabilities that could be exploited.
Network File System (NFS) and Network Information Service (NIS)	Both NFS and NIS have many security problems (such as buffer overflow, potential for denial-of-service attacks, and weak authentication). Also, NFS and NIS are often misconfigured, which could allow local and remote users to exploit the security holes.
Databases	Databases such as MySQL and PostgreSQL are complex applications that can be difficult to configure and secure correctly. These databases have many features that can be misused or exploited to compromise the confidentiality, availability, and integrity of data.
Linux kernel	The Linux kernel is susceptible to many vulnerabilities, such as denial of service, execution of arbitrary code, and root-level access to the system.

Host-security review

When reviewing host security, focus on assessing the security mechanisms in each of the following areas:

>> **Prevention:** Install operating-system updates, secure passwords, improve file permissions, set up a password for a bootloader, and use encryption.

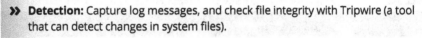

>> **Detection:** Capture log messages, and check file integrity with Tripwire (a tool that can detect changes in system files).

Tripwire started as open-source but no longer is. You can still search for and download the original.

>> **Response:** Make routine backups and develop incident-response procedures.

The following sections review a few of these host-security mechanisms.

Operating system updates

Linux distributions release updates soon. When security vulnerabilities are found, Linux distributions release an update to fix the problem. Many distributions offer online updates that you can enable and use to keep your system up to date. The details of updating the operating system depend on the distribution. (See Book 5, Chapter 4 for information on how to update Linux online.)

File permissions

Protect important system files with appropriate file ownerships and file permissions. The key procedures in assigning file-system ownerships and permissions are as follows:

>> Figure out which files contain sensitive information and why. Some files may contain sensitive data related to your work or business, whereas many other files are sensitive because they control the Linux system configuration.

>> Maintain a current list of authorized users and what they're authorized to do on the system.

>> Set up passwords, groups, file ownerships, and file permissions to allow only authorized users to access the files.

Table 3-2 lists some important system files in Linux, showing the typical numeric permission setting for each file (which may differ slightly depending on the distribution). See Book 6, Chapter 2 for more information on numeric permission settings.

Another important check is for executable program files that have the setuid permission. If a program has setuid permission and is owned by root, the program runs with root privileges no matter who actually runs the program. You can find all setuid programs with the following find command:

```
find / -perm +4000 -print
```

TABLE 3-2   **Important System Files and Their Permissions**

File Pathname	Permission	Description
/boot/grub/menu.1st	600	GRUB bootloader menu file
/etc/cron.allow	400	List of users permitted to use cron to submit periodic jobs
/etc/cron.deny	400	List of users who can't use cron to submit periodic jobs
/etc/crontab	644	Systemwide periodic jobs
/etc/hosts.allow	644	List of hosts allowed to use Internet services that are started with TCP wrappers
/etc/hosts.deny	644	List of hosts denied access to Internet services that are started with TCP wrappers
/etc/logrotate.conf	644	File that controls how log files rotate
/etc/pam.d	755	Directory with configuration files for pluggable authentication modules (PAMs)
/etc/passwd	644	Old-style password file with user account information but not the passwords
/etc/rc.d	755	Directory with system-startup scripts
/etc/securetty	600	TTY interfaces (terminals) from which root can log in
/etc/security	755	Policy files that control system access
/etc/shadow	400	File with encrypted passwords and password expiration information
/etc/shutdown.allow	400	Users who can shut down or reboot by pressing Ctrl+Alt+Delete
/etc/ssh	755	Directory with configuration files for SSH
/etc/sysconfig	755	System configuration files
/etc/sysctl.conf	644	Kernel configuration parameters
/etc/syslog.conf	644	Configuration file for the syslogd server that logs messages
/etc/udev/udev.conf	644	Configuration file for udev — the program that provides the capability to dynamically name hot-pluggable devices and create the device files in the /dev directory
/etc/vsftpd	600	Configuration file for the Very Secure FTP server
/etc/vsftpd.ftpusers	600	List of users who aren't allowed to use FTP to transfer files
/etc/xinetd.conf	644	Configuration file for the xinetd server

File Pathname	Permission	Description
/etc/xinetd.d	755	Directory containing configuration files for specific services that the xinetd server can start
/var/log	755	Directory with all log files
/var/log/lastlog	644	Information about all previous logins
/var/log/messages	644	Main system message log file
/var/log/wtmp	664	Information about current logins

You may want to save the output in a file (append *filename* to the command) and then examine the file for any unusual setuid programs. A setuid program in a user's home directory, for example, is unusual.

Password security

Verify that the password, group, and shadow password files are protected. In particular, the shadow password file has to be write-protected and readable only by root. Table 3-3 shows the password filenames and their recommended permissions.

TABLE 3-3

Ownership and Permission of Password Files

File Pathname	Ownership	Permission
/etc/group	root.root	644
/etc/passwd	root.root	644
/etc/shadow	root.root	400

Incident response

Incident response is the policy that tells you what to do if something unusual happens to the system. The policy tells you how to proceed if someone breaks into your system.

Your response to an incident depends on how you use your system and how important the system is to you or your business. For a comprehensive incident response, remember these key points:

>> Figure out how critical and important your computer and network are and identify who or what resources can help you protect your system.

>> Take steps to prevent and minimize potential damage and interruption.

>> Develop and document a comprehensive contingency plan.

>> Periodically test the contingency plan and revise the procedures as appropriate.

Network-security review

A *network-security review* focuses on assessing the security mechanisms in each of the following areas:

>> **Prevention:** Set up a firewall, enable packet filtering, disable unnecessary inetd or xinetd services, turn off unneeded Internet services, use TCP wrappers for access control, and use SSH for secure remote logins.

>> **Detection:** Use network intrusion detection, and capture system logs.

>> **Response:** Develop incident-response procedures.

Some key steps in assessing the network security are described in the following three subsections.

Services started by inetd or xinetd

Depending on your distribution, the inetd or xinetd server may be configured to start some Internet services, such as Telnet and FTP. The decision to turn on some of these services depends on such factors as how the system connects to the Internet and how the system is being used. Usually, you can turn off inetd and xinetd services by commenting out the line; place a pound sign (#) at the beginning of the line.

If you're using xinetd, you can see which services are turned off by checking the configuration files in the /etc/xinetd.d directory for all the configuration files that have a disable = yes line. (The line doesn't count if it's commented out, which is indicated by a # character at the beginning of the line.) You can add a disable = yes line to the configuration file of any service that you want to turn off.

Also check the following files for any access controls used with the inetd or xinetd service:

>> /etc/hosts.allow lists hosts that are allowed to access specific services.

>> /etc/hosts.deny lists hosts that are denied access to services.

Stand-alone services

Many services, such as apache and httpd (web server), as well as sendmail (mail server), start automatically at boot time, assuming that they're configured to start that way.

In some distributions, you can use the systemctl or chkconfig command to check which of these stand-alone servers is set to start at various run levels. (See Book 5, Chapter 1 for more information about run levels.) Typically, most systems start up at run level 3 (for text login) or 5 (for graphical login). Therefore, what matters is the setting for the servers in levels 3 and 5. To view the list of servers, type **chkconfig --list | more**. When you do a self-assessment of your network security and find that some servers shouldn't be running, you can turn them off for run levels 3 and 5 by typing **chkconfig --level 35 *servicename* off**, where *servicename* is the name of the service you want to turn off.

In some distributions, you can use a graphical user interface (GUI) tool to see which services are enabled and running at any run level. With YaST, for example, click System on the left side of the window and then click Runlevel Editor on the right side of the window.

When you audit network security, make a note of all the servers that are turned on and then try to determine whether they should really *be* on, according to what you know about the system. The decision to turn on a particular service depends on how your system is used (as a web server or as a desktop system, for example) and on how it's connected to the Internet (such as through a firewall or directly).

Penetration test

A penetration test is the best way to tell what services are really running on a Linux system. *Penetration testing* involves trying to get access to your system from an attacker's perspective. Typically, you perform this test from a system on the Internet and try to break in or at least get access to services running on your Linux system.

One aspect of penetration testing is seeing what ports are open on your Linux system. The *port number* is a number that identifies a TCP/IP network connection to the system. The attempt to connect to a port succeeds only if a server is running, or "listening," on that port. A port is considered to be open if a server responds when a connection request for that port arrives.

The first step in penetration testing is performing a *port scan* — the automated process of trying to connect to each port number to see whether a valid response comes back. Many available automated tools can perform port scanning; you can install and use a popular port-scanning tool called nmap (described later in this chapter).

After performing a port scan, you know which ports are open and could be exploited. Not all servers have security problems, but many servers have well-known vulnerabilities. An open port provides a cracker a way to attack your system through one of the servers. In fact, you can use automated tools called *vulnerability scanners* to identify vulnerabilities that exist in your system. (I describe some vulnerability scanners later in this chapter.) Whether your Linux system is connected to the Internet directly (through DSL or cable modem) or through a firewall, use the port-scanning and vulnerability-scanning tools to figure out whether you have any holes in your defenses.

Vulnerability Testing Types

The number-one purpose of penetration testing is to identify vulnerabilities. When you're viewing such a test from this angle, it's important to understand that you have three ways of approaching it: black, white, and gray. These three approaches differ in the amount of information that you assume you have in the beginning. You can use the color with almost any other word — *black box* versus *white box* if a piece of software is doing the testing, for example, *black hat* versus *white hat* if a person is doing the testing, and so on. The following list focuses on the person and uses *box* as the preferred noun:

>> In *black-box testing,* the tests assume no knowledge of the network and look for vulnerabilities that an outsider might stumble across, such as open ports and weak passwords.

Suppose that a bored miscreant came across your network at random and decided to bring it to its knees.

>> In *white-box testing,* the test assumes that the attacker is a knowledgeable insider who's trying to break the system.

Suppose that you just fired a system administrator who wants to get back at you by crashing your network.

>> Between these two extremes lies the realm of *gray-box testing,* which assumes that an insider is behind the problem.

Suppose that someone from shipping is angry about not getting the raise he thought he deserved and wants to make the company pay. The attacker doesn't have the knowledge an administrator would, but he still knows more about the systems than a complete outsider would.

Exploring Security Testing Tools

Many automated tools perform security testing. Some of these tools find the open ports on every system in a range of IP addresses. Others look for the vulnerabilities associated with open ports. Still other tools capture (or *sniff*) those weaknesses and help you analyze them so that you can glean useful information about what's going on in your network.

You can browse a list of the top 100 security tools (based on an informal poll of nmap users) at http://sectools.org. Table 3-4 lists several of these tools by category. I describe a few of the free vulnerability scanners in the next few sections.

TABLE 3-4   **Some Popular Computer-Security Testing Tools**

Type	Names of Tools
Port scanners	nmap, Strobe
Vulnerability scanners	Nessus Security Scanner, SAINT, SARA, Whisker (CGI scanner), ISS Internet Scanner, CyberCop Scanner, Vetescan, Retina Network Security Scanner
Network utilities	Netcat, hping2, Firewalk, Cheops, ntop, ping, ngrep, AirSnort (802.11 WEP encryption-cracking tool)
Host-security tools	Tripwire, lsof
Packet sniffers	tcpdump, Ethereal, dsniff, sniffit
Intrusion detection	aide (Advanced Intrusion Detection Environment), Snort, Abacus portsentry, scanlogd, NFR, LIDSSystems (IDSs)
Log analysis and monitoring tools	logcolorise, tcpdstats, nlog, logcheck, LogWatch, Swatch
Password-checking tool	John the Ripper

TIP

The John the Ripper password-checking tool is one of the best command-line tools an administrator can use to test the strength of user passwords. In most distributions, you have to install it with apt install john, use the unshadow command to create a file containing entries from etc/passwd and etc/shadow, and then look for weaknesses.

nmap (short for *network mapper*) is a port-scanning tool that can rapidly scan large networks and determine what hosts are available on the network, what services they offer, what operating system (and operating-system version) they run, what type of packet filters or firewalls they use, and dozens of other characteristics. You can read more about nmap at http://nmap.org.

If nmap isn't already installed, you can easily install it on your distribution by using the command apt-get install nmap or the software search facility of YaST (find nmap) or any distribution-specific interface you may have.

If you want to try nmap to scan your local-area network, type a command similar to the following (replacing the IP address range with addresses that are appropriate for your network):

```
nmap -O -sS 192.168.0.4-8
```

Following is typical output from that command:

```
Starting nmap 7.60 (http://www.insecure.org/nmap/) at 2018-08-28 16:20 EDT
Interesting ports on 192.168.0.4:
(The 1659 ports scanned but not shown below are in state: closed)
PORT STATE SERVICE
21/tcp open ftp
22/tcp open ssh
111/tcp open rpcbind
631/tcp open ipp
MAC Address: 00:C0:49:63:78:3A (U.S. Robotics)
Device type: general purpose
Running: Linux 3.9.X|3.9.X|3.9.X
OS details: Linux 2.4.18 - 2.6.7
Uptime 9.919 days (since Thu Aug 18 18:18:15 2018)
&#x2026; Lines deleted &#x2026;
Nmap finished: 5 IP addresses (5 hosts up) scanned in 30.846 seconds
```

As you can see, nmap displays the names of the open ports and hazards a guess at the operating-system name and version number.

For a quick scan of your own machine, you can use the IP address of 127.0.0.1 (see Figure 3-1). Ideally, the scan will verify that the ports are closed.

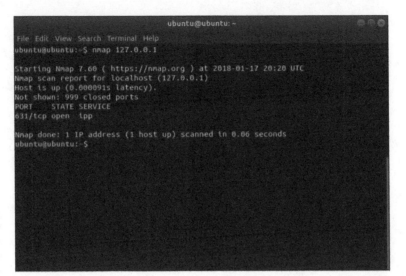

FIGURE 3-1:
You can view any open ports with nmap.

7

Scripting

Contents at a Glance

CHAPTER 1: Introductory Shell Scripting 431

Trying Out Simple Shell Scripts 432

Exploring the Basics of Shell Scripting 433

CHAPTER 2: Working with Advanced Shell Scripting 443

Trying Out sed 443

Working with awk and sed 446

Final Notes on Shell Scripting 450

CHAPTER 3: Programming in Linux 451

An Overview of Programming 452

Exploring the Software-Development Tools in Linux 453

Understanding the Implications of GNU Licenses 473

Chapter **1**

Introductory Shell Scripting

As you've seen throughout many of the preceding chapters, Linux gives you a plethora of small and specialized commands, along with the ability to connect these commands in such a way that one command's output can be used as a second command's input. bash (short for Bourne-Again Shell) — the default shell in most Linux systems — provides this capability in the form of I/O redirection and pipes. bash also includes conditionals such as the if statement that you can use to run commands only when a specific condition is true and the for statement that can repeat the set of commands a specified number of times. You can use these features of bash when writing programs called *shell scripts*: task-oriented collections of shell commands stored in a file.

This chapter shows you how to write simple shell scripts, which are used to automate various tasks. When your Linux system boots, for example, many shell scripts stored in various subdirectories in the /etc directory (such as /etc/init.d) perform many initialization tasks.

Trying Out Simple Shell Scripts

If you're not a programmer, it's common to feel apprehensive about programming. But you can put that apprehension aside: Shell *scripting* (or programming) can be as simple as storing a few commands in a file that can then be executed. In fact, you can have a useful shell program that has in it only a single command.

Shell scripts are popular among system administrators because they can be used to help automate tasks you perform often. If a hard drive seems to be getting full, for example, you may want to find all files that exceed some determined size (say, 5MB) and that have not been accessed in the past 30 days. Once the files are found, you may want to send an email message to all the users identified with those large files, requesting that they archive and clean up those files. You can perform all these tasks with a shell script. You might start with the following find command to identify large files:

```
find / —type f —atime +30 —size +5000k —exec ls -l {} \; > /tmp/largefiles
```

This command creates a file named /tmp/largefiles, which contains detailed information about old files taking up too much space. After you get a list of the files, you can use a few other Linux commands — such as sort, cut, and sed — to prepare and send mail messages to users who have large files to clean up. Instead of typing all these commands manually, place them in a file and create a shell script. That, in a nutshell, is the essence of shell scripts — to gather shell commands in a file so that you can easily perform repetitive system administration tasks. Although you could do all this on the command line without a script file, doing so would require you to type the command — complete with parameters and correct syntax — each and every time.

bash scripts, just like most Linux commands, accept command-line options. Inside the script, you can refer to the options as $1, $2, and so on. The special name $0 refers to the name of the script itself.

Here's a typical bash script that accepts arguments:

```
#!/bin/sh
echo "This script's name is: $0"
echo Argument 1: $1
echo Argument 2: $2
```

The first line runs the /bin/sh program, which subsequently processes the rest of the lines in the script. The name /bin/sh traditionally refers to the Bourne shell — the first Unix shell. In most Linux systems, /bin/sh is a symbolic link to /bin/bash, which is the executable program for bash.

Save this simple script in a file named `simple` and make that file executable with the following command:

```
chmod +x simple
```

Now run the script as follows:

```
./simple
```

It displays the following output:

```
This script's name is: ./simple
Argument 1:
Argument 2:
```

The first line shows the script's name. Because you have run the script without arguments, the script displays no values for the arguments.

Now try running the script with a few arguments, like this:

```
./simple "This is one argument" second-argument third
```

This time, the script displays more output:

```
This script's name is: ./simple
Argument 1: This is one argument
Argument 2: second-argument
```

As the output shows, the shell treats the entire string within the double quotation marks as a single argument. Otherwise, the shell uses spaces as separators between arguments on the command line.

This sample script ignores the third argument (and any others that you might give after it in subsequent attempts) because the script is designed to print only the first two arguments, and nothing references $3 or beyond.

Exploring the Basics of Shell Scripting

Like any programming language, the bash shell supports the following features:

>> Variables that store values, including special built-in variables for accessing command-line arguments passed to a shell script and other special values.

>> The capability to evaluate expressions.

>> Control structures that enable you to loop over several shell commands or execute some commands conditionally.

>> The capability to define functions that can be called in many places within a script. bash also includes many built-in commands that you can use in any script.

The next few sections illustrate some of these programming features through simple examples. (It's assumed that you're already running bash, in which case you can try the examples by typing them at the shell prompt in a terminal window. Otherwise, all you have to do is open a terminal window; bash runs and displays its prompt in that window.)

Storing stuff

You define variables in bash just as you define environment variables. Thus, you may define a variable as follows:

```
count=12 # note no embedded spaces are allowed
```

To use a variable's value, prefix the variable's name with a dollar sign ($). $PATH, for example, is the value of the variable PATH. (This variable is the famous PATH environment variable that lists all the directories that bash searches when trying to locate an executable file.) To display the value of the variable count, use the following command:

```
echo $count
```

bash has some special variables for accessing command-line arguments. As I mention earlier in this chapter, in a shell script, $0 refers to the name of the shell script. The variables $1, $2, and so on refer to the command-line arguments. The variable $* stores all the command-line arguments as a single variable, and $? contains the exit status of the last command the shell executes.

From a bash script, you can prompt the user for input and use the read command to read the input into a variable. Here's an example:

```
echo -n "Enter a value: "
read value
echo "You entered: $value"
```

When this script runs, the read value command causes bash to read whatever is typed in at the keyboard and store that input in the variable called value.

Note: The –n option prevents the echo command from automatically adding a new line at the end of the string that it displays. If that option were not given, Enter a value would be displayed, and the value would be read in on a line following it. This doesn't change the operation in any way at all — only the aesthetics.

Calling shell functions

You can group shell commands that you use consistently into a function and assign that function a name. Later, you can execute that group of commands by using the single name assigned to the function. Here's a simple script that illustrates the syntax of shell functions:

```
#!/bin/sh
hello() {
echo -n "Hello, "
echo $1 $2
}
hello Jane Doe
```

When you run this script, it displays the following output:

```
Hello, Jane Doe
```

This script defines a shell function named hello. The function expects two arguments. In the body of the function, these arguments are referenced by $1 and $2. The function definition begins with hello() — the name of the function, followed by parentheses. The body of the function is enclosed in curly braces — { ... }. In this case, the body uses the echo command to display a line of text.

The last line of the example shows how a shell function is called with arguments. In this case, the hello function is called with two arguments: Jane and Doe. The hello function takes these two arguments and prints a line that says Hello, Jane Doe.

Controlling the flow

In bash scripts, you can control the flow of execution — the order in which the commands are executed — by using special commands such as if, case, for, and while. These control statements use the exit status of a command to decide what to do next. When any command executes, it returns an *exit status:* a numeric value that indicates whether the command has succeeded. By convention, an exit status of zero means that the command has succeeded. (Yes, you read it right: Zero indicates success!) A nonzero exit status indicates that something has gone wrong with the command.

Suppose that you want to make a backup copy of a file before editing it with the vi editor. More important, you want to avoid editing the file if a backup can't be made. Here's a bash script that takes care of this task (the user supplies the path, if necessary, and filename when running the script):

```
#!/bin/sh
if cp "$1" "#$1"
then
vi "$1"
else
echo "Operation failed to create a backup copy"
fi
```

This script illustrates the syntax of the if-then-else structure and shows how the if command uses the exit status of the cp command to determine the next action. If cp returns zero, the script uses vi to edit the file; otherwise, the script displays an error message and exits. By the way, the script saves the backup in a file whose name is the same as that of the original, except for a hash mark (#) added at the beginning of the filename.

TIP

Don't forget the final fi that terminates the if command. Forgetting fi is a common source of errors in bash scripts.

You can use the test command to evaluate any expression and to use the expression's value as the exit status of the command. Suppose that you want a script that edits a file only if it already exists and not create a blank file otherwise, as it normally would. Using test, you can write such a script as follows:

```
#!/bin/sh
if test -f "$1"
then
vi "$1"
else
echo "No such file exists"
fi
```

A shorter form of the test command places the expression in square brackets ([...]). Using this shorthand notation, you can rewrite the preceding script like this:

```
#!/bin/sh
if [ -f "$1" ]
then
vi "$1"
```

```
else
echo "No such file exists"
fi
```

Note: You must have spaces around the two square brackets for this code to work because the left bracket ([) is an alias to test. If you don't leave the space, it's not seen the same as the name of the alias but rather as a part of the name of what you are trying to run.

Another common control structure is the for loop. The following script adds the numbers 1 through 10:

```
#!/bin/sh
sum=0
for i in 1 2 3 4 5 6 7 8 9 10
do
sum=`expr $sum + $i`
done
echo "Sum = $sum"
```

This example also illustrates the use of the expr command to evaluate an expression. It requires white space on both sides of the operand — the plus sign (+), in this case — and doesn't work properly without it.

The case statement is used to execute a group of commands based on the value of a variable. Consider the following script:

```
#!/bin/sh
echo -n "What should I do -- (Y)es/(N)o/(C)ontinue? [Y] "
read answer
case $answer in
y|Y|"")
echo "YES"
;;
c|C)
echo "CONTINUE"
;;
n|N)
echo "NO"
;;
*)
echo "UNKNOWN"
;;
esac
```

Save this code in a file named `confirm` and type **chmod +x confirm** to make it executable. Then try it out like this:

```
./confirm
```

When the script prompts you, type one of the characters y, n, or c and then press Enter. The script displays YES, NO, or CONTINUE, respectively. Here's what happens when you type **c** (and then press Enter):

```
What should I do -- (Y)es/(N)o/(C)ontinue? [Y] c
CONTINUE
```

The script displays a prompt and reads the input you type. Your input is stored in a variable named answer. Then the case statement executes a block of code based on the value of the answer variable. When you type **c**, for example, the following block of commands executes:

```
c|C)
echo "CONTINUE"
;;
```

The echo command causes the script to display CONTINUE.

From this example, you can see that the general syntax of the case command is as follows:

```
case $variable in
value1 | value2)
command1
command2
... other commands ...
;;
value3)
command3
command4
... other commands ...
;;
esac
```

Essentially, the case command begins with the word case and ends with esac. Separate blocks of code are enclosed between the values of the variable, followed by a closing parenthesis and terminated by a pair of semicolons (; ;).

Exploring bash's built-in commands

bash has more than 50 built-in commands, including common commands such as cd and pwd, as well as many others that are used infrequently. You can use these built-in commands in any bash script or at the shell prompt. Table 1-1 describes most of the bash built-in commands and their arguments. After looking through this information, type **help** *command* to read more about a specific built-in command. To find out more about the built-in command test, for example, type the following:

```
help test
```

Doing so displays the following information:

```
test: test [expr]
Exits with a status of 0 (true) or 1 (false) depending on
the evaluation of EXPR. Expressions may be unary or binary. Unary
expressions are often used to examine the status of a file. There
are string operators as well, and numeric comparison operators.
File operators:
-a FILE True if file exists.
-b FILE True if file is block special.
-c FILE True if file is character special.
-d FILE True if file is a directory.
-e FILE True if file exists.
-f FILE True if file exists and is a regular file.
-g FILE True if file is set-group-id.
-h FILE True if file is a symbolic link.
-L FILE True if file is a symbolic link.
-k FILE True if file has its 'sticky' bit set.
-p FILE True if file is a named pipe.
-r FILE True if file is readable by you.
-s FILE True if file exists and is not empty.
-S FILE True if file is a socket.
-t FD True if FD is opened on a terminal.
-u FILE True if the file is set-user-id.
-w FILE True if the file is writable by you.
-x FILE True if the file is executable by you.
-O FILE True if the file is effectively owned by you.
-G FILE True if the file is effectively owned by your group.
(... Lines deleted ...)
```

Where necessary, the online help from the help command includes a considerable amount of detail.

TABLE 1-1   Summary of Built-in Commands in bash Shell

This Function	Does the Following
. *filename* [*arguments*]	Reads and executes commands from the specified *filename* using the optional *arguments*. (Works the same way as the `source` command.)
: [*arguments*]	Expands the *arguments* but doesn't process them.
[*expr*]	Evaluates the expression *expr* and returns zero status if `expr` is true.
alias [*name*[=*value*]...]	Allows one *value* to equal another. You could set *xyz* to run *bg*, for example.
bg [*job*]	Puts the specified *job* in the background. If no *job* is specified, it puts the currently executing command in the background.
break [*n*]	Exits from a `for`, `while`, or `until` loop. If *n* is specified, the *n*th enclosing loop is exited.
cd [*dir*]	Changes the current directory to *dir*.
command [-pVv] *cmd* [*arg*...]	Runs the command *cmd* with the specified arguments (ignoring any shell function named `cmd`).
continue [*n*]	Starts the next iteration of the `for`, `while`, or `until` loop. If *n* is specified, the next iteration of the *n*th enclosing loop is started.
declare [-frxi] [*name*[=*value*]]	Declares a variable with the specified *name* and optionally, assigns it a *value*.
dirs [-l] [+/-*n*]	Displays the list of currently remembered directories.
echo [-neE] [*arg*...]	Displays the arguments, *arg*..., on standard output.
enable [-n] [-all]	Enables or disables the specified built-in commands.
eval [*arg*...]	Concatenates the arguments, *arg*..., and executes them as a command.
exec [*command* [*arguments*]]	Replaces the current instance of the shell with a new process that runs the specified *command* with the given *arguments*.
exit [*n*]	Exits the shell with the status code *n*.
export [-nf] [*name*[=*word*]]...	Defines a specified environment variable and exports it to future processes.
fc -s [*pat*=*rep*] [*cmd*]	Re-executes the command after replacing the pattern *pat* with *rep*.
fg [*jobspec*]	Puts the specified job, *jobspec*, in the foreground. If no job is specified, it puts the most recent job in the foreground.
hash [-r] [*name*]	Remembers the full pathname of a specified command.
help [*cmd*...]	Displays help information for specified built-in commands, *cmd*....
history [*n*]	Displays past commands or past *n* commands, if you specify a number *n*.

This Function	Does the Following
jobs [-lnp] [jobspec...]	Lists currently active jobs.
kill [-s sigspec | -sigspec] [pid | jobspec]...	Ends the process specified.
let arg [arg...]	Evaluates each argument and returns 1 if the last arg is 0.
local [name[=value]...]	Creates a local variable with the specified name and value (used in shell functions).
logout	Exits a login shell.
popd [+/-n]	Removes the specified number of entries from the directory stack.
pushd [dir]	Adds a specified directory, dir, to the top of the directory stack.
pwd	Prints the full pathname of the current working directory.
read [-r] [name...]	Reads a line from standard input and parses it.
readonly [-f] [name...]	Marks the specified variables as read-only so that the variables can't be changed later.
return [n]	Exits the shell function with the return value n.
set [--abefhkmnptuvxldCHP] [-o option] [arg...]	Sets various flags.
shift [n]	Makes the n+1 argument $1, the n+2 argument $2, and so on.
times	Prints the accumulated user and system times for processes run from the shell.
trap [-l] [cmd] [sigspec]	Executes cmd when the signal sigspec is received.
type [-all] [-type |-path] name [name...]	Indicates how the shell interprets each name.
ulimit [-SHacdfmstpnuv [limit]]	Controls resources available to the shell.
umask [-S] [mode]	Sets the file creation mask — the default permission to the mode specified for the files.
unalias [-a] [name...]	Undefines a specified alias.
unset [-fv] [name...]	Removes the definition of specified variables.
wait [n]	Waits for a specified process (n represents its PID) to terminate.

WARNING

Some external programs may have the same name as bash built-in commands. If you want to run any such external program, you must explicitly specify the full pathname of that program. Otherwise, bash executes the built-in command of the same name and never looks for the external program.

Introductory Shell Scripting

Chapter **2**

Working with Advanced Shell Scripting

The preceding chapter introduced you to some of the power available through shell scripting. All the scripts in that chapter are simple bash routines that allow you to run commands and repeat operations a number of times.

This chapter builds upon that knowledge by showing how to incorporate two powerful tools — sed and awk — into your scripts. These two utilities move your scripts to the place where the only limit to what you can do becomes your ability to figure out how to ask for the output you need. Although sed is the stream editor and awk is a quick programming language, they complement each other so well that it's not uncommon to use one with the other. The best way to show how these tools work is to walk through some examples.

Trying Out sed

The following are sample lines of a colon-delimited employee database that has five fields: unique ID number, name, department, phone number, and address.

```
1218:Kris Cottrell:Marketing:219.555.5555:123 Main Street
1219:Nate Eichhorn:Sales:219.555.5555:1219 Locust Avenue
1220:Joe Gunn:Payables:317.555.5555:21974 Unix Way
1221:Anne Heltzel:Finance:219.555.5555:652 Linux Road
1222:John Kuzmic:Human Resources:219.555.5555:984 Bash Lane
```

Imagine that this database has been in existence since the beginning of the company and includes far more than these five entries. Over time, the database has grown to include everyone who now works, or has ever worked, for the company. Several proprietary scripts read from the database, and the company can't afford to be without it. The problem is that the telephone company in one part of the country has changed the 219 prefix to 260, so all entries in the database that use that prefix need to be changed.

This is precisely the task for which sed was created. As opposed to standard (interactive) editors, a *stream editor* works its way through a file line by line and makes changes based on the rules it's given. The rule in this case seems to be to change 219 to 260, but the task isn't quite that simple. To illustrate, if you use the command

```
sed 's/219/260/'
```

the result you get is not completely what you want it to be (all changes are in **bold**):

```
1218:Kris Cottrell:Marketing:260.555.5555:123 Main Street
1260:Nate Eichhorn:Sales:219.555.5555:1219 Locust Avenue
1220:Joe Gunn:Payables:317.555.5555:26074 Unix Way
1221:Anne Heltzel:Finance:260.555.5555:652 Linux Road
1222:John Kuzmic:Human Resources:260.555.5555:984 Bash Lane
```

The changes in the first, fourth, and fifth lines are correct. But in the second line, the first occurrence of 219 appears in the employee ID number rather than in the phone number and was changed to 260. If you wanted to change more than the very first occurrence in a line, you could slap a g (for *global*) into the command:

```
sed 's/219/260/g'
```

That's *not* what you want to do in this case, however, because the employee ID number shouldn't change as a result of this change to the phone prefix. Similarly troublesome, in the third line, a change was made to the address because it contains the value that's being searched for; no change should have been made to this line at all because the employee doesn't have the 219 telephone prefix.

The first rule of using sed is always to identify what makes the location of the string you're looking for unique. If the telephone prefix were encased in parentheses, it would be much easier to isolate. In this database, though, that isn't the case; the task becomes a bit more complicated.

If you said that the telephone prefix must appear at the beginning of the field (denoted by a colon), the result would be much closer to what you want:

```
sed 's/:219/:260/'
```

Again, bolding has been added to show the changes that this command would produce:

```
1218:Kris Cottrell:Marketing:260.555.5555:123 Main Street
1219:Nate Eichhorn:Sales:260.555.5555:1219 Locust Avenue
1220:Joe Gunn:Payables:317.555.5555:26074 Unix Way
1221:Anne Heltzel:Finance:260.555.5555:652 Linux Road
1222:John Kuzmic:Human Resources:260.555.5555:984 Bash Lane
```

Although the accuracy has increased, there's still the problem of the third line in the limited sample (and you don't know how many other lines would be affected in the larger database). Because the colon helped identify the start of the string, it may be tempting to turn to the period to identify the end:

```
sed 's/:219./:260./'
```

But once again, the result still isn't what you hoped for (note the third line):

```
1218:Kris Cottrell:Marketing:260.555.5555:123 Main Street
1219:Nate Eichhorn:Sales:260.555.5555:1219 Locust Avenue
1220:Joe Gunn:Payables:317.555.5555:260.4 Unix Way
1221:Anne Heltzel:Finance:260.555.5555:652 Linux Road
1222:John Kuzmic:Human Resources:260.555.5555:984 Bash Lane
```

The problem, in this instance, is that the period has the special meaning of standing for *any character,* so a match is found whether the 219 is followed by a period, a 7, or any other single character. Whatever the character, it's replaced with a period. The replacement side of things isn't the problem; the search needs to be tweaked. By using the \ character, you can override the special meaning of the period and specify that you're indeed looking for a period and not any single character:

```
sed 's/:219\./:260./'
```

The result becomes

```
1218:Kris Cottrell:Marketing:260.555.5555:123 Main Street
1219:Nate Eichhorn:Sales:260.555.5555:1219 Locust Avenue
1220:Joe Gunn:Payables:317.555.5555:21974 Unix Way
1221:Anne Heltzel:Finance:260.555.5555:652 Linux Road
1222:John Kuzmic:Human Resources:260.555.5555:984 Bash Lane
```

And with that, the mission is accomplished.

Working with awk and sed

The second example to look at involves a legacy database of books that includes the International Standard Book Number (ISBN) of each title. In the old days, ISBN numbers were ten digits and included an identifier for the publisher and a unique number for each book. ISBN numbers are now 13 digits for new books and have been so for several years. Old books (those published before the first of 2007) have both the old 10-digit number and a new 13-digit number that can be used to identify them because the longer number is a variation on the shorter. For this example, to bring the database up to current standards, the existing 10-digit number will stay in the database, and a new field — holding the ISBN-13 number — will be added to the end of each entry.

To come up with the ISBN-13 number for the existing entries in the database, you start with 978 and then use the first 9 digits of the old ISBN number. The 13th digit is a mathematical calculation (a *check digit*) obtained by doing the following:

1. Add all odd-placed digits (the first, the third, the fifth, and so on).

2. Multiply all even-placed digits by 3 and add them.

3. Add the total of Step 2 to the total of Step 1.

4. Find out what you need to add to round the number up to the nearest 10.

   This value becomes the 13th digit.

Consider the 10-digit ISBN 0743477103. It first becomes 978074347710, and then the steps work out like this:

1. $9+8+7+3+7+1=35$.

2. $7*3=21$; $0*3=0$; $4*3=12$; $4*3=12$; $7*3=21$; $0*3=0$; $21+0+12+12+21+0=66$.

3. 66+35=101.

4. 110-101=9.

The ISBN-13 becomes 9780743477109.

The beginning database resembles

```
0743477103:Macbeth:Shakespeare, William
1578518520:The Innovator's Solution:Christensen, Clayton M.
0321349946:(SCTS) Symantec Certified Technical Specialist:Alston, Nik
1587052415:Cisco Network Admission Control, Volume I:Helfrich, Denise
```

And you want the resulting database to change so that each line resembles something like this:

```
0743477103:Macbeth:Shakespeare, William:9780743477109
```

The example that follows accomplishes this goal. It's not the prettiest thing ever written, but it walks through the process of tackling this problem, illustrating the use of awk and sed. I've also included in the steps of having the script write to temporary files so that you can examine those files and see their contents at various stages of the operations. Clean programming mitigates the use of temporary files everywhere possible, but that practice also makes it difficult to follow the action at times. That said, here's one solution out of dozens of possibilities. Read on.

Step 1: Pull out the ISBN

Given the database as it now exists, the first order of business is to pull out the existing ISBN — only the first nine digits, because the tenth digit, which was just a checksum for the first nine, no longer matters — and slap 978 onto the beginning. The nine digits you want are the first nine characters of each line, so you can pull them out by using the cut utility:

```
cut -c1-9 books
```

Because a mathematical operation will be performed on the numbers comprising this value, and because that operation works with each digit, add a space between each number and the next one in the new entry:

```
sed 's/[0-9]/& /g'
```

Now it's time to add the new code to the beginning of each entry (the start of every line):

```
sed 's/^/9 7 8 /'
```

Finally, do an extra step: removing the white space at the end of the line just to make the entry a bit cleaner:

```
sed 's/ $//'
```

Then write the results to a temporary file that you can examine to make sure that all is working as it should. Then the full first step becomes

```
cut -c1-9 books | sed 's/[0-9]/& /g' | sed 's/^/9 7 8 /' | sed 's/ $//' > isbn2
```

Note: The sed operations could be combined in a script file to increase speed and decrease cycles. I'm walking through each operation step by step to show what's going on, however, and am not worried about creating script files for this one-time-only operation.

Examining the temporary file, you see that the contents are as follows:

```
9 7 8 0 7 4 3 4 7 7 1 0
9 7 8 1 5 7 8 5 1 8 5 2
9 7 8 0 3 2 1 3 4 9 9 4
9 7 8 1 5 8 7 0 5 2 4 1
```

Step 2: Calculate the 13th digit

You've taken care of the first 12 digits of the ISBN number. Now you need to compute those 12 digits to figure out the 13th value. Because the numbers are separated by a space, awk can interpret them as fields. The calculation takes several steps:

1. Add all the odd-placed digits:

   x=$1+$3+$5+$7+$9+$11

2. Add all the even-placed digits and multiply by 3:

   y=($2+$4+$6+$8+$10+$12)*3

3. Add the total of Step 2 to the total of Step 1:

   x=x+y

4. Find out what you need to add to round the number up to the nearest 10 by computing the modulo when divided by 10 and then subtracting it from 10.

   The following awk command gets everything in place except the transformation:

   ```
   awk '{ x=$1+$3+$5+$7+$9+$11 ; y=$2+$4+$6+$8+$10+$12 ; y=y*3 ; x=x+y ;
       y=x%10 ; print y }'
   ```

Everything is finished except subtracting the final result from 10, which is the hardest part. If the modulo is 7, for example, the check digit is 3. If the modulo is 0, however, the check digit doesn't become 10 (10 – 0); it stays 0. My solution is to use the transform function of sed:

```
sed 'y/12346789/98764321/'
```

Combining the two operations into one, the second step becomes

```
awk '{ x=$1+$3+$5+$7+$9+$11 ; y=$2+$4+$6+$8+$10+$12 ; y=y*3 ; x=x+y ; y=x%10 ;
   print y }' | sed 'y/12346789/98764321/' > isbn3
```

Examining the temporary file, you see that the contents are

```
9
4
1
5
```

Step 3: Add the 13th digit to the other 12

The two temporary files (one with 12 digits and the other with 1) can now be combined to get the correct 13-digit ISBN number. Just as you used cut in the earlier step, you can use paste now to combine the files. The default delimiter for paste is a tab, but you can change that delimiter to anything with the –d option. I use a space as the delimiter and then use sed to strip the spaces (remember that the isbn2 file has spaces between the digits so that they can be read as fields):

```
paste -d" " isbn2 isbn3 | sed 's/ //g'
```

Finally, add a colon as the first character of each entry to make it easier to append the newly computed ISBN to the existing file:

```
sed 's/^/:/'
```

The entire command becomes

```
paste -d" " isbn2 isbn3 | sed 's/ //g' | sed 's/^/:/' > isbn4
```

Examining the temporary file, you see that the contents are

```
:9780743477109
:9781578518524
:9780321349941
:9781587052415
```

Step 4: Finish the process

The only operation remaining is to append the values in the temporary file to the current database. You use the default tab delimiter in the entry and then strip it out. Technically, you could specify a colon as the delimiter and avoid the last part of the last steps. But you'd rather have your value complete there and be confident that you're stripping characters that don't belong (tabs) instead of adding more characters than should be there. The final command is

```
paste books isbn4 | sed 's/\t//g' > newbooks
```

The final file looks like this:

```
0743477103:Macbeth:Shakespeare, William:9780743477109
1578518520:The Innovator's Solution:Christensen, Clayton M.:9781578518524
0321349946:(SCTS) Symantec Certified Technical Specialist:Alston,
   Nik:9780321349941
1587052415:Cisco Network Admission Control, Volume I:Helfrich,
   Denise:9781587052415
```

Again, you can accomplish this result in many ways. This solution isn't the cleanest, but it does illustrate the down-and-dirty use of sed and awk.

Final Notes on Shell Scripting

As with any other aspect of computing, it takes a while to get used to shell scripting. After you become comfortable writing scripts, however, you'll find that you can automate any number of operations and simplify your task as an administrator. The following tips can be helpful to keep in mind:

>> After you create a script, you can run it automatically on a one-time basis by using at or on a regular basis by using cron.

>> You can use conditional expressions — such as if, while, and until — to look for events to occur (such as certain users accessing a file they shouldn't) or to let you know when something that should be there goes away (a file is removed or a user terminates, for example).

>> You can set permissions on shell scripts in the same way that you set permissions for other files. You can create scripts that are shared by all members of your administrative group, for example. (Use case to create menus based upon LOGNAME.)

» Exploring software-development
tools in Linux

» Compiling and linking programs
with GCC

» Using make

» Debugging programs with gdb

» Understanding the implications of
GNU, GPL, and LGPL

Chapter **3**

Programming in Linux

inux comes loaded with all the tools you need to develop software; often, all you have to do is install them. In particular, Linux has all the GNU software-development tools, such as GCC (C and C++ compiler), GNU make, and the GNU debugger. Whereas the previous two chapters look at some simple tools and shell scripts, this chapter introduces you to programming, describes the software-development tools, and shows you how to use them. Although I provide examples in the C and C++ programming languages, the focus isn't on showing you how to program in those languages but on showing you how to use various software-development tools (such as compilers, make, and debugger).

The chapter concludes with a brief explanation of how the Free Software Foundation's GNU General Public License (GPL) may affect any plans you might have to develop Linux software. You need to know about the GPL because you use GNU tools and GNU libraries to develop software in Linux.

An Overview of Programming

If you've ever written a computer program in any language — even one of the shell scripts from the previous two chapters — you can start writing programs on your Linux system quickly. If you've never written a computer program, however, you need two basic resources before you begin to write code: a look at the basics of programming and a quick review of computers and their major parts. This section offers an overview of computer programming — just enough to get you going.

At its simplest, a *computer program* is a sequence of instructions for performing a specific task, such as adding two numbers or searching for some text in a file. Consequently, computer programming involves *creating* that list of instructions, telling the computer how to complete a specific task. The exact instructions depend on the programming language that you use. For most programming languages, you have to go through the following steps to create a computer program:

1. **Use a text editor to type the sequence of commands from the programming language.**

   This sequence of commands accomplishes your task. This human-readable version of the program is called the *source file* or *source code.* You can create the source file with any application (such as a word processor) that can save a document in plain-text form.

   REMEMBER

   Always save your source code as plain text. (The filename depends on the type of programming language.) Word processors can sometimes put extra instructions in their documents that tell the computer to display the text in a particular font or other format. Saving the file as plain text deletes any and all such extra instructions. Trust me: Your program is much better off without such stuff.

2. **Use a *compiler* program to convert that text file — the source code — from human-readable form into machine-readable *object code.***

   Typically, this step also combines several object code files into a single machine-readable computer program — something that the computer can run.

3. **Use a special program called a *debugger* to track down any errors and find which lines in the source file might have caused the errors.**

4. **Go back to Step 1, use the text editor to correct the errors, and repeat the rest of the steps.**

These steps are referred to as the *edit-compile-debug cycle* of programming because most programmers have to repeat this sequence several times before a program works correctly.

In addition to knowing the basic programming steps, you need to be familiar with the following terms and concepts:

>> *Variables* are used to store different types of data. You can think of each variable as being a placeholder for data — kind of like a mailbox, with a name and room to store data. The content of the variable is its *value*.

>> *Expressions* combine variables by using operators. One expression may add several variables; another may extract a part of a *string* (a series of sequential characters).

>> *Statements* perform some action, such as assigning a value to a variable or printing a string.

>> *Flow-control statements* allow statements to execute in various orders, depending on the value of some expression. Typically, flow-control statements include for, do–while, while, and if–then–else statements.

>> *Functions* (also called *subroutines* or *routines*) allow you to group several statements and give the group a name. You can use functions to execute the same set of statements over and over by invoking the function that represents those statements. Typically, a programming language provides many predefined functions to perform tasks, such as opening (and reading from) a file, and you can create your own functions for similar tasks.

Exploring the Software-Development Tools in Linux

Linux supports all of the following traditional Unix software-development tools:

>> **Text editors** such as vi and emacs for editing the source code. (To find out more about vi, see Book 2, Chapter 6.)

>> A **C compiler** for compiling and linking programs written in C — the programming language of choice for writing Unix applications (though nowadays, many programmers are turning to C++ and Java). Linux includes the GNU C and C++ compilers. Originally, the GNU C compiler was known as GCC, which now stands for *GNU Compiler Collection*. (See a description at http://gcc.gnu.org.)

>> The **GNU make utility** for automating the software *build process* — the process of combining object modules into an executable or a library. (The operating system can load and run an *executable*; a *library* is a collection of binary code that can be used by executables.)

> » A **debugger** for debugging programs. Linux distributions often include the GNU debugger gdb.

> » A **version control system** to keep track of various revisions of a source file. Linux comes with RCS (Revision Control System) and CVS (Concurrent Versions System). Nowadays, most open-source projects use CVS as their version control system, but a recent version control system called Subversion is being developed as a replacement for CVS.

DISTRIBUTION SPECIFIC

You can install these software-development tools in any Linux distribution. In some distributions, the tools are installed by default. If they're not in the distribution you're using, you can type apt-get install gcc and then apt-get install libc6-dev as root in a terminal window (Debian) or choose to install the Development Tools package through the graphical interface (Fedora, SuSE, Ubuntu, and so on).

The next few sections briefly describe how to use these software-development tools to write applications for Linux.

GNU C and C++ compilers

The most important software-development tool in Linux is GCC — the GNU C and C++ compiler. In fact, GCC can compile three languages: C, C++, and Objective-C (a language that adds object-oriented programming capabilities to C). You use the same gcc command to compile and link both C and C++ source files. The GCC compiler supports ANSI-standard C, making it easy to port any ANSI C program to Linux. In addition, if you've ever used a C compiler on other Unix systems, you should feel right at home with GCC.

Using GCC

Use the gcc command to invoke GCC. By default, when you use the gcc command on a source file, GCC preprocesses, compiles, and links to create an executable file. You can use GCC options to stop this process at an intermediate stage, however. You might invoke gcc by using the -c option to compile a source file and to generate an object file, but not to perform the link step.

Using GCC to compile and link a few C source files is easy. Suppose that you want to compile and link a simple program made up of two source files. To accomplish this task, use the following program source code. The task that's stored in the file area.c computes the area of a circle whose radius is specified at the command line:

```
#include <stdio.h>
#include <stdlib.h>
```

```
/* Function prototype */
double area_of_circle(double r);
int main(int argc, char **argv)
{
if(argc < 2)
{
printf("Usage: %s radius\n", argv[0]);
exit(1);
}
else
{
double radius = atof(argv[1]);
double area = area_of_circle(radius);
printf("Area of circle with radius %f = %f\n",
radius, area);
}
return 0;
}
```

You need another file that actually computes the area of a circle. Here's the listing for the circle.c file, which defines a function that computes the area of a circle:

```
#include <math.h>
#define SQUARE(x) ((x)*(x))
double area_of_circle(double r)
{
return M_PI * SQUARE(r);
}
```

For such a simple program, of course, you could place everything in a single file, but this example is a bit contrived to show you how to handle multiple files.

To compile these two files and create an executable file named area, use this command:

```
gcc -o area area.c circle.c
```

This invocation of GCC uses the –o option to specify the name of the executable file. (If you don't specify the name of an output file with the –o option, GCC saves the executable code in a file named a.out.)

If you have too many source files to compile and link, you can compile the files individually and generate *object files* (that have the .o extension). That way, when you change a source file, you need to compile only that file; you just link the compiled file to all the object files. The following commands show how to separate the compile and link steps for the sample program:

```
gcc -c area.c
gcc -c circle.c
gcc -o area area.o circle.o
```

The first two commands run gcc with the -c option compiling the source files. The third gcc command links the object files into an executable named area.

Compiling C++ programs

GNU CC is a combined C and C++ compiler, so the gcc command also can compile C++ source files. GCC uses the file extension to determine whether a file is C or C++. C files have a lowercase .c extension, whereas C++ files end with .C or .cpp.

REMEMBER

Although the gcc command can compile a C++ file, that command doesn't automatically link with various class libraries that C++ programs typically require. Compiling and linking a C++ program by using the g++ command is easy because it runs gcc with appropriate options.

Suppose that you want to compile the following simple C++ program stored in a file named hello.C. (Using an uppercase C extension for C++ source files is customary.)

```
#include <iostream>
int main()
{
using namespace std;
cout << "Hello! This is Linux!" << endl;
}
```

To compile and link this program into an executable program named hello, use this command:

```
g++ -o hello hello.C
```

The command creates the hello executable, which you can run as follows:

```
./hello
```

The program displays the following output:

```
Hello! This is Linux!
```

A host of GCC options controls various aspects of compiling C and C++ programs.

Exploring GCC options

Here's the basic syntax of the gcc command:

```
gcc options filenames
```

Each option starts with a hyphen (–) and usually has a long name, such as -funsigned-char or -finline-functions. Many commonly used options are short, however, such as –c, to compile only, and –g, to generate debugging information (needed to debug the program by using the GNU debugger, gdb).

You can view a summary of all GCC options by typing the following command in a terminal window:

```
man gcc
```

Then you can browse through the commonly used GCC options. Usually, you don't have to provide GCC options explicitly because the default settings are fine for most applications. Table 3-1 lists some of the GCC options you may use.

TABLE 3-1   ## Common GCC Options

Option	Meaning
–ansi	Supports only ANSI-standard C syntax. (This option disables some GNU C-specific features, such as the __asm__ and __typeof__ keywords.) When used with g++, supports only ISO-standard C++.
–c	Compiles and generates only the object file.
–D*MACRO*	Defines the macro with the string "1" as its value.
–D*MACRO=DEFN*	Defines the macro as DEFN, where DEFN is some text string.
–E	Runs only the C preprocessor.
–fallow-single-precision	Performs all math operations in single precision.
–fpcc-struct-return	Returns all struct and union values in memory, rather than in registers. (Returning values this way is less efficient, but at least it's compatible with other compilers.)
–fPIC	Generates position-independent code (PIC) suitable for use in a shared library.
–freg-struct-return	When possible, returns struct and union values registers.

(continued)

TABLE 3-1 *(continued)*

Option	Meaning
–g	Generates debugging information. (The GNU debugger can use this information.)
–I *DIRECTORY*	Searches the specified directory for files that you include by using the #include preprocessor directive.
–L *DIRECTORY*	Searches the specified directory for libraries.
–l *LIBRARY*	Searches the specified library when linking.
–mcpu=*cputype*	Optimizes code for a specific processor. (cputype can take many values; some common ones are i386, i486, i586, i686, pentium, pentiumpro, pentium2, pentium3, and pentium4.)
–o *FILE*	Generates the specified output file (used to designate the name of an executable file).
–00 (two zeros)	Doesn't optimize.
–0 or –01 (letter O)	Optimizes the generated code.
–02 (letter O)	Optimizes even more.
–03 (letter O)	Performs optimizations beyond those done for –02
–0s (letter O)	Optimizes for size (to reduce the total amount of code).
–pedantic	Generates errors if any non-ANSI-standard extensions are used.
–pg	Adds extra code to the program so that, when run, this program generates information that the gprof program can use to display timing details for various parts of the program.
–shared	Generates a shared object file (typically used to create a shared library).
–U*MACRO*	Undefines the specified macros.
–v	Displays the GCC version number.
–w	Doesn't generate warning messages.
–W1, *OPTION*	Passes the *OPTION* string (containing multiple comma-separated options) to the linker. To create a shared library named libXXX.so.1, for example, use the following flag: -W1,–soname,libXXX.so.1.

The GNU make utility

When an application is made up of more than a few source files, compiling and linking the files by manually typing the gcc command can get tiresome. Also, you don't want to compile every file whenever you change something in a single source file. These situations are where the GNU make utility comes to your rescue.

The make utility works by reading and interpreting a *makefile* — a text file that describes which files are required to build a particular program, as well as how to compile and link the files to build the program. Whenever you change one or more files, make determines which files to recompile, and it issues the appropriate commands for compiling those files and rebuilding the program.

Makefile names

By default, GNU make looks for a makefile that has one of the following names, in the order shown:

>> GNUmakefile

>> makefile

>> Makefile

In Unix systems, using Makefile as the name of the makefile is customary because it appears near the beginning of directory listings, while uppercase names appear before lowercase names.

When you download software from the Internet, you usually find a Makefile together with the source files. To build the software, you only have to type **make** at the shell prompt; make takes care of all the steps necessary to build the software. Note that sometimes you may need to run configuration scripts, install additional packages, or add libraries before running make.

If your makefile doesn't have a standard name (such as Makefile), you have to use the −f option with make to specify the makefile name. If your makefile is called myprogram.mak, for example, you have to run make using the following command line:

```
make −f myprogram.mak
```

The makefile

For a program made up of several source and header files, the makefile specifies the following:

>> The items that make creates — usually, the object files and the executable. Using the term *target* to refer to any item that make has to create is common.

>> The files or other actions required to create the target.

>> Which commands to execute to create each target.

Suppose that you have a C++ source file named form.C that contains the following preprocessor directive:

```
#include "form.h" // Include header file
```

The object file form.o clearly depends on the source file form.C and the header file form.h. In addition to these dependencies, you must specify how make converts the form.C file to the object file form.o. Suppose that you want make to invoke g++ (because the source file is in C++) with these options:

» –c (compile only)

» –g (generate debugging information)

» –O2 (optimize some)

In the makefile, you can express these options with the following rule:

```
# This a comment in the makefile
# The following lines indicate how form.o depends
# on form.C and form.h and how to create form.o.
form.o: form.C form.h
g++ -c -g -O2 form.C
```

In this example, the first noncomment line shows form.o as the target and form.C and form.h as the dependent files.

WARNING

The line following the dependency indicates how to build the target from its dependents. This line must start with a tab. Otherwise, the make command exits with an error message, and you're left scratching your head because when you look at the makefile in a text editor, you can't tell the difference between a tab and a space. Now that you know the secret, the fix is to replace the space at the beginning of the offending line with a single tab.

The benefit of using make is that it prevents unnecessary compilations. After all, you can run g++ (or gcc) from a shell script to compile and link all the files that make up your application, but the shell script compiles everything, even if the compilations are unnecessary. GNU make, on the other hand, builds a target only if one or more of its dependents have changed since the last time the target was built. make verifies this change by examining the time of the last modification of the target and the dependents.

make treats the target as the name of a goal to be achieved; the target doesn't have to be a file. You can have a rule such as this one:

```
clean:
rm -f *.o
```

This rule specifies an abstract target named clean that doesn't depend on any-thing. This dependency statement says that to create the target clean, GNU make invokes the command rm -f *.o, which deletes all files that have the .o extension (namely, the object files). Thus, the effect of creating the target named clean is to delete the object files.

Variables (or macros)

In addition to the basic capability of building targets from dependents, GNU make includes many features that make it easy for you to express the dependencies and rules for building a target from its dependents. If you need to compile a large number of C++ files by using GCC with the same options, for example, typing the options for each file is tedious. You can avoid this repetitive task by defining a variable or macro in make as follows:

```
# Define macros for name of compiler
CXX= g++
# Define a macro for the GCC flags
CXXFLAGS= -O2 -g -mcpu=i686
# A rule for building an object file
form.o: form.C form.h
$(CXX) -c $(CXXFLAGS) form.C
```

In this example, CXX and CXXFLAGS are make variables. (GNU make prefers to call them *variables*, but most Unix make utilities call them *macros*.)

To use a variable anywhere in the makefile, start with a dollar sign ($) followed by the variable within parentheses. GNU make replaces all occurrences of a vari-able with its definition; thus, it replaces all occurrences of $(CXXFLAGS) with the string -O2 -g -mcpu=i686.

GNU make has several predefined variables that have special meanings. Table 3-2 lists these variables. In addition to the variables listed in Table 3-2, GNU make considers all environment variables (such as PATH and HOME) to be predefined variables as well.

TABLE 3-2   **Some Predefined Variables in GNU make**

Variable	Meaning
$%	Member name for targets that are archives. If the target is `libDisp.a(image.o)`, for example, $% is `image.o`.
$*	Name of the target file without the extension.
$+	Names of all dependent files with duplicate dependencies, listed in their order of occurrence.
$<	The name of the first dependent file.
$?	Names of all dependent files (with spaces between the names) that are newer than the target.
$@	Complete name of the target. If the target is `libDisp.a image.o)`, for example, $@ is `libDisp.a`.
$^	Names of all dependent files, with spaces between the names. Duplicates are removed from the dependent filenames.
AR	Name of the archive-maintaining program (default value: `ar`).
ARFLAGS	Flags for the archive-maintaining program (default value: `rv`).
AS	Name of the assembler program that converts the assembly language to object code (default value: `as`).
ASFLAGS	Flags for the assembler.
CC	Name of the C compiler (default value: `cc`).
CFLAGS	Flags that are passed to the C compiler.
CO	Name of the program that extracts a file from RCS (default value: `co`).
COFLAGS	Flags for the RCS co program.
CPP	Name of the C preprocessor (default value: `$(CC) –E`).
CPPFLAGS	Flags for the C preprocessor.
CXX	Name of the C++ compiler (default value: `g++`).
CXXFLAGS	Flags that are passed to the C++ compiler.
FC	Name of the FORTRAN compiler (default value: `f77`).
FFLAGS	Flags for the FORTRAN compiler.
LDFLAGS	Flags for the compiler when it's supposed to invoke the linker `ld`.
RM	Name of the command to delete a file (default value: `rm –f`).

A sample makefile

You can write a makefile easily if you use the predefined variables of GNU make and its built-in rules. Consider, for example, a makefile that creates the executable xdraw from three C source files (xdraw.c, xviewobj.c, and shapes.c) and two header files (xdraw.h and shapes.h). Assume that each source file includes one of the header files. Given these facts, here's what a sample makefile may look like:

```
##########################################################
# Sample makefile
# Comments start with '#'
#
##########################################################
# Use standard variables to define compile and link flags
CFLAGS= -g -O2
# Define the target "all"
all: xdraw
OBJS=xdraw.o xviewobj.o shapes.o
xdraw: $(OBJS)
# Object files
xdraw.o: Makefile xdraw.c xdraw.h
xviewobj.o: Makefile xviewobj.c xdraw.h
shapes.o: Makefile shapes.c shapes.h
```

This makefile relies on GNU make's implicit rules. The conversion of .c files to .o files uses the built-in rule. Defining the variable CFLAGS passes the flags to the C compiler.

TECHNICAL STUFF

The target named all is defined as the first target for a reason: If you run GNU make without specifying any targets in the command line (see the make syntax described in the following section), the command builds the first target it finds in the makefile. By defining the first target all as xdraw, you can ensure that make builds this executable file, even if you don't explicitly specify it as a target. Unix programmers traditionally use all as the name of the first target, but the target's name is immaterial; what matters is that it's the first target in the makefile.

How to run make

Typically, you run make simply by typing the following command at the shell prompt:

```
make
```

When run this way, GNU make looks for a file named GNUmakefile, makefile, or Makefile — in that order. If make finds one of these makefiles, it builds the first target specified in that makefile. If make doesn't find an appropriate makefile, however, it displays the following error message and exits:

```
make: *** No targets specified and no makefile found. Stop.
```

If your makefile happens to have a different name from the default names, you have to use the -f option to specify the makefile. The syntax of the make command with this option is

```
make -f filename
```

where *filename* is the name of the makefile.

Even when you have a makefile with a default name such as Makefile, you may want to build a specific target out of several targets defined in the makefile. In that case, you have to use the following syntax when you run make:

```
make target
```

If the makefile contains the target named clean, for example, you can build that target with this command:

```
make clean
```

Another special syntax overrides the value of a make variable. GNU make uses the CFLAGS variable to hold the flags used when compiling C files, for example. You can override the value of this variable when you invoke make. Here's an example of how you can define CFLAGS as the option -g -02:

```
make CFLAGS="-g -02"
```

In addition to these options, GNU make accepts several command-line options. Table 3-3 lists the GNU make options.

TABLE 3-3   ## Options for GNU make

Option	Meaning
−b	Ignores the variable given but accepts that variable for compatibility with other versions of make.
−C *DIR*	Changes to the specified directory before reading the makefile.
−d	Prints debugging information.
−e	Allows environment variables to override definitions of similarly named variables in the makefile.
−f *FILE*	Reads FILE as the makefile.
−h	Displays the list of make options.
−i	Ignores all errors in commands executed when building a target.
−I *DIR*	Searches the specified directory for included makefiles. (The capability to include a file in a makefile is unique to GNU make.)
−j *NUM*	Specifies the number of jobs that make can run simultaneously.
−k	Continues to build unrelated targets, even if an error occurs when building one of the targets.
−l *LOAD*	Doesn't start a new job if load average is at least *LOAD* (a floating-point number).
−m	Ignores the variable given but accepts that variable for compatibility with other versions of make.
−n	Prints the commands to execute but does not execute them.
−o *FILE*	Does not rebuild the file named *FILE*, even if it is older than its dependents.
−p	Displays the make database of variables and implicit rules.
−q	Does not run anything, but returns 0 (zero) if all targets are up to date, 1 if anything needs updating, or 2 if an error occurs.
−r	Gets rid of all built-in rules.
−R	Gets rid of all built-in variables and rules.
−s	Works silently (without displaying the commands as they execute).
−t	Changes the time stamp of the files.
−v	Displays the version number of make, licensing information, and a copyright notice.
−w	Displays the name of the working directory before and after processing the makefile.
−W *FILE*	Assumes that the specified file has been modified (used with −n to see what happens if you modify that file).

The GNU debugger

Although make automates the process of building a program, that part of programming is the least of your worries when a program doesn't work correctly or when a program suddenly quits with an error message. You need a debugger to find the cause of program errors. Linux includes gdb — the versatile GNU debugger with a command-line interface.

Like any debugger, gdb lets you perform typical debugging tasks, such as the following:

>> Set a breakpoint so that the program stops at a specified line.

>> Watch the values of variables in the program.

>> Step through the program one line at a time.

>> Change variables in an attempt to correct errors.

The gdb debugger can debug C and C++ programs.

Preparing to debug a program

If you want to debug a program by using gdb, you have to ensure that the compiler generates and places debugging information in the executable. The debugging information contains the names of variables in your program and the mapping of addresses in the executable file to lines of code in the source file. gdb needs this information to perform its functions, such as stopping after executing a specified line of source code.

TIP

To make sure that the executable is properly prepared for debugging, use the -g option with GCC or G++. You can do this task by defining the variable CFLAGS in the makefile as

```
CFLAGS= -g
```

Running gdb

The most common way to debug a program is to run gdb by using the following command:

```
gdb progname
```

progname is the name of the program's executable file. After progname runs, gdb displays the following message and prompts you for a command:

```
GNU gdb (GDB) 7.5.91.20130417-cvs-ubuntu
Copyright (c) 2013 Free Software Foundation, Inc.
License GPLv3+: GNU GPL version 3 or later ___<http://gnu.org/licenses/gpl.html>
This is free software: you are free to change it and redistribute it.
There is NO WARRANTY, to the extent permitted by law. Type "show copying" and
    "show warranty" for details.
This GDB was configured as "i686--linux-gnu".
For bug reporting instructions, please see:
http://www.gnu.org/software/gdb/bugs/.
(gdb)
```

You can type gdb commands at the (gdb) prompt. One useful command, help, displays a list of commands, as the next listing shows:

```
(gdb) help
List of classes of commands:
aliases -- Aliases of other commands
breakpoints -- Making program stop at certain points
data -- Examining data
files -- Specifying and examining files
internals -- Maintenance commands
obscure -- Obscure features
running -- Running the program
stack -- Examining the stack
status -- Status inquiries
support -- Support facilities
tracepoints -- Tracing of program execution without stopping the program
user-defined -- User-defined commands
Type "help" followed by a class name for a list of commands in that class.
Type "help all" for the list of all commands.
Type "help" followed by command name for full documentation.
Command name abbreviations are allowed if unambiguous.
(gdb)
```

To quit gdb, type q and then press Enter.

gdb has a large number of commands, but you need only a few to find the cause of an error quickly. Table 3-4 lists the commonly used gdb commands.

TABLE 3-4 ## Common gdb Commands

This Command	Does the Following
break *NUM*	Sets a breakpoint at the specified line number, *NUM*. (The debugger stops at breakpoints.)
bt	Displays a trace of all stack frames. (This command shows you the sequence of function calls so far.)
clear *FILENAME: NUM*	Deletes the breakpoint at a specific line number, *NUM*, in the source file *FILENAME*. clear xdraw.c:8, for example, clears the breakpoint at line 8 of file xdraw.c.
continue	Continues running the program being debugged. (Use this command after the program stops due to a signal or breakpoint.)
display *EXPR*	Displays the value of an expression, *EXPR* (consisting of variables defined in the program), each time the program stops.
file *FILE*	Loads the specified executable file, *FILE*, for debugging.
help *NAME*	Displays help on the command named *NAME*.
info break	Displays a list of current breakpoints, including information on how many times each breakpoint is reached.
info files	Displays detailed information about the file being debugged.
info func	Displays all function names.
info local	Displays information about local variables of the current function.
info prog	Displays the execution status of the program being debugged.
info var	Displays all global and static variable names.
kill	Ends the program you're debugging.
list	Lists a section of the source code.
make	Runs the make utility to rebuild the executable without leaving gdb.
next	Advances one line of source code in the current function without stepping into other functions.
print *EXPR*	Shows the value of the expression *EXPR*.
quit	Quits gdb.
run	Starts running the currently loaded executable.
set variable *VAR=VALUE*	Sets the value of the variable *VAR* to *VALUE*.
shell *CMD*	Executes the shell command *CMD* without leaving gdb.

This Command	Does the Following
step	Advances one line in the current function, stepping into other functions, if any.
watch *VAR*	Shows the value of the variable named *VAR* whenever the value changes.
where	Displays the call sequence. Use this command to locate where your program died.
x/*F ADDR*	Examines the contents of the memory location at address *ADDR* in the format specified by the letter *F*, which can be o (octal), x (hex), d (decimal), u (unsigned decimal), t (binary), f (float), a (address), i (instruction), c (char), or s (string). You can append a letter indicating the size of data type to the format letter. Size letters are b (byte), h (halfword, 2 bytes), w (word, 4 bytes), and g (giant, 8 bytes). Typically, *ADDR* is the name of a variable or pointer.

Finding bugs by using gdb

To understand how you can find bugs by using gdb, you need to see an example. The procedure is easiest to show with a simple example, so the following, dbgtst.c, is a contrived program that contains a typical bug:

```
#include <stdio.h>
static char buf[256];
void read_input(char *s);
int main(void)
{
char *input = NULL; /* Just a pointer, no storage for string */
read_input(input);
/* Process command. */
printf("You typed: %s\n", input);
/* ..._*/
return 0;
}
void read_input(char *s)
{
printf("Command: ");
gets(s);
}
```

This program's main function calls the read_input function to get a line of input from the user. The read_input function expects a character array in which it returns what the user types. In this example, however, main calls read_input with an uninitialized pointer — the bug in this simple program.

Build the program by using gcc with the –g option:

```
gcc –g –o dbgtst dbgtst.c
```

Ignore the warning message about the gets function being dangerous; I'm trying to use the shortcoming of that function to show how you can use gdb to track down errors.

To see the problem with this program, run it and type test at the Command: prompt:

```
./dbgtst
Command: test
Segmentation fault
```

The program dies after displaying the Segmentation fault message. For such a small program as this one, you can probably find the cause by examining the source code. In a real-world application, however, you may not immediately know what causes the error. That's when you have to use gdb to find the cause of the problem.

To use gdb to locate a bug, follow these steps:

1. **Load the program under** gdb.

   Type gdb dbgtst, for example, to load a program named dbgtst in gdb.

2. **Start executing the program under** gdb **by typing the** run **command, and when the program prompts for input, type some input text.**

   The program fails as it did previously. Here's what happens with the dbgtst program:

```
(gdb) run
Starting program: /home/edulaney/swdev/dbgtst
Command: test
Program received signal SIGSEGV, Segmentation fault.
0x400802b6 in gets () from /lib/tls/libc.so.6
(gdb)
```

3. **Use the** where **command to determine where the program died.**

   For the dbgtst program, this command yields output similar to the following:

```
(gdb) where
#0 0x400802b6 in gets () from /lib/tls/libc.so.6
#1 0x08048474 in read_input (s=0x0) at dbgtst.c:16
#2 0x08048436 in main () at dbgtst.c:7
(gdb)
```

The output shows the sequence of function calls. Function call #0 — the most recent one — is to the gets C library function. The gets call originates in the read_input function (at line 16 of the file dbgtst.c), which in turn is called from the main function at line 7 of the dbgtst.c file.

4. **Use the list command to inspect the lines of suspect source code.**

In dbgtst, you may start with line 16 of dbgtst.c file, as follows:

```
(gdb) list dbgtst.c:16
11 return 0;
12 }
13 void read_input(char *s)
14 {
15 printf("Command: ");
16 gets(s);
17 }
18
(gdb)
```

After looking at this listing, you can tell that the problem may be the way read_input is called. Then you list the lines around line 7 in dbgtst.c (where the read_input call originates):

```
(gdb) list dbgtst.c:7
2 static char buf[256];
3 void read_input(char *s);
4 int main(void)
5 {
6 char *input = NULL; /* Just a pointer, no storage for string */
7 read_input(input);
8 /* Process command. */
9 printf("You typed: %s\n", input);
10 /* ... */
11 return 0;
(gdb)
```

At this point, you can narrow the problem to the variable named input. That variable is an array, not a NULL (which means zero) pointer.

Fixing bugs in gdb

Sometimes, you can fix a bug directly in gdb. For the example program in the preceding section, you can try this fix immediately after the program dies after displaying an error message. An extra buffer named buf is defined in the dbgtst program, as follows:

```
static char buf[256];
```

You can fix the problem of the uninitialized pointer by setting the variable input to buf. The following session with gdb corrects the problem of the uninitialized pointer. (This example picks up immediately after the program runs and dies due to the segmentation fault.)

```
(gdb) file dbgtst
A program is being debugged already. Kill it? (y or n) y
Load new symbol table from "/home/edulaney/sw/dbgtst"? (y or n) y
Reading symbols from /home/edulaney/sw/dbgtst ... done.
(gdb) list
1 #include <stdio.h>
2 static char buf[256];
3 void read_input(char *s);
4 int main(void)
5 {
6 char *input = NULL; /* Just a pointer, no storage for string */
7 read_input(input);
8 /* Process command. */
9 printf("You typed: %s\n", input);
10 /* ... */
(gdb) break 7
Breakpoint 2 at 0x804842b: file dbgtst.c, line 7.
(gdb) run
Starting program: /home/edulaney/sw/dbgtst
Breakpoint 1, main () at dbgtst.c:7
7 read_input(input);
(gdb) set var input=buf
(gdb) cont
Continuing.
Command: test
You typed: test
Processm exited normally.
(gdb)q
```

As the preceding listing shows, if the program is stopped just before read_input is called and the variable named input is set to buf (which is a valid array of characters), the rest of the program runs fine.

After finding a fix that works in gdb, you can make the necessary changes to the source files and make the fix permanent.

Understanding the Implications of GNU Licenses

You have to pay a price for the bounty of Linux. To protect its developers and users, Linux is distributed under the GNU GPL (General Public License), which stipulates the distribution of the source code.

The GPL doesn't mean, however, that you can't write commercial software for Linux that you want to distribute (either for free or for a price) in binary form only. You can follow all the rules and still sell your Linux applications in binary form.

When writing applications for Linux, there are a number of licenses that may apply (MIT and BSD, for example), but you should be aware of two licenses:

>> The **GNU General Public License** (GPL), which governs many Linux programs, including the Linux kernel and GCC.

>> The **GNU Library General Public License** (LGPL), which covers many Linux libraries.

WARNING

The following sections provide an overview of these licenses and some suggestions on how to meet their requirements. Don't take anything in this book as legal advice. Instead, you should read the full text for these licenses in the text files on your Linux system and then show these licenses to your legal counsel for a full interpretation and an assessment of their applicability to your business.

The GNU General Public License

The text of the GNU General Public License (GPL) is in a file named COPYING in various directories in your Linux system. Type the following command to find a copy of that file in your Linux system for various items:

```
find /usr -name "COPYING" -print
```

After you find the file, you can change to that directory and type more COPYING to read the GPL. These are examples of the license accompanying code, and you can find other examples at www.gnu.org/copyleft/gpl.html.

The GPL has nothing to do with whether you charge for the software or distribute it for free; its thrust is to keep the software free for all users. GPL requires that the software be distributed in source-code form and stipulates that any user can copy and distribute the software in source-code form to anyone else. In addition, everyone is reminded that the software comes with absolutely no warranty.

The software that the GPL covers isn't in the public domain. Software covered by GPL is always copyrighted, and the GPL spells out the restrictions on the software's copying and distribution. From a user's point of view, of course, GPL's restrictions aren't really restrictions; the restrictions are benefits because the user is guaranteed access to the source code.

WARNING

If your application uses parts of any software that the GPL covers, your application is considered a *derived work*, which means that your application is also covered by the GPL and that you must distribute the source code to your application.

Although the GPL covers the Linux kernel, the GPL doesn't cover your applications that use the kernel services through system calls. Those applications are considered to be normal use of the kernel.

If you plan to distribute your application in binary form (as most commercial software is distributed), you must make sure that your application doesn't use any parts of any software the GPL covers. Your application may end up using parts of other software when it calls functions in a library. Most libraries, however, are covered by a different GNU license, which is described in the next section.

You have to watch out for only a few of the library and utility programs that the GPL covers. The GNU dbm (gdbm) database library is one of the prominent libraries that GPL covers. The GNU bison parser-generator tool is another utility that the GPL covers. If you allow bison to generate code, the GPL covers that code.

TECHNICAL STUFF

Other alternatives for the GNU dbm and GNU bison aren't covered by GPL. For a database library, you can use the Berkeley database library db in place of gdbm. For a parser-generator, you may use yacc instead of bison.

The GNU Library General Public License

The text of the GNU Library General Public License (LGPL) is in a file named COPYING.LIB. If you have the kernel source installed, a copy of COPYING.LIB file is in one of the source directories. To locate a copy of the COPYING.LIB file on your Linux system, type the following command in a terminal window:

```
find /usr -name "COPYING*" -print
```

This command lists all occurrences of COPYING and COPYING.LIB in your system. The COPYING file contains the GPL, whereas COPYING.LIB has the LGPL.

The LGPL is intended to allow use of libraries in your applications, even if you don't distribute source code for your application. The LGPL stipulates, however, that users must have access to the source code of the library you use — and that users can use modified versions of those libraries.

The LGPL covers most Linux libraries, including the C library (libc.a). Thus, when you build your application on Linux by using the GCC compiler, your application links with code from one or more libraries that the LGPL covers. If you want to distribute your application in binary form only, you need to pay attention to LGPL.

One way to meet the intent of the LGPL is to provide the object code for your application and a makefile that relinks your object files with any updated Linux libraries the LGPL covers.

REMEMBER

A better way to satisfy the LGPL is to use *dynamic linking*, in which your application and the library are separate entities, even though your application calls functions that reside in the library when it runs. With dynamic linking, users immediately get the benefit of any updates to the libraries without ever having to relink the application.

You can find the newest version of the license, GPLv3, and a Quick Guide to it at www.gnu.org/licenses/quick-guide-gplv3.html.

Linux
Certification

Contents at a Glance

CHAPTER 1: **Studying for the Linux Essentials Certification Exam** 479

Overview of Linux Essentials 479
The Linux Community and a Career in Open Source 480
Finding Your Way on a Linux System 482
The Power of the Command Line 483
The Linux Operating System 485
Security and File Permissions 486

CHAPTER 2: **Studying for the CompTIA Linux+ Powered by LPI Certification Exams** 489

Overview of the CompTIA Linux+ Exams 489
System Architecture 490
Linux Installation and Package Management 492
GNU and Unix Commands 494
Devices, Linux File Systems, Filesystem Hierarchy Standard 495
Shells, Scripting, and Data Management 497
User Interfaces and Desktops 498
Administrative Tasks 500
Essential System Services 501
Networking Fundamentals 502
Security 504

CHAPTER 3: **Other Linux Certifications** 507

Vendor-Neutral Certifications 507
Vendor-Specific Certifications 508

Chapter **1**

Studying for the Linux Essentials Certification Exam

Just as you can attain many levels of degrees through an educational institution (associate's, bachelor's, master's, and doctorate degrees), you can achieve multiple levels of Linux certification. This book is written primarily for the Linux+ certification from CompTIA and the LPI LX0-103 and LX0-104 exams. As such, it also covers everything you need to know to study and pass LPI's lower-level certification, known as Linux Essentials.

This chapter provides an overall look at the exam and then explores the topics in each of the domains.

Overview of Linux Essentials

The Linux Essentials Certificate of Achievement was created by the Linux Professional Institute (LPI) to appeal to the academic sector. Students taking semester-based classes in Linux may not get through all the topics necessary to pass the two exams (LX0-103 and LX0-104) that are necessary to gain the Level 1 certification, but LPI still wanted to recognize and authenticate their knowledge. This program was created through international collaboration with a classroom focus in mind. As of this writing, the current version is 1.5, and the exam code is 010-150.

REMEMBER

Linux Essentials is a certificate of achievement, intended to be a much lower-level (subset) certification than the Level 1 certification. Although Linux Essentials is recommended, it's not required for any of the LPIC professional certification or any other certifications.

The exam has five domains, called *topics.* Table 1-1 shows these topics and their weightings. It's important to note that weightings are always subject to change; it's not uncommon for them to be tweaked a bit over time.

TABLE 1-1   ### Domains on the Linux Essentials Exam

Topic	Weighting
The Linux Community and a Career in Open Source	7
Finding Your Way on a Linux System	9
The Power of the Command Line	9
The Linux Operating System	8
Security and File Permissions	7

The sections that follow look at each of these topics in more detail.

The Linux Community and a Career in Open Source

Table 1-2 shows the subtopics, weight, description, and key knowledge areas for this topic.

Here are the top ten items to know as you study for this domain:

>> Linux is the best-known example of open-source software so far developed (and still in development).

TABLE 1-2   **Breakout of Topic 1**

Subtopic	Weight	Description	Key Areas
Linux Evolution and Popular Operating Systems	2	Knowledge of Linux development and major distributions	Open-source philosophy, distributions, and embedded systems (The distributions to be cognizant of include Android, Debian, Ubuntu, CentOS, openSUSE, and Red Hat.)
Major Open Source Applications	2	Awareness of major applications and their uses and development	Desktop applications, server applications, development languages, and package management tools and repositories (Topics include OpenOffice.org, LibreOffice, Thunderbird, Firefox, GIMP, Apache HTTPD, NGINX, MySQL, NFS, Samba, C, Java, Perl, shell, Python, dpkg, apt-get, rpm, and yum.)
Understanding Open Source Software and Licensing	1	Open communities and licensing open-source software for business	Licensing, Free Software Foundation (FSF), and Open Source Initiative (OSI) (Topics include GPL, BSD, Creative Commons, Free Software, FOSS, FLOSS, and open-source business models.)
ICT Skills and Working in Linux	2	Basic Information and Communication Technology (ICT) skills and working in Linux	Desktop skills, getting to the command line, industry uses of Linux, and cloud computing and virtualization (Topics include using a browser, privacy concerns, configuration options, searching the web, and saving content.)

» The *shell* is the command interpreter that resides between the user and the operating system. Although many shells are available, the most common today is the bash shell.

» A plethora of applications and tools is available for use with the various Linux distributions. Many of these tools are also open-source.

» The Apache Software Foundation distributes open-source software under the Apache license Free and Open Source (FOSS).

» The Free Software Foundation (FSF) supports the free (open source) software movement and copyleft under the GNU General Public License. *Copyleft* makes it possible for modifications to be made to software while preserving the same rights in the produced derivatives.

» The Open Source Initiative (OSI) also supports the open-source software movement, as do the GNOME Foundation, the Ubuntu Foundation, and many other organizations.

- » OpenOffice.org was a popular suite of open-source office-productivity software. LibreOffice is a fork of OpenOffice that has eclipsed it in popularity.

- » Samba makes it possible for Linux systems to share files with Windows-based systems.

- » Thunderbird is a popular mail and news client created by the Mozilla Foundation.

- » Many web browsers are available for Linux, and one of the most popular is Mozilla Firefox.

Finding Your Way on a Linux System

Table 1-3 shows the subtopics, weights, descriptions, and key knowledge areas for this topic.

TABLE 1-3 **Breakout of Topic 2**

Subtopic	Weight	Description	Key Areas
Command Line Basics	3	Using the Linux command line	Basic shell, command-line syntax, variables, globbing, and quoting (Topics include bash, echo, history, PATH env variables, export, and type.)
Using the Command Line to Get Help	2	Running help commands and navigation of the various help systems, man, and info	The topics include: man files, `info` command, `/usr/share/doc`, and locate
Using Directories and Listing Files	2	Navigating home and system directories and listing files in various locations	Files, directories, hidden files and directories, home directory, and absolute and relative paths (Topics include common options for `ls`, recursive listings, cd, . and .., home, and –.)
Creating, Moving, and Deleting Files	2	Creating, moving, and deleting files under the home directory	Files and directories, case sensitivity, and simple globbing and quoting (Topics include `mv`, `cp`, `rm`, `touch`, `mkdir`, and `rmdir`.)

Here are the top ten items to know as you study for this domain:

>> Regular expressions – often referred to as *globbing* – can be used with the shells available in Linux to match wildcard characters. Among the possible wildcards, the asterisk (∗) matches any number of characters; the question mark (?) matches only one character.

>> Linux is a case-sensitive operating system.

>> Files can be hidden by preceding their names with a single period (.). In pathnames, however, a single period (.) specifies this directory, and two periods (..) signifies the parent directory.

>> Absolute paths give the full path to a resource, whereas relative paths give directions from where you're currently working. An example of an absolute path is /tmp/eadulaney/file, and an example relative link is ../file.

>> Files can be copied by using cp or moved by using mv. Files can be deleted with rm, and directories (which are created with mkdir) can be removed with rmdir. Recursive deletion can be done with rm -r.

>> To change directories, use the cd command. When this command is used without parameters, it moves you to your home directory. To see what directory you're currently working in, use the pwd (present working directory) command.

>> The ls command has a plethora of options allowing you to list files. The –a option lists all files (including hidden files).

>> Help is available through the manual pages (accessed with the man command) and info (which shows help files stored below /user/info).

>> The whatis command shows what manual pages are available for an entry, and whereis shows the location of the file and all related files (including any manual pages).

>> Many standard utilities allow you to enter the name of the executable followed by "--help" to obtain help only on the syntax.

The Power of the Command Line

Table 1-4 shows the subtopics, weights, descriptions, and key knowledge areas for this topic.

TABLE 1-4

Breakout of Topic 3

Subtopic	Weight	Description	Key Areas
Archiving Files in the Command Line	2	Archiving files in the user home directory	Files, directories, archives, and compression (Topics include tar as well as common tar options, gzip, bzip2, zip, and unzip.)
Searching and Extracting Data from Files	3	Searching and extracting data from files in the home directory	Command-line pipes, I/O redirection, and basic regular expressions (Topics include grep, less, cat, head, tail, sort, cut, and wc.)
Turning Commands into a Script	4	Turning repetitive commands into simple scripts	Basic shell scripting and awareness of common text editors (Topics include #!, /bin/bash, variables, arguments, for loops, echo, and exit status.)

Here are the top ten items to know as you study for this domain:

» Standard input (stdin) is traditionally the keyboard, and standard output (stdout) is traditionally the monitor. Both can be redirected, as can standard error (stderr), by using the symbols >, >>, <, and |.

» Commands can be joined on the command line by the semicolon (;), and each command runs independently. You can also use the pipe (|) to send the output of one command as the input of another command.

» The cut command can pull fields from a file, and the fields can be combined by using either paste or join. The latter offers more features than the former and can be used with conditions.

» The wc command can count the number of lines, words, and characters in a file.

» The grep utility (and its counterparts egrep and fgrep) can be used to find matches for strings within files.

» The find command can be used to search the system for files/directories that meet any number of criteria. When these entities are found, the xargs command can be used to look deeper within them for other values (such as in conjunction with grep).

» You can use the tar command (which can combine multiple files into a single archive) to do backups.

» In addition to archiving, you can compress files with the gzip or pack command. To uncompress files, use uncompress, gunzip, or unpack.

» Variables can be given at the command line and referenced as $1, $2, and so on, or entered into the executing file with the read command.

» Logic can be added to scripts by testing conditions with test or [. Commands can execute through if-then-fi deviations or looping (while, until, or for). You can use the exit command to leave a script or use break to leave a loop.

The Linux Operating System

Table 1-5 shows the subtopics, weights, descriptions, and key knowledge areas for this topic.

TABLE 1-5   **Breakout of Topic 4**

Subtopic	Weight	Description	Key Areas
Choosing an Operating System	1	Knowledge of major operating systems and Linux distributions	Windows, Mac, and Linux differences; distribution lifecycle management (Topics include GUI versus command line, desktop configuration; maintenance cycles, and Beta and Stable.)
Understanding Computer Hardware	2	Familiarity with the components that go into building desktop and server computers	Hardware (Topics include motherboards, processors, power supplies, optical drives, peripherals, hard drives and partitions, /def/sd*, and drivers.)
Where Data Is Stored	3	Where various types of information are stored on a Linux system	Programs and configuration, packages and package databases, processes, memory addresses, system messaging, and logging (Topics include ps, top, free, syslog, dmesg, /etc/, /var/log/, /boot/, /proc;, /dev/, and /sys/.)
Your Computer on the Network	2	Querying vital networking settings and determining the basic requirements for a computer on a local area network (LAN)	Internet, network, routers, querying DNaS client configuration, and querying network configuration (Topics include route, ip route show, ifconfig, ip addr show, netstat, /etc/resolv.conf, /etc/hosts, IPv4, IPv6, ping, and host.)

Here are the top ten items to know as you study for this domain:

>> When run, every command spans at least one process; processes can be viewed with ps or top (which updates the display dynamically).

>> Jobs can run in the foreground or background and be moved between the two. Jobs running in the foreground can be suspended by pressing Ctrl+Z.

>> IPv4 uses 32-bit addresses, each divided into four octets. The first octet identifies the class of address (A, B, or C). The address can be public or private.

>> The ifconfig utility can be used to see the current IP configuration of the network cards.

>> The ping utility is an all-purpose tool for testing connectivity. It sends echo messages to a specified host to see whether that host can be reached. You can use ping with the loopback address (127.0.0.1) to test internal configuration.

>> The route utility displays the routing table and allows you to configure it.

>> The netstat utility shows the current status of ports – those that are open, listening, and so on.

>> The system log is /var/log/messages, and this log is where the majority of events are written to by the system log daemon (syslogd). Messages routed there can be viewed with the dmesg command.

>> The logrotate command can be used to automatically archive log files and perform maintenance as configured in /etc/syslog.conf.

>> You can manually write entries to log files by using the logger command.

Security and File Permissions

Table 1-6 shows the subtopics, weights, descriptions, and key knowledge areas for this topic.

Here are the top ten items to know as you study for this domain:

>> File and directory permissions can be changed with the chmod command (which accepts numeric and symbolic values).

>> Adding 1000 to standard permissions turns on the sticky bit; adding 2000 turns on the SGID permission. Adding 4000 turns on the SUID permission.

TABLE 1-6   **Breakout of Topic 5**

Subtopic	Weight	Description	Key Areas
Basic Security and Identifying User Types	2	Understanding various types of users on a Linux system	Root, standard, and system users (Topics include /etc/passwd, /etc/group, id, who, w, sudo, and su.)
Creating Users and Groups	2	Creating users and groups on a Linux system	User and group commands, and user IDs (Topics include /etc/passwd, /etc/shadow, /etc/group, /etc/skel, id, last, useradd, groupadd, and passwd.)
Managing File Permissions and Ownership	2	Understanding and manipulating file permissions and ownership settings	File/directory permissions and owners (Topics include ls –l, ls –a, chmod, and chown.)
Special Directories and Files	1	Understanding special directories and files on a Linux system, including special permissions	Using temporary files and directories, and symbolic links (Topics include /tmp, /var/tmp, Sticky Bit, ls –d, and ln –s.)

>> Links are created with the ln command. A *hard link* is nothing more than an alias to a file (sharing the same inode). The ln –s command creates a symbolic link that's an actual file with its own inode. The symbolic link contains a pointer to the original file and can span file systems; the hard link can't.

>> User accounts can be added by manually editing the configuration files or using the useradd command; they can be removed with userdel.

>> The groupadd utility can be used to create groups, and groupdel can be used to remove groups. Groups can be modified with groupmod, and users can be moved from one group to another with the newgrp command.

>> Passwords are changed with the passwd command. Older systems stored passwords in /etc/passwd; now passwords are stored in /etc/shadow, where they're more secure.

>> To see who logged on most recently and may still be on the network, you can use the last command.

Studying for the Linux Essentials Certification Exam

» The su command allows you to become another user (returning with exit). If no other username is specified, the root user is implied — hence, the su for *superuser*.

» Use sudo instead of su when you want to run a command as another user (usually, root) without becoming that user.

» The who command shows who's logged on; the w command shows information combining who with uptime.

Chapter 2

Studying for the CompTIA Linux+ Powered by LPI Certification Exams

The preceding chapter examines the Linux Essentials exam — the lower-level certification offered by the Linux Professional Institute (LPI). Although it's not a requirement, that certification should be viewed as a stepping stone to a higher-level exam. The Linux+ certification exam from CompTIA — consisting of the LPI LX0-103 and LX0-104 exams — is an ideal example of such a high-level test.

In this chapter, I provide an overview of the two exams and then explore the topics in each of the domains.

Overview of the CompTIA Linux+ Exams

The official name of the certification in question is CompTIA Linux+ Powered by LPI, and although that's a mouthful to say, it's also a meaningful addition to a résumé. The certification is awarded by CompTIA; it consists of two exams by the

LPI: LX0-103 and LX0-104. Accordingly, at the time of taking the exams, a candidate can choose to have the test scores forwarded to LPI and gain the Level 1 certification (LPIC-1) at the same time.

TIP

Records are separately maintained by LPI and CompTIA. If you choose not to forward your scores, you can be Linux+-certified but not LPIC-1 certified.

Each of the two exams consists of 60 questions that must be answered in 90 minutes. The passing score is 500 on a scale from 200 to 800, and it's highly recommended — but not required — that candidates have 12 months of Linux administration experience. Finally, it's necessary to pass the LX0-103 exam before sitting for the LX0-104 exam.

There are four domains on one exam and six on the other. Table 2-1 shows the domains on each test, along with their prospective weightings.

The sections that follow look at each of these topics in more detail.

TABLE 2-1   **Domains on the Linux+ Exams**

Exam	Domain	Weighting
LX0-103	101 System Architecture	14%
	102 Linux Installation and Package Management	18%
	103 GNU and Unix Commands	43%
	104 Devices, Linux Filesystems, Filesystem Hierarchy Standard	25%
LX0-104	105 Shells, Scripting, and Data Management	17%
	106 User Interfaces and Desktops	8%
	107 Administrative Tasks	20%
	108 Essential System Services	17%
	109 Networking Fundamentals	23%
	110 Security	15%

System Architecture

Table 2-2 shows the subtopics, weights, descriptions, and key knowledge areas for this topic.

TABLE 2-2   **Breakout of Domain 101**

Subtopic	Weight	Description	Key Areas
Determine and configure hardware settings	2	Conceptual understanding of kernel loading options and boot steps	Be able to work with peripherals, storage devices, and the tools you use to configure them.
Boot the system	3	Walking through the boot process	Know common boot commands, the boot sequence, and boot logs.
Change runlevels/boot targets and shutdown or reboot system	3	Changing to single-user mode, shutting down and rebooting the system, and knowing that you should alert users to changes in the run level and to the need for properly terminating processes	Set the default run level, change run levels, and know how to terminate.

To adequately address these topics, focus on the following files, terms, and utilities: /dev, /etc/init.d, /etc/inittab, /proc, /sys, /var/log/messages, BIOS, bootloader, dmesg, init, kernel, lsmod, lspci, lsusb, modprobe, shutdown, and telinit.

Here are the top ten items to know as you study for this domain:

>> The system log is /var/log/messages, and this log is where the majority of events are written to by the system log daemon (syslogd). Messages routed there can be viewed with the dmesg command.

>> The logrotate command can be used to automatically archive log files and perform maintenance as configured in /etc/syslog.conf.

>> You can manually write entries to log files by using the logger command.

>> The init daemon is responsible for maintaining proper running of daemons at specified run levels. The system attempts to go to the run level specified as the default in the /etc/inittab file upon each boot.

>> Run levels can be changed with the init and shutdown commands.

>> Valid run levels defined as standards are 0 (power off), 1 (single-user mode), 2 (multiple user without Network File System), 3 (multiple user with NFS), 5 (X environment), and 6 (reboot).

>> The lsmod command is used to list loaded modules. The insmod command is used to install a module. The rmmod command is used to remove a module from the system. The modinfo command shows information about a module.

» The `modprobe` utility can probe and install a module and its dependents, whereas the `depmod` utility determines and shows any module dependencies that exist.

» Kernel software is typically named `linux–x.y.z`, where *x.y.z* represents the version number.

» The `make config` command executes a command-line-oriented view and allows you to respond interactively with the kernel build.

Linux Installation and Package Management

Table 2-3 shows the subtopics, weights, descriptions, and key knowledge areas for this topic.

TABLE 2-3 **Breakout of Domain 102**

Subtopic	Weight	Description	Key Areas
Design hard disk layout	2	Designing a disk-partitioning scheme for a Linux system	Allocate file systems and swap space, tailoring the design to the intended use of the system.
Install a boot manager	2	Selecting, installing, and configuring a boot manager	Interact with the bootloader, GRUB Legacy, and GRUB 2.
Manage shared libraries	1	Determining the shared libraries that executable programs depend on and installing them when necessary	Identify shared libraries, typical locations, and how to load.
Use Debian package management	3	Knowing the Debian package tools	Install, upgrade, and uninstall Debian binary packages, and obtain package information such as version, content, dependencies, package integrity, and installation status.
Use RPM and Yum package management	3	Knowing the RPM and Yum tools	Install, upgrade, and remove packages with RPM and Yum; determine what files a package provides; and find the package a specific file comes from.

To adequately address these topics, focus on the following files, terms, and utilities: /(root) file system, /boot/grub/menu.1st, /etc/apt/sources.list, /etc/ld.so.conf, /etc/yum.conf, /etc/yum.repos.d/, /home file system, /var file system, apt-cache, apt-get, aptitude, dpkg, dpkg-reconfigure, grub-install, LD_LIBRARY_PATH, ldconfig, ldd, MBR, mount points, partitions, rpm, rpm2cpio, superblock, swap space, yum, and yumdownloader.

Here are the top ten items to know as you study for this domain:

>> The ldd command is used to see what shared libraries a program depends on.

>> The ldconfig command is used to update and maintain the cache of shared library data. You can see the current cache by using the command ldconfig -p.

>> Popular package managers include Red Hat's Package Manager (rpm) and Debian's (dpkg). The purpose of both is to simplify working with software.

>> Options available with rpm include -i (for installing packages), -e (for removing packages), -q (for querying what packages belong to what files), -b (for building a package), and -p (to print/display information).

>> With dpkg, you use the dselect command to use the graphical interface. You can also use command-line options that include -i (to install packages), -1 (to list information about the package), -r (to remove the package), and -c (to list all files in the package).

>> The Advanced Packaging Tool (apt) was designed as a front end for dpkg but now works with both .deb and .rpm packages.

>> Yum (Yellow dog Updater, Modified) can be used at the command line to download rpm packages.

>> The superblock contains information about the type of file system, the size, the status, and metadata information.

>> The GRUB (an acronym for GNU's Grand Unified Bootloader) bootloader allows multiple operating systems to exist on the same machine and let a user to choose which one he or she wants to boot on startup. The latest version is GRUB 2.

>> Linux uses both a swap partition and a swap file for swap space. The swapon command can be used to toggle designated swap space on and off. Areas for swap space can be created with mkswap.

GNU and Unix Commands

Table 2-4 shows the subtopics, weights, descriptions, and key knowledge areas for this topic.

TABLE 2-4   **Breakout of Domain 103**

Subtopic	Weight	Description	Key Areas
Work on the command line	4	Interacting with shells and commands, using the command line and the bash shell	Use single shell commands and one-line command sequences, modify the shell environment and use/edit command history, and invoke commands inside and outside the defined path.
Process text streams using filters	3	Applying filters to text streams	Send text files and output streams through text utility filters.
Perform basic file management	4	Using the basic Linux commands to manage files and directories	Copy, move, and delete files and directories individually and recursively.
Use streams, pipes, and redirects	4	Redirecting streams and connecting them, including standard output, standard input, and standard error	Pipe the output of one command to the input of another, and send output to both stdout and a file.
Create, monitor, and kill processes	4	Performing basic process management	Run jobs in the foreground and background, send signals to processes, monitor active processes, and select and sort processes for display.
Modify process execution priorities	2	Managing process execution priorities	Run programs with higher and lower priorities than the default, and change the priority of a running process.
Search text files using regular expressions	2	Understanding regular expressions and how to use them	Create simple regular expressions and perform searches through the file system and/or through files.
Perform basic file editing operations using vi	3	Understanding vi navigation, editing, copying, deleting, and so on	Use basic vi modes to insert, edit, copy, delete, and find text.

To adequately address these topics, focus on the following files, terms, and utilities: &, ., bash, bg, bzip2, cat, cp, cpio, cut, dd, echo, egrep, env, exec, expand, export, fg, fgrep, **file, file globbing,** find, fmt, free, grep, gunzip, gzip, **head, history, jobs,** join, kill, killall, ls, man, mkdir, mv, nice, nl, nohup, od, paste, pr, ps, pwd, regex(7), renice, rm, rmdir, sed, set, sort, split, tail, tar, tee, top, touch, tr, uname, unexpand, uniq, unset, uptime, vi, wc, and xargs.

Here are the top ten items to know as you study for this domain:

>> When run, every command spans at least one process, and processes can be viewed with ps or top (which continues to update the display dynamically).

>> Jobs can run in the foreground or background and can be moved between the two. Jobs running in the foreground can be suspended by pressing Ctrl+Z.

>> Files can be copied by using cp or moved by using mv. Files can be deleted with rm, and directories (which are created with mkdir) can be removed with rmdir. Recursive deletion can be done with rm -r.

>> To change directories, use the cd command. When used without parameters, this command moves you to your home directory. To see what directory you're working in, use the pwd (present working directory) command.

>> The ls command has a plethora of options that allow you to list files. The -a option lists all files (including hidden files).

>> The cut command can pull fields from a file, and the fields can be combined by using either paste or join. The latter offers more features than the former and can be used with conditions.

>> The wc command can count the number of lines, words, and characters in a file.

>> The grep utility (and its counterparts egrep and fgrep) can be used to find matches for strings within files.

>> The find command can be used to search the system for files/directories that meet any number of criteria. When these entities are found, the xargs command can be used to look deeper within them for other values (such as in conjunction with grep).

>> It's possible to convert data from one value to another by using utilities. The most popular utilities include tr (translate) and sed (the stream editor).

Devices, Linux File Systems, Filesystem Hierarchy Standard

Table 2-5 shows the subtopics, weights, descriptions, and key knowledge areas for this topic.

TABLE 2-5

Breakout of Domain 104

Subtopic	Weight	Description	Key Areas
Create partitions and file systems	2	Configuring disk partitions	Use various mkfs commands to set up partitions and create file systems, and manage MBR partition tables.
Maintain the integrity of file systems	2	Maintaining a standard file system and the extra data associated with journaling	Know file system monitoring, integrity, and repair, and monitor free space and inodes.
Control mounting and unmounting of file systems	3	Configuring the mounting of file systems	Manually mount and unmount and configure removable file systems, and configure file system mounting on bootup.
Manage disk quotas	1	Managing user quotas	Configure quotas, and generate, edit, and check reports.
Manage file permissions and ownership	3	Controlling file access with permissions and ownership	Change the file-creation mask, work with special files, and use the group field to grant file access to group members.
Create and change hard and symbolic links	2	Managing links to a file	Use links to support system administration and be able to differentiate between copying and linking files.
Find system files and place files in the correct location	2	Appreciating the Filesystem Hierarchy Standard (FHS)	Understand the correct location of files and the purpose of important directories.

To adequately address these topics, focus on the following files, terms, and utilities: /etc/fstab, /etc/updated.conf, /media, chgrp, chmod, chown, debugfs, df, du, dump32fs, e2fsck, edquota, ext2/ext3/ext4, find, fsck, ln, locate, mke2fs, mkfs, mkswap, mount, quota, quotaon, reiserfs v3, repquota, tune2fs, type, umask, umount, updated, vfat, whereis, which, xfs, and xfs tools.

Here are the top ten items to know as you study for this domain:

>> File and directory permissions can be changed with the chmod command (which accepts numeric and symbolic values).

>> The owner of a group can be changed with the chown command, whereas the chgrp command allows changing the group associated with a file.

>> The du command can show how much of a disk is used.

>> The df command shows how much of a disk is free.

- The main tool for troubleshooting disk issues is fsck, which can check file system structure, including inodes.

- To mount file systems, use the mount command, and to unmount them, use umount. To have mounting occur automatically at startup, add the entries to /etc/fstab.

- Quotas can restrict the amount of space users or groups can use on the disk. Quotas are initialized with the quota command, and they're toggled on and off with quotaon and quotaoff. Quotas can be changed with edquota, and reports can be generated with repquota.

- When files are created, the default permissions are equal to 666 minus any umask values. The default permissions for directories is equal to 777 minus any umask values.

- The mke2fs utility can be used to make the file system.

- Linux supports numerous file systems, including ext2, ext3, ext4, and reiserfs.

Shells, Scripting, and Data Management

Table 2-6 shows the subtopics, weights, descriptions, and key knowledge areas for this topic — the first of the 104 exam.

TABLE 2-6   **Breakout of Domain 105**

Subtopic	Weight	Description	Key Areas
Customize and use the shell environment	4	Modifying global and user profiles	Set environment variables and work within bash, set the command search path, and maintain skeleton directories for new user accounts.
Customize or write simple scripts	4	Customizing existing bash scripts and writing new ones	Be able to write code that includes loops and tests as well as command substitution and conditional mailing.
SQL data management	2	Querying databases and manipulating data with SQL	Know basic SQL commands and perform basic data manipulation.

To adequately address these topics, focus on the following files, terms, and utilities: /etc/profile, ~/.bash_login, ~/.bash_logout, ~/.bash_profile, ~/.bashrc, ~/.profile, alias, delete, env, export, for, from, function, group by, if, insert, join, lists, order by, read, select, seq, set, test, unset, update, where, and while.

Here are the top ten items to know as you study for this domain:

» Logic can be added to scripts by testing conditions with test or [. Commands can execute using by if-then-fi deviations or through looping (while, until, or for). You can leave a script with the exit command or leave a loop with break.

» Variables can be given at the command line and referenced as $1, $2, and so on, or entered into the executing file with the read command.

» The alias command can be used to create an alias for a command to operate by another name (such as being able to type dir and have ls -l performed).

» Environmental variables can be viewed with the env command.

» Variables can be added to the environment by using the set command and export; they're removed by using unset.

» The /etc/profile configuration file is executed whenever a user logs in.

» For those using the bash shell, the shell first looks for .bash_profile; if it doesn't find that profile, it looks for .bash_login.

» When the bash user logs out, the shell looks for .bash_logout and executes any commands found there.

» Whereas other configuration files run only when the user logs in or out, the .bashrc file can execute each time a shell is run.

» Shell scripts must have executable permissions to run or must be called by a shell (as in sh script). The normal exit status of any script or application is 0; anything else signifies a non-normal exit.

User Interfaces and Desktops

Table 2-7 shows the subtopics, weights, descriptions, and key knowledge areas for this topic.

To adequately address these topics, focus on the following files, terms, and utilities: /etc/initab, /etc/x11/xorg.conf, braille display, DISPLAY, emacspeak, gdm configuration files, gestures, GOK, high contrast desktop themes, kdm configuration files, large screen desktop themes, mouse keys, on-screen reader, orca, screen magnifier, screen reader, slow/bounce/toggle keys, sticky/repeat keys, X, xdm configuration files, xdpyinfo, xhost, and xwininfo.

TABLE 2-7   **Breakout of Domain 106**

Subtopic	Weight	Description	Key Areas
Install and configure X11	2	Installing and configuring X11	Have a basic understanding of X Window configuration as well as the X font server.
Set up a display manager	2	Setting up and customizing a display manager	Work with XDM (X Display Manager), GDM (Gnome Display Manager), and KDM (KDE Display Manager), and be able to do basic configuration of LightDM.
Accessibility	1	Knowing and being aware of accessibility technologies	Understand assistive technology (AT) and keyboard settings (such as those possible with AccessX). The topics also include visual settings and themes.

Here are the top ten items to know as you study for this domain:

>> The emacspeak speech interface is one of the most popular speech interfaces available for Linux.

>> The xdpyinfo utility can be used to view information about an X server. It can be used with the all option to see information about all the extensions supported by the server.

>> Window information for X can be viewed with the xwininfo utility. Using the –all option shows all the possible information.

>> The server access-control program for X is xhost. This program is used to connect to a host across the network and work within the graphical interface.

>> The X Display Manager (xdm) is the default display manager included with the X Window System.

>> The /etc/x11/xorg.conf file is the X configuration file used for initial setup.

>> Several AT projects have been developed for both KDE (KDE Accessibility Project) and GNOME (GNOME Accessibility Projects).

>> Orca is a screen reader from the GNOME project intended to help people who are blind or impaired. Orca works with Mozilla Firefox, Thunderbird, OpenOffice.org/LibreOffice, and other applications.

>> The GNOME onscreen keyboard reader (GOK) is another assistive technology that works with XML files and can dynamically create keyboards to adapt to a user's needs.

>> *Slow keys* can be configured for a keyboard preference to accept input only if a key is held, which prevents accidental presses from counting as input. *Bounce keys* can be configured to ignore fast duplicate key presses; *sticky keys* can be used to simulate simultaneous key presses.

Administrative Tasks

Table 2-8 shows the subtopics, weights, descriptions, and key knowledge areas for this topic.

TABLE 2-8 **Breakout of Domain 107**

Subtopic	Weight	Description	Key Areas
Manage user and group accounts and related system files	5	Adding, removing, suspending, and changing user accounts	Work with user and group accounts, including those created for special purposes and limited accounts.
Automate system administration tasks by scheduling jobs	4	Using cron and anacron	Run jobs at regular intervals and at specific times by using cron and anacon.
Localization and internationalization	3	Localizing a system in a language other than English as well as time zone settings, local settings, and environment variables.	Understand why LANG=C is useful in scripts, and know how to configure local settings and environment variables.

To adequately address these topics, focus on the following files, terms, and utilities: /etc/at.allow, /etc/at.deny, /etc/cron, /etc/cron.allow, /etc/cron.deny, /etc/crontab, /etc/group, /etc/localtime, /etc/passwd, /etc/shadow, /etc/skel, /etc/timezone, /usr/bin/locale, /usr/share/zoneinfo, /var/spool/cron/*, ASCII, at, atq, atrm, chage, crontab, date, **environment variables**, groupadd, groupdel, groupmod, iconv, ISO-8859, passwd, tzconfig, tzselect, Unicode, useradd, userdel, usermod, and UTF-8.

Here are the top ten items to know as you study for this domain:

>> Users can be added by manually editing the configuration files or by using the useradd command (and users can be removed with userdel).

>> The groupadd utility can be used to create groups, and groupdel can be used to remove groups. Groups can be modified with groupmod, and users can be moved from one group to another with the newgrp command.

>> To schedule a job to run only once in unattended mode, you can use the at command.

>> Scheduled jobs can be viewed with the atq command and deleted before execution with atrm.

» Restrictions can be placed on who can use the at service (atd) by creating an at.allow file and placing only valid usernames below it.

» You can create an at.deny file — instead of at.allow — and place in it the names of users who can't use that at service (meaning that everyone not listed there can still use it).

» If you need to schedule an unattended job to run at any sort of regular interval, you can create a crontab (cron table) entry for it.

» crontab files are read by the cron daemon, which looks every minute to see whether any jobs need to run.

» Restrictions can be placed on who can use cron by creating a cron.allow or a cron.deny file.

» There are six fields to each entry in the cron tables: the minute the job is to run (0 to 59), the hour the job is to run (0 to 23), the day of the month (1 to 31), the month of the year (1 to 12), the day of the week (0 to 6), and the path to the executable that is to run.

Essential System Services

Table 2-9 shows the subtopics, weights, descriptions, and key knowledge areas for this topic.

TABLE 2-9   **Breakout of Domain 108**

Subtopic	Weight	Description	Key Areas
Maintain system time	3	Properly maintaining the system time and synchronizing the clock	Using NTP configuration and the pool.ntp.org service.
System logging	2	Configuring the syslog daemon	Configure the logging daemon (syslog) to send log output to a server, work with logrotate, and know about rsyslog and syslog-ng.
Mail Transfer Agent (MTA) basics	3	Using commonly available MTA programs	Be able to perform basic forward and alias configuration on a host.
Manage printers and printing	2	Managing print queues and user print jobs	Use both CUPS and legacy LPD.

To adequately address these topics, focus on the following files, terms, and utilities: /etc/cups, /etc/localtime, /etc/ntp.conf, /etc/timezone, /usr/share/zoneinfo, ~/.forward, CUPS config files/tools/utils, date, exim, hwclock, klogd, logger, lpd legacy interface (lpr, lprm, lpq), mail, mailq, newaliases, ntpd, ntpdate, pool.ntp.org, postfix, qmail, sendmail, syslog.conf, and syslogd.

Here are the top ten items to know as you study for this domain:

>> The Network Time Protocol (NTP) daemon (ntpd) maintains the time on all servers using NTP.

>> The hwclock command can be used to display the date and time of a system's hardware clock (also known as the *real-time clock*).

>> The time zone is configured in the /etc/timezone file. Local time is likewise configured in /etc/localtime.

>> The sendmail service is a general-purpose SMTP program used for sending e-mail between servers.

>> The mailq command shows a list of messages in the mail queue and works sendmail.

>> The newaliases command builds a database for the mail aliases file.

>> Mail can be forwarded from one e-mail address to another by using a .forward file.

>> Line printers are rarely used anymore, but support for them remains. The primary utilities associated with them were/are as follows: lpr (to submit a print job), lpq (to see the print queue), and lprm (to remove queued print jobs).

>> The Common Unix Printing System (CUPS) is the most common printing interface used on Linux today. It provides support for the line-printer daemon as well as for Server Message Block (SMB).

>> The kernel logging daemon (klogd) logs Linux kernel messages.

Networking Fundamentals

Table 2-10 shows the subtopics, weights, descriptions, and key knowledge areas for this topic.

TABLE 2-10   **Breakout of Domain 109**

Subtopic	Weight	Description	Key Areas
Fundamentals of Internet protocols	4	Demonstrating proper understanding of TCP/IP	Know networking fundamentals and be able to identify common TCP and UDP ports.
Basic network configuration	4	Viewing, changing, and verifying configuration settings on clients and hosts	Manually and automatically configure network interfaces and set a default route.
Basic network troubleshooting	4	Troubleshooting networking issues on clients and hosts	Debug problems associated with the network configuration.
Configure client-side DNS (Domain Name Service)	2	Configuring DNS on a client/host	Modify the order in which name resolution is done, query remote servers, and configure DNS.

To adequately address these topics, focus on the following files, terms, and utilities: /etc/hostname, /etc/hosts, /etc/nsswitch.conf, /etc/resolv.conf, /etc/services, dig, ftp, host, hostname, ifconfig, ifdown, ifup, netstat, ping, route, telnet, tracepath, and traceroute.

Here are the top ten items to know as you study for this domain:

>> IPv4 uses 32-bit addresses divided into four octets. The first octet identifies the class of address (A, B, C). The address can be public or private.

>> The ifconfig utility can be used to see the current Internet Protocol (IP) configuration of the network cards.

>> The ping utility is an all-purpose tool for testing connectivity. It sends echo messages to a specified host to see whether it can be reached. ping can be used with the loopback address (127.0.0.1) to test internal configuration.

>> Instead of using ping, you can use traceroute to see the route taken to reach a particular host.

>> The route utility displays the routing table and allows you to configure it.

>> The netstat utility shows the current status of ports — those that are open, those that are listening, and so on.

>> The name of the network host is configured in /etc/hostname and can be viewed with the hostname command.

>> You can remotely log in to another host with telnet, but it's highly recommended that this utility no longer be used due to very weak security.

>> FTP servers can be used to transfer files from one host to another.

>> DNS is used for resolving names to addresses. Utilities that can be used in conjunction with it include dig (for DNS lookup).

Security

Table 2-11 shows the subtopics, weights, descriptions, and key knowledge areas for this topic.

TABLE 2-11   **Breakout of Domain 110**

Subtopic	Weight	Description	Key Areas
Perform security administration tasks	3	Reviewing system configuration to ensure host security	Understand local security policies as well as how to discover open ports on a system.
Set up host security	3	Knowing how to set up a basic level of host security	Understand TCP wrappers and shadow passwords.
Securing data with encryption	3	Understanding key techniques that secure data	Know how to use OpenSSh 2 and GnuPG.

To adequately address these topics, focus on the following files, terms, and utilities: /etc/hosts.allow, /etc/hosts.deny, /etc/inetd.conf, /etc/inetd.d/*, /etc/init.d/*, /etc/inittab, /etc/nologin, /etc/passwd, /etc/shadow, /etc/ssh/ssh_host_dsa_key, /etc/ssh/ssh_host_rsa_key, /etc/ssh_known_hosts, /etc/sudoers, /etc/xinetd.conf, /etc/xinetd.d/*, ~/.gnupg/*, ~/.ssh/authorized_keys, ~/.ssh/id_dsa, ~/.ssh/id_rsa, chage, find, gpg, id_dsa.pub, id_rsa.pub, lsof, netstat, nmap, passwd, ssh, ssh_host_dsa_key.pub, ssh_host_rsa_key.pub, ssh-add, ssh-agent, ssh-keygen, su, sudo, ulimit, and usermod.

Here are the top ten items to know as you study for this domain:

>> Adding 1000 to standard permissions turns on the sticky bit, whereas 2000 turns on the SGID permission, and 4000 turns on the SUID permission.

>> Links are created with the ln command. A *hard link* is nothing more than an alias to a file (sharing the same inode). A symbolic link is created with ln -s and is an actual file with its own inode. The symbolic link contains a pointer to the original file and can span file systems (whereas the hard link can't).

» Passwords are changed with the passwd command. Older systems stored passwords in /etc/passwd, but passwords are now in /etc/shadow, where they're more secure.

» To see who logged on most recently and may still be logged on, you can use the last command.

» The su command allows you to become another user (returning with exit). If no other username is specified, the root user is implied — hence, su for *superuser*.

» To run a command as another user (usually, root) rather than become that user, use sudo instead of su.

» The who command shows who is logged on; the w command shows information combining who with uptime.

» You can limit which hosts can remotely connect by using either a hosts. allow file (only those hosts specifically listed can connect) or a hosts.deny file (only those hosts specifically listed can't connect).

» The ulimit utility can show the limit on the number of open files allowed in Linux. You can change that value by using this same command.

» The usermod command changes attributes for a user and modifies the user account.

Chapter **3**

Other Linux
Certifications

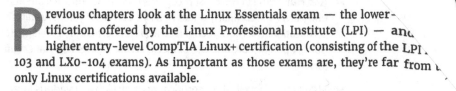

P revious chapters look at the Linux Essentials exam — the lower-~~
tification offered by the Linux Professional Institute (LPI) — an~
higher entry-level CompTIA Linux+ certification (consisting of the LPI ~
103 and LX0-104 exams). As important as those exams are, they're far from ~
only Linux certifications available.

In this chapter, I look first at other vendor-neutral certifications and then at some
of the most popular vendor-specific Linux certifications.

Vendor-Neutral Certifications

Just as the CompTIA Linux+ Powered by LPI certification is a great entry-
level authentication of basic knowledge, so are most other certifications from
CompTIA. The only operating-system-specific one that CompTIA offers is Linux+,
but it also offers such certifications as A+ (hardware), Network+ (computer
networking), and Security+ (host and client security). All these certifications are
well recognized and represented in the market and are good choices to add to a
résumé.

...so offers certifications above the LPIC-1 level. LPIC-2, which requires passing another two exams (referenced as 201 and 202: exam codes 201-450 and 202-..., respectively), focuses on such advanced topics as network configuration, file storage, troubleshooting, and system security. LPIC-3 is for senior-level administrators and allows you to specialize in a particular area of focus after you attain the LPIC-2 certification. Each exam you choose to take homes in on a specific area of expertise, such as virtualization and high availability or security.

Some other vendor-neutral Linux certifications once existed and were popular, but most of them have now fallen by the wayside (are no longer offered or no longer kept current). Although those certifications may have value for those who currently hold them, they should be avoided by those who are currently looking to have a third party authenticate their knowledge and skills.

ndor-Specific Certifications

Several vendors offer certifications that authenticate specialization in their specific distributions of Linux. Following are three of those vendors and their most popular certifications:

>> **Red Hat:** Some of the most recognized certifications are from Red Hat. At the entry level, the company offers Red Hat Certified System Administrator (RHCSA) certification. The more recognized Red Hat Certified Engineer (RHCE) certification builds upon RHCSA, and the pinnacle certification is Red Hat Certified Architect (RHCA).

>> **SUSE:** From Novell, SUSE certification is available at various levels: SUSE Certified Administrator (SCA), SUSE Certified Engineer (SCE), and SUSE Enterprise Architect (SEA). Both SCA and SCE are available in several tracks: Enterprise Linux, OpenStack Cloud, Enterprise Storage, and Systems Management. To become SEA-certified, you must have two of the SCE certifications, three SCA certifications, and one certification from any other track.

>> **Oracle:** Oracle, the company that acquired Sun Microsystems and its rich history of Linux, offers both Oracle Certified Associate (OCA) and Oracle Certified Professional (OCP) certifications.

Index

Special Characters

– (hyphen), 113–114

! (exclamation point) command

  FTP command, 225

  repeating commands, 92

(pound sign; hash mark)

  comments, 192, 237, 253

  HTML anchors, 207, 209

* (asterisk), 90–91

. (single dot), 111

. . (dot-dot), 111

; (semicolon), 86

? (question mark)

  displaying list of commands, 225

  HTML queries, 209

  wildcard, 90–91, 102

[ ] (brackets), 90–91

\ (backslash), 86

{ } (curly braces), 237

| (pipe feature), 100–101

~ (tilde character), 111

" " (quotation marks), 62, 85, 91, 433

A

absolute paths, 483

acpid service, 243

ad hoc mode, 183

ADSL (asymmetric DSL), 157

Advanced Encryption Standard (AES), 184

Advanced Packaging Tool (APT), 52–54, 124, 493

alias command, 93, 440, 498

apache service, 243

Apache Software Foundation, 481

Apache Web Server, security vulnerabilities, 418

apache2 server, 240, 243

apmd service, 243

append command, 225

application gateway, 375

Application layer (of TCP/IP), 168

application-proxy gateway firewall, 404–405

apropos command, 93

APT (Advanced Packaging Tool), 52–54, 124, 493

apt–get package installer, 12, 52

ARPANET, 169, 260

ascii command, 225

Aspell application, 124

asterisk (*), 90–91

asymmetric DSL (ADSL), 157

AT Attachment (ATA), 32

at commands, 310–312, 500

atd daemon program, 243, 310

audio players, 129, 131

authentication

  defined, 375

  GNU Privacy Guard, 389–396

  PAMs, 383–384

  RADIUS servers, 184

  security vulnerabilities, 418

autoconf package, 17

autofs service, 243

automake package, 17

automated backups, 347–348

awk language, 446–450

B

backdoor, defined, 375

backing up and restoring files

  commercial utilities, 343

  overview, 341

  before partitioning, 33

  selecting strategy and media, 342

  tape archiver

backing up and restoring files *(continued)*
   automated backups, 347–348
   incremental backups, 347
   multivolume archive, 345–346
   overview, 343
   single-volume archive, 343–345
   tapes, 346
backslash (\), 86
Bandwidth Place, 164
bash shell. *See also names of specific commands*
  built-in commands, 439–441
  changing default shell, 84
  commands
   arguments, 62, 85–86
   automatic command completion, 89
   backslash character, 86
   for checking disk-space use, 120–121
   combining, 86–87
   concatenating with semicolons, 86
   for date and time display, 96, 99
   for directory listings and permissions, 112–114
   for directory management, 93, 117
   for file archiving and compression, 95
   for file management, 93, 116–117
   for file processing, 94–95, 100–102
   for file system management, 96
   for file system navigation, 110–111
   for finding abbreviations, 93
   for finding files, 93–94, 118–119
   for finding help, 93
   format and syntax for, 62, 85
   I/O redirection, 87–89
   for mounting and unmounting drives, 119–120
   for process management, 95, 97–98, 101
   repeating previously typed commands, 91–92
   for user management, 96–97, 114–116
   wildcards, 90–91
  controlling flow of execution, 435–438
  defined, 17, 61
  defining variables, 434–435
  general discussion, 60–61
  opening terminal window, 61, 83–84

  opening virtual consoles, 84
  shell scripts, 62, 102–104
bastion host, 375
batch files, 102
bc calculator, 17
bg command, 95, 440
/bin directory, 107, 334
/bin subdirectory, 109
binary command, 225
BIND DNS, 262–263, 267–268, 418
Binutils package, 17
bison parser-generator tool, 474
bit bucket (/dev/null), 89
black-box testing, 424
block devices, 306
BogoMIPS metric, 58, 60
/boot directory
  defined, 107, 334
  /grub file, 294
  /grub/menu.1st file, 294, 420
  /System.map file, 294
  /vmlinuz file, 294
bootloaders, defined, 57
boot messages, 58
bounce keys, 499
brackets ([ ]), 90–91
break command, 440, 468
broadband over power lines (BPL), 155
BRU utility, 343
bt command, 468
buffer overflow, 375
bye command, 225

C

C shell, 84
CA (certificate authority), 376
CA ARCserve Backup for Linux utility, 343
cable modem connections
  compared to DSL, 156
  connection diagram and notes, 164–166
  data-transfer speeds, 163–164

defined, 155

general discussion, 154

overview of function, 162–163

caching name server

defined, 267

/etc/named.conf file, 268–270

localhost.zone file, 276

reverse-mapping zone, 277

root zone file, 274–276

RR formats, 271–274

starting, 277

testing, 277–278

zone-file formats, 270–271

cal command, 96, 99

Calc program, 124, 126–127

calculators, 124, 128–129

calendar applications, 128

Canonical, 73

canonical names, 266

Carrier-Sense Multiple Access/Collision Detection (CSMA/CD), 173

cat command, 86, 89, 94, 102–103, 303

cd command

defined, 93, 440

FTP, 225

navigating directories with, 111–112, 483, 495

writing shell scripts, 102–103

CD/DVD drives

block devices, 306

burning discs, 129, 132–133

configuration and management of, 24, 51

file system, 106

system requirements, 31–32

cdrdao program, 132–133

cdrecord program, 132

CD-ROM drives, 106, 306

central processing unit. *See* CPU

certificate authority (CA), 376

certificates, defined, 376

certification. *See* Linux certification

chage command, 379

chains (iptables command), 408–410

character devices, 306–307

check digit, 446

chgrp command, 329, 385

chkconfig command, 293

chmod command, 93, 103–104, 114–115, 225, 385, 486, 496

chown command, 93, 116, 329, 496

chsh command, 84, 96

Cinnamon variation of GNOME, 73–74

clear command, 468

Click-N-Run web-based interface, 12

Clipboard manager (Klipper), 76

close command, 225

command command, 440

command line, defined, 62

COMMAND.COM command interpreter, 84

commercial backup utilities, 343

Common Unix Printing System (CUPS), 502

Common Vulnerabilities and Exposures (CVE), 417

compilers

defined, 452

GCC, 21, 454–458

compress command, 95

CompTIA A+ certification, 507

CompTIA Linux+ exams

LX0-103, 490–497

LX0-104, 497–505

overview, 489–490

CompTIA Network+ certification, 507

CompTIA Security+ certification, 507

computer security

application gateway, 375

audits

common vulnerabilities, 417–418

host-security review, 418–422

methodology, 416–424

network-security review, 422–424

nontechnical aspects of, 414–415

overview, 413–414, 416–417

security testing tools, 425–427

technical aspects of, 415

vulnerability testing types, 424

computer security *(continued)*

  authentication, 375

  backdoor, 375

  bastion host, 375

  buffer overflow, 375

  certificate authority, 376

  certificates, 376

  chage tool, 379

  confidentiality, 376

  cracker, 376

  DDoS, 376

  decryption, 376

  digital signature, 376

  DMZ, 376

  DoS, 376

  dual-homed host, 376

  encryption, 376

  exploit tools, 376

  find tool, 379

  firewall, 376

  hash, 376

  host, 377

  integrity, 377

  IP spoofing, 377

  IPSec, 377

  logic bombs, 377

  lsof tool, 379

  netstat tool, 379

  nmap tool, 379

  nonrepudiation, 377

  packet, 377

  packet filtering, 377

  packet sniffers, 200, 378, 425

  passwd tool, 379

  perimeter network, 377

  PKI, 377

  port scanning, 377

  proxy server, 377

  public key cryptography, 377

  screening router, 378

  setuid program, 378

  spyware, 378

  su tool, 379

  sudo tool, 379

  symmetric key encryption, 378

  threat, 378

  Trojan horse, 378

  ulimit tool, 379

  usermod tool, 379

  virus, 378

  vulnerabilities, 378

  war-dialing, 378

  war-driving, 378

  worm, 378

concatenation

  of command options, 114

  of commands, 86

Concurrent Versions System (CVS), 21, 454

conditional expressions, 450

confidentiality, 376

configuration files

  /etc/fstab file, 338

  mail servers, 246–254

  TCP/IP networks, 191–195

continue command, 440, 468

Coreutils package, 17

cp command, 90–91, 93, 116

cpio command, 17, 95

CPU (central processing unit)

  defined, 9, 23

  system requirements, 32

  viewing top processes, 297–298

crackers, defined, 376

cron jobs, 313–315, 347

cron service, 243

crond service, 243

crontab command, 312–315, 347, 501

CSMA/CD (Carrier-Sense Multiple Access/Collision Detection), 173

CUPS (Common Unix Printing System), 502

curly braces ({ }), 237

cut command, 94, 484, 495

CVE (Common Vulnerabilities and Exposures), 417

CVS (Concurrent Versions System), 21, 418, 454

Cyber Alert System (US-CERT), 380

D

DATA command, 247

date command, 96, 99

dd command, 94

DDoS (distributed denial of service) attacks, 366, 369, 376

DEB files (Debian package files), 51–52

Debian
  automatically starting servers, 293
  configuring network at boot, 201
  DEB files, 51–52
  file sharing with NFS, 339
  installing missing applications, 124
  installing Samba, 359
  installing software, 52–54
  Internet super server, 236
  mounting CD-ROM, 338
  needed information before installing, 30
  releases of, 14
  run levels, 289
  starting NFS server, 356
  starting servers automatically at boot, 241–242
  text mode installation, 40
  turning off stand-alone servers, 397

debuggers
  defined, 452
  GNU debugger, 17, 21, 466–472

DEC (Digital Equipment Corporation), 174

declare command, 440

decryption, 376, 395–396

delete command, 225

delete through newline (dnl) macro, 248–249

dependencies, 55

depmod command, 308

derived work, 474

DES encryption, 325

/dev directory, 107, 334

device drivers, defined, 305

device files
  block devices, 306
  character devices, 306–307
  network devices, 307

overview, 305–306
  udev program, 307

/dev/null (bit bucket), 89

df command, 96, 120–121, 496

DHCP (Dynamic Host Configuration Protocol), 170, 178, 234

dial-up Internet connections, 154, 156

diff command, 17, 94

dig (Domain Internet Groper) utility, 264–265

digiKam application, 130–131

Digital Equipment Corporation (DEC), 174

digital signatures, 376

Digital Subscriber Line. *See* DSL

digital-camera tools, 129

dir command, 225

directories. *See also* files and directories
  cd command, 483
  current, 110
  defined, 105
  home, 110
  pwd command, 483
  referring to name of, 111
  standard directories, 334
  top level, 107–108

dirs command, 440

disconnect command, 225

disk performance and usage, 300–302

display adapters (video cards), 33

DISPLAY environmental variable, 328

distributed denial of service (DDoS) attacks, 366, 369, 376

DistroWatch.com, 11

dmesg command, 58

DMZ, 376

dnl (delete through newline) macro, 248–249

DNS (Domain Name System)
  BIND system, 262–263, 267–268, 418
  configuring
    caching name server, 267–278
    primary name server, 278–280
    resolver, 266–267
  defined, 170, 234, 259

DNS (Domain Name System) *(continued)*
  function of, 259–260
  hierarchical domain names, 261–262
  name servers, 260–264
  port number, 234
  resolver library, 264
  utility programs, 264–266
Domain Internet Groper (dig) utility, 264–265
DoS, 376
DOS disk partition, mounting, 348–351
DOS floppy disks, 349–350
dot-dot (. .), 111
dotted-decimal (dotted-quad) notation, 170
Draw program, 124
drive administration and management, 23–24
driver modules, 308–309
DSL (Digital Subscriber Line)
  compared to cable, 156
  connection diagram and notes, 159–161
  data-transfer speeds, 158
  defined, 155
  general discussion, 154
  overview of function, 156–157
  selecting providers and plans, 158–159
  variations of, 157–158
du command, 96, 120–121, 301–302, 496
dual-homed host, 376
DVD/CD drives
  block devices, 306
  burning discs, 129, 132–133
  configuration and management of, 24, 51
  file system, 106
  system requirements, 31–32
Dynamic Host Configuration Protocol (DHCP), 170, 178, 234
dynamic linking, 474

E

echo command, 440
ed text editor
  commands, 143–144

defined, 17, 140
deleting text, 142
editing text, 141
modes, 141
navigating within, 142
replacing text, 143
saving changes, 143
edit-compile-debug cycle, 452
emacs editor, 16, 17, 21
emacspeak speech interface, 499
email
  as Internet service, 20, 154
  mail servers
    configuration file, 246–254
    delivery mechanism, 247
    delivery testing, 246–247
    file contents, 254–257
    installing, 245
enable command, 440
encryption, 185–188, 325, 376, 395–396
end of file (EOF) marker, 346
environment variables (users), 326–328
Epiphany web browser, 210
ESSIDs (SSIDs), 185, 188
/etc directory
  /aliases file, 257
  /apache2/ httpd.conf file, 294
  /apt/ sources.list file, 294
  /at.allow file, 294
  /at.deny file, 294
  /bash.bashrc file, 294
  /bashrc file, 294
  /cron.allow file, 313, 420
  /cron.deny file, 313, 420
  /crontab file, 420
  /cups/cupsd.conf file, 294
  defined, 107, 334
  /exports file, 355, 356
  /fonts file, 295
  /fstab file, 295, 337–339
  /group file, 295, 324, 421
  /grub.conf file, 295

/host.conf file, 192–193, 264, 266

/hosts file, 192, 295

/hosts.allow file, 192, 194, 295, 398–399, 411, 420

/hosts.deny file, 192, 195, 295, 411, 420

/httpd/conf/httpd.conf file, 295

/inetd.conf file, 411

/init.d file, 295

/init.d/* file, 411

/init.d/rcS file, 295

/inittab file, 288–291, 295, 411

/issue file, 295

/lilo.conf file, 295

/login.defs file, 295

/logrotate.conf file, 420

/mail/access file, 255

/mail/access.db file, 255

/mail/certs file, 256

/mail/helpfile file, 253, 255

/mail/local-host-names file, 255

/mail/mailertable file, 255

/mail/relay-domains file, 255

/mail/sendmail.cf file, 246–254

/mail/trusted-users file, 255

/mail/userdb.db file, 255

/mail/virtusertable file, 255

/modprobe.conf file, 295, 309

/modules.conf file, 295

/mtab file, 295

/named.conf file, 268–270

/networks file, 192–193

/nologin file, 411

/nsswitch.conf file, 192, 195

/pam.d file, 420

/passwd file, 295, 323, 324, 411, 420, 421

/profile file, 295

/profile.d file, 295

/rc.d file, 420

/rc.d/rc.sysinit file, 295

/resolv.conf file, 192–194, 264, 266

/samba/smb.conf file, 358, 360

/samba/smbusers, 358

/securetty file, 420

/security file, 420

/services file, 235

/shadow file, 296, 383, 411, 420, 421

/shells file, 296

/shutdown.allow file, 420

/skel file, 296

/ssh file, 420

/ssh/ssh_config component, 400

/ssh/sshd_config component, 400

/sysconfig file, 296, 420

/sysctl.conf file, 296, 420

/syslog.conf file, 420

/termcap file, 296

/udev file, 296

/udev/udev.conf file, 420

/vsftpd file, 420

/vsftpd.ftpusers file, 420

/X11 file, 296

/X11/xorg.conf file, 296

/xinetd.conf file, 296, 411, 420

/xinetd.d file, 411, 421

/yum.conf file, 296

Ethernet. *See also* networking and Internet connections

  advantages of, 172–173

  cables, 174–175

  connection diagram and notes, 175–176

  origin of, 174

  overview of function, 173

eval command, 440

Evolution mail client, 247

exchanging keys (GPG), 393–394

exclamation point (!) command

  FTP command, 225

  repeating commands, 92

exec command, 440

executable files, 103, 114, 388, 453

exim service, 245

exit command, 440

expand command, 94

exploit tools, 376

export command, 440

expressions
  conditional, 450
  defined, 453
  regular, 483

Ext3 file system, 309

external hard drive, as backup media, 342

F

fc command, 440

fdformat command, 96

fdisk command, 96

Fedora
  automatically starting servers, 293
  configuring network at boot, 201
  configuring Samba, 359
  /etc/fstab file, 339
  file sharing with NFS, 339
  installing software, 54
  Internet super server, 236
  mail server, 249
  restarting NFS service, 340
  run levels, 289
  starting servers automatically at boot, 241
  text mode installation, 40
  turning off stand-alone servers, 398

Fedora Media Writer, 35

fg command, 95, 440

FHS (Filesystem Hierarchy Standard), 14, 335

fiber-to-the-curb (FTTC), 155

fiber-to-the-home (FTTH), 155

fiber-to-the-premise (FTTP), 155

file command, 94, 468

file sharing
  configuration and management of, 25
  with NFS
    exporting file system with, 354–356
    mounting, 357
    overview, 353–354
  with Samba
    configuring, 359–360
    installing, 359
    overview, 357–359
    resources for, 361

file systems
  backing up and restoring files, 341–348
  commands
    for checking disk-space use, 120–121
    for directory listings and permissions, 112–114
    for directory management, 117
    for file management, 116–117
    for file system navigation, 110–111
    for finding files, 118–119
    for mounting and unmounting drives, 119–120
    for user management, 114–116
  configuration and management of, 25
  defined, 105
  drive letters, 106
  /etc/fstab file, 337–339
  filenames, 106–107
  file-system hierarchy
    FHS, 335
    overview, 333
    standard directories, 334
    /usr directory, 334
    /var directory, 334
  mounting
    DOS disk partition, 341
    NFS file system, 341
    NTFS partition, 351
    overview, 336–337
    Windows disk partition, 348–351
  NFS
    exporting with, 340, 354–356
    file sharing with, 339–340
    mounting, 341
  overview, 331–333
  pathnames, 106–107, 333
  root directory, 105–107

File Transfer Protocol. *See* FTP

file transfer utilities, as Internet service, 20

files and directories. *See also* directories
  copying, 483, 495
  GPG encryption and authentication utility, 389–396
  hiding, 483
  monitoring log files, 396

moving, 483, 495

overview, 384

ownership, 385–386

setting default permission, 386–387

setting user ID permission, 388

Filesystem Hierarchy Standard (FHS), 14, 335

FileZilla FTP client

  downloading, 218, 220

  uploading/downloading files, 221

find command, 93, 118, 379, 484, 495

Findutils package, 17

finger utility, 17

firewalls

  application-proxy gateway firewall, 404–405

  characteristics of, 403

  defined, 25, 376

  overview, 402

  packet filter firewall, 403–404

  stateful inspection firewall, 404

  ufw, 406

fixed wireless broadband (FWB; WiMAX), 155

flow of execution (scripting), 435–438

flow-control statements, 453

fold command, 94

FORWARD chain, 408–410

. forward file, 256–257

FOSS (Free and Open Source), 481

frames (packets), 173, 377

Free and Open Source (FOSS), 481

free command, 95

Free Software Foundation (FSF), 15, 481

freeDB.org, 131

fsck command, 96, 497

FTP (File Transfer Protocol)

  anonymous, 217

  command-line client, 223–227

  defined, 170, 234

  GUI clients

    FileZilla, 218, 220–221

    gFTP, 218

    web browsers, 218, 221–223

  overview, 217

  port numbers, 234

ftp command, 223–224

FTTC (fiber-to-the-curb), 155

FTTH (fiber-to-the-home), 155

FTTP (fiber-to-the-premise), 155

functions (subroutines; routines), 435, 453

FVWM graphical user interface, 69

FWB (fixed wireless broadband), 155

G

g++ (GNU C++) compiler, 21

gawk package, 17

gcc (GNU C compiler), 17, 21, 454–458

gcj (GNU compiler for Java), 21

gdb debugger. *See* GNU debugger

gdbm library, 17, 474

gedit text editor, 137–139

General Public License (GPL), 473–474

get command, 225

gettext utilities, 17

gFTP FTP client

  downloading, 218

  uploading/downloading files, 219–220

GGv (GNOME Ghostview), 133–135

ghostscript interpreter, 17

ghostview application, 17

The GIMP (GNU Image Manipulation Program), 18–19, 133–134

The GIMP User Manual (GUM), 134

globbing (regular expressions), 483

GNOME (GNU Object Model Environment) graphical user interface

  alternatives to, 69

  calculator, 128–129

  CD player, 131

  Cinnamon variation, 73–74

  contextual menu, 71

  defined, 18

  desktop for, 70–74

  gedit text editor, 137–139

GNOME (GNU Object Model Environment) graphical user interface *(continued)*
general discussion, 10, 16, 19, 69–70
help viewers, 22
logging out, 65
MATE variation, 74
opening terminal window, 84
Unity variation, 73
virtual consoles, 84
web browser, 210
GNOME Ghostview (GGv), 133–135
GNOME onscreen keyboard reader (GOK), 499
GNU C compiler (gcc), 17, 21, 454–458
GNU C Library, 18
GNU C++ compiler (g++), 21
GNU compiler for Java (gcj), 21
GNU dbm (gdbm) database library, 474
GNU debugger
commands, 468–469
defined, 17, 21
finding bugs, 469–471
fixing bugs in, 471–472
gdb debugger, 466–472
overview, 466
preparing to debug, 466
running, 466–467
GNU Image Manipulation Program (The GIMP), 18–19, 133–134
GNU licenses
General Public License, 473–474
Library General Public License, 13, 15, 474–475
GNU Object Model Environment graphical user interface. *See* GNOME graphical user interface
GNU Privacy Guard. *See* GnuPG encryption and authentication utility
GNU profiling (gprof) utility, 21
GNU Project, 15
GNU software
list of well-known, 17–18
overview, 15–16
GNUchess game, 18
Gnumeric graphical spreadsheet, 18

GnuPG (GNU Privacy Guard) encryption and authentication utility
encrypting/decrypting messages, 395–396
exchanging keys, 393–394
generating key pairs, 392
overview, 389–391
signing files, 394–395
GOK (GNOME onscreen keyboard reader), 499
Google Chrome web browser, 210
Google Groups, 42
GParted partition editor, 33–34
GPG encryption and authentication utility. *See* GnuPG encryption and authentication utility
GPL (General Public License), 473–474
gpm service, 243
gprof (GNU profiling) utility, 21
GRand Unified Bootloader (GRUB), 41, 57–58, 286–287, 493
graphical user interfaces. *See* GUIs
gray-box testing, 424
grep utility, 18, 62, 85, 91, 94, 100, 484, 495
groff document formatting system, 18
groupadd utility, 325, 487, 500
groups
changing file ownership, 328–329
overview, 324–325
setting default values for, 325
groups command, 96
growisofs program, 132
GRUB (GRand Unified Bootloader), 41, 57–58, 286–287, 493
gtk+ GUI toolkit, 18
GUIs (graphical user interfaces)
applications and, 16–19
exploring, 27
tools
editing configuration file, 359
managing user accounts with, 320–321
system administration, 316–318
GUM (*The GIMP User Manual*), 134
gunzip command, 95
gzip utility, 18, 95

H

halt command, 95
hard drives
  file system, 106
  system requirements, 32
hard limits (user accounts), 321
hard links, 487, 504
hard mount, 357
hardware, defined, 9, 23
hash (message digest), defined, 376
hash command, 225, 440
hash mark (#; pound sign)
  comments, 192, 237, 253
  HTML anchors, 207, 209
hdparm program, 300–301
HDSL (high-bit-rate DSL), 158
help command, 225, 440, 468
HELP command, 253
hiding NAT, 406
high-bit-rate DSL (HDSL), 158
history command, 91–92, 440
/home directory, 108, 334
HOME environmental variable, 328
host, defined, 377
host addresses, 170, 192
host security, 373–374
  files and directories
    changing ownerships and permissions, 385–386
    GnuPG encryption and authentication utility, 389–396
    monitoring log files, 396
    overview, 384
    reviewing permissions, 419–421
    setting default permission, 386–387
    setting user ID permission, 388
    viewing ownerships and permissions, 385
  incident response, 421–422
  operating system updates, 419
  overview, 381, 418–419
  passwords
    overview, 382

    PAMs, 383–384
    reviewing, 421
    shadow passwords, 382–383
  tools, 425
host utility, 264–266
HOSTNAME environmental variable, 328
hosts.allow file, 505
hosts.deny file, 505
hot-plug devices, 24
HTML (Hypertext Markup Language), 206
HTTP (Hypertext Transfer Protocol), 170, 206, 212, 220, 234
httpd server, 20, 240, 243
hwclock command, 502
hyphen (–), 113–114

I

IANA (Internet Assigned Numbers Authority), 235
id command, 96
IDE (Integrated Drive Electronics), 32
identification number (ID), 324
IDSL (Integrated Services Digital Network DSL), 157
IEEE (Institute of Electrical and Electronics Engineers), 174, 181
IETF (Internet Engineering Task Force), 171, 260
ifconfig utility, 196, 486, 503
ifup command, 201
image command, 225
IMAP (Internet Messages Access Protocol), 171
IMAPv4 (Internet Messages Access Protocol version 4)
  defined, 234
  inetd server, 236
  port number, 234
Impress program, 124, 127–128
incident response, 421–422
incremental backups, 347
indent package, 18
inetd server, 236–237, 397, 398, 422
info break command, 468
info command, 93, 468

infrastructure mode, 183, 186

init 0 command, 65

init daemon, 491

innd service, 243

INPUT chain, 408–410

insmod command, 308, 309, 491

Institute of Electrical and Electronics Engineers (IEEE), 174, 181

Integrated Drive Electronics (IDE), 32

Integrated Services Digital Network DSL (IDSL), 157

Intel, 174

Intel Pentium microprocessors, 9, 11, 14

in.telnetd server, 20

International Organization for Standardization (ISO), 261

International Standard Book Number (ISBN), 446–449

Internet Assigned Numbers Authority (IANA), 235

Internet connections
  configuration and management of, 25
  connection options
    broadband over power lines, 155
    cable modem, 154–155
    dial-up, 154, 156
    Digital Subscriber Line, 154–155
    fiber-to-the-home, 155
    fixed wireless broadband, 155
    satellite Internet access, 155
  general discussion, 19, 153
  Internet overview, 154
  local-area networks
    wired, 167–179
    wireless, 181–190
  network management
    configuration files for TCP/IP networks, 191–195
    configuring network at boot, 201–202
    troubleshooting TCP/IP networks, 196–200
  setting up
    cable modem, 162–166
    Digital Subscriber Line, 156–161

Internet Engineering Task Force (IETF), 171, 260

Internet Messages Access Protocol (IMAP), 171

Internet Messages Access Protocol version 4. See IMAPv4

Internet services (network applications)
  client/server architecture
    defined, 229–230
    Internet super servers, 235–239
    overview, 229–230
    port numbers, 233–235
    stand-alone servers, 239–244
    TCP/IP and sockets, 230–233
  common, 20
  defined, 229
  /etc/hosts.allow file, 194
  /etc/hosts.deny file, 195
  overview, 19–20
  port numbers and, 170–172

Internet super servers, 235–236, 398

Intrusion detection, 425

IP addresses, 169–170, 192, 193. See also Domain Name System; URLs

IP Security Protocol (IPSec), 377

IP spoofing, 377

IPSec (IP Security Protocol), 377

iptables commands, 25, 407–410

IPv4 (IP version 4), 486, 503

IPv6 (IP version 6), 171

ISBN (International Standard Book Number), 446–449

isdn service, 243

ISO (International Organization for Standardization), 261

ISOLINUX bootloader, 58

J

jobs, scheduling
  one-time jobs, 310–312
  recurring jobs, 312–315

jobs command, 441

John the Ripper password-checking tool, 425

K

K scripts, 292

K3b optical disc burner, 132–133

KDE (K Desktop Environment) Plasma graphical user interface

bottom panel

  configuring, 81

  general discussion, 76, 78–79

  icons, 80–81

  Main Menu button (Application Starter), 79–80

calculator, 128–129

CD player, 131

configuring desktop, 81–82

contextual menus, 77–78, 81

general discussion, 10, 19, 69, 75

help viewers, 22

KickOff application launcher, 79–80

KWrite text editor, 139–140

logging out, 65

opening terminal window, 84

origin of, 76

terminology confusion, 75–76

virtual consoles, 84

web browser, 210

Kernel Interface table, 198

Kernel IP routing table, 196

kernel logging daemon (klogd), 502

key pairs, generating, 392

keyboards

configuration and management of, 24

system requirements, 32

kill command, 95, 97–98, 441, 468

Kimball, Spencer, 133

Klipper (Clipboard manager), 76

klogd (kernel logging daemon), 502

Knopper, Klaus, 12

Knoppix

boot commands for troubleshooting, 42–45

Internet super server, 236

root user, 286

starting servers automatically at boot, 241–242

text mode installation, 40

Konqueror web browser, 210

Kontact application, 124, 128

ksyms command, 308

KWrite text editor, 139–140

L

LANANA (Linux Assigned Names And Numbers Authority), 306

LANs (local-area networks)

setting up with cable, 165–166

setting up with DSL, 159–160

wired (Ethernet)

  advantages of, 172–173

  cables, 174–175

  connecting to Internet, 178–179

  connection diagram and notes, 175–176

  overview of function, 173

  TCP/IP, 167–179

wireless

  configuring access points, 185–186

  configuring network cards, 186–187

  connection diagram and notes, 184–185

  encryption, 185–188

  infrastructure and ad hoc modes, 183

  security specifications, 183–184

  standards for, 181–183

last command, 505

lcd command, 225

ldconfig command, 493

ldd command, 95, 493

less command, 18, 94

let arg command, 441

LGPL (Library General Public License), 13, 15, 474–475

/lib directory, 108, 334

/lib subdirectory, 109

libpng library, 18

library, defined, 453

Library General Public License (LGPL), 13, 15, 474–475

LibreOffice suite

Calc, 126–127

defined, 482
general discussion, 123–125
Impress, 127–128
Writer, 125–126
LILO bootloader, 41, 57–58
LindowsOS, 12
links
  dynamic linking, 474
  hard links, 487, 504
  symbolic links, 504
  web browsing, 206–207
Linux
  booting, 57–59
  commercial, for-profit distribution, 13
  computer compatibility, 11
  configuring, 26–27
  general discussion, 1
  installing
    burning media, 30
    common problems, 39–40
    general discussion, 26, 29
    hardware information, 30–33
    Live distributions, 34–35
    partitioning, 30–31, 33–34
    rebooting, 31
    setting up to boot from DVD/CD drive, 30
    text mode installation, 40
    USB distributions, 35–37
  logging in, 58–59
  logging out, 65
  multiuser, multitasking feature of, 10
  shutting down, 64–65
  standards for, 14
  system administration
    drives, 23–24
    file sharing, 25
    file systems, 25
    networking, 25
    overview, 23
    peripherals, 24
  troubleshooting
    common problems, 39–40

fatal signal 11 error message, 45
kernel boot options, 48
Knoppix boot commands, 42–45
reboot problems, 45–47
X Window System, 40–42
version numbers, 13–14
Linux applications. *See also names of specific applications*
for graphics and imaging, 133–135
installing missing, 124
for multimedia, 129–133
for office, 124–129
overview, 123–124
Linux Assigned Names And Numbers Authority (LANANA), 306
Linux certification
  CompTIA Linux+ exams
    LX0-103, 490–497
    LX0-104, 497–505
    overview, 489–490
  Linux Essentials Certificate of Achievement
    "Finding Your Way on a Linux System" topic, 482–483
    "Linux Community and a Career in Open Source" topic, 480–482
    "Linux Operating System" topic, 485–486
    "Power of the Command Line" topic, 483–485
    "Security and File Permissions" topic, 486–488
  vendor-neutral certifications, 507–508
  vendor-specific certifications, 508
Linux distributions. *See also specific names of distributions*
  components of
    applications, 16, 19
    GNU software, 15–18
    GUIs, 16, 19
    Internet services, 19–20
    network compatibility, 19
    online documentation, 22
    overview, 10–11
    software-development tools, 20–21
  Debian GNU/Linux, 12
  Fedora, 12

Gentoo, 12
Knoppix, 12
Linspire, 12
Live distributions, 11
MEPIS Linux, 12
open-source nature of, 11
Slackware, 12
SUSE, 13
Ubuntu, 13
version numbers, 13–14
Linux Essentials Certificate of Achievement
"Finding Your Way on a Linux System" topic, 482–483
"Linux Community and a Career in Open Source" topic, 480–482
"Linux Operating System" topic, 485–486
"Power of the Command Line" topic, 483–485
"Security and File Permissions" topic, 486–488
Linux kernel
boot options, 48
defined, 10
security vulnerabilities, 418
starting (booting), 58
version numbers, 13–14
Linux Standard Base (LSB), 14–15, 335
list command, 468
listen queue, 233
Live distributions, 30, 33–35
ln command, 93
local command, 441
local-area networks. *See* LANs
localhost.zone file, 276
locate command, 93, 119
log analysis, 425
log files
monitoring, 396
syslogd server and, 109
logger command, 486, 491
logic bombs, 377
LOGNAME environmental variable, 328
logout command, 441
logrotate command, 486, 491

/lost+found directory, 108
LPJ metric, 60
lpr command, 94
ls command
combining shell commands, 86
defined, 93, 495
for directory listings and permissions, 112, 114
FTP, 225
servers that can be started and stopped manually, 240
LSB (Linux Standard Base), 14–15, 335
lsmod command, 308, 491
lsof utility, 379
LX0-103 exam, 490–497
LX0-104 exam, 497–505

M

m4 macro processor, 18, 248–250
macros, defined, 248
MAIL environmental variable, 328
MAIL FROM: command, 247
mail servers
configuration file
complexity of, 246
m4 macro processor, 248–250
macro file, 250–253
overview, 247–248
syntax, 253–254
delivery mechanism, 247
delivery testing, 246–247
file contents, 254–257
general discussion, 245
installing, 245
mail transport agents (MTAs), 245
mail user agents (MUAs), 245
mailq command, 502
major device numbers, 305–306
make utility, 18, 21, 453, 458–465, 468, 492
man command, 22, 93, 118
man page (manual page), 22
masquerading feature, 407

master zone statements, 270

MATE variation of GNOME, 74

Math program, 124

Mattis, Peter, 133

MD5 encryption, 325, 383–384

mdelete command, 225

mdir command, 226

/media directory, 108, 334

message digest (hash), defined, 376

Metcalfe, Robert M., 174

mget command, 226

mice
  configuration and management of, 24
  system requirements, 32

MIMO (multiple-input-multiple-output) access
    points, 183

minor device numbers, 305–306

mitigation approach to security, 371–372

mkdir command, 93, 115, 117, 226

mke2fs utility, 497

mkfs command, 96

mknod command, 96

mkswap command, 96

mls command, 226

/mnt directory, 108, 334

Mockapetris, Paul, 260

modinfo command, 308, 491

modprobe command, 308, 309, 492

monitors, system requirements for, 32

monolithic program, 308

more command, 63, 94, 100, 303

mount command, 96, 119

mounting
  defined, 336–337
  DOS disk partition, 348–351
  filesystems, 497
  hard mount, 357
  mount point, 337, 341
  NFS, 341, 357
  NTFS partition, 351
  soft mount, 357
  Windows disk partition, 348–351

Mozilla Firefox web browser
  bookmarking, 211
  as FTP client, 221–223
  history, 211
  home page, 213
  installing, 210
  menus, 212–213
  navigating within, 211
  Pocket cache, 211
  screen shots, 211
  search engine, 211, 215
  security, 212–214
  starting, 210
  status bar, 212
  surfing with, 214–215
  tabbed browsing, 210
  toolbars, 210–212

Mozilla Mail, 247

Mozilla Thunderbird, 482

mput command, 226

MTAs (mail transport agents), 245

MUAs (mail user agents), 245

multiple-input-multiple-output (MIMO)
    access points, 183

multivolume archive, backing up and
    restoring, 345–346

mv command, 93, 116–117

N

name servers
  caching name server, 267–278
  defined, 260
  named daemon, 243, 263, 269, 277
  primary name server, 278–280

name service switch (NSS), 195, 266

NAT (Network Address Translation) routers,
    159, 165, 178–179, 184–185, 405–406

National Vulnerability Database, 417

Nautilus File Manager, 132

Nautilus graphical shell, 19

ncurses package, 18

NetBIOS, 171

netstat utility, 198–199, 379, 486, 503

Network Address Translation (NAT) routers, 159, 165, 178–179, 184–185, 405–406

network addresses, 170

network applications (Internet services)
  client/server architecture
    defined, 229–230
    Internet super servers, 235–239
    overview, 229–230
    port numbers, 233–235
    stand-alone servers, 239–244
    TCP/IP and sockets, 230–233

network cards, system requirements for, 32

network devices, 307

Network File System. *See* NFS

Network Information Service (NIS), 418

Network layer (of TCP/IP), 168–169

network mapper tool, 426

Network News Transfer Protocol (NNTP), 171

network protocols, 19

network security
  enabling packet filtering
    iptables command, 407–410
    security level configuration tool, 406–407
  firewalls
    application-proxy gateway firewall, 404–405
    characteristics of, 403
    overview, 402
    packet filter firewall, 403–404
    stateful inspection firewall, 404
  general discussion, 374–375
  inetd server, 422
  Internet super servers, 398
  key security files, 411
  NAT, 405–406
  OpenSSH software, 399–401
  overview, 422
  penetration testing, 423–424
  stand-alone servers, 397–398
  stand-alone services, 423
  TCP wrapper, 398–399
  tools, 425

xinetd server, 422

network service, 243

Network Time Protocol. *See* NTP

networking and Internet connections
  configuration and management of, 25
  connection options
    broadband over power lines, 155
    cable modem, 154–155
    dial-up, 154, 156
    Digital Subscriber Line, 154–155
    fiber-to-the-home, 155
    fixed wireless broadband, 155
    satellite Internet access, 155
  general discussion, 19, 153
  Internet overview, 154
  local-area networks
    wired, 167–179
    wireless, 181–190
  network management
    configuration files for TCP/IP networks, 191–195
    configuring network at boot, 201–202
    troubleshooting TCP/IP networks, 196–200
  setting up
    cable modem, 162–166
    Digital Subscriber Line, 156–161

networking service, 243

newaliases command, 502

news/alerts, security, 379–380

next command, 468

NFS (Network File System)
  defined, 234
  exporting file system with, 340, 354–356
  file sharing with, 339–340
  mounting, 341, 357
  overview, 25, 353–354
  port number, 234
  RPC facility, 172
  security issues, 340, 354
  security vulnerabilities, 418

nfs service, 243

nfslock service, 243

nfsserver service, 243
nice command, 95
NIS (Network Information Service), 418
nl command, 94
nmap tool, 379
nmbd NetBIOS name server, 358
nmblookup command, 358
NNTP (Network News Transfer Protocol), 171
nonrepudiation, 377
NSS (name service switch), 195, 266
NTFS (NT File System) partition, 33, 351
NTP (Network Time Protocol)
  daemon (ntpd), 502
  defined, 234
  port number, 234

O

OCA (Oracle Certified Associate) certification, 508
OCP (Oracle Certified Professional)
    certification, 508
one-time jobs, scheduling, 310–312
online documentation, 22
open command, 226
Open Secure Shell (OpenSSH) software, 399–401
Open Secure Sockets Layer (OpenSSL)
    software, 418
Open Source Initiative (OSI), 11, 481
OpenOffice, 482
open-source, defined, 11
OpenSSH (Open Secure Shell) software, 399–401
OpenSSL (Open Secure Sockets Layer)
    software, 418
openSUSE, 13
operating systems
  defined, 9–10
  purpose of, 10
/opt directory, 108, 334
/opt subdirectory, 109
Oracle Certified Associate (OCA) certification, 508
Oracle Certified Professional (OCP)
    certification, 508
Orca screen reader, 499
$ORIGIN directive, 270–271

OSI (Open Source Initiative), 11, 481
OUTPUT chain, 408–410
ownerships and permissions
  /etc/passwd file, 421
  files and directories
    changing, 385–386
    commands, 112–116
    key system files, 420
    viewing, 385
  scripting, 450
  for users and groups, 328–329

P

package managers, 493
packet filter firewall, 403–404
packet filtering, 377
packet sniffers (sniffers), 200, 378, 425
packets (frames), 173, 377
PAMs (pluggable authentication modules),
    383–384
PARC (Xerox Palo Alto Research Center), 174
passwd command, 96, 287, 379, 487
passwords
  changing, 505
  host-security review, 421
  John the Ripper password-checking tool, 425
  overview, 382
  PAMs, 383–384
  resetting root password, 286–287
  shadow passwords, 382–383
paste command, 94
patch command, 18, 94
PATH environmental variable, 328
pathnames, 106–107, 333
pcmcia service, 243
PEM (Privacy Enhanced Mail), 256
penetration testing, 423–424
perimeter network, 377
peripherals
  configuration and management of, 24
  defined, 23
Perl, 21

permissions. *See* ownerships and permissions

persistent storage, defined, 36

Physical layer (of TCP/IP), 168–169

PID (process ID), 97–98

ping utility, 197, 486, 503

pipe feature (|), 100–101

pixels, defined, 32

PKI (Public Key Infrastructure), 377

pluggable authentication modules (PAMs), 383–384

Point-to-Point Protocol (PPP) connections, 307

POP3 (Post Office Protocol version 3), 171, 234

popd command, 441

port address translation, 406

port number, 423

port scanners, 425

port scanning, 377, 423–424

portmap service, 244

port-scanning tool, 397

POSIX (Portable Operating System Interface) standards, 14

Post Office Protocol version 3 (POP3), 171, 234

postfix service, 245

pound sign (#; hash mark)
  comments, 192, 237, 253
  HTML anchors, 207, 209

PPP (Point-to-Point Protocol) connections, 307

PPPoE (PPP over Ethernet), 161

print EXPR command, 468

printenv command, 95

printers
  configuration and management of, 24
  setting up, 48–51
  system requirements, 33

Privacy Enhanced Mail (PEM), 256

/proc file system
  /acpi file, 304
  /bus file, 304
  /cmdline file, 304
  /cpuinfo file, 302–303, 304
  defined, 108, 302
  /devices file, 304

/dma file, 304

/driver/rtc file, 304

/filesystems file, 304

/ide file, 304

/interrupts file, 304

/ioports file, 304

/kcore file, 302, 304

/kmsg file, 304

/loadavg file, 304

/locks file, 304

/meminfo file, 304

/misc file, 304

/modules file, 304

/mounts file, 304

/net file, 304

/partitions file, 304

/pci file, 304

/scsi file, 304

/stat file, 305

/swaps file, 305

/sys file, 305

/uptime file, 305

/version file, 305

process ID (PID), 97–98

programming. *See* scripting

prompt command, 226

protocols, defined, 19

proxy server, 377

ps ax command, 97–98, 101

ps command, 63–64, 95

pstree command, 95

public key encryption
  defined, 377
  digital signatures, 390–391
  GPG
    encrypting/decrypting messages, 395–396
    exchanging keys, 393–394
    generating key pairs, 392
    signing files, 394–395
  overview, 389–390

Public Key Infrastructure (PKI), 377

pushd command, 441

put command, 226

pwd command, 93, 110, 226, 441, 483

Python, 21

Q

QTParted GUI tool, 31

question mark (?)

　displaying list of commands, 225

　HTML queries, 209

　wildcard, 90–91, 102

quit command, 226, 468

QUIT command, 247

quotas (user accounts), 321, 497

quotation marks (" "), 62, 85, 91, 433

R

RADIUS (Remote Authentication Dial-In User
　Service) servers, 184

RADSL (rate-adaptive DSL), 158

RAM (random-access memory), 23, 32

rate-adaptive DSL (RADSL), 158

RCPT TO: command, 247

RCS (Revision Control System), 18, 21, 454

read command, 441

readonly command, 441

reboot command, 95

recurring jobs

　automated backups, 347

　scheduling, 312–315

recv command, 226

Red Hat Certified Architect (RHCA), 508

Red Hat Certified Engineer (RHCE), 508

Red Hat Certified System Administrator
　(RHCSA), 508

Red Hat (Linux distribution), 12

Red Hat Package Manager (RPM) format,
　12, 51–52

Red Hat Security Center, 380

regular expressions (globbing), 483

relative paths, 483

Remote Authentication Dial-In User Service
　(RADIUS) servers, 184

remote login and access

　as Internet service, 20, 154

　with OpenSSH software, 399–401

remote name daemon control (rndc) utility, 269

rename command, 226

Rendezvous Directory Service, 172

resolver library, 193, 263, 264, 266

resource records (RR), 270–273

restart command, 240

return command, 441

reverse lookups, 265

Revision Control System (RCS), 18, 21, 454

RHCA (Red Hat Certified Architect), 508

RHCE (Red Hat Certified Engineer), 508

RHCSA (Red Hat Certified System
　Administrator), 508

Rhythmbox audio player, 131–132

risk analysis

　mitigation approach, 371–372

　overview, 368

　probability and effect, 370

　security policy, 370–371

　threats, 369

　vulnerabilities, 369

rm command, 93, 117

rmdir command, 93, 117, 226

rmmod command, 308, 491

rndc (remote name daemon control) utility, 269

/root directory, 105–107, 108, 333, 334

root user and account (superuser), 59, 65, 97,
　285–286

route spoofing, 403

route utility, 196, 486, 503

routines (functions), 435, 453

RPM (Red Hat Package Manager) format, 12,
　51–52

RR (resource records), 270–273

run command, 468

run levels, 288–289, 291

/run subdirectory, 110

rwx permissions, 113–114

S

S scripts, 292

Samba
  configuring, 359–360
  defined, 25, 482
  general discussion, 357–359
  installing, 359
  resources for, 361

samba service, 244

SANS Institute, 417

satellite Internet access, 155

SAX2 program, 82

/sbin directory
  defined, 108, 334
  /hotplug program, 307
  ifconfig command, 196
  ifup command, 201
  route command, 196
  /udev program, 307

/sbin subdirectory, 109

SCA (SUSE Certified Administrator), 508

SCE (SUSE Certified Engineer), 508

scheduling jobs
  one-time jobs, 310–312
  recurring jobs, 312–315

screening router, 378

scripting
  bash built-in commands, 439–441
  calling shell functions, 435
  conditional expressions, 450
  controlling flow of execution, 435–438
  defining variables, 434–435
  GNU licenses
    General Public License, 473–474
    Library General Public License, 474–475
  overview, 431–433, 453
  sed stream editor
    awk language and, 446–450
    overview, 443–446
  setting permissions, 450
  software-development tools, 453–472
    GCC utility, 454–458

GNU debugger, 466–472
GNU make utility, 458–465
overview, 453–454

SCSI (Small Computer System Interface) controllers, 32

SDSL (symmetric DSL), 158

SEA (SUSE Enterprise Architect), 508

Secure Shell (SSH), 172, 184, 220, 234

security. *See also* computer security
  enabling packet filtering, 406–407
  establishing security framework
    business requirements, 368
    overview, 366–368
    risk analysis, 368–372
  host security
    files and directories, 384–396
    overview, 373–374, 381
    passwords, 382–384
  importance of, 366
  network security
    firewalls, 402–405
    Internet super servers, 398
    key security files, 411
    NAT, 405–406
    OpenSSH software, 399–401
    overview, 374–375
    packet filtering, 406–410
    stand-alone servers, 397–398
    TCP wrapper, 398–399
  news and updates, 379–380
  overview, 365
  physical security, 287
  security testing tools, 425–427
  terminology, 375–378
  tools, 379

security policy, 370–371

sed stream editor
  awk language and, 446–450
  converting data with, 94, 495
  defined, 18
  overview, 443–446

segment violations, 45

semicolon (;), 86

send command, 226

sendmail server

  configuration file

    complexity of, 246

    m4 macro processor, 248–250

    macro file, 250–253

    overview, 247–248

    syntax, 253–254

  defined, 20, 244, 502

  delivery mechanism, 247

  delivery testing, 246–247

  file contents, 254–257

  installing, 245

  security vulnerabilities, 418

server processes, 235

service-configuration utility, 242–243

set command, 441

set user ID (setuid/suid) permission, 388

set variable command, 468

setuid program, 378, 388

SHA-512 encryption, 325

shadow passwords, 382–383

/share subdirectory, 109

Sharutils package, 18

shell CMD command, 468

SHELL environmental variable, 328

shells. *See also* bash shell

 C shell, 84

 calling shell functions, 435

 defined, 481

 OpenSSH software, 399–401

 SSH, 172, 184, 220, 234

shift command, 441

shutdown command, 95

Shuttleworth, Mark, 73

signing files, 394–395

SIGSEGV [Segment Violation Signal] (signal 11) errors, 45

Simple Mail Transfer Protocol (SMTP), 170, 234, 247

Simple Network Management Protocol (SNMP), 172, 231, 234, 418

single dot (.), 111

single-volume archive, backing up and restoring, 343–345

size command, 226

slow keys, 499

Small Computer System Interface (SCSI) controllers, 32

smb service, 244

smbadduser program, 358

smbcacls program, 358

smbclient Windows client, 358

smbcontrol program, 358

smbd SMB server, 358

smbfs service, 244

smbmount program, 358

smbpasswd program, 358

smbprint script, 358

smbstatus command, 358

smbtar program, 358

smbumount program, 359

SMTP (Simple Mail Transfer Protocol), 170, 234, 247

sniffers (packet sniffers), 200, 378, 425

SNMP (Simple Network Management Protocol), 172, 231, 234, 418

snmpd service, 244

sockets

 attributes of, 230

 client/server architecture, 232–233

 connectionless protocols, 231–233

 connection-oriented protocols, 231–233

 datagram sockets, 231

 defined, 230

 stream sockets, 231

soft limits (user accounts), 321

soft mount, 357

software

 defined, 9

 installing, 51–54

 software build process, 453

Software utility, 54

software-development tools

 GCC, 454–458

general discussion, 453–454

GNU debugger, 466–472

GNU make utility, 458–465

overview, 20–21

Sony PlayStation, 11

sort command, 94, 101

sound cards

configuration and management of, 24

system requirements, 33

source code/source file, 11, 452

source-based distribution, defined, 12

spamassassin service, 244

split command, 94, 102

/spool subdirectory, 110

spyware, 378

/src subdirectory, 109

/srv directory, 108, 334

SSH (Secure Shell), 172, 184, 220, 234

ssh service, 244

sshd service, 20, 244

SSIDs (ESSIDs), 185, 188

Stallman, Richard, 15

stand-alone servers

general discussion, 239

network-security review, 423

starting and stopping manually, 240

starting automatically at boot

general discussion, 240–241

GUI service-configuration utilities, 241–242

list of services, 243–244

systemctl command, 241

update-rc.d command, 241–242

turning off, 397–398

standard directories, 334

standard error (stderr), 87–89

standard input (stdin), 87–88, 484

standard output (stdout), 87–88, 484

start command, 240

startup scripts, 291–292

state table, 404

stateful inspection firewall, 404

statements

defined, 453

flow-control, 453

master zone, 270

static NAT, 405

status command, 226, 240

stderr (standard error), 87–89

stdin (standard input), 87–88, 484

stdout (standard output), 87–88, 484

step command, 469

sticky keys, 499

stop command, 240

su command, 96, 97, 488, 505

su utility, 379

subroutines (functions), 435, 453

Subversion control system, 418

sudo command, 379, 488, 505

superblock, 493

superuser (root user and account), 59, 65, 97, 285–286

SUSE

automatically starting servers, 293

configuring network at boot, 202

configuring Samba, 359–360

digiKam application, 130–131

/etc/fstab file, 338

file sharing with NFS, 339

installing software, 55

Internet super server, 236, 238

Linux certifications, 508

mail server, 247–248

partitioning, 31

run levels, 289

setting up firewall, 407

starting servers automatically at boot, 241

text mode installation, 40

turning off stand-alone servers, 398

wireless network configuration, 189

SUSE Certified Administrator (SCA), 508

SUSE Certified Engineer (SCE), 508

SUSE Enterprise Architect (SEA), 508

swapoff command, 96

swapon command, 96, 493

swapping, defined, 300

symbolic links, 504

symmetric DSL (SDSL), 158

symmetric key encryption, 378

Synaptic Package Manager, 53

sync command, 96

/sys directory, 108

sysfs file system, 307

syslog service, 244

syslogd service, 244

system administration

  administrators, 283

  backups, 284

  boot process

    automatically starting servers, 293–294

    /etc/inittab file, 288–290

    general discussion, 287

    init program, 288–289

    manually starting and stopping servers, 292–293

    run levels, 288–289, 291

    startup scripts, 291–292

  configuration files, 294–296

  defined, 283

  device drivers, 305

  device files

    block devices, 306

    character devices, 306–307

    network devices, 307

    overview, 305–306

    udev program, 307

  driver modules, 308–309

  GUI tools, 316–318

  hardware management, 284

  network status monitoring, 285

  operating system and utility management, 284

  printing system management, 284

  scheduling jobs, 310–315

  security monitoring, 285

  security setup, 285

  software installation, 284

  startup and shutdown, 284–285

system performance monitoring

  defined, 284

  disk performance and usage, 300–302

  general discussion, 296–297

  top utility, 297–298

  uptime command, 298–299

  viewing system information, 302–305

  vmstat utility, 299–300

task automation, 284

user account management

  defined, 284

  logging in as root user, 285

  resetting root password, 286–287

  su – command, 285–286

system log, 486, 491

System Monitor utility, 200, 202, 316–318

system-config-printer tool, 48–51

systemctl command, 241

T

tac command, 94

tail command, 94

tar (tape) archiver program

  automated backups, 347–348

  backups, 25

  defined, 18, 95

  incremental backups, 347

  multivolume archive, 345–346

  overview, 343

  single-volume archive, 343–345

  tapes, 346

Tcl/Tk (Tool Command Language and toolkit), 21

TCP wrappers, 237, 398–399

tcpd program, 236–237

tcpdump utility, 199–200

TCP/IP (Transmission Control Protocol/Internet Protocol)

  client/server architecture

    connectionless protocols, 231

    connection-oriented protocols, 231

    general discussion, 230

configuration files
/etc/host.conf file, 192–193
/etc/hosts file, 192
/etc/hosts.allow file, 192, 194
/etc/hosts.deny file, 192, 195
/etc/networks file, 192–193
/etc/nsswitch.conf file, 192, 195
/etc/resolv.conf file, 192–194
four-layer model of, 167–169
general discussion, 19, 167
Internet services, 170–172
IP addresses, 169–170
origin of, 169
port numbers, 170–172
troubleshooting networks
connectivity to host, 197
GUI tools for, 200
IP routing table, 196–197
network interfaces, 196
network status, 198–199
sniffing network packets, 199–200
telinit command, 291
Telnet, 172, 234, 247
telnet command, 247
Temporal Key Integrity Protocol (TKIP), 184
TERM environmental variable, 328
testparm program, 359
texinfo utilities, 18
text editors
defined, 453
ed text editor, 17, 140–144
gedit text editor, 137–139
GUI-based, 137–140
vi text editor, 140, 145–149
text terminal (command-line interface), 15
TFTP (Trivial File Transfer Protocol), 172, 235
threats, security, 369, 378. See also security
tilde character (~), 111
time utility, 18
times command, 441
TKIP (Temporal Key Integrity Protocol), 184
/tmp directory, 108, 334, 432

/tmp subdirectory, 110
Tool Command Language and toolkit (Tcl/Tk), 21
top utility, 95, 297–298
Torvalds, Linus, 1, 11, 60
touch command, 93
tr utility, 94, 101, 495
Transmission Control Protocol/Internet
Protocol. See TCP/IP
Transport layer (of TCP/IP), 168
trap command, 441
Tripwire, 396
Trivial File Transfer Protocol (TFTP), 172, 235
Trojan horse, 378
tty command, 96
type command, 93, 441

U

Ubuntu
automatically starting servers, 293
configuring network at boot, 201
installing missing applications, 124
installing Samba, 359
installing software, 52–54
Internet super server, 236
latest version of, 14
network configuration tool, 177
PPPoE DSL connections, 161
root user, 286
run levels, 289
starting servers automatically at boot, 241–242
System Monitor utility, 200, 202, 316–318
text mode installation, 40
turning off stand-alone servers, 397
udev program, 307
UDP (User Datagram Protocol), 231
ufw (Uncomplicated Firewall), 406
ulimit utility, 379, 441, 505
umask command, 386–387, 441
umount command, 96
unalias command, 93, 441
uname command, 63, 95

Uncomplicated Firewall (ufw), 406

uncompress command, 95

Uniform Resource Locators. *See* DNS; in URLs

uniq command, 94

Unity variation of GNOME, 73

Unix systems, 417

unloading device driver modules, 309

unmount command, 120, 337

unmounting
  commands for, 119–120
  DOS floppy disks, 350–351

unset command, 441

update-rc.d command, 241–242, 293–294

updates
  operating system updates, 419
  security, 379–380

uptime command, 63, 298–299

URLs (Uniform Resource Locators). *See also* DNS
  defined, 207
  directory path, 208
  domain name, 208
  filename, 209
  HTML anchor, 209
  port number, 208
  protocol, 207–208

U.S. Computer Emergency Readiness Team (US-CERT), 380

USB distributions
  configuring PC to boot from USB, 36–37
  creating bootable flash drives, 35–36
  general discussion, 35
  working from, 37

USB drives
  as backup media, 342
  configuration and management of, 24, 51

US-CERT (U.S. Computer Emergency Readiness Team), 380

user command, 226

User Datagram Protocol (UDP), 231

user file-creation mask, 386

useradd command, 322, 500

usermod command, 379, 505

users
  changing file ownership, 328–329
  environment variables, 326–328
  /etc/passwd file, 323–324
  managing user accounts
    with commands, 322–323
    with GUI tools, 320–321
  setting default values for, 325

/usr directory
  /bin directory, 334
  /bin/scp component, 400
  /bin/slogin component, 400
  /bin/ssh component, 400
  /bin/ssh-keygen component, 400
  defined, 108
  /games directory, 334
  hierarchy of, 334
  /include directory, 334
  /lib directory, 334
  /libexec directory, 334
  /local directory, 334
  /sbin directory, 334
  /sbin/sshd component, 400
  /share directory, 334
  /src directory, 334
  subdirectories of, 109

V

/var directory
  defined, 108
  hierarchy of, 334
  /log/apache2 file, 296
  /log/boot.msg file, 296
  /log/cron file, 296
  /log/dmesg file, 296
  /log/httpd file, 296
  /log/messages file, 296
  subdirectories of, 109–110
  /log system file, 421
  /log/lastlog system file, 421
  /log/messages system file, 421
  /log/wtmp system file, 421
  /var/cache directory, 335

/var/crash directory, 335
/var/lib directory, 335
/var/lock directory, 335
/var/log directory, 335, 396
/var/mail directory, 335
/var/opt directory, 335
/var/run directory, 335
/var/spool directory, 335
/var/tmp directory, 335
/var/yp directory, 335
variables
  defined, 453
  defining, 434–435
  managing, 498
VDSL/VHDSL (very-high bit-rate DSL), 158
vendor-neutral certifications, 507–508
vendor-specific certifications, 508
version control systems, 454
Very Secure FTP daemon (vsftpd) server, 20,
    238–239, 244, 397
very-high bit-rate DSL (VDSL/VHDSL), 158
vi text editor
  commands, 148–149
  defined, 140
  deleting text, 147–148
  editing text, 148–149
  modes, 146
  navigating within, 146–149
  saving changes, 147
  starting, 145
video cards (display adapters), 33
virus, defined, 378
vmstat utility, 299–300
vsftpd (Very Secure FTP daemon) server, 20,
    238–239, 244, 397
vulnerability scanners, 425
vulnerability testing, 417–418, 424. See also
    computer security

W

wait command, 441
Wall, Larry, 18
war-dialing, 378

war-driving, 378
watch VAR command, 469
wc command, 95, 100, 484, 495
web browsers
  defined, 205–206
  Epiphany, 210
  as FTP clients, 218, 221–223
  Google Chrome, 210
  Konqueror, 210
  Mozilla Firefox
    bookmarking, 211
    history, 211
    home page, 213
    installing, 210
    menus, 212–213
    navigating within, 211
    Pocket cache, 211
    screen shots, 211
    search engine, 211, 215
    security, 212–214
    starting, 210
    status bar, 212
    surfing with, 214–215
    tabbed browsing, 210
    toolbars, 210–212
  overview, 209
web browsing
  links, 206–207
  standards for, 206
  URLs, 207–209
web servers
  client/server architecture
    defined, 229–230
    Internet super servers, 235–239
    overview, 229–230
    port numbers, 233–235
    stand-alone servers, 239–244
    TCP/IP and sockets, 230–233
  defined, 206
  overview, 209
WEP (Wired Equivalent Privacy), 183–184
whatis command, 93, 483
where command, 469

whereis command, 94

which command, 94

white-box testing, 424

who command, 488, 505

Wi-Fi (Wireless Fidelity), 181. *See also* wireless local-area networks

Wi-Fi Alliance, 183

Wi-Fi Protected Access 2 (WPA2), 184

Wi-Fi Protected Access (WPA), 184

WiMAX (fixed wireless broadband), 155

WIMP (windows, icons, mouse, and pointer), 60

winbind service, 244

winbindd server, 359

Windows disk partition, mounting, 348–351

Wired Equivalent Privacy (WEP), 183–184

Wireless Fidelity (Wi-Fi), 181. *See also* wireless local-area networks

Wireshark packet sniffer, 200

WLANs (wireless local-area networks)
  configuring access points, 185–186
  configuring network cards, 186–187
  connection diagram and notes, 184–185
  encryption, 185–188
  infrastructure and ad hoc modes, 183
  security specifications, 183–184
  standards for, 181–183

World Wide Web
  as Internet service, 20, 154
  overview, 205–206

worm, defined, 378

WPA (Wi-Fi Protected Access), 184

WPA2 (Wi-Fi Protected Access 2), 184

Writer program, 124–126

X

X Display Manager (xdm), 499

X Window System
  creating configuration file, 41–42
  defined, 10
  general discussion, 14
  troubleshooting, 40–42

Xandros File Manager, 132

xdm (X Display Manager), 499

xdpyinfo utility, 499

Xerox Palo Alto Research Center (PARC), 174

x/F ADDR command, 469

Xfce graphical user interface, 69

xfs service, 244

xhost program, 499

xinetd server, 236–239, 244, 397, 398, 422

XMMS audio player, 131–132

xwininfo utility, 499

Y

YaST Control Center, 55, 359–360

YaST installation and configuration tool, 13, 189, 242, 247–248

ypbind service, 244

Yum tool, 493

Z

zcat command, 95

zless command, 95

zmore command, 95

zone files, 270, 274–277

About the Author

Emmett Dulaney is a university professor and columnist for *Certification Magazine*. An expert on operating systems and certification, he is the author of *CompTIA Security+ Study Guide*, *CompTIA A+ Complete Study Guide*, and *CompTIA Network+ Exam Cram*.

Publisher's Acknowledgments

Senior Acquisitions Editor: Katie Mohr
Project Editor: Charlotte Kughen
Copy Editor: Kathy Simpson
Technical Editor: Guy Hart-Davis
Editorial Assistant: Matthew Lowe
Sr. Editorial Assistant: Cherie Case

Production Editor: Magesh Elangovan
Cover Image: © pedrosek/Shutterstock

Leverage the power

Dummies is the global leader in the reference category and one of the most trusted and highly regarded brands in the world. No longer just focused on books, customers now have access to the dummies content they need in the format they want. Together we'll craft a solution that engages your customers, stands out from the competition, and helps you meet your goals.

Advertising & Sponsorships

Connect with an engaged audience on a powerful multimedia site, and position your message alongside expert how-to content. Dummies.com is a one-stop shop for free, online information and know-how curated by a team of experts.

- Targeted ads
- Video
- Email Marketing

- Microsites
- Sweepstakes sponsorship

20 MILLION PAGE VIEWS
EVERY SINGLE MONTH

15 MILLION UNIQUE
VISITORS PER MONTH

43% OF ALL VISITORS ACCESS THE SITE
VIA THEIR MOBILE DEVICES

700,000 NEWSLETTER SUBSCRIPTIONS
TO THE INBOXES OF
300,000 UNIQUE INDIVIDUALS EVERY WEEK

# of dummies

Custom Publishing

Reach a global audience in any language by creating a solution that will differentiate you from competitors, amplify your message, and encourage customers to make a buying decision.

- Apps
- Books
- eBooks
- Video
- Audio
- Webinars

Brand Licensing & Content

Leverage the strength of the world's most popular reference brand to reach new audiences and channels of distribution.

For more information, visit **dummies.com/biz**

PERSONAL ENRICHMENT

Staying Sharp

9781119187790
USA $26.00
CAN $31.99
UK £19.99

Facebook

9781119179030
USA $21.99
CAN $25.99
UK £16.99

Guitar

9781119293354
USA $24.99
CAN $29.99
UK £17.99

Investing

9781119293347
USA $22.99
CAN $27.99
UK £16.99

Beekeeping

9781119310068
USA $22.99
CAN $27.99
UK £16.99

Digital Photography

9781119235606
USA $24.99
CAN $29.99
UK £17.99

Meditation

9781119251163
USA $24.99
CAN $29.99
UK £17.99

Pregnancy

9781119235491
USA $26.99
CAN $31.99
UK £19.99

Samsung Galaxy S7

9781119279952
USA $24.99
CAN $29.99
UK £17.99

iPhone

9781119283133
USA $24.99
CAN $29.99
UK £17.99

Crocheting

9781119287117
USA $24.99
CAN $29.99
UK £16.99

Nutrition

9781119130246
USA $22.99
CAN $27.99
UK £16.99

PROFESSIONAL DEVELOPMENT

Windows 10

9781119311041
USA $24.99
CAN $29.99
UK £17.99

AutoCAD

9781119255796
USA $39.99
CAN $47.99
UK £27.99

Excel 2016

9781119293439
USA $26.99
CAN $31.99
UK £19.99

QuickBooks 2017

9781119281467
USA $26.99
CAN $31.99
UK £19.99

macOS Sierra

9781119280651
USA $29.99
CAN $35.99
UK £21.99

LinkedIn

9781119251132
USA $24.99
CAN $29.99
UK £17.99

Windows 10

9781119310563
USA $34.00
CAN $41.99
UK £24.99

SharePoint 2016

9781119181705
USA $29.99
CAN $35.99
UK £21.99

Fundamental Analysis

9781119263593
USA $26.99
CAN $31.99
UK £19.99

Networking

9781119257769
USA $29.99
CAN $35.99
UK £21.99

Office 2016

9781119293477
USA $26.99
CAN $31.99
UK £19.99

Office 365

9781119265313
USA $24.99
CAN $29.99
UK £17.99

Salesforce.com

9781119239314
USA $29.99
CAN $35.99
UK £21.99

Coding

9781119293323
USA $29.99
CAN $35.99
UK £21.99

Learning Made Easy

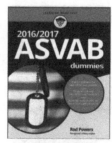
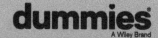

Small books for big imaginations

9781119177173
USA $9.99
CAN $9.99
UK £8.99

9781119177272
USA $9.99
CAN $9.99
UK £8.99

9781119177241
USA $9.99
CAN $9.99
UK £8.99

9781119177210
USA $9.99
CAN $9.99
UK £8.99

9781119262657
USA $9.99
CAN $9.99
UK £6.99

9781119291336
USA $9.99
CAN $9.99
UK £6.99

9781119233527
USA $9.99
CAN $9.99
UK £6.99

9781119291220
USA $9.99
CAN $9.99
UK £6.99

9781119177302
USA $9.99
CAN $9.99
UK £8.99

Unleash Their Creativity

dummies.com

dummies
A Wiley Brand